DEVELOPING
WORK AND STUDY SKILLS

DEVELOPING
WORK AND STUDY SKILLS

LINDA LEE-DAVIES

WITH IT SKILLS SECTION BY
SUSAN BAILEY

THOMSON
™

Australia • Brazil • Canada • Mexico • Singapore • Spain • United Kingdom • United States

THOMSON

Developing Work and Study Skills
Linda Lee-Davies, IT Skills Section by Susan Bailey

Publishing Director	**Commissioning Editor**	**Editorial Assistant**
John Yates	Geraldine Lyons	James Clark
Senior Production Editor	**Manufacturing Manager**	**Marketing Manager**
Alissa Chappell	Helen Mason	Leo Stanley
Typesetter	**Production Controller**	**Cover Design**
Interactive Composition Corporation	Maeve Healy	Harris Cook Turner
Text Design	**Printer**	
Design Deluxe, Bath, UK	C & C Offset Printing Co., Ltd	

British Library Cataloguing-in-Publication Data
A catalogue record for this book is available from the British Library

This book is dedicated to Mum and Dad

Two straightforward, hardworking people, they gave me the greatest gift you can pass on to any child – independence. Their strong work ethic, having stayed with me throughout employment, will be passed on to my own son Peter and the many thousands of students I have the privilege of guiding.

Linda Lee-Davies

I would like to dedicate this book to my lovely husband Andrew, children Jade and Joel, and all my family, as a thank you for all their tremendous support. In life we must strive to improve and support the lives of others to *make a difference*. This book helps all students who read it enhance their skills and make a difference to their own lives.

Susan Jane Bailey

Brief contents

Contents

The title of the book, in terms of the order of the wording, establishes the priority from the outset. It is not a book which purely assists with study in higher education, although of course it covers the essentials. The book focuses on preparing the reader for improvement and success in the working world and instilling a sense and culture of perpetual self-development for a life-time.

There is no presumption that the student is straight from further education, although this is catered for well, so it is written to also include the mature student in work studying part-time or by distance learning. Whatever the background of the student, it is presumed they are a manager or a potential manager and all of the chapters are geared to helping them maximise their study towards the aim of self-improvement in this area.

I have deliberately ensured a duality to each chapter. This is not just to attract the mature market and cater for the more diverse nature of student intake, but also to give the student without work experience an insight into the working world and what they will need to equip themselves for it, in real terms not ideological ones. As an experienced recruiter over all levels and across the UK, I interviewed many hundreds of new graduates. Although impressed with their knowledge of their subject, I was left unimpressed and of the opinion that the majority were not equipped with the skills and attitude for entering the working world. This is why I have gone much further than simply providing basic job application and interview techniques in the content.

I also met many hundreds of very clever managers with no or few paper qualifications and who wanted to better themselves. They were no less bright than I but feared the academic world. I wanted to open this up more for them. Experience should count as qualification and this book attempts to help potential candidates to look at that side of the equation too.

All chapters have the final goal of job and management success in mind. Whether studying to enter work at this level or improving a current level, the material goes beyond aiming for a good mark in an assignment. The material is written to not only improve the performance of students during their university stay but to be applied directly to the working world from the minute they start. The purpose of a group presentation at university, for instance, takes on a new meaning when directly related to a future management role.

As international travel becomes more common in many management roles, I have also kept a cross cultural awareness throughout the book. It is not possible to cover all cultural differences each time but I felt it important to ensure a healthy approach to diversity in all respects to give the student or manager the best start. Respect for the differences of others is a key theme throughout the text, whether at the individual or local level or in international dealings.

I have also introduced the student to the concept of self-audit from the start. The SWOTPLOT and other audit tools are geared to accustom them to this approach which is more and more common in management/leadership roles and now also in academia at all levels, following recent government initiatives. By knowing themselves they are not only more able to focus on appropriate areas for their self improvement but are better placed to understand others. This approach familiarises them with the PDP – personal development plan – and helps them use this tool more effectively throughout their working life.

In addition, therefore, to advising at different levels of ability, the chapters can be used to complete actions derived from the self-audit tools. The self-audit tools in this book do not merely take a snapshot of the participant, they direct them towards self improvement from the start and in turn they direct the self-improvement itself. Action planning is encouraged and the chapters are designed for quick access to appropriate topics. Equally the chapters gain work momentum as they progress chronologically, giving the reader more and more parallels with successful employment. Lifelong learning is promoted throughout.

This approach means that the text serves well during study, a worthwhile investment in itself, but it can also be used well after study is over to help in the workplace. This gives it an extended and very useful shelf life.

The IT skills section of the book is separated in Part 6 for easy reference. It is written in an enthusiastic and accessible way and I have ensured page space for well over 250 screen examples in this section alone to aid reader understanding. The needs of the student of all ages and types are taken into account and the same lifelong learning ethic is threaded through its content too. Susan Bailey has brought many of the technical techniques needed for work and study to life. Her own preface to the section explains this is in more detail.

Linda Lee-Davies

At home as well as in the workplace, the use of information technology (IT) and information systems (IS) is universal. Software like Microsoft Office© is a common and essential tool. The IT skills section will explain the main principles underlying IT and IS, and the basic concepts and techniques behind Microsoft© Office and related software. It will provide common sense advice and a range of techniques to support your learning.

In each chapter you will find tips throughout the text and exercises at the end of each section. The highlighting and reinforcing of these key items will act as an aide-memoir as you practice your skills and familiarise yourself with the jargon. In addition the companion website contains a glossary of terms and extra material to enhance this IT skills section. The attainment of these skills will support you throughout your life and career, and prepare you for an ever changing workplace. These techniques are the key to adaptability in lifelong learning and flexible working. You can dip in and out of the chapters and the website, and use each section to develop initial skills in a particular area.

The main aims of the **IT skills section** is that you should be able to:

- understand the basic principles and terms used in IT and IS
- undertake straightforward exercises in Microsoft© Office programs and related software.
- acquire the key skills needed in today's working and learning environments.

This section will support new students come from a range of backgrounds,

- School leavers
- Those who work in industry and commerce
- Those who have been away from the workplace for some time
- Mature students

Whenever you embark on something new and different, you relate it to something you already know. You move from "known" to "unknown". Working with Microsoft Office© or any other suite of programs requires tactics, especially if you are a new user. This section will enable you to take small steps using illustrated examples.

The chapters here allow you to experiment without getting bogged down with too much technical detail. They are suitable for all ages. Education is now a life-long pursuit open to all.

Realistically it is not possible to learn word processing, spreadsheet techniques, presentation and database skills prior to enrolling onto a new course. What your tutor needs from you may be smartly presented documents and crisp presentations. In addition you may be required to get your head around figures and formulae, graphs and charts, and you may also be involved with the manipulation of data and databases. Therefore you need a starting point A starting point so that you can cope with the requirements of your course, whilst building up confidence to try something new. That is the way in which these chapters are designed.

The first section deals with making the best use of the electronic (e-) support mechanisms that exist within Further and Higher Education, including on-line facilities and email. The second section helps you to produce smart documents using Microsoft Word©. The third section is in three parts, it considers Microsoft Excel©, firstly as a data management tool, secondly as a facilitator of graph and chart creation and thirdly as a manipulator of facts, figures, formulae and statistics. The fourth section looks at data capture and databases using Microsoft Access©, whilst the fifth is concerned with producing simple but effective presentations using Microsoft PowerPoint©. Throughout the text, key words used to manipulate data and found on toolbars will be shown in bold and underlined in the appropriate place. E.g. **Tools**

A final point is to always take advantage of the free or low cost courses that are available to you at your college, university or through your workplace. Practice makes perfect and **you** *"can make a difference"* to your life by enhancing your capabilities and enriching your experience. The ball is in your court!

Susan Bailey

Acknowledgements

Thanks to contributors

Editorial Consultant, Florence Lee
Administrative Support, Jane Getliffe and Jenny Brown

Thanks to reviewers

Andrew Aston – Southampton Solent University
Stewart Dunlop – Galway Mayo Institute of Technology
Tan Yoke Eng – Canterbury Christchurch University
Tricia Price – University of Westminster
Nigel Richardson – London College of Communication

LINDA LEE-DAVIES
BA (Hons) MBA, PGCTHE

*Senior Lecturer in Organisational Behaviour
and Human Resource Management*

Linda is currently lecturing at Northampton Business School within the University of Northampton. Responsible for a wide portfolio of delivery from undergraduate to postgraduate level, Linda also heads the commercial, part-time management suite through to and including MBA. With a keen research interest and published papers in leadership as well as a passion for promoting personal development planning, she particularly focuses on working with a mix of local, national and international business clients to keep material relevant and useful to the workplace.

Before moving to an academic position four years ago, Linda held a senior role in a large recruitment firm where, in addition to business diagnostics, development and direction setting, she groomed managers for leadership positions. Following a BA in business Linda gained her MBA at Henley Management College and is now conducting doctoral studies in leadership and management.

linda.lee-davies@northampton.ac.uk

SUSAN BAILEY
Cert. Ed., M.Sc., MBCS

Principal Lecturer and Field Chair in Information Sciences

Susan is currently lecturing at Northampton Business School within the University of Northampton. She is responsible for a wide portfolio of delivery from undergraduate to postgraduate level and is Course Leader for the BA in information systems. Susan overseas QA provision within her field and also has special responsibility for the students' Personal Development Portfolio (PDP) requirements. Susan's research interests and published papers are in usability and user centred design with special attention to the older user. Susan also works with local businesses and is involved with Knowledge Transfer Partnership (KTP) in the area.

Before joining the university four years ago, Susan ran her own company and through this provided software training and support for a range of industrial and commercial outlets. Prior to that she worked for Texas Instruments (TI) as a microprocessor training officer. Susan held a range of other senior posts in computer aided design (CAD), QA provision and marketing whilst at TI.

Susan also enjoys fundraising, singing and photography. She has been married to Andrew for 33 years and has two grown up children.

Susan.Bailey@northampton.ac.uk

Walk through tour

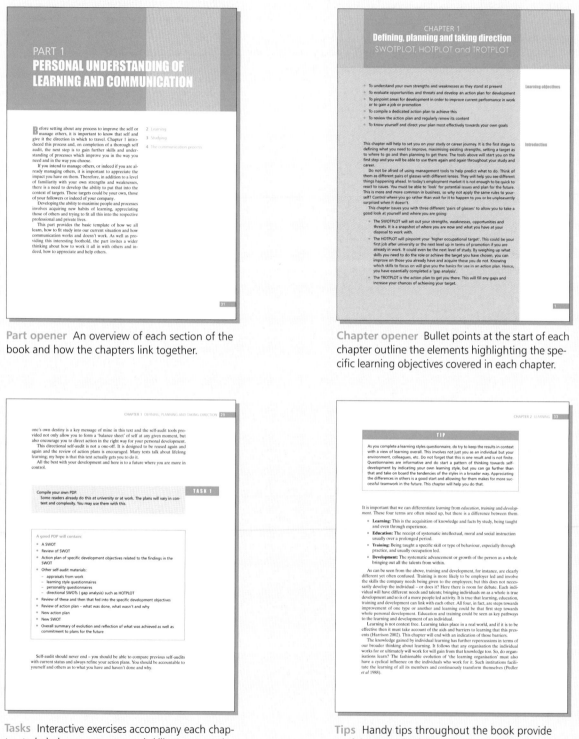

Part opener An overview of each section of the book and how the chapters link together.

Chapter opener Bullet points at the start of each chapter outline the elements highlighting the specific learning objectives covered in each chapter.

Tasks Interactive exercises accompany each chapter, to help hone your personal skills as you read.

Tips Handy tips throughout the book provide useful practical information for work and study.

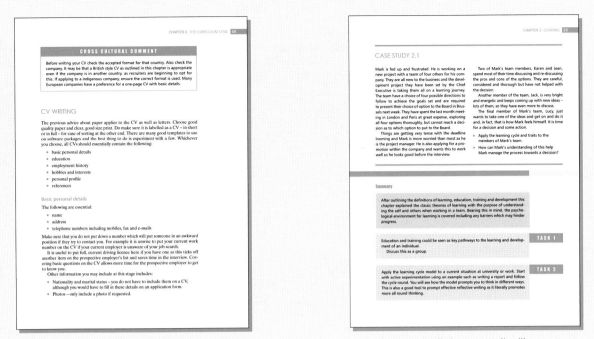

Cross cultural comments Helpful advice on how to approach work and study across cultural barriers.

Case studies Realistic case studies illustrate how key skills issues relate to the real world.

Summaries Briefly recap and review the main concepts and key points covered.

Visit the companion website at
www.thomsonlearning.co.uk/lee-davies
to find valuable teaching and learning material including:

For lecturers

- Notes on case studies and chapter tasks
- PowerPoint slides

For students

- Multiple choice questions
- Weblinks
- Chapter overviews
- Online glossary for the IT skills section

THOMSON

YOUR LEARNING SOLUTIONS PARTNER

About Us | Customer Support/Order | Contact Us | Online Resources | Site Map

STUDENTS

ABOUT THE BOOK
INSTRUCTORS
STUDENTS

Multiple choice questions
Weblinks
Chapter overviews
Glossary

Student's Resources

Multiple choice questions
To test your knowledge of the book, on a chapter-by-chapter basis.

Weblinks
These web links will help you to explore further the material provided within the text.

Chapter overviews
Explains what is covered in the chapter.

Glossary
For the IT skills section.

Developing Work and Study Skills
Linda Lee Davies with Susan Bailey
1844802256

Home | Thomson Learningp

Copyright, Terms & Conditions | Privacy Policy | Webmaster

CHAPTER 1

Defining, planning and taking direction
SWOTPLOT, HOTPLOT and TROTPLOT

- To understand your own strengths and weaknesses as they stand at present
- To evaluate opportunities and threats and develop an action plan for development
- To pinpoint areas for development in order to improve current performance in work or to gain a job or promotion
- To compile a dedicated action plan to achieve this
- To review the action plan and regularly renew its content
- To know yourself and direct your plan most effectively towards your own goals

This chapter will help to set you on your study or career journey. It is the first stage to defining what you need to improve, maximising existing strengths, setting a target as to where to go and then planning to get there. The tools above will start you on the first step and you will be able to use them again and again throughout your study and career.

Do not be afraid of using management tools to help predict what to do. Think of them as different pairs of glasses with different lenses. They will help you see different things happening ahead. In today's employment market it is not enough to be quick to react to issues. You must be able to 'look' for potential issues and plan for the future. This is more and more common in business, so why not apply the same rules to yourself? Control where you go rather than wait for it to happen to you or be unpleasantly surprised when it doesn't.

This chapter issues you with three different 'pairs of glasses' to allow you to take a good look at yourself and where you are going:

- The SWOTPLOT will set out your strengths, weaknesses, opportunities and threats. It is a snapshot of where you are now and what you have at your disposal to work with.
- The HOTPLOT will pinpoint your 'higher occupational target'. This could be your first job after university or the next level up in terms of promotion if you are already in work. It could even be the next level of study. By weighing up what skills you need to do the role or achieve the target you have chosen, you can improve on those you already have and acquire those you do not. Knowing which skills to focus on will give you the basics for use in an action plan. Hence, you have essentially completed a 'gap analysis'.
- The TROTPLOT is the action plan to get you there. This will fill any gaps and increase your chances of achieving your target.

SWOTPLOT

Table 1.1 shows a blank SWOTPLOT grid. We will consider how to fill this in by looking at each heading in turn.

Strengths

Put in at least three but preferably six strengths you have. If you cannot think of any get a friend, colleague, manager or lecturer to help.

Suggestions How would other people describe you? This is not a time to be modest. If you or those helping you think it may be one of your strengths, put it down.

Examples of strengths are: confident, hard-working, trustworthy, finisher, motivated, articulate, organised, approachable, understanding, decisive, thorough, gregarious, good team player, target orientated, methodical, creative, innovative, accurate, imaginative, persistent, flexible, stable, quick to react to change, outgoing, supportive, able to cope with pressure.

Do not unthinkingly copy from the examples – only put them in if they really apply to you. To get the most out of the SWOTPLOT you must put things as they are – *not* as you wish them to be. Make sure your chosen strengths really reflect you.

Weaknesses

What are your particular weaknesses? Enter up to six but do not go overboard – try to balance each with a strength.

Suggestions Be really honest without being too self-persecuting. Also try to word them in as positive a way as possible so they lend themselves to you thinking of a way to develop a plan to improve or allow for them.

Examples of weaknesses are: less organised than is desirable, not always able to manage time effectively, money management/finance problems (particularly if you are a student), not confident at public speaking/presentations, inadequate attention paid to detail, less creative than you would like, too reactive to others, easily influenced, poor written skills in terms of spelling/grammar, not assertive enough, less confident than desirable, prone to worry.

Think about these very carefully as they will form the basis of a forward action plan. Cover all aspects of your life – not just the course you are on or the job you are in. Think of work, study, family, friends and previous times where you have been aware of some disappointment or awareness of your own limitations – and we all have them. It is important for you to accept this, as some things can be improved but others you may have to accept and learn to work around. Such recognition and definition is part of the personal development process. We gain more and more confidence by learning to accept ourselves and working with what we have.

Table 1.1 SWOTPLOT – blank

	Strengths **S**	Weaknesses **W**	Opportunities **O**	Threats **T**
Points arising **P**				
List **L**				
Obligation **O**				
Time **T**				

Opportunities

Write down your opportunities – now and in the future – again cover all aspects of your life: work, family, study, hobbies, social, etc. Think of everything in terms of a chance to use your strengths and develop your weaknesses.

Suggestions Examples of opportunities are: the course of study you are on or potential courses which may help, pending/potential promotion at work, a chance to take part in a presentation/public speaking, projects at work or university, a social engagement, sports, a due assignment or report, support from family, job interview, company growth/change, previous mistakes – by you and other people – that you can learn from.

As you work through all the aspects of your life, try to view things with a 'glass half full' approach (an optimistic approach) to get the most out of this section. In this case, rose tinted glasses are good – the more positive you are here, the better your action plan will be for the future.

At this stage a positive outlook can be the difference between seeing something as an opportunity or a threat. Of course, in some cases, the same thing can be both an opportunity and a threat.

Threats

What may stand in your way? What may prevent you from doing what you want to? The word threat suggests something sinister – but this is not always the case. Often threats are simple and innocent things in our lives – things which are not necessarily harmful or distressing but which limit our ability to progress in the way we had originally planned. It is quite acceptable to put something under the heading of threat which is pleasant but which may have repercussions to your career or future plans. Remember this is nothing to do with being nasty or resentful – it is about being realistic and dealing with what comes our way in a positive way.

Also, of course, some threats are sinister – don't be frightened – write them down and then they can be dealt with. The 'ostrich' technique will not serve you well here – you need to be as transparent as possible and to face up to whatever the threat is.

Suggestions Examples of threats are: family crises, lack of money, friends wanting to go out, maternity, paternity, not getting on with a boss, redundancy, bullying, lack of willpower, working while studying, studying while working, lack of privacy, lack of time, family versus work/study, fear of failure, self perception, lack of confidence.

It is also acceptable to have the same item under both 'opportunity' and 'threat' in order to get the most well rounded outcome from your set of anchor points.

Tables 1.2 and 1.3 are examples of SWOTPLOTs initially filled in by a student and a manager/potential manager respectively. We will now consider how the rest of the grid should be completed to turn it into an action plan.

Table 1.2 SWOTPLOT (student example)

	Strengths **S**	Weaknesses **W**	Opportunities **O**	Threats **T**
	Reliable Methodical Willing Cooperative Hard-working Flexible	Confidence Time management Distraction Organisation Assertion	Group presentation Assignment due Weekend work Family support Friends	No money Social life Weekend work Fear of failure Time management
Points arising **P**				
List **L**				
Obligation **O**				
Time **T**				

Table 1.3 SWOTPLOT (manager/potential manager example)

	Strengths S	Weaknesses W	Opportunities O	Threats T
	Fairly confident Articulate Approachable Team worker Hard-working Understanding	Presentations Time management Saying yes too often Written skills	Regular meetings Annual conference Change at work Colleagues Course of study	Financial commitments Growing family Time Fear of failure Not enough belief in self
Points arising P				
List L				
Obligation O				
Time T				

Points arising

Using the phrase 'which means that' after the items entered in your SWOT, enter points for preservation or attention. This highlights its repercussions and links to direction. Use a positive viewpoint and think of ways to overcome the negative. For example, if you know that a particular weakness for you, as for many others, is a lack of presentation skills, then you could seek a chance to enter into group work or a project or situation which commits you to doing some presentation work. If you feel you say 'yes' to too many things, then a focus on assertiveness is in order.

Interpret your SWOT entries by changing their order and by switching the phrases around too; for example, time management becomes manage time. This technique gets you thinking actively about a solution and turning it into an action. Alternatively, ask yourself a question about it or use a phrase like 'need a chance to' which makes it positive and proactive and takes it from the 'talk' stage to the 'walk' stage.

List

List *specific* ways or options to achieve or deal with the points which have arisen. For instance, extending the examples above, a project, meeting or conference where you can start presenting and an assertiveness course or some instruction. Feel free to list alternatives for the same point to give yourself choice. Again ask yourself questions to help. None of this is about exactness, it is about direction and the SWOTPLOT will help you evolve a direction for yourself. You can then keep building on it, so it does not matter if you have not included everything at this stage.

Obligation

Obligate yourself now to a specific action for each point by adding a verb to your chosen list of options or a specific outlet. For example *attend* a weekly/monthly meeting or *take part in* a group presentation for assessment and *book* an assertiveness course or *read* about assertiveness. Make a choice from any list of actions and state a precise intention related to a real and specific thing. Change your approach here to an active one by choosing a direct verb such as take/attend/chair a weekly meeting. The idea is to give yourself a realistic target that you will be able to achieve.

Time

Give each item an exact time. For example for a weekly/monthly meeting, put the date in the plan and in your diary. For the assertiveness course, put a time limit on it, such as three months, so that it becomes an action and does not remain an intention. However, do not just put 'three months' in – also look up the date in your diary, list it and enter the obligation in your diary for follow up. If the worst case scenario is that you have not managed to do what you set to do at least you can reschedule it and not forget it.

Table 1.4 SWOTPLOT (student example)

	Strengths S	Weaknesses W	Opportunities O	Threats T
	Reliable Methodical Willing Cooperative Hard-working Flexible	Confidence Time management Distraction Organisation Assertion	Group presentation Assignment due Weekend work Family support Friends	No money Social life Weekend work Fear of failure Time management
Points arising P	Need a chance to organise or audit within a group or project	Need to build confidence Need to address use of time Need to say no	Use weekend work to improve experience Assignment Presentation coming up	Budgeting Balance work, social life and university Organise time and face failure
List L				
Obligation O				
Time T				

Table 1.5 SWOTPLOT (manager/potential manager example)

	Strengths S	Weaknesses W	Opportunities O	Threats T
	Fairly confident Articulate Approachable Team worker Hard-working Understanding	Presentations Time management Saying yes too often Written skills	Regular meetings Annual conference Change at work Colleagues Course of study	Financial commitments Growing family Time Fear of failure Not enough belief in self
Points arising P	Need a chance to build confidence and use verbal skills	Improve written skills Be assertive Manage time Present	Pick a meeting Can I do anything at the conference? What courses can I take?	Split time between family and work Build more confidence in self
List L				
Obligation O				
Time T				

Table 1.6 SWOTPLOT (student example)

	Strengths S	Weaknesses W	Opportunities O	Threats T
	Reliable Methodical Willing Cooperative Hard-working Flexible	Confidence Time management Distraction Organisation Assertion	Group presentation Assignment due Weekend work Family support Friends	No money Social life Weekend work Fear of failure Time management
Points arising P	Need a chance to organise or audit within a group or project	Need to build confidence Need to address use of time Need to say no	Use weekend work to improve experience Assignment Presentation coming up	Budgeting Balance work, social life and university Organise time and face failure
List L	Organise involvement in group work or project Is there a group assignment coming up?	Assertiveness course Time management course How do I use my time?	Reflect on work experience Relate study to work and assignment Take part in a presentation	Look at finances and how I spend my time Think about what can go right as well as wrong
Obligation O				
Time T				

Table 1.7 SWOTPLOT (manager/potential manager example)

	Strengths S	Weaknesses W	Opportunities O	Threats T
	Fairly confident Articulate Approachable Team worker Hard-working Understanding	Presentations Time management Saying yes too often Written skills	Regular meetings Annual conference Change at work Colleagues Course of study	Financial commitments Growing family Time Fear of failure Not enough belief in self
Points arising P	Need a chance to build confidence and use verbal skills	Improve written skills Be assertive Manage time Present	Pick a meeting Can I do anything at the conference? What courses can I take?	Split time between family and work Build more confidence in self
List L	Front line project with team	Refresh on rules of writing Assertiveness course Presentations course Time management course	What meeting shall I take? What shall I do at the conference? What course is best for what I need?	How do I split my time? Think about what can go right as well as wrong? Learn from my mistakes
Obligation O				
Time T				

Table 1.8 SWOTPLOT (student example)

	Strengths **S**	Weaknesses **W**	Opportunities **O**	Threats **T**
	Reliable Methodical Willing Cooperative Hard-working Flexible	Confidence Time management Distraction Organisation Assertion	Group presentation Assignment due Weekend work Family support Friends	No money Social life Weekend work Fear of failure Time management
Points arising **P**	Need a chance to organise or audit within a group or project	Need to build confidence Need to address use of time Need to say no	Use weekend work to improve experience Assignment Presentation coming up	Budgeting Balance work, social life and university Organise time and face failure
List **L**	Organise involvement in group work or project Is there a group assignment coming up?	Assertiveness course Time management course How do I use my time?	Reflect on work experience Relate study to work and assignment Take part in a presentation	Look at finances and how I spend my time Think about what can go right as well as wrong
Obligation **O**	Be organiser and auditor in next group assignment	Book an assertiveness course Read about assertiveness Go on a time management course Analyse and plan my time	Write about work experience Use this in next assignment Find out when next presentation is and make sure I have a key role in it	Analyse my time Plan my time Analyse my finances Plan my finances List everything that can go well in a presentation Read about presentations or go on a course
Time **T**				

Table 1.9 SWOTPLOT (manager/potential manager example)

	Strengths S	Weaknesses W	Opportunities O	Threats T
	Fairly confident Articulate Approachable Team worker Hard-working Understanding	Presentations Time management Saying yes too often Written skills	Regular meetings Annual conference Change at work Colleagues Course of study	Financial commitments Growing family Time Fear of failure Not enough belief in self
Points arising **P**	Need a chance to build confidence and use verbal skills	Improve written skills Be assertive Manage time Present	Pick a meeting Can I do anything at the conference? What courses can I take?	Split time between family and work Build more confidence in self
List **L**	Front line project with team	Refresh on rules of writing Assertiveness course Presentations course Time management course	What meeting shall I take? What shall I do at the conference? What course is best for what I need?	How do I split my time? Think about what can go right as well as wrong? Learn from my mistakes
Obligation **O**	Isolate next project and lead it	Read about writing skills Book assertiveness course Go on presentations course Book time management course	Look up next suitable meeting – chair it Present with others at the conference Book a course of study e.g. CMS	Analyse my time Make a time plan List my mistakes and see what learnt Analyse rights and wrongs in meeting I chair
Time **T**				

Table 1.10 SWOTPLOT (student example)

	Strengths S	Weaknesses W	Opportunities O	Threats T
	Reliable Methodical Willing Cooperative Hard-working Flexible	Confidence Time management Distraction Organisation Assertion	Group presentation Assignment due Weekend work Family support Friends	No money Social life Weekend work Fear of failure Time management
Points arising P	Need a chance to organise or audit within a group or project	Need to build confidence Need to address use of time Need to say no	Use weekend work to improve experience Assignment Presentation coming up	Budgeting Balance work, social life and university Organise time and face failure
List L	Organise involvement in group work or project Is there a group assignment coming up?	Assertiveness course Time management course How do I use my time?	Reflect on work experience Relate study to work and assignment Take part in a presentation	Look at finances and how I spend my time Think about what can go right as well as wrong
Obligation O	Be organiser and auditor in next group assignment	Book an assertiveness course Read about assertiveness Go on a time management course Analyse and plan my time	Write about work experience Use this in next assignment Find out when next presentation is and make sure I have a key role in it	Analyse my time Plan my time Analyse my finances Plan my finances List everything that can go well in a presentation Read about presentations or go on a course
Time T	Date of next group assignment – here and in diary	Book now – enter on list of things to do in diary Read now Go on course within month – date here and in diary Plan time now	Write now – finish by Friday – date here and in diary Date of next assignment Date of presentation	Analyse and plan now List now Read about presentations by next Monday Date of presentation course here and in diary

Table 1.11 SWOTPLOT (manager/potential manager example)

	Strengths S	Weaknesses W	Opportunities O	Threats T
	Fairly confident Articulate Approachable Team worker Hard-working Understanding	Presentations Time management Saying yes too often Written skills	Regular meetings Annual conference Change at work Colleagues Course of study	Financial commitments Growing family Time Fear of failure Not enough belief in self
Points arising **P**	Need a chance to build confidence and use verbal skills	Improve written skills Be assertive Manage time Present	Pick a meeting Can I do anything at the conference? What courses can I take?	Split time between family and work Build more confidence in self
List **L**	Front line project with team	Refresh on rules of writing Assertiveness course Presentations course Time management course	What meeting shall I take? What shall I do at the conference? What course is best for what I need?	How do I split my time? Think about what can go right as well as wrong? Learn from my mistakes
Obligation **O**	Isolate next project and lead it	Read about writing skills Book assertiveness course Go on presentations course Book time management course	Look up next suitable meeting – chair it Present with others at the conference Book a course of study e.g. CMS	Analyse my time Make a time plan List my mistakes and see what learnt Analyse rights and wrongs in meeting I chair
Time **T**	Date of next project here and in diary	Read now Book now Put date of courses here and in diary	Date of next meeting – here and in diary Date of conference Date of course of study	Analyse above now Plan now and have complete before (date) List now Analyse meeting elements (date) before meeting

As you complete your SWOTPLOT, you can feel the evolution and can create a focus and sense of direction for yourself – something you can now undertake at any time. There is a lot you can do with this work – it does not stop here. Remember it is ongoing. Personal development is ongoing and learning is for life.

You have created a basic action plan from the original SWOT. The tool only leaves room for bullet points and a good exercise is to expand on the actions and list further tasks around them. Come on, really talk yourself into them! Another very useful exercise is to write about the whole process and reflect on what you have found out. Write in terms of 'I' and just talk about it as you go through each box. You should be able to write a couple of sides of A4 in this way or more! This will firm up the commitments and give you valuable experience of reflective writing – a skill now used more and more in assessment for study and for assessment at work at all levels. There are examples of reflective writing below but remember it is about *you*. Some guidelines are also given.

Having evolved an action plan, you need to check what you have and haven't done. Tick off your achievements and analyse your development. Equally, look at why some things were not achieved and how you can prevent that barrier arising again.

A useful tip is to list a set of action points – similar to the actions in the minutes of a meeting. Also set yourself a deadline to check what has been achieved.

Reflective writing

With the increase in portfolio work assessment from undergraduate level to reflective sections of reports at MBA level, reflective writing is a skill to get to grips with early on. Because it is personal and because it is written more freely than an essay or business report, it can be difficult to approach. Some people even think it is a bit silly or fluffy! Whatever the opinion, it is becoming more of a necessity to master this skill. In fact, one must be able to switch from the scientific/factual approach of report writing to the more holistic/emotional approach of reflective work. Both of these skills are now key in both the academic and business worlds and it is not enough to be good at just one of them.

The key to reflective writing is to avoid pure description. Just talking about what happens will not impress and will probably bore the reader. As the name suggests, it is the reflection which counts and this means showing what effect things have had on the writer, what it means to them and where it will take them. Evolution is the way to succeed with reflective writing and this should be demonstrated very clearly in the text. Showing your understanding of the situation you are writing about and how it can be used elsewhere is important. Demonstrating development at different levels and talking about it retrospectively as well as taking it forward shows a management mentality prepared to keep learning as well as being able to constructively criticise the self.

Figure 1.1 is a good cross check. As you are writing, check to see if you have covered the directions and levels.

This model encourages you to think about your self and your own evolution as well as that of those around you. You can replace the vertical entries with the appropriate people who surround you to suit your particular situation. However you do it, the key is to see the effect on others as well as yourself and to think about the past, present and future in all cases. This will demonstrate mature reflection of a holistic nature.

To make life easier when faced with portfolio compilation, make quick notes on different bits of paper as things happen and file them away. These will prompt creative flow later. Once writing, write as you speak and worry about editing later.

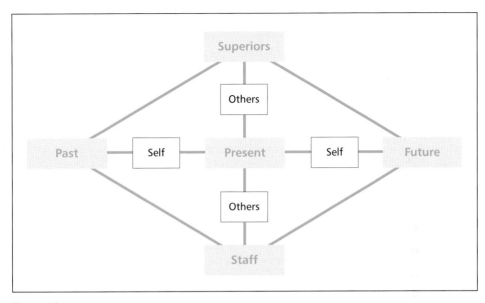

Figure 1.1 Reflective cross check

Feelings are good in this type of production – write how you feel. Even if you do not know how to phrase something, write down a word which covers it and you can make the sentences make sense later. This way you will capture the natural essence of the writing and it will be truly reflective instead of a mini business report or essay.

REFLECTIVE WRITING (student example)

November 200*

I have just completed my first group assignment which involved a joint report and a presentation. It was not the most enjoyable experience I have had since starting university and, frankly, I would have preferred to do it on my own, but I can clearly see the reason for having to do it in terms of preparing me for the future workplace. I have also had to overcome some personal fears in doing the presentation and feel much stronger for doing so.

We were split into groups at the beginning of term with over five weeks before the assignment was due in. We all thought this was plenty of time which was a mistake. All of us underestimated how difficult it was going to be to get everyone together at the same time and how much research and planning would be needed in order to get a good grade. There were five in my group and from the start there was a lot of arguing. Two members of the group were particularly bad and were always arguing as to what was the priority – it was clear they were battling to lead the group and I think they cost the group a lot of time with this. Me, I just wanted a quiet life and to know what I needed to do – do it and thought everyone else would do the same. It did not work out like this. Another member of the group kept failing to do their bit and when they did do things, it was always at the last minute. This was really annoying and we made sure they knew it.

Two weeks before the deadline the group finally got it together – following a very big argument. Each person went away and completed an allocated task and we all met the day before the due date to pull it and the presentation together. We got a C and a C+ respectively and learnt a lot in the process.

(continued)

I know now that it is normal to argue in groups and this is reflected in Tuckman's theory of form, storm, norm and perform. (Harvard ref). However, our group stayed in this stage for too long and cost us a grade or two in the process. If we had 'normed' earlier we could have increased the depth of our work and even enjoyed it more. With the benefit of hindsight, I can see how we could have achieved this. We could have had an agenda and each chaired the meeting in turn so everyone had a chance to be responsible for the whole group. This would have solved the arguing – particularly between the two 'leaders'. Also I could have taken on more responsibility this way. I can see I was only interested in my bit and getting it done and didn't really see the whole picture at all. In addition to this if the group had been more encouraging to the member who needed it rather than excluding them, they may have been more productive and also enjoyed it more. If Adair's theory is applied to this situation it can be seen that each individual concentrated more on themselves rather than the task in question and the team as a whole.

This imbalance is clearly seen with hindsight and it would be a good idea to apply this tool to the situation earlier to 'test' what is being achieved and what level of balance there is. I can see what a good lesson this is for a future management career. If I can predict what may happen within a group and indeed put measures in to check the progress of a group, then I have more chance of succeeding with any teams I am in charge of.

From a personal and emotional point of view, I really gained a lot from doing the presentation, although it was very hard. As a group we did not prepare enough. We did get our PowerPoint® slides done but it was clear they were patched together from different sources and lacked consistency. Also some of the slides were difficult to read as we put too much information on them. We spent a lot of time setting up as we did not know how to use the equipment in the room. I was very nervous and felt sick that morning. I took in lots of notes on A4 and could feel my hands shaking as I read it out. This was in the feedback – I was reading with my head down. I did feel good though that I got through it as I thought I was going to bottle out at the last minute and the lecturer praised me for overcoming my nerves well. I have since done another presentation in another module and felt I had really improved. It wasn't perfect as I still read a bit – but I definitely looked up more at the audience and came across with a bit more confidence. I am really going to work on this and feel I have learnt a lot in terms of skills for the workplace. Being able to give a confident presentation is important in management. I now make sure I can use the equipment, prepare well in advance and make notes on numbered cards to help me look more professional.

REFLECTIVE WRITING (manager/potential manager example)

Meeting performance analysis

I have just chaired my first formal meeting and have mixed feelings about the outcome. A number of things went very well but I am not sure if I asserted myself well enough throughout and did not achieve the overall objective.

The meeting drew together a mix of staff from my team with the purpose of discussing the merging of three registration systems into one. Two members represented each system, with representatives from IT, Marketing and Finance present. The minutes of the meeting will be forwarded to the operations director and regional management team.

Technically the meeting went very well. Paperwork went out well in advance and everyone came equipped to discuss the issue. Housekeeping matters such as venue, equipment, etc. went smoothly and I had had a number of attachments forwarded before the meeting so could set up people quickly with anything they wanted to display as a presentation to the group. I was really pleased about this as I had worried a great deal about things going wrong – even down to the food not arriving. All this went well.

I stuck to the agenda closely and each team had a fair opportunity to present the strengths of their particular system to the others. Marketing, Finance and IT also presented the factors important to their departments. This took some time but all were well informed and I thought this would progress to a healthy debate and final decisions about what to include in the final system. I opened the floor for debate – dreading silence – and in fact was pleasantly surprised at the immediate interest and passion. However, it became clear that each team was simply safeguarding their own system as it currently stood and the floor divided. One particular team were far more vocal than others and it was clear things were getting out of control. I did manage to quieten everyone down and ask for input towards one system. Although I received a few ideas, I felt by this time there was a reluctance and the spirit I had hoped for and thought was developing through the presentations was lost. I also suspected that although a few had not spoken up much during the meeting they had left unhappy and would talk about it in a more covert way.

This was certainly a baptism of fire and I feel, as chair, I could have controlled a number of things in a better way.

Up to the point of the debate everyone was happy and contributing well. This good work was undone by the arguing. On consideration, I could have made a small presentation myself, as chair, to state the objective again and to guide everyone to contribute to that – rather than fight for their own system. I could then have split the cohort up into mixed teams and set each team the task of contributing four key things towards the final system. At the end of the group work – where each had also had the chance to get to know others better – I could have written the ideas up on a board and encouraged a healthy brainstorm. By standing up at the head, I would have naturally asserted my authority but yet still guided the ideas from the floor to a point where they are used. I could have encouraged the ideas to be owned and agreed by the group and ensured that names were attributed to the ideas and these printed in the minutes for the senior team to see. I could also have asked for and set up a working party – made up of a representative from each opposing team to see the work through to implementation.

The action of writing this reflection of events had helped me focus on what I need to do and in fact, I will do it before sending the minutes off to the senior team. I will reconvene a shorter meeting where I will do the above and ensure all parties leave satisfied and well represented. This can be added to minutes. It will be clear then that not only has each individual contributed well but that we operated well as a whole team and indeed managed to achieve the task set and start implementation. I will also sport my ability to constructively criticise my own actions and lead the team in the same direction as the company.

HIGHER OCCUPATIONAL TARGET

Make a list of all the skills needed for the next stage that you wish to be at. The best way to approach this if it is job related is to take the job description of the role you aspire to and list all the skills necessary to do it. Table 1.12 provides a grid to enable you to perform this analysis.

- Handy skills: Enter the desirable skills you need for this target or role.
- Obligatory skills: Enter the essential skills you need for this target or role.
- Tick: Tick those you have and make note of those which you do not have or which may need improving.

Table 1.12 HOTPLOT		
Handy skills H	Obligatory skills O	Tick if have them T

This personal management tool is really easy and quick to fill in and it is also useful to complete one when applying for new roles and before an interview as a personal audit. Being prepared will help you anticipate likely interview questions and ensure you appear more confident in terms of your direction.

Table 1.13 illustrates a completed HOTPLOT and serves as an example for both student and management needs.

Table 1.13 HOTPLOT

Handy skills H	Obligatory skills O	Tick if have them T
IT literacy – spreadsheet and PowerPoint®	Presentation	✔ ✔
Administrative	Report writing	✔ ✔
Business development	Supervisory	✔ ✔
Chairing	Motivational	✔ ✔
	Organisational	✔
	Performance management	✔
	Client facing	✔

As an alternative to ticking the skills you could grade yourself. Use whatever system helps you the most. You could even change the tool and tick the skills you haven't got – it is up to you. If you look at the completed HOTPLOT you can see that the obligatory skills form the spine of your findings as they run down the middle of the tool. This is the first focus and actions will pivot from there. The example HOTPLOT indicates that a priority for development would be presentational skills and mastering performance management.

Where you have the required skills and have ticked them, you need to be able to explain how you acquired them and how you can demonstrate them if questioned at an interview, so take the opportunity to make some notes about this now. It is also a good idea to think of practical examples which demonstrate your claim. Make a note of these too and you will not be caught out at interview.

If you have not gained some of the obligatory skills to date then what are you going to do to get them? The next management tool will help you with this.

In the example above two of the handy skills are there and two are not. Apply the same approach as above to these and bear in mind that these can be useful leverage in terms of competitive advantage at interview.

The findings from this management tool can now be transported to the TROTPLOT. This is going to commit you to action to achieve the skills you need to help ensure you travel in the direction you wish to go.

TROTPLOT

This management tool is similar to the SWOTPLOT but is much more specific in nature in terms of its direction. It is your choice whether you use all the tools or a mix of them to suit yourself. Once again, we will look at each section of the grid in turn.

Target skills

Transfer to this square from the HOTPLOT: target skills are the skills you have pinpointed as not having.

Refine existing skills

Enter here the existing skills you have that need further development. If you are using this specifically for an application or interview then also put in the skills you have ticked on the HOTPLOT as having already acquired so you can start thinking of examples. In addition, you can think about how to keep and refine them for the role in question.

Opportunities

Have you any opportunities to gain or develop or even observe someone else doing the skills you have highlighted?

Table 1.14 TROTPLOT				
	Target skills T	Refine existing skills R	Opportunities O	Threats T
Points arising P				
List L				
Obligation O				
Time T				

Threats

What might stand in your way? This applies to work, home, family, social life – anything which may be a factor in preventing you gaining the skills shortages you have identified.

From this point completion of the grid is the same as for the SWOTPLOT.

- Points arising: Using the phrase 'which means that' enter points for preservation or attention.
- List: List specific ways to achieve these ideas.
- Obligations: Obligate yourself now to a specific action for each point.
- Time: Give each item an exact time scale.

You can also write in over two boxes if it suits: see Table 1.15. As long as the analysis is made and a direction and time commitment entered, you can use the tool as you like. The idea is to achieve action points for a plan.

You can also add in any additional material from your original SWOTPLOT in the appropriate places and you will have the start of a tailored action plan. The SWOTPLOT is tailored to you in general, the TROTPLOT to a specific direction, for example an interview, and the two together ensure you are aware of your needs and development but most importantly have directed them exactly to where you want to go.

In addition to directing actions more specifically and highlighting points to bring up at interview for example, the TROTPLOT, as do the other tools, gives you the ammunition to be able to talk about yourself.

This is useful when applying for jobs but it also works to increase your confidence on an ongoing basis. As we get to know ourselves better, we are more able to accept both our strengths and weaknesses and this helps with the image we portray in everyday life. It can create either satisfaction or acceptance and these show because they lead to self-perpetuating virtuous circle rather than the more negative vicious one.

A good way of starting this off is to use the tools in this chapter. Take one of them and talk out loud to yourself about yourself. Talk about what you see and ad lib; even more ideas may occur to you as you open yourself up for more creative thinking.

This practice means that when you are required to represent yourself in the future – such as at interview – it will sound naturally confident because it comes from within rather than it being something you have tried to memorise before the event.

Sometimes people can be sceptical about the value of these kinds of tools – not usually those with a management mentality, it has to be said, but more often those who do not follow it through – and it is important to note that even more value comes from their use over time. Students and managers in the past have found such audits or personal portfolios of great use when looking back a year later. They can then see how far they have come. In order to achieve the greatest clarity of hindsight, there are a few more steps to be taken.

ACTION AUDIT

Once the tools are completed, date them and keep them. Then it is a good idea – especially for portfolio work – to create a list of the action points you derived from the

Table 1.15 TROTPLOT

	Target skills T	Refine existing skills R	Opportunities O	Threats T
	Presentation Business development Chairing Performance management	IT ☆ Admin Report writing Supervisory Motivational Organisational Client facing	Meeting/group work in three weeks New company in town New team	Holiday period Family commitments Lack of confidence
Points arising P	Need to read/train in presentation and try to do one What new business can I get? Need to chair meetings What is performance management?	Add database skills to portfolio Analyse time management Increase client work	Need to plan and work up to meeting/group work Need to research new company Need to assess what new team needs and get to know them	Need to plan around holidays Inform family of my needs Find a way to build confidence
List L				
Obligation O	Presentation at meeting in three weeks – commit now Analyse new business and get client visits – two weeks Chair next meeting – three weeks – date in diary Get book on performance management now and read within two weeks	Book database training now for next month Analyse time now – replot and plan for next fortnight Client visits as to left	Having committed to presentation and chair for next meeting – assess all requirements and book now New company client visit within three weeks Team building meeting in one week	Set up holiday planner and plan work before and after for team – NOW Give family my timetable Book first singing lesson for next week – always wanted to do this
Time T				

☆ Ensure that I note examples of each of these for interview questions

tools. From this create yourself an **action check list** where you can tick off the actions as you complete them. Even better, create a more rigorous **action audit** where you review the results and create further actions from them as well as indicate why you have not done something and what you are going to do about it.

For portfolio work at all levels a physical **action plan** compiled following a personal analysis is always a good idea and is often specified in the marking criteria. Many successful managers and students plot these in the form of charts/tables where they plot the action over time. See Table 1.16 for an example.

Table 1.16 Action audit – ACE chase

| Action | Completed? | Excuse/evaluation |
A	C	E

Tailor the action audit to suit by adding further rows for further actions. Alternatively make up one of your own. As long as an audit is carried out the exact format does not matter.

Periodic comparisons are of great use and read very well in portfolio work. Comparing two SWOTPLOTS done at different times works well. Of even more value is to assess the action plans and evolve them.

If you have not been set a target then set your own to do another SWOTPLOT and review your progress. Quarterly reviews work well but make sure you review at least once annually.

HOTPLOTs and TROTPLOTs can be done whenever needed for the focus needed.

Summary

This chapter has provided several tools for personal audit and progression. Personal analysis for the present is achieved through the SWOTPLOT which leads on to an action plan based on those present findings.

- Reflective writing is encouraged and examples are provided.
- A gap analysis is described to direct actions towards career goals. A progressive audit is made through the HOTPLOT, taking into consideration both current jobs and those the reader may be aiming for in the future.
- Specific direction towards those aims is then achieved through the TROTPLOT and these actions are audited through the ACE chase. This portfolio of audit tools provides a thorough insight into the self and career needs now and for the future.
- The tools are tasks in themselves and the reader is effectively the case study in this chapter. Tips on how to use the tools and fill them in are clearly given throughout the chapter. The chapter is devoted to self diagnosis in the spirit that progression as well as managing and leading others is based on a good sound knowledge of self.

References and further reading

Pedler, M., Burgoyne, J. and Boydell, T. (2001) *A Manager's Guide to Self Development*, Berkshire: McGraw-Hill Education.

Websites

www.mindtools.com/swot.html
www.quintcareers.com/SWOT_Analysis.html

ENDNOTE: PERSONAL DEVELOPMENT PLANNING

Personal development planning (PDP) is here to stay. Development is no longer about being in the right place at the right time or simply about gaining paper qualifications. These, especially the latter, are still important but effective personal development requires the gaining and refining of certain skills that are simply not examined in the usual formal way. These are the things which give you the edge at interview and in the workplace. Where paper qualifications are important, they are the basic currency only. The currency of differentiation comes from competency in many of the extra skills covered in this book. These are the skills which not only help you to achieve the basic currency but which help you stand out form the crowd.

Largely, these skills come down to 'communication' – our communication with others in different forms, and, of course, our communication with ourselves. By improving these lines of communication we head towards a greater likelihood of success. By knowing ourselves we can proactively channel our energies in the right direction and endeavour to improve things appropriate to our needs and the situation. By knowing some of the rules in the different forms of communications with others, we can avoid misunderstandings and, furthermore, we can understand others in order to help develop them also.

Effective PDP is proactive – we take charge of the direction of development by regular evaluation, action planning and review. We naturally do all of these things for our businesses but so rarely take the time to invest the same audit to ourselves. We can audit our businesses to prevent them going in the wrong direction, and can apply the same rules to ourselves to prevent us going in the wrong direction.

This should become a life habit. Personal development planning should be a natural part of working life and getting into the habit of doing it is not as difficult as it seems. Often when staff are faced with PDP they are reluctant. It is unknown territory and can seem a waste of time to someone who cannot see what great results can be achieved. Also, if superiors misuse them at bad appraisals that also cultivates suspicion.

Admittedly, self-audit can be laborious. Like any data collection it can be a little tedious – filling in questionnaires, forms, etc. It is what you read into that data and then what you do with it that counts. This is the same in business and the same when writing essays and reports for academia – it is the analysis of those findings which educates towards a direction more likely to be correct for the individual.

This book attempts to provide many of the basics needed to study well in higher education and develop in the workplace and it is hoped that the direct links to the workplace make it 'real'. More than that though, I really hope to inspire the reader with a healthy attitude towards personal development planning. Taking charge of one's own destiny is a key message of mine in this text and the self-audit tools provided not only allow you to form a 'balance sheet' of self at any given moment, but also encourage you to direct action in the right way for your personal development.

This directional self-audit is not a one-off. It is designed to be reused again and again and the review of action plans is encouraged. Many texts talk about lifelong learning; my hope is that this text actually gets you to do it.

All the best with your development and here is to a future where you are more in control.

TASK 1

Compile your own PDP.

Some readers already do this at university or at work. The plans will vary in content and complexity. You may use them with this.

A good PDP will contain:

- A SWOT
- Review of SWOT
- Action plan of specific development objectives related to the findings in the SWOT
- Other self-audit materials:
  - appraisals from work
  - learning style questionnaires
  - personality questionnaires
  - directional SWOTs (gap analysis) such as HOTPLOT
- Review of these and then that fed into the specific development objectives
- Review of action plan – what was done, what wasn't and why
- New action plan
- New SWOT
- Overall summary of evolution and reflection of what was achieved as well as commitment to plans for the future

---

Self-audit should never end – you should be able to compare previous self-audits with current status and always refine your action plans. You should be accountable to yourself and others as to what you have and haven't done and why.

Some academic modules are now specifically geared towards this and the assessment is in effect a PDP. Don't undervalue these. For example, some students studying specific material such as marketing, accountancy, etc. may wonder what the value of doing personal development is at the time. In my recruitment experience there is no sector which does not require these generic skills – all individuals likely to take up any position of responsibility have a duty to their future team to round themselves for the role. Aim for your own balance. You deserve to succeed.

PART 1
PERSONAL UNDERSTANDING OF LEARNING AND COMMUNICATION

Before setting about any process to improve the self or manage others, it is important to know that self and give it the direction in which to travel. Chapter 1 introduced this process and, on completion of a thorough self audit, the next step is to gain further skills and understanding of processes which improve you in the way you need and in the way you choose.

If you intend to manage others, or indeed if you are already managing others, it is important to appreciate the impact you have on them. Therefore, in addition to a level of familiarity with your own strengths and weaknesses, there is a need to develop the ability to put that into the context of targets. These targets could be your own, those of your followers or indeed of your company.

Developing the ability to maximise people and processes involves acquiring new habits of learning, appreciating those of others and trying to fit all this into the respective professional and private lives.

This part provides the basic template of how we all learn, how to fit study into our current situation and how communication works and doesn't work. As well as providing this interesting foothold, the part invites a wider thinking about how to work it all in with others and indeed, how to appreciate and help others.

CHAPTER 2
Learning

Learning objectives

- To understand the different ways in which we learn
- To appreciate the differences in others
- To understand one's own learning ability
- To understand barriers to learning

Introduction

In order to understand learning many texts start with an introduction to a learning styles questionnaire (LSQ). These questionnaires pinpoint your learning preferences rather than your learnt habits and are very useful in helping you understand yourself. However, they do not tend to encourage a healthy overview of learning across different levels and an appreciation of the differences in others is also important for your development.

This chapter sets out to broaden this approach. It is important to know the basics of the classic theories, so an awareness of where and how learning takes place is established. It is also a good idea to do an LSQ at some point, both to experience it and to isolate your own trends – although not as a first step. A good adaptation of the classic LSQ can be found in the text indicated at the end of this chapter. Also indicated are several internet sites which will relieve any curiosity.

> **TIP**
>
> As you complete a learning styles questionnaire, do try to keep the results in context with a view of learning overall. This involves not just you as an individual but your environment, colleagues, etc. Do not forget that this is one result and is not finite. Questionnaires are informative and do start a pattern of thinking towards self-development by indicating your own learning style, but you can go further than that and take on board the tendencies of the styles in a broader way. Appreciating the differences in others is a good start and allowing for them makes for more successful teamwork in the future. This chapter will help you do that.

It is important that we can differentiate *learning* from *education*, *training* and *development*. These four terms are often mixed up, but there is a difference between them.

- **Learning:** This is the acquisition of knowledge and facts by study, being taught and even through experience.
- **Education:** The receipt of systematic intellectual, moral and social instruction usually over a prolonged period.
- **Training:** Being taught a specific skill or type of behaviour, especially through practice, and usually occupation led.
- **Development:** The systematic advancement or growth of the person as a whole bringing out all the talents from within.

As can be seen from the above, training and development, for instance, are clearly different yet often confused. Training is more likely to be employer led and involve the skills the company needs being given to the employees; but this does not necessarily develop the individual – or does it? Here there is room for debate. Each individual will have different needs and talents; bringing individuals on as a whole is true development and so is of a more people led activity. It is true that learning, education, training and development can link with each other. All four, in fact, are steps towards improvement of one type or another and learning could be that first step towards whole personal development. Education and training could be seen as key pathways to the learning and development of an individual.

Learning is not context free. Learning takes place in a real world, and if it is to be effective then it must take account of the aids and barriers to learning that this presents (Harrison 2002). This chapter will end with an indication of those barriers.

The knowledge gained by individual learning has further repercussions in terms of our broader thinking about learning. It follows that any organisation the individual works for or ultimately will work for will gain from that knowledge too. So, do organisations learn? The fashionable evolution of 'the learning organisation' must also have a cyclical influence on the individuals who work for it. Such institutions facilitate the learning of all its members and continuously transform themselves (Pedler *et al* 1988).

THE KOLB LEARNING CYCLE

The cyclical nature of learning was outline by David Kolb in the 1980s. Kolb (1984) developed a famous model which showed learning to be cyclical and to consist of four stages.

- **Active experimentation** **(Acting/doing)**
  This involves learning through doing. Previous thoughts and ideas are applied at this stage into a practical situation where trial and error gives rise to further thoughts and ideas which can be followed through the whole cycle.

- **Concrete experiences** **(Feeling)**
  Following active experimentation, one has now gained concrete experience in terms of the development of feelings. These feelings are then used as a reference point for future actions.

- **Reflective observation** **(Watching)**
  Reflecting upon previous experiences and feelings is important here. Watching, listening and actively thinking through issues ensure that careful consideration is made before taking action.

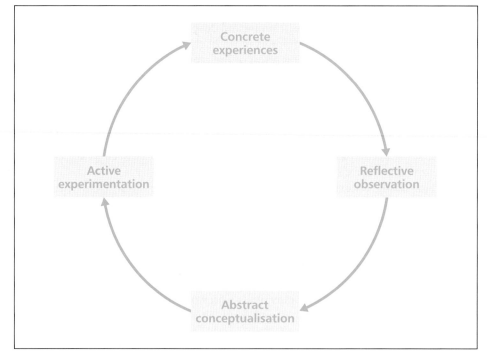

Figure 2.1 The Kolb Learning Cycle

Source: Kolb 1984. Adapted with permission of Pearson Education

- **Abstract conceptualisation   (Thinking)**
  This is where theories for the future are developed. Using reflections, an analysis is undertaken which, as the name suggests, conceptualises in the abstract. That is, the individual thinks through the repercussions and applies what has been learnt to similar situations in order to increase the success of the idea. Logical thought and modelling ideas in the air then give rise to new things to try out . . .

And so back to active experimentation where they are actually tried out and so on, in a circular fashion.

Although Kolb's model does simplify matters somewhat and very tidily places learning into only four categories, it does get across the message that learning is a process and an ongoing cycle made up of a mixture of elements and these should be considered whether studying or managing others or both.

Kolb went on to define four types of learner within this cycle:

- *Diverger* – learns best through feeling and watching
- *Assimilator* – learns best through watching and thinking
- *Converger* – learns best through thinking and doing
- *Accommodator* – learns best though doing and feeling

These are placed on his cycle in Figure 2.2 for clarity.

Peter Honey and Alan Mumford (1986) simplified this further and created four learning types that carried one main attribute from each of the four stages on the

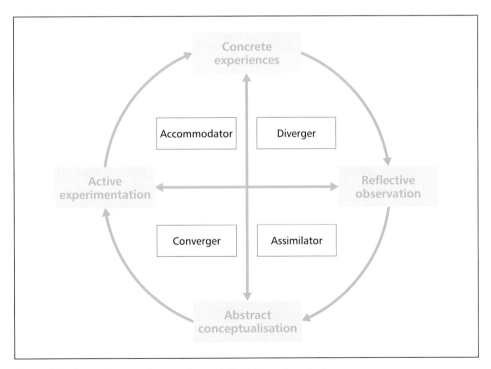

Figure 2.2 The Kolb Learning Cycle and Kolb Learning Styles

Source: Kolb 1984. Adapted with permission of Pearson Education

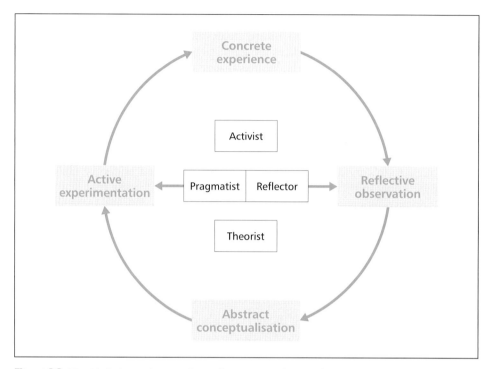

Figure 2.3 The Kolb Learning Cycle and Honey and Mumford Learning Styles

Source: Adapted by the author from Kolb (1984) Honey & Mumford (1986)

learning cycle. These types are often found in LSQs and are, from the top of the cycle clockwise, as follows:

- Activist
- Reflector
- Theorist
- Pragmatist

The learning preferences of these types can be deduced from their titles but illustrated more fully in horoscope fashion the tendencies are:

- **Activist**
  Activists learn best by jumping straight into things, acting first and considering the consequences later. They like immediate experiences and have an open mind towards anything new. Not the best at longer-term implementation, activists will look for something else to do once the initial excitement has died down. Activists like the limelight.

- **Reflector**
  Reflectors will think things though very carefully before making a decision. They like to have all the facts and comments from different experiences together first and will go on to make an 'educated' decision in their own time. They will think strategically and try to incorporate the views of others.

- **Theorist**

  Theorists like logic and will think matters through in a linear way. With a tendency to perfectionism they like to apply sound theories to their observations. They prefer to be intellectually stretched and work in a structured environment. Theorists are not comfortable with the subjective or flippancy.

- **Pragmatist**

  Pragmatists just want to put ideas into practice and experiment. With a dislike for open ended discussion they will roll their sleeves up and have a go to see if something works. They like being given previous examples of success.

There are a number of advantages and disadvantages to each particular trait and these are covered well by Lashley and Best (2001) for those who wish to study this further.

As an overview, in Figure 2.4 the traits can be divided into thinkers and doers (backwards and forwards). Reflectors think backwards at what has happened and theorists forwards to what could happen. Activists are involved and doing it while pragmatists offer to have a go at doing something new.

TIP

Remember this is a general look at the traits and in real life it is not cut and dried – there are grey areas too.

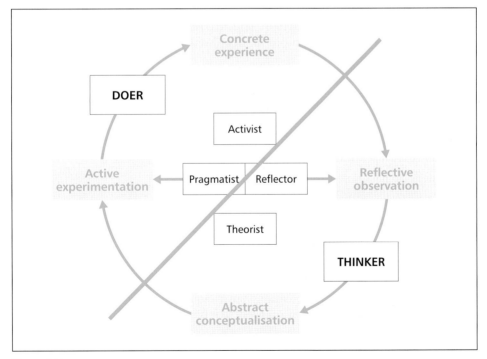

Figure 2.4

Source: Adapted by the author: Kolb (1984) Honey and Mumford (1986)

POSITIVE ASSOCIATION FOR POSITIVE LEARNING

Learning and memory are inextricably linked (Mullins 2002). Our attitude to learning is affected by our past and many other things. Often we set about learning for a sense of achievement and it should be a positive experience. Daniel Goleman (1996, p. 85) states that, 'memory is state specific'. He outlines the benefits of positive association with events and it is easy to see how this must link to more effective learning. He links ability to mood state in terms of creating those future memories: 'people in good moods have a perceptual bias that leads them to be more expansive and positive in their thinking.' He also suggests that being in a good mood will make us able to think in a more flexible way and indeed in a more complex way, therefore finding solutions more readily. This is food for thought when considering our own learning and that of our staff or future staff, not just in terms of the stages on the learning cycle and the style of learning but also the internal and external factors which influence learning.

There are a number of factors which can influence the speed of learning as well as the enjoyment of learning (Mullins 2002). Internal factors such as the emotions and memory, alluded to above, and external factors such as our environment and reward can have a direct influence on the quantity and quality of learning.

BARRIERS TO LEARNING

Just as there are ways to promote more effective learning, it follows that certain barriers to learning must exist. Mumford (in Beardwell and Holder, 2001) identified ten specific blocks to learning:

- Perceptual – inability to see there is a problem
- Cultural – conditioning about the way things are done already
- Emotional – anxiety can impede learning
- Motivational – a lack of willingness to risk take
- Cognitive – previous bad learning experiences
- Intellectual – limited ability
- Expressive – ineffective communication skills
- Situational – a lack of opportunity
- Physical – time, place, etc. inappropriate
- Specific environment – unsupportive colleagues/superiors

These blocks can be interpreted in a number of different ways to the above but are useful in terms of analysing the learning environment for yourself or staff. You can begin to predict what may stand in your way so it is not a surprise and, indeed you can work on eradicating likely barriers.

CASE STUDY 2.1

Mark is fed up and frustrated. He is working on a new project with a team of four others for his company. They are all new to the business and the development project they have been set by the Chief Executive is taking them all on a learning journey. The team have a choice of four possible directions to follow to achieve the goals set and are required to present their choice of option to the Board in Brussels next week. They have spent the last month meeting in London and Paris at great expense, exploring all four options thoroughly, but cannot reach a decision as to which option to put to the Board.

Things are getting very tense with the deadline looming and Mark is more worried than most as he is the project manager. He is also applying for a promotion within the company and wants this to work well so he looks good before the interview.

Two of Mark's team members, Karen and Jean, spend most of their time discussing and re-discussing the pros and cons of the options. They are careful, considered and thorough but have not helped with the decision.

Another member of the team, Jack, is very bright and energetic and keeps coming up with new ideas – lots of them, so they have even more to discuss.

The final member of Mark's team, Lucy, just wants to take one of the ideas and get on and do it and, in fact, that is how Mark feels himself. It is time for a decision and some action.

- Apply the learning cycle and traits to the members of Mark's team.
- How can Mark's understanding of this help Mark manage the process towards a decision?

Summary

After outlining the definitions of learning, education, training and development this chapter explained the classic theories of learning with the purpose of understanding the self and others when working in a team. Bearing this in mind, the psychological environment for learning is covered including any barriers which may hinder progress.

TASK 1

Education and training could be seen as key pathways to the learning and development of an individual.

Discuss this as a group.

TASK 2

Apply the learning cycle model to a current situation at university or work. Start with active experimentation using an example such as writing a report and follow the cycle round. You will see how the model prompts you to think in different ways. This is also a good tool to prompt effective reflective writing as it literally promotes more all round thinking.

TASK 3

Having had an outline of the four learning styles of Honey and Mumford, try to plot yourself on the model and think about what this means in terms of who you work or study with.

Complete an LSQ and compare the actual results with those you expected to test how accurate your self-perception is.

In addition to thinking about yourself, apply the facts to groups, thinking about how one style can help another.

TASK 4

Bearing in mind positive association, work in groups to outline how you can make your learning as positive an experience as possible.

TASK 5

Apply the learning barriers to your own situation. You can re-interpret the meaning of each block – the important thing is to look for potential issues. Write a short reflective piece on your findings which outlines how you are going to deal with them. Not all the barriers will apply.

References and further reading

Beardwell, I. and Holden, L. (2001) *Human Resource Management – a Contemporary Approach*, Harlow: FT Prentice Hall.

Brooks, I. (2003) *Organisational Behaviour*, Harlow: FT Prentice Hall.

Goleman, D. (1996) *Emotional Intelligence*, London: Bloomsbury.

Harrison, R. (2002) *Learning and Development*, CIPD Enterprises Ltd.

Honey, P. and Mumford, A. (1986) *The Manual of Learning Styles*, Peter Honey Publications.

Kolb, D. (1984) *Experiential Learning*, Prentice Hall.

Lashley, C. and Best, W. (2001) *12 Steps to Study Success*, London: Continuum.

Mullins, L. (2002) *Management and Organisational Behaviour*, Harlow: FT Prentice Hall.

Pedler, M., Boydell, T. and Burgoyne, J. (1988) *Learning Company Project*: *A Report on Work Undertaken October 1987 to April 1988*, Sheffield Training Agency.

Torrington, D. and Hall, L. (1998) *Human Resource Management*, Prentice Hall.

Websites

www.infed.org/biblio/b-learn.htm
www.support4learning.org.uk/education/lstyles.htm
www.emtech.net/learning_theories.htm
www.peterhoney.com

CHAPTER 3
Studying

- To identify the best times and environment for study
- To use study time most effectively and productively
- Refine reading skills appropriate to purpose
- Learn how to engineer and channel thinking and creativity

The previously discussed learning theory can now be applied to effective study. It is also useful to refer to the chapter on time management in this book.

There are two key themes to maximising the effectiveness of study:

- positive psychology
- prudent preparation

Incorporated within these are a number of other considerations and particular skills that it is necessary to acquire:

- where and when to study
- reading skills
- note-taking skills
- thinking skills – logical and creative

WHERE AND WHEN TO STUDY

This will vary for every person but the advice is always to try and find a set place to work if you can. If you are able to isolate an area in the house which can remain as you left it that is great. This area can then be personalised with items that stimulate a positive feeling and this makes it easier to sit down and get straight on with the work.

In many cases individuals are not able to secure their own space in a house and are fighting against the demands of others in the household. Shared computers are an issue, as is the use of the dining room table. The latter will always need clearing just as you get to a productive bit of work. Large trays are very useful in these instances. Work can then be left in the order you need it, books open at the place you left them and everything can simply be shifted in one go. Piling up work and closing books to clear away bring negative psychology to the situation and you will have to push yourself to open them again and get re-motivated.

The rule of thumb question is can you sit back down and quickly get on with the work without setting up each time and re-reading material? If not, think around this issue and set up as best you can.

The tray system works well in terms of its ease of transportation but also – particularly in families – creates a good study ethic or culture. If Mum or Dad is studying in an organised way which becomes part of the household routine, then children absorb this and often join in with their own work in a similar no fuss and less tense fashion. Fewer arguments ensue when everything is easily transportable. Demonstrably huffing and puffing as you pack up bags and close books does not have the same effect and may in fact give the wrong impression about healthy study and lifelong learning.

TIP
Remember to have your study plan visible and plan to avoid and prevent interruptions.

Good lighting is vitally important in the study area. You should also check your working environment for its ergonomics – the physical efficiency of your work area and seating position. Hunching over your work makes the job more tedious. Laptops can be a prime cause of both back ache and eye strain. Trying to work with a laptop on a coffee table for instance can be very tiring on the eyes and back and you will feel worse for wear the following day. Working little and often can help to combat these problems so try to break your work up into chunks that suit your schedule.

At university or college many of the same rules apply. Quiet study areas in the library are invaluable as you can often have the peace of anonymity in the company of others doing the same thing. You will be surprised how much you can get done in a planned study session of an hour working on your own in the library – it is a good practice to make such sessions a regular part of your schedule. Campus is an ideal place to make the most of studying with others in group work too.

When you study will also depend on your timetable and body clock. There is little point fighting against nature to squeeze in study. For instance if you are an owl rather than a lark, promising yourself you will get up early every morning to do an hour is unrealistic and bound to fail. Your study plan must fit around your working or university week. Plot this out on one sheet of paper and consider it carefully for a suitable study time, bearing in mind your best and most productive time of day. Each day will vary with differing commitments. Don't forget to build in your social life as well – little point planning a heavy stint on a Saturday morning if Friday is a regular late night out.

All your study sessions do not have to be exactly the same length of time. It is just as useful to have the odd half hour slot in addition to a couple of hours. If you follow the rule of being ready to work straight away without procrastinating, you can be very productive in short slots and cumulatively these can really add up. It is better to do shorter stints at peak productive times than nothing at all. All too often these potentially productive units are wasted as it is presumed they are not long enough.

Manage expectations – your own and those of others. Having put considerable effort into your planning, you need to ensure the time units are indeed used as they were meant to be. As already mentioned, communicating and including the people around you in your plans can have the desired effect but respect their time too in return. If you say you are going to start at a particular time, then do so – they then know where they stand. If you say you will finish at a particular time, then do so – as a mark of respect. If you go over the time too often, those around you will see the study process as a negative one that takes something away from them. Follow the golden rule of 'under-promise and over-deliver'. If you have promised to stop at a particular time then make sure the time you have stated allows you more than enough to cover what you need. Finish at least on time in their eyes or earlier as a surprise – looking eager to be involved in what they are doing rather than giving them the full story on what a difficult session you have had.

A potential creator of tension and the cause of arguments, in families particularly, is the squeezing of extra value for yourself in someone else's time, which they subconsciously regard as theft.

Your respect will be returned in the manner you delivered it. If you have considered other family members carefully, they will quickly start to do the same for you and help to make it easier for you to study.

Managing your own expectations is also key. This is partly achieved by setting out clearly the task for each session, but apply to yourself the rules discussed above. If you have promised yourself you will do something then do it. Make sure the promise is realistic in the first place and then achieve it or more. The principle of the 'baker's dozen' applies well here. A 'baker's dozen' is not twelve but more. In medieval times there were harsh penalties if tradespeople under-delivered in terms of the weight or quantity of their goods. To ensure against this, they always provided more than the agreed amount so twelve loaves from the baker would actually be thirteen. This principle can be used in working and study life.

You will feel better if you do not let yourself down. However you justify to yourself why something is not done – and we can all be very good at doing that – if you know in your heart you could have done more you will feel dissatisfied. It is also good to groom a 'baker's dozen' mentality anyway so it almost becomes the default. Decide which kind of person you want to be – the *nearly there person* who doesn't quite hit the target and probably does not get promoted as readily or the *clearly there person* who achieves the target and more!

Approach your selected workplace with the four T's.

- *Temperament* – positive and ready
- *Task* – measured and with direction
- *Tools* – everything you need in place
- *Time* – an allocated time to stick to

Now if you are anything like me you may also add a fifth T . . .

- *Tuckshop* – supply of biscuits, etc.

READING SKILLS

A core skill for effective study is the ability to read in the right way. Contrary to taught practice in schools, this is not cover to cover nor from the beginning to the end of a text.

Re-thinking the use of books is crucial to an effective use of time and maximum information gathering. For the purposes of adult education and lifelong learning, books and other study texts need to be treated very differently from novels and leisure reading. Study texts should be approached in an organised and, frankly, quite ruthless way. A broad range of reading is required in higher education and goes beyond one core text. There just is not the time to pour over everything in detail, so a system needs to be adopted to gain the necessary breadth.

Start 'speed reading'

A simple management tool has been created to help with the process of speed reading. Try it a couple of times and you will see how the practice can benefit you and even become a 'norm' for you. It will feel a bit awkward at first but bear with it.

Always start any reading exercise with an objective in mind. You need to have a focus so you naturally find information to match your needs. To gain breadth, try to read conflicting texts and articles to get different views.

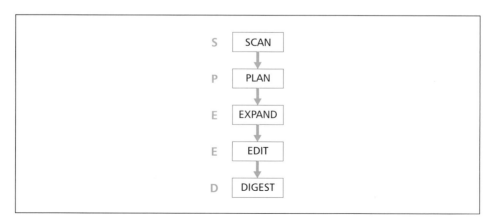

Figure 3.1 Speed reading

Scan Get an overview of the book or article by running your eye down the pages quickly. Look at the cover and contents as well as chapter headings, summaries and, yes, the pictures.

This scan will identify large chunks of the book you don't need and importantly indicate where those you need are. This is all done with your objective in mind. If you are looking for a particular argument also look for the opposite argument during your scan.

Plan Now you have isolated the material likely to be use to you, plan which exact pieces of the book you will read further. Think about the order in which you will do this. Mark any particular bits that seem to oppose or complement each other.

Expand Now you can actually read the planned pieces in detail to get what you need. Remember to do this expansion with your objective in mind or you will waste time. As well as content collection, also take on board the flavour of the writing and what you think of how the author has dealt with the topic. Being able to comment on or critique the content helps you to understand it better and takes you to a higher level of more active reading.

Edit Make useful notes for yourself – perhaps on clearly marked bookmarks. These should give the main points, indicate any quotes that could be used, what arguments to take and link back to your main purpose. They should also have key words outlined or detailed separately so you can skim through these when you need to. A good tip is to note some main points on another piece of paper and attach it to the front of the book so you can quickly source a particular theme more readily.

You can see as you make notes that you are drawing in your 'expanded' reading more tightly. This is important in terms of memory retention.

Digest A good practice is always to go back and check your notes and marked sections, which does three things: it (a) checks your understanding of the content; (b) ensures you are more likely to remember it for longer; and (c) checks whether you have stuck to your objective and retrieved from the process what you set out to. This keeps the reading exercise active at all stages, saves time in terms of increasing your ability to remember what you have read and helps with closure so you can turn to another book with a fresh mind.

NOTE-TAKING AND NOTE-MAKING SKILLS

Note-taking

Note-taking has changed considerably in the last few years. With more and more lecture delivery being made on PowerPoint® and the introduction of student web boards, access to the main themes of the lessons is already done for the student. Lecturers like myself regularly supply students with comprehensive and easy to print out notes on the web boards. Also, the sequence of delivery is easily followed over the course of the terms as documents are accessible in date order. Losing notes is no longer an issue as they can easily be accessed and used.

This may be convenient and the notes may be in a professional format but there are drawbacks. With students aware that a lot of the work is going to be done for them, they may not always make the effort to make their own notes and understand the content. As this is a key factor in recall, they are potentially deprived of a necessary memory retentive vehicle.

It is a good idea for students to print the notes off before the lecture, read them through once to have an 'anchor' and then use them to make appropriate notes on. This will help with listening and understanding. The notes made are additions to the basic material and will take students to a higher level of understanding beyond the old fashioned way of scribbling as much as possible in a lecture. This had its own advantages but times have changed. The drawback of the new media is that there is sometimes the temptation to think 'Oh, I'll just print off the notes so I don't need to think too hard.' It may even be tempting to fail to show up. Resist these temptations as you will deprive yourself of the most effective way to log and lodge the information and then you will have to cram and panic, using more time than you would have needed to in order to re-do the work. It is best to have your notes in a format where you are refreshing your memory rather than adding new material at the last minute.

In an effort to help students, I will vary when I put material on the web board and carefully consider what material I do put on it. I will give clear instruction as to what to do and do encourage a number of sessions where full note-taking is needed. I do this to help levels of understanding and also to maintain some writing skills. Students can find a three-hour written exam a bit of a shock for the writing hand when they have become used to keyboard input.

So note-taking must be appropriate to the lecturer and situation. Also bear in mind that you are note-taking in order to remember – recall is the key objective and, as we have already seen in learning and general study, memory works by association – hopefully positive association.

The trend now is that you are less likely to be note-taking in order to create a document which you take away and learn, having virtually written everything put in front of you. It is more likely that you will be given material for and before the lesson which you learn and the purpose of note-taking becomes one of maximising future recall.

The key objectives of note-taking which will maximise their use are summarised in Figure 3.2.

It is a good idea to get into the practice of identifying key words that should activate a series of other pieces of information, much like a database.

Notes should be brief, not a full story that you will never go back to in earnest. In the process of writing them make sure they can be read back easily. Order them in a relevant way to your studies on that particular module, both for ease of reference and so they can be added to with ease. Equally, store them in such a way that they can be moved about according to the needs of the time. Highlight main points in the notes so you have several levels of reference and reading. For example, it is useful for exam revision to have highlighted points in the notes which activate the further detail and those further notes then activate a deeper knowledge and so on. Also use marks, shapes, colour, arrows, etc. to guide yourself around your notes.

Remember –   your notes and the printouts are your record for future reference

Ensure understanding – note-taking in the right way will help your understanding of the topic

Concentration –   the act of note-taking means you have to concentrate

Organisation –   your notes will assist planning for study and assignments and be a good starting point for further research

Recall –   they should help you remember

Demonstration –   the notes can be shown to others and used to discuss/debate issues for more creative thinking

Figure 3.2 RECORD

TIP

Think of your record system as a database where a key word phrase or search activates a wealth of information.

If your notes do not do any of the above for you – you are doing them incorrectly.

Note-making

Note-making can be seen to be the even more proactive derivative of note-taking. It is used when the purpose of recall is not the priority. It is the start of a more creative process, not of retrieving data but making new data.

Spider diagrams, spray diagrams or pattern notes are useful for this process. Now more commonly brought together as mind mapping, it has become quite fashionable again to put ideas together in this way. Specific software packages make it easy to store information and e-mail it to fellow students or colleagues.

Putting notes together on one page in this format allows a more strategic approach as well as a tactical one. The detail of sections of subjects can be noted but it is also possible to see potential areas for consideration in this way and think forward rather than retrospectively. This leads very nicely on to thinking – both logical and creative.

THINKING

Logical and creative thought should be used together for best effect. The mind maps mentioned above start us along that road. The logical notes on a situation provide the base for the potential, i.e. the creative thinking.

Logical thinking

Often when given a project, assignment or problem, we charge ahead in haste and jump to conclusions. Stopping to think things through logically will save time in the long run and give rise to better answers and solutions. A linear analysis where things are broken down, links highlighted and facts differentiated from any assumptions will help to identify trends and enable deduction from the given data.

Start by defining the issue in hand then categorise what you know already and analyse it for trends, etc. This helps to isolate what you do not know.

Taking a problem solving approach, ask:

- What exactly is the problem, issue or task?
- What do I know already?
- How does that fit together and what does it show in terms of trends, etc.?
- What information do I lack and need to know to go further?

This logical approach ensures you gain any extra information and do not proceed without it, so reducing error. This is pure logic and from here we go into the territory of blended logic where a little creativity starts to creep into the process, albeit in a logical manner. These four logical questions are in essence retrospective and we need our process to help us think ahead, so we must start considering what options we have and the pros and cons of each. The next question, therefore, is:

- What are my options?

Logically list each option and make a list of pros and cons for each one – this can be done in a table or any other convenient format. From here you can analyse the resulting pros and cons and enter into the territory of conceptualisation – remember you are thinking through possibilities in a logical way.

TIP

Test out these theories on paper by working through causes and effect to possible solutions and then a chosen solution.

Creative thinking

It is easy to see the natural progression from logical thought to creative thought having set the base for it. Now the purpose is to push the situation to its full potential by thinking through all options in a different way.

One of the more well-known ways of thinking creatively is *brainstorming*. This technique makes very positive use of lateral thinking and channels the creative energy of those present.

A few basic rules will maximise the output:

- The atmosphere has to be right. People must not feel restricted or think they may look stupid – encourage any idea and plenty of them.

- Quantity is probably more important than quality in brainstorming, especially in the early stages.
- Make sure the ideas land somewhere and are written down for all to see to inspire further thought.
- Brainstorm at a fast pace as it winds up the thinking process and feels more exciting.
- Never criticise any input. All ideas are good even if they are impractical – they may spark off thoughts for something more practical.
- Encourage wild card ideas for the same reason. This also stretches the parameters of the minds working on the problem, encouraging them to think more widely.
- Enjoy the brainstorming session and evaluate the ideas later, with an open mind.

TIP

Leave evaluation of the ideas until after the brainstorm has finished – never do it as you go along as it will dampen enthusiasm.

Consider how extreme catwalk fashion can be. It is accepted that many of the outfits will not be worn but the ideas flow through to the general garments worn once the impact has been made. This is how initially wild ideas from a brainstorm can generate sound ideas to be taken forward and implemented.

Another creative thinking technique is simply to ask yourself questions – active questions. By answering them you begin to talk yourself through various situations.

The familiar who?, where?, what?, how?, why? and when? questions always serve a situation well. Most of these used several times will help to prompt more lateral thinking.

Thinking through different levels, times or through the eyes of different people – known as dimension shifting – is another technique to help creative thinking. The model used in Chapter 1 for reflective writing is a good example of how using these prompts can make us think things through in a different way. So do think before, during and after. Do think at all levels of people that the situation may affect.

TIP

Imagine things from all sorts of different perspectives as if you were able to fly around it. Make a check list to help but look at it from the top, from below, from a distance, rotate it, make it disappear, make it bigger, etc. The idea is to bring your thinking to really free levels to maximise the likelihood of better ideas.

These techniques help to form the good habit of questioning everything, which sets off higher levels of thought in itself. Being able to think at different levels, in different ways and from other perspectives than your own make for better studying and potentially better marks. Such creative approaches will allow you to make adaptations to classic theories as well as apply them at different levels for effect and create interesting, imaginative and more holistic work.

CASE STUDY 3.1

Helen has three assignments due in the next fortnight. She is in her first term of university, it is nearing the end of term and she is panicking that she has left everything until the last minute. Helen lives in halls and has made a big effort to get in with the crowd. Trouble is, there is always a party or something going on and she does not like to miss out. She has everything needed for her study laid out in her room. There is no particular order but everything is there. Helen has taken her maximum allowance of books out from the library and does not know where to start. Every time she gets started with study there is a knock at the door and a friend wants her to do something or go out. She is getting very worried and the stress is beginning to affect what little concentration she has.

- Advise Helen on how she could control her study more and get more out of it.

CASE STUDY 3.2

Serena has just hurried home from work. It has been a very stressful day. She has picked up the children from after school care and as they all come bundling through the front door the phone rings. She throws down all the bags, lunch boxes, coats and various artistic creations from the kids and answers the phone. Then she goes into the kitchen to make the family meal and sees the kids have just helped themselves to a quick sandwich in the meantime. The bread and honey are all over the kitchen table where she was studying last night and left her books open ready to do some more this evening. The kids have also changed the order of her piles of paper and some of the notes are on the floor. Serena has a management report due for her Certificate of Management Studies programme. She had made good progress last night with her primary research results and analysis of secondary data and feels she will have to start all over again. Serena often works in the kitchen in the evening while clearing up and getting the lunch boxes, etc. ready for the following day. She also finds it useful for access to the biscuits and coffee. She will have to spend time clearing up the mess and resorting her notes before she can start up again.

- Serena has a busy life. How can she help herself further to ensure quality study time and output?
- How can she get others to help her?
- The management report she has to write requires her to show innovative thought in the recommendations if she is to get a really good mark – what can Serena do to increase her creativity?

Summary

A realistic look at study has been made in this chapter, from creating the right environment for study to a portfolio of skills including reading, note-taking and creative thinking which make that study more effective. The speed reading section is of particular help in saving time and avoiding wasted effort.

TASK 1

Pick up a book and speed read it. If you get the chance, get into groups after you have done this and tell each other about the book you have read.

TASK 2

Analyse your study environment and make three positive improvements to it.

Reference

Lashley, C. and Best, W. (2001) *12 Steps to Study Success*, London: Continuum.

Websites

www.how-to-study.com
www.studygs.net
www.ucc.vt.edu/stdysk/stdyhlp.html

CHAPTER 4
The communication process

Learning objectives

- To understand the repercussions of bad communication
- To understand the benefits of good communication
- To diagnose where communication may break down
- To learn and practise the steps for good communication

Introduction

Later chapters in this book will cover many types of personal communication in more detail. In order to best understand and improve each of these types, however, it is necessary to understand the process of communication itself and particularly where that process can fail.

Where communication starts and how it ends as well as how the communication is transmitted and subsequently received is crucial to the degree of success. The process itself would appear to be relatively simple, making one wonder why it so often goes wrong. What becomes evident is that just as it can take very little for things to go wrong, it is equally easy to do little things to help ensure they go right.

THE ELEMENTS OF THE COMMUNICATION PROCESS

The communication process is essentially made up of five elements. Each of these factors dictates or indicates the level of understanding achieved and each has an effect on the other. The five elements are:

- the sender or initiator
- the task involved and timeframe
- the medium of the communication
- the recipient
- the required action

Figure 4.1 illustrates the elements which make up the whole causal loop of communication.

Between the sender and the recipient there are many ways in which the process can be delayed, altered or even halted and the ultimate outcome is a clear indicator of the degree of success.

From the initial transmission to the limitations of the time and task itself, to the choice of medium in which to transmit, to the situation and ability of the recipient to

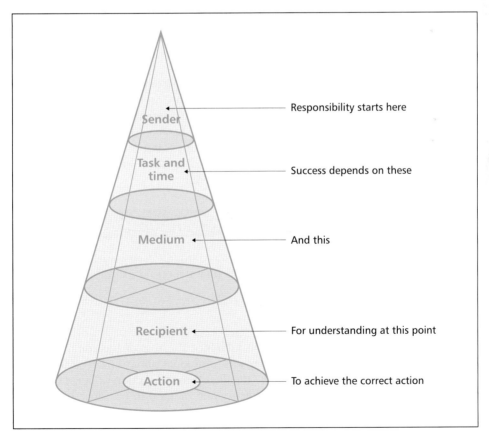

Figure 4.1 The communication process

receive, there is a lot of potential for confusion to occur. This may result in the incorrect action or even no action taking place. There are many variations at each stage of the process, but by taking each stage aside it may be possible to isolate potential blocks in the process to ensure greater success. It is important to understand that responsibility starts *and stays* with the initial sender, as the result of their transmission depends entirely on their choices and level of staying power to see the process through.

Sender

Responsibility starts here. The sender is responsible for the whole communication process and its ultimate result. It is not good enough to abdicate this as soon as possible for comfort. The relief of release can be more important to some people than the actual success of transmission. Some simply do not want the responsibility and literally dump the message without thought. How many times have you been preoccupied with another task when an inconsiderate sender verbally flings something at you? You are not in a position to really take in the details but their relief is more important to them than your understanding, resulting in a high probability of misunderstanding, which in its turn takes more time and trouble. These senders cost companies money.

The sender has three aims:

- to be received
- to be understood
- to initiate the correct action

All decisions within the communication process stem from trying to achieve these three aims and the sender should identify in advance precisely the action required in order to most successfully achieve it and also anticipate potential misunderstandings.

If faced with an inconsiderate sender, throw the hot coal back at them. Politely make them relay the message to you in a form to suit you, for example ask them to write down the full details in an e-mail to you. Do not let them walk away smugly with relief while you worry about another thing to remember.

TIP

If you are the sender, follow your transmission through each stage to see what happens – although it is going a bit far to do what the guy in the cartoon is doing.

Task and time

The information or instruction itself will influence the rest of the communication process. It is at this stage that the sender will form ideas about how to transmit the message. Another key influence is time – the likely time the action will take or a time constraint or deadline will dictate the urgency and method of transmission. For example, an urgent item for a meeting deadline a few hours away is not likely to arrive unless the sender chooses exactly the right words and exactly the right way to transmit the message.

© Fran / Cartoonstock.com

Medium

The medium is the channel of transmission. Any benefit gained in the process so far is completely cancelled out if the wrong medium is chosen. The sender must ensure that the medium can lead to the required action. A message note left on a very untidy desk is unlikely to lead to success. The sender must also contemplate 'appropriateness'. It has been known for staff in some companies to receive bad news by group e-mail for instance. What might be thought of as a fast and efficient medium can become a vehicle of personal insult when content and contact are not in line.

TIP
Compare several media in your mind before sending a message. This prevents you defaulting to a habit medium.

TIP
Ask the recipient what medium they prefer.

Recipient

Even after the above stages have been successfully accomplished, there is still plenty of room for things to go wrong. The level of the recipient's ability to actually receive the message must be taken into account by the sender. This can be affected by many factors: the recipient may be preoccupied with something else or may have poor listening skills, which will inevitably impede the communication process. The ability of the sender to assess this is key and will help to avoid pitfalls. Addressing the communication process in a proactive way reduces the chance of error by compensating early in the process. The sender should also introduce check mechanisms to ensure the right message has been received. Asking for feedback is a simple and effective way of doing this. Remember, it is the achievement of the fullest possible understanding which is the priority, not the release of the responsibility.

TIP

Check understanding. Ask the recipient for feedback.

ACTION

The crucial test of good communication is whether it has elicited the required action. If it hasn't then a review of all the stages in the process must be undertaken. The default of presumption by the sender that something in the process could have been different or improved is a good thing and carries through the responsibility.

There are four likely action outcomes from the communication process, illustrated in Figure 4.2:

- desired
- delayed

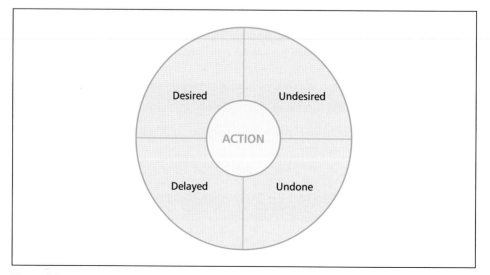

Figure 4.2 The four action outcomes

- undesired
- undone

Desired action

This is also the desired outcome. The full action required by the sender has been achieved in exactly the expected way and at the expected time. This outcome indicates that the stages of the communication process were effective and that the sender was in tune with the recipient in terms of deciding their delivery and content. The sender can walk away satisfied, knowing they have done their job well.

Delayed action

This is where the correct action has taken place in all respects except for the timing. Full understanding of the task in hand has been achieved but misunderstanding has occurred as to the urgency.

Undesired action

An action has taken place but it is incomplete or incorrect. Full misunderstanding has occurred, possibly with costly consequences. Time and effort have been put into the wrong thing completely. This will result not only in frustration but also demotivation. If recipients put their effort into something and then discover it is not what was expected, they are going to feel let down and unappreciated. Worse still would be if the sender did not accept responsibility for the misunderstanding and indicated that it was the recipient's fault.

Undone action

A complete mix up has occurred and no action is done or even underway. The instruction was so vague that no one has started anything towards the required action.

Whether effective or not, the choices made by the sender have a causal effect on the outcome and type of action resulting from it. This is seen in the causal loop of communication shown in Figure 4.3.

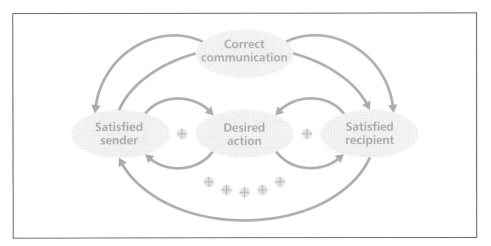

Figure 4.3 Triple causal loop of communication

STEPS FOR COMPETENT COMMUNICATION

C   Clarify your thoughts and ideas before starting the communication process

O   Objective: set each time so each transaction has clear purpose

M   Measure the physical/environmental setting for potential barriers

M   Monitor the receiving ability of the recipient

U   Understand others as well as set out to be understood

N   Note what is necessary for each stage of the process to work

I   Implement each stage with the possibility of review in case change is needed

C   Consult others where appropriate and ask questions

A   Assume responsibility for the success of the process from the start

T   Test recipient understanding and watch response

I   Indicate priorities to help outcome and check timings are clear

O   Orchestrate the future actions of the recipient

N   Never leave the process to run itself – follow it up to check progress

BARRIERS TO THE COMMUNICATION PROCESS

In addition to competencies which increase the success of the process there are factors which have a direct impact on it in a more negative way. Although this chapter is devoted to the emphasis of the positive ways to ensure an effective communication process, consideration must be made of the possible hurdles that slow or interrupt the process. A collection of potential barriers is provided for your interpretation:

Time, tone, jargon, knowledge level of sender or recipient, confidence, attitude, body language, level of interpersonal skills of sender or recipient, assumptions, preconceptions, waffle, level of planning undertaken, length of message, context, mood of sender or recipient, language, culture, fear of rejection, personality, motivation, ability, training, environment, distraction, personal issues, hierarchical position, technology, corporate culture, levels of empowerment, corporate structure.

The last few barriers in the collection take us into the territory of corporate communication. Just as individual psychology and socio-cultural elements (Rouse and Rouse 2002) can affect communication from the bottom up, corporate structure, culture and ability can impede the communication process from a top down perspective.

Whilst this chapter is not the place to explore this further, it is recommended that some reading is undertaken on organisational behaviour in general as part of a personal development programme for preparing oneself for the working world or progressing through it. A number of texts are suggested at the end of the chapter.

CASE STUDY 4.1

Anya is sitting in a sales management meeting with eight of her colleagues from around the region. They are reporting figures to their regional manager. Her phone rings for the fourth time that morning and she bustles off most importantly to answer it. She has the air of indispensability but no one is fooled. They are annoyed by the interruptions and the regional manager has a private word with her. Defensively, Anya states that her team have let her down and just can't get on with the tasks she has left them to do. She describes how she left on her desk a list of tasks for the day scribbled out for them to sort between themselves. Two customers are irate and have now complained and want to speak to her directly because they have not heard back from the staff in the branch as promised. This means she will have to make two further calls to the customers and also ring the office anyway for all the details. She will have to miss some of the meeting to do this. She blames her staff.

- Is Anya right to blame her staff?
- What could Anya have done differently to ensure good communication through the branch?
- What, in terms of the business and staff satisfaction, would have been the positive outcomes of clear and effective communication in this instance?
- What is your opinion of Anya's conduct in general?

Summary

In this chapter we have studied the key elements of the communication process and considered the positive outcomes of using it well and the negative outcomes of overlooking where it can go wrong. The causal nature of communication has been illustrated and a series of steps towards competent communication isolated. Barriers to communication were highlighted with a view to preventing them blocking the process.

TASK 1

Working in groups, take six of the barriers listed above or suggest your own. Explain how they impact on the communication process using real working examples. Do not leave it there though – explain how you would positively overcome them.

TASK 2

Take a picture or collection of shapes that no one has seen before. With your back to your group describe it to them for them to draw how they see it. This exercise has been done most commonly with a group of rectangles in the past (Leavitt and Bahrani 1988 in Rees and Porter 2003) to prove the variety of interpretation by the recipient as well as illustrate the barriers to communication.

TASK 3

Take three recent examples of communication with different media and apply the communications process to them. Analyse where you as an individual could have improved any part of that process and how that would appear in the outcome.

References and further reading

Brooks, I. (2003) *Organisational Behaviour*, Harlow: FT Prentice Hall.
Mullins, L. (2002) *Management and Organisational Behaviour*, Harlow: FT Prentice Hall.
Rees, W. D. and Porter, C. (2003) *Skills of Management*, London: Thomson Learning.
Rouse, M. J. and Rouse, S. (2002) *Business Communications*, London: Thomson Learning.

Websites

www.natcom.org
http://library.thinkquest.org

PART 2
WRITTEN COMMUNICATIONS

Part 2 brings together a number of the key writing skills. Geared for both business and study, the four chapters give basic templates and rules for good communication using this media. The basics are thought out carefully to set lifelong ground rules but are then built on to show how even written communication is key in selling ideas and, of course, the self, in a job interview.

Intertwined with the helpful structures and tips are transferable habits which can be applied to any written piece. The letter writing structure can be transported to any type of letter for work and the report writing is valuable for both study and business.

Chapter 8 then feeds in a number of things to make life easier when writing under pressure. Working to deadlines of any kind can make remembering such things as rules of grammar difficult. Thus, the part ends with a comprehensive set of checks and a structure to assist creative thinking and writing and avoid that empty 'blank page terror' feeling.

Learning objectives

- To understand the principles of writing effective letters in general
- To write effective job application letters
- To fill in application forms properly

© John Morris / Cartoonstock.com

"Just a second while I get your letter out of my file."

Introduction

Letter writing as a whole is an art – or is it a science? The creative use of language as an art in the letter can be completely lost if the science of layout, glance mechanisms and psychological prompts are not used to ensure it is read as intended and for full effect.

There are many types and purposes of letters so it is perhaps best to concentrate on one particular type to establish a basic set of rules that can then be adapted according to need. Keeping to a simple policy will save you time leafing through examples of different letters where there is a temptation to copy rather than create one's own original. This will encourage the skill to develop naturally over time and with practice. Original content will shine through.

One of the most useful letters to study is the job application letter. Not only will most of us use this at some time but the psychology behind its layout and content can then be transferred to business letters in general, where there are essentially four main types – good news, bad news, persuasion and information (Rouse and Rouse 2002).

THE APPLICATION LETTER

There are a few fundamental rules to consider. I mention these as the recipient of many thousands of such letters in over 15 years in recruitment. I am still regularly surprised at the oversights made by many applicants – at all levels.

Appearance

Paper and envelope Where possible, it is advisable to use unfolded A4 paper. This should ensure your cover letter is all on one page unless you are asked to write more. It also furnishes the best glance down the page. There is a high likelihood that not all of it will be read fully by a busy employer who has many letters to get through.

TIP
A5 size paper is for personal notes, thank you letters to aunties, etc.

Use plain paper in all cases in the best weight you can afford. White or cream should be the first choice, but blue and grey quality paper can be acceptable too. Paper should be unlined and not perforated; do not use patterned or themed paper.

The envelope size should be in keeping with the paper size, so use A4 where possible. The application content should be cleanly extracted face up from the envelope allowing reading to start as easily as possible. If a smaller envelope has to be used, the DL size is appropriate where the letter is folded into three sections across its width and opens out easily for the reader. The letter should not be folded into quarters and squeezed into an envelope any smaller than DL. This would minimise the impact of all the hard work spent on the letter content.

TIP
Leave really small envelopes for the milkman!

Typed or handwritten? There is no doubt that typed letters are easier to read and this is especially useful if you have poor handwriting. Ensure the font size suitable and clear: the usual minimum is 12 point, while anything bigger than 14 point looks like the letter is shouting its way out of the envelope.

If you write well – particularly with an ink pen – this can sometimes give you an edge. It looks very professional when accompanied by a typed CV and gives a personal touch. Do space the letter carefully – it should not be too high nor look squashed at the end so there is very little room to sign off elegantly.

> ### TIP
>
> Good handwriting is still very much appreciated so feel free to maximise this talent if you have it.

Giving some thought to the appearance of your letter ensures the most positive psychological start as it makes its entrance. The content needs to be broken down more scientifically if we are to manipulate the reader just that bit further toward the action we require.

Content

Your address Depending on your age, you will have had different instructions from your school days. Classic teaching puts the personal address on the right and bear in mind that many employers will be of that school. It is also acceptable to position the address centrally on the paper now, as if using your own headed noted paper.

Recipient's address The business address goes on the left-hand side of the page and this rule applies whichever position you choose for your own address.

Always ensure names are spelt correctly – this is vital to continuing the positive psychology started by the general overall impression.

Date This can be on the left or the right, but make sure you do date the letter.

Reference line – bold including codes and numbers This should include any job numbers or a code you have been given and which should be quoted. This helps the recipient identify who should deal with your letter. The reference line is generally positioned under the salutation (see below).

With this top part of the letter in order and having caused no offence with incorrect spelling of names, etc. you are ready to allow the content to go to work. This still needs a scientific touch as well as the artful use of words.

Pacing and spacing the content Essentially there are three parts to a good application letter:

- Salutation
- Explanation
- Lift and Line up for interview/or purpose

Yes, the letter should **SELL** you to the employer and make them want to read your curriculum vitae (CV) in a positive frame of mind.

Salutation Strictly the salutation is the 'Dear whoever' bit. For our purposes, we are going to extend consideration of the salutation to the first paragraph of the letter.

- Try to avoid Dear Sir etc. and get a name whenever possible. Phone up the company and make sure you have the correct spelling.
- Accurately fill out the reference line with the job details and code – double check accuracy here too (see above).

- Get straight to the point, for example: Please consider this letter an application for . . . as advertised in . . . and when . . .
- Keep the official stuff short and precise and go to a second paragraph as soon as you can to drag the eye downwards to the more interesting content.

Explanation 1 In five or six lines explain what you can offer to the role. Do not get carried away and give your life history – you are aiming to outline a 'fit' only.

Use some wording or terms from the advert and explain where you are and how that relates to the new role. For example: 'Currently finishing a Certificate in Management Studies, I am keen to secure a management role which uses my up-to-date knowledge and specific work experience. A hard-working and team-spirited individual, I am very eager to secure a progressive position in . . .'

Explanation 2 Now write five or six lines indicating what they can do for you. This could be training where appropriate, the size of the company, giving you a team to run, allowing you to gain further experience with them. The idea is to paint a partnership where it is that evident that you fit and that the benefits will be equal for both sides.

Starting a new paragraph indicate what you have enclosed, for example 'I have enclosed my CV for your consideration' and then in the same paragraph go on to 'lift and line up'.

Lift and line up! You now need to *lift* up the spirit of the whole thing and *line up* all thoughts towards an interview in this case (or to any other purpose of the letter in other cases). Remember the letter does not get you the job – although it can make you lose it – the letter's purpose, along with the CV, is to get an interview.

To lift your letter up, make sure the last paragraph is upbeat and enthusiastic – sound like you want the job without going too far.

To line up, it is not a bad idea to use the word 'interview' in the last sign off sentence as it leaves the right flavour with the reader, as they go to your CV with that word in their head. This may look like psychological manipulation, but it does mean the reader goes on to the CV in the right spirit.

A sentence which incorporates a lift and line up, and even a fit, might be something like: 'I would be delighted to attend an interview to discuss my enthusiasm and suitability for this post'.

Sign off carefully

- Remember to use 'Yours faithfully' where there is no name in the salutation and 'Yours sincerely' where there is – this is a commonly made mistake although everyone professes to know this rule
- Leave room to actually sign in ink *and* write or type your full name underneath
- You can indicate enclosures beneath this

This is a basic template for a good quality application letter. As previously indicated, the principles can be applied to other types of letter.

> **TIP**
>
> Read the advert carefully – some ask for you to write about yourself more extensively. Essentially do whatever the advert tells you to do.

There is one golden rule about the application form:

FILL IT IN! – even if you are including a CV.

There is nothing more annoying for a busy employer or personnel department than to receive an application form with the sections left blank and a CV attached. Some put 'see CV' all over the form – not even 'please see CV'. It really is not wise to make any more work for the employer than you have to. Filling in the form they have provided even where it means repeating some of the information makes it easier for them to find the match they require. The more obstacles you put in their way, the less likely they are to find the matches they need to put you on the 'YES' pile and so you get put on the 'No' pile just because you could not be bothered. It is tedious but it does help. You can cut and paste into a soft copy very often to help ease the burden, so try this.

CASE STUDY 5.1

Curtis has just scurried to the post box with a quickly put together application for a great job which would take him to the next stage of his career. If he gets it in the post tonight it will arrive the day after the deadline on the advert. Phew! As his handwriting is very poor he has typed it and his letter reads thus. . . .

Home address

Alpha Ltd
Uptown
Brightchester

Date
Ref: Application for manager's position

Dear Mr Goodchance

I have enclosed my CV as application for the above position.

I am currently in a very busy role as a deputy manager working for XYZ Ltd and often work long hours to ensure I get the work done. More than qualified for the position above, I am eager to take the next step up.

I look forward to hearing from you

Yours faithfully

Curtis Clotbottom

● What could Curtis do to improve his application letter?
As a group re-write the letter and read it out.

Summary

This chapter has set out to ingrain good letter writing skills so they become the norm. By pointing out the psychological effect of the layout as well as the words, using a good basic template can become habit. The chapter focused on the application letter, describing useful skills for the reader to use inside and outside of work with tips and methods that are easily transfered to all types of letter writing.

Using the advice from this chapter, write your own application letter leaving blank spaces for job title, etc. Keep this as a template for your future use.

TASK 1

References and further reading

Aamodt, M. and Raynes, R. (2001) *Human Relations in Business*, Belmont, CA: Wadsworth.
Morris, M. and Smith, H. (1999) *Business Writing*, London: Orion Business Books.
Rouse, M. J. and Rouse, S. (2002) *Business Communications*, London: Thomson Learning.
Seely, J. (1998) *The Oxford Guide to Writing and Speaking*, Oxford: Oxford University Press.

Website

englishplus.com/grammar/letrcont.htm

CHAPTER 6

The curriculum vitae

Learning objectives

- To write an effective CV
- To present your own strengths in the most effective way
- To increase promotion and employment opportunities

Introduction

Curriculum vitae (CV) is Latin and literally means the running order of life. This is not, however, how you write a CV. In the USA and Europe the CV is called a résumé, a more accurate title. British CVs tend to run to two or three pages, while most European CVs are only one page.

CROSS CULTURAL COMMENT

Before writing your CV check the accepted format for that country. Also check the company. It may be that a British style CV as outlined in this chapter is appropriate even if the company is in another country, as recruiters are beginning to opt for this. If applying to a indigenous company, ensure the correct format is used. Many European companies have a preference for a one-page CV with basic details.

CV WRITING

The previous advice about paper applies to the CV as well as letters. Choose good quality paper and clear, good size print. Do make sure it is labelled as a CV – in short or in full – for ease of sorting at the other end. There are many good templates to use on software packages and the best thing to do is experiment with a few. Whichever you choose, all CVs should essentially contain the following:

- basic personal details
- education
- employment history
- hobbies and interests
- personal profile
- references

Basic personal details

The following are essential:

- name
- address
- telephone numbers including mobiles, fax and e-mails

Make sure that you do not put down a number which will put someone in an awkward position if they try to contact you. For example it is unwise to put your current work number on the CV if your current employer is unaware of your job search.

It is useful to put full, current driving licence here if you have one as this ticks off another item on the prospective employer's list and saves time in the interview. Covering basic questions on the CV allows more time for the prospective employer to get to know you.

Other information you may include at this stage includes:

- Nationality and marital status – you do not have to include them on a CV, although you would have to fill in these details on an application form.
- Photos – only include a photo if requested.

Education

This is best presented backwards!

- Start with your most current qualification – including anything you are currently studying. Bolding this out often works well
- Make sure dates and establishments are as clear as the qualifications. Put in grades where you think they will be important
- Training courses can also be added here if you wish – or create another section for them if you have a long list

Employment history

This is also done backwards.

- List your current or most recent work experience first and on the first page wherever possible
- Make dates and establishments clear
- Dates should all be on the same side and zig-zag (one date clearly leads into another and there are no obvious gaps)
- Explain all gaps to pre-empt red flagging at interview. This saves time at interview and helps to establish a positive psychology
- Do not be too narrative; bullet points may be best
- Allocate most space to the most recent or most appropriate role that fits with the one you are applying for; devote less and less space to each job as you go back in time
- Cover as big a range of skills as you can: e.g. organisation, motivation (self and others), working within time constraints, management, team work, projects, responsibility, deputising, etc.
- As well as who you report to, outline who else you deal with in the company to show breadth
- Group temporary assignments together, unless there are some that do you particular justice or are particularly relevant
- Use bold type for job titles in particular as part of a glance mechanism for the ten-second speed read
- Use active words and reflect what was in the original advert in places in a subtle way

Hobbies and interests

First of all, make sure you have some hobbies and interests. Their purpose on the CV includes the following:

- They need to show a mix of sedentary pursuits and team work
- They need to reflect the culture of the company too but of course be truthful
- Watch for county-level commitments, etc. as these can be an interview red flag in some cases

- Community or charity work is always a big plus
- Note that whatever you write the interviewer may pick out as an ice-breaker at the interview – so if you write 'current affairs', make sure you have read the papers beforehand

Personal profile

The personal profile is important at any age but is particularly so for graduates and those applying for management roles.

> **TIP**
>
> You need to get across a human message in what could be a very big pile of applications.

Depending on fashion the profile can be at the beginning of the CV or near the end. Currently it is more usual to place the profile at the end, leaving the human element as one of the last reads for the prospective employer. This means that once the basic currency of qualifications and experience is established, the personality adds an edge. Bear the following points in mind when compiling your personal profile:

- It is best written in third person as if someone else has written it – in fact get someone else to write it if you can
- Take eight strengths and get a colleague to compile a paragraph around them
- Reflect the advert/internal specification of the position you are applying for

> **TIP**
>
> Make the time to isolate and compile good examples of your strengths so that when you get asked for some at interview you have them ready to talk about rather than having to make something up as you go along.

References

References can be added at the end or you can indicate that they are available on request.

The format described in this chapter is a blend of the reverse chronological and functional CV (Seely 1998) maximising on the benefits of both.

CV check list

- Make sure all pages are named
- Staple the CV together but leave the letter loose on top
- There is little need for posh covers as, particularly in big companies, these are torn off for photocopying purposes

- Check how the CV works when someone glances through it
- Obviously use your computer's spell checker
- Finally
  - don't send applications in late
  - don't lie
  - don't be modest

CASE STUDY 6.1

In this chapter you are the case study.

- Compare your existing CV with the recommendations above and make amendments.

Summary

This chapter is devoted to writing the most effective CV possible. By looking at structure and content, it assists the reader to channel their own information into the most effective format possible for internal promotion or for external job applications.

TASK 1

Using eight listed strengths or your SWOTPLOT, get a friend to compose a five to six line profile of you in the third person.

References and further reading

Higginbottom, G. (2001) *CVs for Graduates*, How to Books.
McGee, P. (2002) *Writing a CV That Works*, How to Books.
Seely, J. (1998) *The Oxford Guide to Writing and Speaking*, Oxford: Oxford University Press.

Websites

www.handsoncv.co.uk
www.cv-service.org
www.your-job-cv.co.uk

CHAPTER 7
Report and essay writing

Learning objectives

- To understand the structure and content of reports and essays for academia and for business
- To ensure that the best and most effective content is used within both formats
- To understand the differences of report, essay writing and portfolio work and the writing styles required

Introduction

Understandably, writing reports and essays is a key worry for students. They do not have a monopoly on concern, however, as business puts a great amount of pressure on staff to compile concise and competitive reports for use internally and externally. The advantage is that once you have got to grips with the basics the skills never leave you. This is one discipline worth putting some effort into.

REPORTS

The report owes its origins to the world of work (Lashley and Best 2001) but is now also a common feature in the academic world. This makes sense because it is important for graduates to enter the working world with the skills to produce reports and an experienced working person should also be able to transfer their report writing skills to the world of academia and obtain that currency in reverse.

Of all the media used in academia, the report is one of the most restrictive structures to work with because certain items must be placed in certain sections. Knowing what goes where is important for maximum marks and the discipline is also useful in the working world in terms of ensuring completeness. Also, once this particular skill is mastered, other academic media will benefit. The dissertation is a larger extension of the report format and the skills of critique and debate are also welcome in a good essay.

Title page

The title or heading should indicate the full nature of the report. In the case of an assignment this could be the assignment question itself.

This page should also contain information for identification.

- name
- course
- due date
- tutor/lecturer

For assignments a front sheet should be used if provided by your tutors.

TIP

For business reports reference numbers can be added, a circulation list used and an indication of confidentiality can be included.

Contents page

The contents page needs to show how the report is divided and where individual sections may be found. The sections and sub-sections are numbered, usually using the decimal point system. You can add the page numbers as well for ease of use.

Example contents page

1.0 Summary/executive summary

2.0 Literary review (optional at this level)

3.0 Introduction

4.0 Method

5.0 Findings

    5.1 Main section heading

    5.2 Main section heading

    5.3 Main section heading

        5.3.1 First sub heading of section 5.3

        5.3.2 Second sub heading of section 5.3

6.0 Conclusion

7.0 Recommendations

Appendices

Bibliography

Index (in larger reports)

Glossary (if necessary)

This layout will help the reader locate sections that are appropriate to them as well as making you look highly efficient and organised. A list of Appendices can be added after the contents page in bigger reports.

TIP

Overall the report should: 'Tell them what you are going to say'
                                  'Say it'
                                  'Tell them you have said it'

THE LAYOUT

1.0 Summary/executive summary

This should give a brief idea of the whole report. It is essentially a precis of the report itself.

TIP

Formal reports are <u>usually</u> written in an impersonal style:
e.g. The resulting figures showed . . .
    It was evident that . . .
    It was considered to be . . .

The summary should also whet the appetite for what is to come – so make it interesting. Look on it as a management overview. Needless to say although it appears at the beginning of the report, it is usually written at the end.

2.0 Literary review

This is optional and usually for use with larger reports which have involved a lot of research. It is essentially the author's comment on the texts used to compile the report. This would not usually be included in a commercial report which would go straight into the introduction. This section is an opportunity to demonstrate academic breadth and prowess. Don't worry managers – your chance to show your prowess and experience comes later.

3.0 Introduction

This should begin with a description of the subject area. It can, in the case of an assignment, break the title down and highlight areas that as a result should be discussed. The introduction should give a clear indication of *what* the report is going to cover and its objectives.

Some reports use a Terms of Reference section which is basically a statement of who asked for the information and what it is supposed to cover. The introduction can do all this as a whole if you wish.

TIP

It is also a good idea, in the introduction, to state the results you hope to achieve from the findings. Some very successful report writers set out to prove a theory and they put their head on the line and declare it.

Needless to say if you make such a commitment you must see it through. Make sure you do try to prove it, or if findings have gone the other way, be brave enough to say so.

4.0 Method

Having relayed *what* you are going to do, tell the readers *how* you are going to do it. Explain clearly how you are going to tackle, or have tackled the topic in question. This could be as simple as explaining the intended order of your text and what each section will look at, to detailing your intentions to interview a CEO, gather hundreds of statistics, questionnaires, etc.

Stating your intent to use particular types of research or models, theories and concepts in a certain way is recommended. There are three particular areas you can hone into to illustrate the choices you are making for the report:

- primary research
- secondary research
- use of concepts, models and theories

A subtle touch appears when you evidently make a judgement about the better direction to follow in order to clarify things for the reader using some or all of these categories.

Primary research This consists of interviews, questionnaires, etc. which extract original information as yet unavailable to you. It is material you have personally collected straight from its source.

You can state in your method exactly what you have chosen to undertake and give an indication of the size of the sample.

Secondary research This consists of data collection too but utilising that which already exists within the company, published national reports, etc. Using these at different levels – corporate, local, national, international – will show good comparative thinking.

In both primary and secondary research the findings can be *quantitative* – something you can count – or *qualitative* – requiring comment or opinion. This aspect should be borne in mind when compiling a questionnaire and thinking about the types of outcome desired for the report.

TIP

It can be useful to word the introduction and the method in the future tense to show your intentions. This also has the key positive bonus of preventing you from writing about the findings in these sections, which is a common mistake. In the introduction or the method, do not talk about anything you found out, only about what you are going to do and how. The executive summary, on the other hand, should cover the whole report and therefore encapsulate the findings.

Use of models, concepts and theories The third area to explain is that of using established theories, concepts or models to prove or disprove points or to compare approaches and to gain a view for discussion. These can stem from a literary review, where one is used, but are also useful in work reports. As with the SWOTPLOT, etc. you used in Chapter 1, models etc. are merely different glasses to look through to gain a better understanding of what you are looking at, or even a different view.

Using contrasting theories is a good idea to help create a rounded approach, as is adapting the model to suit the company. Still quote the source but indicate the adaptation by author. Even better, get innovative and create your own models to view your issues. Remember, though, in the method state your intention to use them and compare them – leave the actual results for the next bit!

5.0 Findings

This section is for the facts and results from your primary, secondary and conceptual research. It is used to illustrate research, explain and apply theory and present contrasting evidence in order to come to the fairest conclusion you can. You do not conclude here though – just present the findings and their influence.

It is a good idea to show different opinions and views and, when looking at the theory, more marks are obtained for applying that theory to the subject rather than just repeating what you have been taught.

As you illustrate your knowledge, do show a management overview and an understanding of different levels of staff in the company and recognise that the same matter can often be read in different ways. For example, utilise phrases such as: 'This would suggest that . . .', 'Alternatively, it could be decided that . . .'.

The following tips can enhance the readability of your report and make it more useful for your readers:

- Use clear models or diagrams to break up the text – ensuring that they are all labelled and sourced (Figure 1, etc.). Long lists and tables should be put in appendices and referred to in the text.
- Make reference to all sources by use of the Harvard system, for example using phraseology such as 'In the text Porter (1986) said . . .'. At the end in the bibliography and in alphabetical order by surname, list all referenced works in a consistent format: Porter, M. (1986) *Title of book*, Place of publication: Publisher.
- Abbreviations can be used as long as they are explained in full the first time they are mentioned, e.g. Certificate of Management Studies (CMS).
- Technical words: think of your reader and explain these when you first introduce them. Remember that in industry, the public sector, etc. your report may go to a wide audience of varying backgrounds.
  - Check your spelling, grammar and readability. It does not reflect well on you if you get these wrong. The next chapter deals with this.
  - Avoid bias, be factual and be objective. Opinions should be presented in an informed and balanced way.
  - Do try to refer back to your purpose from time to time to show that you are in control.

6.0 Conclusion

This is the place for the conclusion in academic reports but in commercial reports the conclusion is often the final section.

If used before any recommendations in an academic report, it is in effect a summary of the findings and a means to highlight arising problems and so a lead into your management recommendations.

If used after any recommendations in a commercial report, it is again a summary but of the findings and recommendations together and more along the lines of the 'tell them you've said it' rule. It should also be more dramatic in commercial contexts.

As well as commenting on arising problems etc., you can also be seen to constructively criticise your own work. For instance, it shows a healthy management attitude to say that more research into a certain area could have been done. This may even be a recommendation.

7.0 Recommendations

This is your opportunity to express an opinion but remember to keep to a third person approach and avoid bias. It should go without saying that your recommendations should relate directly to your findings and again be in keeping with the original purpose of the report. Mirroring the findings is a useful tip. A good way of ensuring this is to copy and paste the findings into the recommendations section and then write over the top of the findings with the appropriate recommendation.

> ### TIP
>
> Bear in mind that this is the section where you get to show off your management head. The whole report should reflect this to an extent, but this is where you are seen to not just reproduce information, but to apply it and propose solutions to arising problems.

Appendices

This is the place for long lists, large tables, etc. which constitute the background information you refer to.

If you have circulated a questionnaire, the results can be tabulated in an appendix and perhaps referred to in the main text with a graph. An example of the questionnaire itself can also be included in the appendices.

The appendices show the depth of your study and research for your management report without making the reader go through each and every detail in the text.

References

Ensure you always list the books/journals etc. that you use. As indicated above, it is usual to use the Harvard system as illustrated.

Plagiarism This is the attempt to use another person's work as your own and is in effect theft. Acknowledge all of your sources by referencing them correctly as shown. Except for direct quoting use your own words. Packages exist now which can isolate text and source them to internet sites, so if you do try this you are quite likely to be caught out. Start as you mean to go on and source everything.

> ### CROSS CULTURAL COMMENT
>
> It can be easy to get caught in the trap of apparent plagiarism, especially where English is not your first language. When sourcing quotes and ideas from the internet, for instance, ensure you clearly attribute the text to its particular author.

> ### TIPS
>
> - Use double line spacing
> - Do not put your report in a bulky folder
> - You can highlight appendix references in the text for easier housekeeping
> - Use a marker as you write and make notes to yourself so you can pick up easily without reading whole thing again which wastes time

DISSERTATIONS

The dissertation is almost a longer and more thorough version of the report. Whilst some of the tips for report writing more than apply to such a document, it is highly recommended that students attend specific tutorials on this topic and read specifically around research methods for best effect. This book could not devote the time and attention needed to do it full justice so some further reading is listed at the end of the chapter.

ESSAY WRITING

The essay is still most commonly used in academia and is much more fluid than the report. It is still necessary to ensure a beginning, a middle and an end and to apply the 'tell 'em' rule, as previously indicated but there is more flexibility as to its structure, giving you more control.

Essentially you decide the structure based on the actual question and the arguments you wish to present. Terms such as account for, compare, evaluate, explain or discuss will be used and help to determine how you sequence your text (Lashley and Best 2001).

Depending on the initial request, you may decide to interweave some contrasting points to come to a conclusion at the end of an essay or you may block your arguments together and then conclude. Examples of each method are given in Figures 7.1 and 7.2.

Figures 7.1 and 7.2 offer two simple examples of a rough structure to follow. You decide the headings and you decide the structure to ensure your answer is presented in the best possible light.

However you format it, your essay should always actually answer the question set. Carefully break down the question first and ensure you know exactly what you are

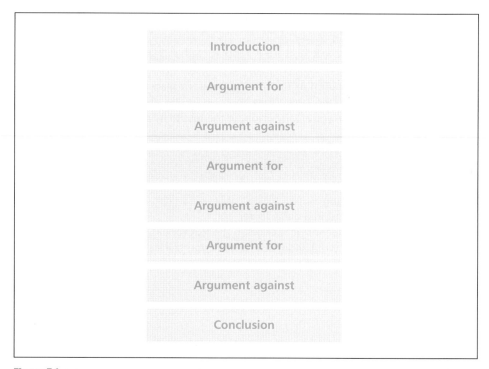

Figure 7.1 Interwoven essay example

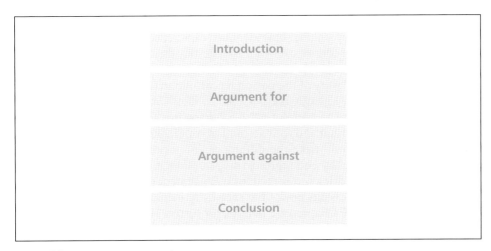

Figure 7.2 Block essay example

tackling for the marks. It is easy to get diverted or misunderstand the question and so spend a lot of time for nothing.

As with reports, a range of opinion should be sported with evidence of breadth in reading sources and the essay should be written in third person. Remember, the level of your critical argument will dictate your marks.

The use of concepts, theories, etc. is the same as for reports and the same rules for referencing and plagiarism apply. An essay should flow well and lead logically into a conclusion. As with reports, your conclusion should be born of the content of the essay – nothing new should be introduced at the end.

Although you have more freedom as to the structure and sequencing of material in an essay, remember that this will contribute to the marks and is worth thinking about it carefully. The ease with which the points you are making can be found will make all the difference. Do not make the reader search for the answer to the question. Make it really clear that you have answered it. It is not a bad idea to refer back to the points in the question from time to time in the essay.

PORTFOLIO WRITING

The portfolio is used more and more for work courses and for modules at university. Currently assessment by portfolio is very fashionable. Examinations, reports and essays assess a snapshot of what you know, but a portfolio offers tangible proof of the development of thought and personal skills. For this reason it is tackled in a very different way. Each portfolio brief will be different and the actual content will be determined by specific assessors. Read these as carefully as an essay or report brief.

However, you will have even more freedom with this medium. Often the sequence and structure are once again down to you, so careful consideration is necessary. Portfolios often contain a lot of personal content and some are entirely devoted to personal development. For this you will need to master reflective writing and the model and tips given in Chapter 2 will help greatly with this. The content should not only address the set brief but also look at different levels as advised by the model and the work should show the 'evolution' of the author. Demonstrating how you have developed over time or will develop in the future by gaining some identified experiences is a good ploy for marks and the more you indicate control over your own destiny the better. Remember, reflection is not just retrospective in this instance: good reflection contains projection!

People are often more wary of the personal portfolio than anything and find it the hardest thing to write. Frequently the personal content can be written in 'I' or first person form. However, be careful not to be too narrative and just relay events. It is your analysis that is important and your account of your feelings and learning and how that will be used which will make the difference. Treat portfolio writing as a completely different skill to essay and report writing but take it just as seriously. Perfecting the art of reflective writing is essential for management progress. It is not enough just to possess one of the skills now – the successful manager/leader needs to have both at their disposal. See Chapter 1, Endnote, for further tips on PDPs.

Summary

Effective report writing is as important in academia as it is in business. This chapter gives a sound structure in which to achieve the best marks at university as well as a format which translates well into business. In addition to looking at the content and structure of reports, the chapter looks at the differences required for essay writing and portfolio work. Reflective writing in the latter is emphasised and a good comparison is made of all three media.

TASK 1

Compare an existing report you have with the template offered in this chapter.

TASK 2

As a group compare a set of reports (at least three) and give them grades out of 20. Justify your marking criteria and discuss why the highly marked ones succeeded and why those with a low mark did not.

References and further reading

Lashley, C. and Best, W. (2001) *12 Steps to Study Success*, London: Continuum.
Morris, M. and Smith, H. (1999) *Business Writing*, London: Orion Business Books.
Rouse, M. J. and Rouse, S. (2002) *Business Communications*, London: Thomson Learning.
Seely, J. (1998) *The Oxford Guide to Writing and Speaking*, Oxford: Oxford University Press.

Websites

www.surrey.ac.uk/Skills/pack/report.html
www.accaglobal.com/publications/studentaccountant/43905
planet.tvi.cc.nm.us/ba122/Reports/ReportWriting.htm

CHAPTER 8
General writing skills

- To write in a readable style to impress
- To develop your own method for creative writing skills
- To form a discipline for checking the quality of work produced

This chapter is dedicated to helping you develop your writing skills in general. It will then also serve as a kit for your future use and reference as the principles can be transferred to many different types of writing. It is also very much written in the spirit of assuming oversight through busy-ness rather than a lack of knowledge in the first place. The best of us make the most straightforward of errors when we are in a hurry.

WRITING TERROR

I have diagnosed, and named, two grave conditions with regard to writing:

- blank page terror
- error terror

I have put together this kit to help overcome both conditions. Although it is not designed to turn you into a writer overnight, it will help you write in a better way.

Blank page terror!! Writing for impact

- Think before you start – questions to ask yourself
- Some basic rules of producing good, readable text

Error terror!! Check it, check it and check it . . .

- Proof-reading – grammar and spelling tips
- Layout

Think of all writing as selling. Whether writing an essay or a business report you need to ensure your ideas are captured in an articulate and attractive way for the best mark possible or to get the business.

Writing to sell

Writing to sell imposes its own disciplines. You know before you start that you have to make an immediate and favourable impression on your potential customer. You need to distinguish what you have to offer from other similar products. And you need to do it as quickly as possible – the average attention span of someone reading a sales message is around 15 seconds. If you haven't stimulated interest in that time you have failed. (Morris and Smith 1999, p. 74)

Blank page terror!! (BPT)

Just where do you start?

Think before you start – questions to ask yourself Know the answers to the following questions and the text will start writing and organising itself.

The reader

- What kind of reader am I trying to impress?
- What is of most interest to them?
- How do I speak to them?

The reason

- Why am I writing this?
- What objectives do I have?

The rubrik

- What are the instructions?
- What is the question or the title of an essay asking for?
- What is the necessary template/structure I need to work to?

Jot down some answers to these questions and cut and paste over templates to work to. For instance if writing a report, paste over the template of headings and write under each heading a few notes to yourself to get you started. If you get into the habit of creating a template to work to each time, you need never worry about BPT.

Some basic rules of producing good text

- Use short words and sentences
- Do not use jargon and technical language
- Check readability – Gunning's Fog Index (Seely 1998)
- Use the active voice, not the passive voice

Examples of active and passive voice:

- ABC Ltd won a large part of this new market (ACTIVE)
- A large part of this new market has been won by ABC Ltd (PASSIVE)

This is easy to spot – if the subject comes before the verb then the sentence is usually *active*. If the verb comes before the subject then the sentence is usually *passive*.

You can also look for various forms of the verb 'to be' in the sentence (is, are, was, were, will be, have been, should be, has been, etc.). This can lead to a sentence being identified as *passive*.

- Use the positive voice and positive words
- Make the text reader focused rather than writer focused
- Make the text gender neutral. Avoid 'his' and 'her'; this can usually be achieved by applying the plural

Examples of gender weighted and gender neutral phrasing:

- Each candidate for this position must file his/her application before . . . SINGULAR and GENDER WEIGHTED.
- All candidates for this position must file their applications before . . . PLURAL and GENDER NEUTRAL.

CROSS CULTURAL COMMENT

Idioms and clichés should be avoided. Idioms are specific to one language, e.g. 'eat their words'. Bear in mind that with the internet global appeal should be considered.

CASE STUDY 8.1

A vertically challenged individual of feminine dispo-sition placed her posterior on a proximate herba-ceous mound simultaneously masticating a quantity of separated lacteal fluid. An insidious approach was made by a large arachnid taking up a parallel position which resulted in a most hasty departure by the fore-mentioned individual experiencing extremely high levels of circulatory adrenalin.

- What is this a 'fogged' version of?

Gunning's Fog Index

This is a mathematical calculation created by Robert Gunning to assess readability (Seely 1998).

- Take a sample of your writing about 100 words long ending with the end of a sentence.
- Count all the words of three syllables or more (e.g. Bar'ris'ter) = number of long words (NLW).
- Work out the average sentence length (ASL)
- Apply this formula:

$$(ASL + NLW \times 0.4) = \text{FOG INDEX}$$

- A total of about 15 shows an easily readable style for graduate calibre, 20 is for the highly literate.

ERROR TERROR! CHECK IT, CHECK IT AND CHECK IT!

Proof-reading

Lindsell-Roberts (1999, p. 90) states, 'Proof-reading is akin to quality control'. How-ever, do not rely on computer spell checks alone.

- Check all names, addresses and telephone numbers – every time. This is where many mistakes are made as we get used to the numbers, etc. and skip over checking them when the ad comes back from the setters. Also, it is basic respect to check any other names such as client names. There is just no excuse for them to be wrong.
- Check all dates – very carefully. Also if you name the day with the date – check that it matches against the calendar.
- Check all numbers. Common mistakes are too many noughts and decimal points in the wrong places. For example Argos once advertised a TV for £2.99 on the internet.

Benjamin (1997) gives us a few pointers on dealing with numbers in text:

- Write out numbers under ten in full.
- Use numerals for numbers greater than ten.

The exception to this is when you begin a sentence with a number: always write it out in full. (*Source:* Words at Work, © Susan Benjamin (1997), reprinted by permission of Basic Books.)

Benjamin also advises about these common confusions:

- When to use *among* or *between*
  - use among when you are writing about three or more parties
  - use between when you are discussing two parties
- When to use *amount* or *number*
  - use amount when you are discussing volume
  - use number when you are discussing things you can count
- When to use *fewer* or *less*
  - Use fewer for things you can count
  - Use less for volume or degree

(*Source*: *Words at Work*, © Susan Benjamin (1997), reprinted by permission of Basic Books.)

- Check for words which sound alike (homophones – see box)

Homophones

Accept	to take
Except	other than
Advice	recommendation
Advise	to give an opinion
Affect	to influence
Effect	to result/bring about
Complement	to complete or add to something
Compliment	to praise
Eminent	well-known
Imminent	immediate
Ensure	to make certain
Insure	to protect against
Moral	lesson relating to right or wrong
Morale	spirit
Principal	school official, main, first in rank
Principle	a rule
Respectfully	in a respectful manner
Respectively	in the order listed
Should of	this is not correct English
Should have	this is correct
Stationary	fixed in place
Stationery	paper products

When in any doubt – look it up!

Source: Words at Work, © Susan Benjamin (1997), reprinted by permission of Basic Books.

- Check for repeated words, e.g. The the
- Check for omissions
- Check speeling (just kidding!)
- Check all plurals and re-check when making changes to sentences

Obviously this check list encompasses plurals, the correct use of suffixes and doubling final consonants. Naturally, I hear you say! Let's look at these last two points in more detail.

When adding a suffix, when do you lose and when do you retain the final 'e' or the final 'y'?

- *Lose* the 'e' when the suffix begins with a vowel – e.g. Us**able**
- *Keep* the 'e' when the suffix begins with a consonant – e.g. Care**less**
- *Lose* the 'y' to an 'i' when adding a suffix if a consonant precedes it – e.g. Ea**sily**
- *Keep* the 'y' when the 'y' is preceded by a vowel – e.g. Depl**oys**

When should you double final consonants?

- If the word has one syllable, double it – e.g. chop to chopped.
- Double the final consonant in a word ending in a single vowel and consonant together – e.g. refer to referred, transfer to transferred.
- DO NOT double the final consonant in words with three or more syllables – e.g. benefited.

Still on spelling, we must mention IE and EI. Lindsell-Roberts (1999) gives us this rhyme to help. Most of us know the first two lines:

Put i before e, (yield, field)

Except after c, (deceit, receive)

Or when sounded like a,

As in neighbour or weigh.

And except seize and seizure,

And also leisure.

Weird, height and either,

Forfeit and neither.

Grammar

One could do a whole handout on grammar, but, as above, let us look at what is most likely to go wrong so you can spot it in your proof-reading.

Seely (1998, p. 158) puts us on the right track: 'One of the causes of problems when writing sentences, especially long sentences, is the verb.'

Confusions can occur in meaning when the verb is not finite A finite verb shows the tense, number (singular or plural) and person. Seely gives the following example:

> In late September in Herefordshire, during those last magic days of summer, **walking** through the fields by the river Wye!

So here you can see the verb relates to no one, has no tense and we do not know if it singular or plural. He then changes this to:

> In late September in Herefordshire, during those last magic days of summer, I used to love walking through the fields down by the river Wye!

Although this is a very simple way of analysing it, it does illustrate quite a common problem in copywriting. Ask yourself what tense, number and person are indicated by the verb as an easy way to check that a sentence makes sense.

Lack of agreement Lack of agreement is where the subject and the verb do not agree and it can be most annoying for readers. For example:

> Several members of the Board, including LLD, **has visited** the students in the past year.

Obviously the verb should agree with the plural subjects and not LLD and should be **have visited**!

Note that using either/neither in the subject can often make this even more difficult. Look out for the mixed singular and plural subject. For example:

> Either LLD or her assistant **is** the person to take charge of this lesson.

This is quite straightforward, as both are singular but *the verb must actually agree with the subject that comes immediately before it*. So:

> Either LLD or her students **are** to blame.

The same applies to the person of the verb:

> Either Carole or I **am** going to look after you.
> Either you or Carole **is** going to look after me.

The split infinitive Finally, the split infinitive: 'To boldly go . . .' These can be annoying. An infinitive is the part of the verb that has 'to' with it and the two parts should be kept together wherever possible. However, do not assume that all split infinitives are necessarily wrong – they are permissable to avoid ambiguity or excessive artificiality.

Punctuation

- Check that commas make sense of the sentence
- Check apostrophes are used correctly:
  - Mr Reed's lecture
  - Mr Jones's lecture
  - The co-members' opinions (plural)
  - Women's rights (plural without an s)
  - Boys' school

Beware of contraction confusion! Contraction is what happens when two words become one, with one or more letters being discarded. The discarded letters are replaced with an apostrophe. For example:

- its – possessive **its** has no more bits
- it's is the contraction of **it is**

- they're is the contraction of they are and is frequently confused with **their** and **there**

I know this is very primitive but these are the most common mistakes I see. It is not usually because people do not know them but because they do not spend the time being a bit more careful.

TIPS
• Look for missing brackets and quotation marks.
• Look out for correct use of colons, semi-colons, etc.
• Look for missing question marks at the end of questions.

Benjamin (1997) helps out with traffic signals to clarify where to use full stops, colons, etc.

TIP		
Traffic sign	**Punctuation mark**	**Meaning**
Red light	full stop	stop
Blinking red	colon	stop, then proceed
Blinking yellow	semi-colon	proceed cautiously
Yellow	comma	slow down
Green	nothing	proceed

Source: Words at Work, © Susan Benjamin (1997), reprinted by permission of Basic Books.

Thinking in this simple way will make it easier to check for correct punctuation. Sometimes when things are elementary we overlook them more easily.

Finally, consider these tips:

- Get someone else to check your work
- Read it aloud
- Read it in a different order
- Leave it a while and read it again

LAYOUT

In addition to the verbal content you need to consider whether the words are presented in an attractive and eye-catching way. Rupert Morris and Harriet Smith (1999, p. 33) sum it up thus:

> Don't just read the words; look at the whole page.
>> Check that you have appropriate headings to catch the eye.
>>> Think about white space and all-round readability.

White space

White space refers to areas of the page deliberately left blank for effect, for example between paragraphs or sections, around lists or displayed items. Lindsell-Roberts (1999, p. 46) points out a few reasons for using white space:

> White space makes the document inviting and approachable.
>> It provides contrast and a resting place for the reader's eyes.
>>> A document with ample white space creates the impression that it's easy to read.

The typeface

Consider the choice of font and use of bolding and underlining. Look at 'justifying' the text or leaving it 'ragged right'. Think about the use of lower and upper case as well as italics. 'WOB' (white on black) can be quite powerful. Lines, borders, colour and shadowing are also available. All these effects are useful – just do not overdo things. Highlighting too many things will dilute the importance of the things you are really trying to attract the eye to. However, don't forget to headline.

Bear in mind the reader will not necessarily read every word. What can they pick up with a quick glance? Ensure the text is set with a glance mechanism – anchors of highlighted text which guide the eye through the main points of the page.

Conclusion

Morris and Smith (1999, p. 131) conclude very appropriately:

- Understanding your readers is the key to your success – listen to them, find out what they want, and then write for them.
- Use simple, active language – avoid jargon, abstract nouns, and management-speak.
- Listen to what you write – think of your writing as a conversation.
- Learn the tricks of the trade – grammar and punctuation – and use them effectively.
- Organise your writing – start with the message, promote the key ideas, then build up the rest of the content.
- Make sure what you have written is easy on the eye.

Above all, write with purpose – it will make all the difference. (Morris and Smith 1999)

Summary

Starting with blank page terror and how to deal with it, this chapter gets the reader writing from scratch by asking questions and setting up a structure within which to be creative. To supplement this some rules about readability are covered.

Error terror is tackled so that a retrospective look at all pieces of work is made and some basic checks become the norm in a busy world where error is easy. Proof-reading, spelling, grammar and the overall look of the work is covered in a straight-forward way which can be used for reference in the future.

TASK 1

In groups pick a simple nursery rhyme and 'fog' it – have fun.

TASK 2

Write an advert for your own job or that of someone you know.

TASK 3

Collect 20 adverts between a group of you from a selection of publications and compare them for phrases, structure, impact, etc. Discuss and prepare a short sit down presentation as to their strengths and weaknesses.

References and further reading

Benjamin, S. (1997) *Words at Work*, Reading, Massachussetts: Perseus Books.
Blamires, H. (1997) *The Cassell Guide To Common Errors In English*, London: Cassell.
Lindsell-Roberts, S. (1999) *Business Writing For Dummies*, Foster City, CA, USA: IDG Books.
Morris, R. and Smith, H. (1999) *Business Writing*, London: Orion Business Books.
Seely, J. (1998) *The Oxford Guide To Writing & Speaking*, Oxford: Oxford University Press.
Whitcut, J. (1997) *The Oxford Better Word Power*, Oxford: Oxford University Press.
Marketing-magic.biz/archives/...writing-advertising-copy.htm

Website

www.uri.edu/cels/pls/logan/teaching/html/ev533/fog.htm

PART 3
ONE TO ONE COMMUNICATIONS

With the current or future workplace in mind, this part contains a set of key personal skills for better effectiveness. A deliberate focus on interviewing has been made with multiple ends in mind. The focus is on the one to one interview and how to fare as well as possible as the interviewee and as the interviewer. Being able to interview well both ways is key to future success.

Getting a job through interview success is a popular topic with most but often neglected is the art of effectively interviewing others – which is not always taught and can fill the new manager with dread. A thorough look at this in this part gives much food for thought. Although the pivot in this part is the job interview, the skills are transferable to many study and workplace situations.

The interviewing focus is advanced with questioning techniques, listening skills, body language and assertiveness so one to one communication is rounded and the individual is encouraged to think carefully about how they appear to others.

While the skills discussed in this part apply to a one to one situation, they create a firm basis for expanding communication techniques to more complicated contexts.

CHAPTER 9

Interviewing skills as an interviewee

Learning objectives

- To be prepared for interviews whether internal or external
- To improve performance at interview
- To maximise interview time
- To prepare for assessment centres
- To prepare for panel interviews

Introduction

However you look at it, the interview process is a performance – in part anyway. There are certain lines to learn and stage directions to follow. The interview is not the place to make big statements about non-conformance to society norms. In the main there are codes to follow and failure to do this will usually result in failure to get the job.

As an interviewee it is important to respect and of course expect the potential diversity of interviewer ahead of you. You will not necessarily know how competent they themselves are at interviewing and indeed you may have to compensate for any inability on their part. The codes of conduct for interview will act as a safety net for most eventualities in this case. You do not necessarily know what particular beliefs, biases, etc. the interviewer may have, so following the codes of conduct for interview will help to keep you within safe selection territory. Remember that is what they are doing – selecting the right person for the job – so everything you can do to 'fit' that job is important. Your appearance, language including body language, attitude, etc. will all be judged and usually very quickly at interview.

> **TIP**
>
> Also remember that the interview is for you too. You are interviewing the company to see if they suit you – classily of course – but it is important to acknowledge the process is a two way one.

PREPARATION

Well done – you have successfully got to interview stage! Now the work really starts and it is important you prepare carefully. You need to prepare for a number of eventualities and this should have started at your letter and CV writing stage.

You should, of course, have kept the original advert as an anchor reference. Closely study the wording of the advert again now and take on board the 'culture' of the company from it. Do a quick gap analysis on yourself in terms of the advert. Of the things it asks for, consider which ones are your strengths and which ones need working on. Complete a HOTPLOT for the job in question by which time you will have semi-interviewed yourself – excellent preparation. It will also give you some answers to the likely questions ahead.

Carefully read any material sent to you. Do not leave this until the last minute. Reading the night before or on the day should be refresher reading. Get to know the company from the information sent and note the wording of the enclosures and start slipping some of it into your vocabulary before the day.

If very little is sent to you, research the company yourself. You should do this in any case. It is really easy to research companies on the internet and you can get a lot of information now. Don't overlook aspects such as the corporate colours and culture, which you can then reflect in your material and manner at the interview. You can phone the company beforehand and ask for any corporate literature before the event. Pro-activity like this will be noted when you mention it at interview. In fact some companies leave it open to see what you do and what you turn up with.

> **TIP**
>
> Prepare answers for the obvious questions ahead. See below for the mainstay questions that you really should have answers for. Use the results of your SWOTPLOT, HOTPLOT and TROTPLOT in Chapter 1 to form the basis for your answers.

Appearance

Obviously this should be smart. A good deal of care should be taken to dress appropriately for the company you are attending so that you walk through the door *in* your outfit not *after* your outfit. It should not wear you and should not be particularly memorable save for being appropriate and classy. Be careful about wearing brand new clothes you are not used to. The clothes can look stiff and make you look the same and it can be embarrassing to try putting your hand in the pocket of a jacket that is still stitched up. In general, classic dress works best with no particular attention drawn to any particular part of your body. Good grooming is important and the first statement made about you in person. It is you the person who needs to shine through and if you look accomplished, apparently without trying, you are more likely to succeed. Don't overdo it – it is just as bad to look as if you have tried too hard.

TIPS

Gents

No white socks

Polished shoes

Suit fabric and tie – classy and forgettable. One should not be able to remember the pattern on a suit

If possible wear a shirt with cuff links; cuffs should show a little

Minimise jewellery. Best not to wear earrings, etc.

Tidy/clean hair and trimmed nails

Ladies

Avoid short skirts, low tops and very high heels

Classy and conservative is best

Suits can look good, but if wearing a trouser suit try not to look too manly

Hair is best away from face and any fiddling

Make-up and nail varnish should be day colours only – avoid anything too heavy or dark as it can look cheap

Always wear 'hose', – i.e. tights etc. Bare legs are a no-no at interview

Closed shoes are most appropriate, even in summer and there should be no scuffs or chips on heels

Limit jewellery to tasteful and toned down pieces

Underwear should not be visible in any way – e.g. dark bras under white shirts or skirts/trousers so tight that you suffer VPL (visible panty line)

In all cases make sure you are 'lint' free by brushing down. Hairs – especially pet hairs – look shabby. Watch for marks, hanging threads or small holes in the clothes. If you have made repairs (e.g. buttons) make sure they are sewn with the right thread. Finally apply perfume and after shave carefully – when you are nervous it is easy to put on that bit extra for luck as if it is a magical potion to protect. It is not – rather than protect you, it can send the wrong message.

Your clothes can also affect your posture; how they fit you may affect the way you stand, sit and move. Ensure the length of skirts or fit of trousers does not affect the simple act of sitting with poise and elegance. Check this by trying it out in front of a mirror. It is not a bad idea anyway to use a hand mirror with a big mirror to check the 'view' from the back. Jacket lines, hair lines, etc. can be checked this way.

Also if the company you are attending for interview has a uniform, for example with a navy theme, then an effort to adopt the look will help 'fit' you to the culture.

Portfolio

Take a copy of your CV, application, letter and corporate information, etc. in a neat portfolio for reference. Ensure you are able to carry this easily and find things easily within it without fumbling. Memorise the order for easy extraction and only keep in there what you need on the day.

THE INTERVIEW

The journey

If it is close enough, go and sound out the site beforehand. If not, do as much homework as you can before you go. Work out your journey and transport options carefully and allow room for delays and errors. If you intend to drive, work out parking well ahead. Contact the company beforehand and have directions sent to you.

It is better to arrive nearby early and grab a coffee than be late, but do not be much too early for the interview itself. It is as rude to be overly early for an appointment as it is to be late. Obviously never be late. There is nothing worse than listening to the dramatic run down of events by a rushed and red-faced individual who basically did not manage their time well. Often the story is embellished with a little extra drama anyway as if to validate the lateness. Remember how you cope with your time and events is one of the factors being judged. Should the unavoidable really happen even though you set aside plenty of time, and this will be very rare, then a call to reception is good manners. When you do arrive, adopt a calm exterior and resist the temptation to dramatise the event. Calmly relay what was outside of your control and planning and resume with the interview mode as soon as you can.

Reception

Go into interview mode the minute you enter the building From the outset, treat everyone with respect – including and especially the receptionist. Some interviewers place themselves in reception or watch to see what you do and how you conduct yourself. There is nothing worse than someone who is rude to administrative staff and treats them as underlings. This shows a lack of respect or possible 'New Manager Syndrome', that is: 'I just got some power and am not mature enough to know what to do with it'.

If you are laden with coats, etc. ask if you can leave them in reception. Sort out visitors' tags and try not to look awkward.

Sit carefully on edge of seating, ready to get up gracefully. Some reception furniture can make for an undignified start if you are not careful. Squidgy chairs and sofas are impossible to get up from with poise and some leather ones make a lovely rude noise as you rise. Spend this time looking around for extra information about the company.

Place anything you are carrying in a place where you can pick it up seamlessly and leave your hand free for the handshake as you rise to your feet. Make sure you have a decent handshake.

Don't use your mobile while you are waiting – it looks insecure. Switch it off. Be careful about accepting coffee, etc. as it can affect the freshness of your breath.

The room

Walk into the room confidently and carefully assess your seating in the first few seconds as you say hello and shake hands. As you sit down draw the chair slightly to angle or closer if necessary. Try not to sit straight on like a rabbit in headlights!

Place your portfolio in front of you for easy access. If it is a briefcase, lean it carefully on the side of your chair for easy opening. Try not to have bags/cases on the floor where you have to bend right over when sitting down to retrieve things. If you squash the diaphragm in your chest, you will emerge from the move breathless and sound less confident.

Questions

Have assertive and interesting replies ready for the basic, obvious questions.

Why do you want the job? Avoid the twee answers like 'I like working with people'. Answers which incorporate using your existing skills and then developing them are best. The rule here is that your answer will be similar to the content of your original application letter. That would have contained what you had to offer them and also what they could do for you. This combination is good in any answer. Use your SWOTPLOT, HOTPLOT and TROTPLOT outcomes to format answers which sound confident and two way. This is in addition to highlighting any other particular aspects of the job which suit you such as travel, working with a diverse customer base, etc.

Where do you see yourself in five years? Avoid answers like 'sitting in your chair!' – it is old hat and not as clever as you think. From the initial diagnostics gained in Chapter 1, work out a realistic plan of development which results in showing your ambition but within a real setting. Reference to management responsibility increasing is always good if it is appropriate for the position. Also the indication that this will be with the same company is reassuring for them, so this is your opportunity to get the word 'loyalty' into the equation. The aim is to make them see you as an investment rather than someone travelling through their system.

What are your strengths and weaknesses? You should have this ammunition at hand following the exercises in Chapter 1. Have at least eight strengths at your disposal. However, don't just reel them off in a list and make sure you have a practical example for every one of them. It is quite common to be asked to give an example of how this showed in your current or previous work life. Have these examples prepared as there is nothing more embarrassing than not being able to think of one on the spot and nothing more annoying of thinking of the best answer as you walk down the stairs after the interview.

With regard to weaknesses, have some so you do not sound too arrogant but needless to say do not go overboard. Have fewer weaknesses than strengths and present them as areas for development or training. Weaknesses such as impatience and taking too much on can be quite attractive to some recruiting audiences.

What would you like the company to do for you? Work out training, development and progression needs beforehand. A candidate who knows exactly what they want from a company always looks better. Again, in terms of loyalty, it doesn't hurt to indicate a need for stability to show that you are aware that it is a two way arrangement.

What sets you apart from other applicants? What are your unique selling points? Take some of your strengths and really try to work this out. What do you do really well? Don't be modest. Apart from traits such as quickness to learn, ability to manage diversity or to operate well under pressure, think of energy giving traits: your positive attitude, ability to inspire and motivate others, etc. – these can be a real vote swinger.

As well as having good answers, think about how you answer. A short silence beforehand is quite acceptable and then when you answer make good eye contact. Do not answer before they have finished asking the question.

Hypothetical questions are also fashionable. These are 'What would you do if . . .?' questions. Think them through and answer with a management mentality. A good rule of thumb with hypothetical questions is to try and get a good mix in your answer about the tasks, team and individual and how that fits in with the corporate purpose, people and productivity.

Ask questions politely throughout the interview at appropriate moments unless otherwise instructed not to. This helps you to deal with things as they occur and drive the interview in the direction you wish it to go as well as making you look enthusiastic and interested. This approach also prevents the awful bit at the end when you try to think of something clever after everything has been discussed – you can also say that you have asked about things throughout the interview and that these were dealt with very well.

Presentations

It is not unusual to be asked to do a presentation at interview. Chapter 15 covers this in more detail for you, but here are a few tips:

- Do your PowerPoint® slides in corporate colours and get the company's logo from the internet
- Save your presentation in several versions and call beforehand to check what equipment you will be using
- Take handouts – they look professional and can serve as a back-up if the technology fails

ASSESSMENT CENTRES

These are large-scale recruitment events generally staged in hotels, training centres, etc. It is worth being prepared for such an event and regarding them as an extended interview. They often last a day – sometimes longer – and you have to be on your best behaviour all this time. They can also be held internally in a company for management talent spotting. They are the *Pop Idol* of the recruitment world and usually involve:

- group work
- presentations
- tests
- interviews

Observers are assigned to watch your performance in each of these tasks and mark you. The marks across the range are collated in what is called the 'wash-up' at the end of the day when you have gone and these, with comments from the observers, are discussed in detail.

To succeed at such an event:

- Always enter each and every task with enthusiasm – even if you think it is silly – remember you are being watched for your reactions to things

- Demonstrate your 'teaminess' at all times by referring to peers in presentations, etc.

- Make sure you have as much energy in the afternoon as the morning, stamina is important – fake it if necessary and collapse later

- Be as much on your guard during lunch and 'nod and grin' times as you are for the exercises. You are still being watched. Presume you are being watched at all times. It is not unheard of for assessors to stand outside the room you are meeting in first thing and watch to see if you introduce yourself to people you do not know.

- Drinks afterwards or overnight are dangerous. Drink enough to be sociable if you wish to but keep well within your limit. This is not the time to show how many you can sink.

PSYCHOMETRIC TESTS

Psychometric tests include personality and ability tests, such as maths, comprehension, etc. In the case of personality tests, answer honestly with the real answer and not what you think you should say – there are trips in the system to catch you out. If you have to take an ability test, remember that accuracy and speed are equally important.

THE PANEL INTERVIEW

Panel interviews can be thought of as cruel but they are a fact of life. As with the individual interview, positioning is important – only this time they can see more of you. Remember to turn the chair slightly as you sit down and pay attention to your posture and attire as indicated above. Address all parties as you relay your answers. By moving your eye contact to each person as you talk – calmly and smoothly rather than like a deliberate nodding dog – you are forming a 'relationship' with each person on the panel. Pretend you have a piece of invisible thread attached to each member and remember to pull each one throughout the interview.

You need to try to address all likely hidden agendas. It is likely that with several interviewers on the panel one or two may have other agendas. Your recruitment may be secondary to how well they themselves perform when questioning you in front of their boss. In order to do this they may even be overly interrogative to make themselves look good. Keep calm and answer fully and respectfully – even if you think the questions a little bizarre. The golden rule is not to challenge them in this setting. By making them look as good as possible in front of their boss you are more likely to get their support for your application. Think of it as gaining votes. As you work your way through the interview try to have 'reached' all panel members in some way to help steer their vote towards you. There also does still exist the 'good guy/bad guy' technique, where one panel member questions you while another watches you closely for your reaction, including your body language.

THE EXIT AND THE AFTERMATH

Give some thought beforehand to making a graceful exit. After you have been through a gruelling interview, running out of the building is tempting. Keep calm, collect everything you came with and ensure good handshakes on exit. There is nothing more embarrassing than forgetting your bag and having to return for it. Thank the interviewer/s and, of course, thank the receptionist. It does not hurt to make a fuss over the latter if they have been helpful and if this is audible it can show good grace and manners. Don't overdo it though.

Follow up

- A thank you note can work well if you do not get the job and keeps bridges open.
- Politely ask why you did not get the job and what you can improve on.
- If you come away from the interview unhappy that you were not asked something crucial the only person to blame is yourself. You should have brought it up in some way.

Don't forget these last points:

- The interview is a two way process.
- You are there to assess them too and ask them questions.
- To ask what the next stage is.

It is a good idea to read the next chapter on how to interview someone else. By seeing things in reverse you can gain some empathy for the interviewer and perhaps predict what will be judged.

CROSS CULTURAL COMMENT

When attending interviews abroad learn some basic greetings in the local language to show good manners. It may feel odd but the gesture will be appreciated.

CASE STUDY 9.1

This one is another self case study. Take a particular interview you have attended for any job and really go through it with a fine-tooth comb. Picture yourself before, during and after the interview and compare with the notes in this chapter. List all the things you could have done differently.

- Work out all your answers for the basic questions indicated in the chapter.

Summary

In addition to emphasising the need for thorough preparation for interview, this chapter briefs the potential candidate on appearance, dealing with reception and what questions to prepare answers for. Presentations at interview are now commonplace and this is covered along with the approach necessary for successful performance at assessment centres and panel interviews.

TASK 1

As a group, discuss your various interview experiences ready to share with a seminar group.

References and further reading

Amos, J. (2004) *Handling Tough Job Interviews*, How to Books

Bremner, M. (1992) *Modern Etiquette*, Chancellor Press

Hawthorne, R. (1997) *Do's and Don'ts, An Anthology of Forgotten Manners*, London: Pavilion Books

Lees, J. and DeLuca, M. (2003) *Job Interviews: Top Answers to Tough Questions*, McGraw-Hill Education

Morgan, J. (1996) *Debrett's New Guide to Etiquette and Modern Manners*, London: BCA.

Websites

www.job-interview.net

www.alec.co.uk/interview

www.quintcareers.com/intvres.html

www.businessballs.com/interviews.htm

CHAPTER 10
Interviewing skills as an interviewer

Learning objectives

- To maximise use of interview time as an employer
- To recruit the best candidates for the role
- To plan the interview time effectively
- To direct questions to gain maximum information in the minimum time
- To review your own interviewing performance
- To increase staff retention through more effective recruitment

Introduction

The interview process is a complicated process and an expensive one. Choosing candidates carefully is essential, but companies do not want to waste time interviewing unnecessarily, and interview time must be used prudently and effectively. The longest interviews are not necessarily the best ones. Lack of direction in the interview can lead to making the wrong choices. This in turn is costly in terms of candidate unsuitability, consequently affecting productivity or quality of service or resulting in a higher staff turnover which is crippling for the business.

More and more managers are, quite rightly, judged on their staff retention and the quality of their teams and performance. Key to this is effective recruitment and key to recruitment are good interviewing and selection skills. The interview process is not watertight, however much you train for it and practise it. Most managers can put their finger on one recruit who did extremely well at interview and seemed to transform into a devil on starting the job itself. Whilst this cannot be eliminated completely there are methods which help reduce this possibility, starting with preparation before the interview itself and a structured use of time within the interview. By adopting good management techniques early on you can save your company a lot of money and inconvenience. The interview process is only one part of a long domino effect. The cost of recruiting and interviewing the candidate is one thing, but to invest in training in someone who does not stay long is very expensive.

PREPARATION BEFORE THE INTERVIEW

This key part of the interview process is often overlooked. It starts long before you meet the candidate, not five minutes before they arrive. Never hurriedly grab a CV, skim through it and think you can wing it. Your aim should be to take the reins of control right from the word go.

The first step is to plan wisely and keep the number of interviews to a minimum. Be realistic – most interviews last between 45 minutes and an hour, depending on the level – and the process is a very tiring one. Leave gaps between each interview to allow you to write up notes and psychologically prepare for the next one. Conveyor belt interviewing is bad enough but to do it without coming up for air is a mistake which in itself courts more mistakes.

> ### TIP
>
> Six to eight interviews for one position is more than enough – more than that and your selection at the paperwork stage needs some attention.

© John Morris / Cartoonstock.com

"I agree Hepworth you do have drive, ambition and self-confidence, but what we're looking for is ability."

Depending on economic climes, you will receive varying responses to your adverts. If response is poor it may reflect the job market but also take a good look at the quality and circulation of the advert. It is not wise just to interview to make up numbers. Interview those that meet your criteria and if necessary re-advertise – it is cheaper than making a recruitment mistake in the long run.

If you receive large quantities of applications, you can expand on the basic yes–no approach for interviews.

- Set up three piles for the applications:

  YES   MAYBE   NO

- Then act according to how many YES applications you have.
  - TOO MANY: put all the MAYBEs in the no pile and ruthlessly reassess the YES pile to the right number.
  - TOO FEW: Look again at the MAYBEs, but don't be too generous – it is better to interview a few good candidates than lots of poor ones.
- NEVER LOOK AGAIN AT THE NO PILE. Send them all a polite letter of rejection wishing them all the best in their search for future employment.

This, and the way I have geared these interview guidelines, will help in your overall analysis of the form. It is accepted that some companies/organisations have particular procedures for selection and these are respected. The guidelines here are general ones and the methods used in, for instance, the public sector may be different. This being the case, make your own mind up about the particular features you are able to use within any corporate structures you must follow.

SYSTEMATIC ANALYSIS

A good application contains an abundance of information about the applicant, which you should absorb before the meeting. It is important to have a system of looking through the CV or application form several times and for different things on each occasion and this starts from the level of trouble the candidate has taken to produce a good quality CV or fill in the application prompts. Then systematically go through the following steps.

Look for gaps Look for gaps specifically in the order of dates. Dates should be set out clearly so you can 'zig-zag' through them and red flag any doubtful periods. It is important to ascertain reasons for the gaps. It might be as innocent as a gap year, family commitments, etc. but this is a key area to clear up. Of course a really good CV would not have raised the doubt in the first place.

Look for patterns in the information Is there a pattern in their study subjects, for example are they arts or science led? Has the candidate maintained a consistent level of achievement?

Look for type of jobs Have they held management roles, or roles similar to the one applied for? Do the job changes represent real progression and how does the most recent one fit with the role they want with you?

Look for type of organisation Is there a pattern in the type of company they have worked for – large or small, private or state owned?

Look for job importance Has each job given increased responsibility?

Look for number of jobs Recently it has become more acceptable to move jobs for promotion more often but within limits – look for unsettled candidates and job hopping.

Look for salary progression Has the salary increased as it should have? Are they earning what they should be? How does it sit with the package you are offering?

Look for a career plan The development and comments shown in the CV should give clues to the candidate's aspirations and motivation. How realistic are they?

Look for interests Is there a pattern in the type of sport, hobby or interest pursued? Is it active or passive? Social or solitary? Do the interests reflect work or compensate for it? Do they require substantial commitment? Would they interfere with work?

In this way and covering many other topics such as health, geography, etc. you can earmark areas for proactive discussion in the interview to give the meeting direction. This is in addition to matching any key criteria required for the job itself – which should go without saying.

This preparation not only helps screen the right applicants to select them for interview but also ensures that the interview time is fully and properly used. Spending time in the interview asking questions which are already answered on the CV while overlooking the red flag areas you could have highlighted beforehand are a waste of recruitment time. Such omission tempts fate and the wrong recruits may emerge to cost you and to embarrass you later. Also by not skimping on this vital preliminary stage you are less likely to get side tracked in the interview and less likely to forget the questions you intended to ask.

INTRODUCTIONS

Before you meet, greet and seat your applicant, a little more preparation is necessary.

- Be smart – first impressions work both ways.
- Be tidy – ensure that the interview room/area is neat, uncluttered and will accommodate a comfortable interview.
- Be prompt – try not to leave the applicant waiting around. Your interview timing should be set to allow some time in between. It is best to stick to times and set the good example you will expect from them if you recruit them. You must stay in control of this time.
- No interruptions – make sure you will not be disturbed. Apart from it being rude to take phone calls etc., it is good management to communicate your plans to your staff and delegate responsibilities so that your time is entirely devoted to the interview. This includes holding calls and ensuring your computer screen is switched off if you are at your desk. It is distracting when an e-mail come in and you may be tempted to peek to see who it is from while the interviewee is talking.
- No barriers – clearing the desk is not just a good physical process but it will also create good psychology in terms of the two way communication you will be trying to encourage.

> **TIP**
>
> Overall, use your introduction to create the right impression of yourself and your company. Even if this candidate is not the right person for your job they are a walking, talking advertisement for your company and how they are treated and what they see will be relayed outside to other potential applicants and of course customers.

This puts you in a good position to judge them and form your first impression of them. This is important, especially if you are interviewing for a front-line role involving clients and customers. Their handshake, demeanour, etc. are all important in the overall picture and you can use this point of introduction to establish what they would like to be called, for example shortened versions of their name.

THE INTERVIEW PLAN

The following can be used as a basic interview procedure:

1 A good introduction, break the ice and create a rapport with the candidate quickly.

2 Set out and agree the interview structure.

3 Describe your company and the job as well as how it fits into the company/management structure.

4 Question the candidate on his/her background and qualifications, assessing their experience and aims.

5 Invite questions from the candidate.

   YOUR SAFETY STOP POINT!!

   If the candidate is by now obviously unsuitable you can save your time and theirs by terminating here.

6 Question the candidate further covering any areas of doubt you have and tackling any sensitive issues – this is the best time for sensitive issues as bringing them up any earlier would have put the candidate off.

7 Sum up.

8 Outline the next stage in your recruitment process.

9 Thank them for coming and finish the interview.

10 Write up your notes and thoughts as soon after the interview as you can.

1. A good introduction, break the ice and create a rapport with the candidate quickly

The hobbies and interests section on the candidate's CV is usually a good place to start for this. As previously indicated, this is their first impression of you and the company too. Ensure the approach is friendly and calm. Letting them know how busy you are by acting in a rushed and officious manner will not put them at ease. Remember you want to extract as much information from the candidate as you can in the minimum time – this will not happen if you go at them with an aura of tension around you.

2. Set out and agree the interview structure

This is not just for housekeeping purposes. This is also an exercise in the management of their expectations. It is best not to promise an hour for instance at the outset. If you get to half an hour and know the candidate is not right for the job then it is a waste of time to fill up the remaining time. Indicate the preliminary and investigatory nature of this first sitting and that it may not last very long – say 20 minutes to half an hour. This way, if it only lasts this long they are not disappointed and if it lasts more then they feel great as they have gone over your indicated time so feel they have done well whether they get the job or not.

Here is an example. The interviewer, having completed Step 1, says:

Now, I would just like to outline the structure and purpose of this first session. It is a short preliminary session before a more extensive second interview for those who have the qualifying criteria for the post. I would like to introduce you to our company and outline the job to you and perhaps if I do that first you can then give me a run down of your experience which fits the vacancy. This may last 20–30 minutes and I will liaise with my colleagues regarding a shortlist for the longer second interview.

You should also set out your policy regarding questions from the candidate at this point. Either invite them to ask questions throughout – as long as you can control the time – or state that there will be time later.

Every candidate is a walking advertisement for your company and especially those who attend an interview with you. This is why it is crucial to create the right impression and leave them feeling good. Using the time as per the interview structure will help, as will using the question plan shown later in the chapter to ensure you maximise use of the time and leave them in the right frame of mind. Even if they do not get the job, they may still evangelise the merits of the company to their mates in the pub.

3. Describe your company and the job as well as how it fits into the company/management structure

It is important that this is done early on in the interview. As indicated above all candidates advertise your company in some way. This is your opportunity to ensure candidates are informed in a positive way. This done in tandem with the job description, fit, etc. and sets the scene. It also serves, partly selfishly, as a matching mechanism. By hearing yourself talk through the details you are setting up what key matching criteria you require for the post and set about matching in your mind against those criteria rather than basing your judgement on whether you happen to like the candidate.

4. Question the candidate on his/her background and qualifications, assessing their experience and aims

Now the candidate is informed and warmed up they are more likely to offer a richer level of information and feel more relaxed about talking about themselves. It is important to stick to a question plan as suggested later in the chapter as getting key information out of them regarding their human/management/team abilities is vital and requires more than easy and bland questions about qualifications. It is important to quickly get to grips with what makes them tick and what they are like under pressure. Questions put in a certain order will help to achieve this as will using the correct types of question technique. Techniques are discussed in Chapter 12.

5. Invite questions from the candidate

You can encourage candidates to ask questions as you go along and this can create a very good atmosphere. This really only works well if you have some interviewing experience. If you are less experienced, you may need to control the timing of questions from the candidate.

It does take time to relax and develop good interviewing skills. This structure and the question plan are designed to help you do that. The key is to perfect the art of listening as well as questioning so you are not worrying and thinking about your next question for the candidate but are actually listening to their answer and incorporating it into your line of questioning. An inability to do this makes you look amateur and foolish.

Safety stop point!! If the candidate is by now obviously unsuitable you can save your time and theirs by terminating here

This sounds cruel, but if you have followed the order of questioning suggested below and listened carefully then you will know by now how the candidate matches the job in question. If they clearly do not there is no point in continuing.

Having managed their expectations of time at the beginning of the structure there should be no disappointment or surprise at stopping gracefully and kindly here. This should be the 20–30 minute mark and they should exit happily feeling they have had the 'value' stated. Sum up and show them out nicely having thanked them and explained the next stage in the overall process (note the depersonalisation).

6. Question the candidate further covering any areas of doubt you have and tackling any sensitive issues

Now they have made it past the safety stop point they must be worth further questioning. You can drill into their qualifications more and deal with any red flag/sensitive issues in detail. The question plan helps with this.

7. Sum up

This is vital to show you have been listening and healthily reassures them of your interest in them. This is done enthusiastically whether you feel they are right for the job or not.

8. Outline the next stage in your recruitment process

Make it clear to the candidate what will happen next. How and when they will hear from you is key to their management and to the level of respect they will hold for the company even if they do not get the job. It is a good idea to check outgoing 'No' letters to see if you are happy they are customer friendly.

9. Thank them for coming and finish the interview

Remember it is their time too and they are interviewing you and your company.

10. Write up your notes and thoughts as soon after the interview as you can

This is especially important if you are interviewing a number of candidates or if you have a period of time between the interview and the actual selection. In addition to the obvious comments you might make about the candidate in terms of their matching criteria and skills, also make a note of the examples they used to illustrate them. This really helps with recall and more effective matching. You will also be surprised how much you forget about your interviewees in a short time, so write down everything you can now. Also a diagram of where they fit into their company is very helpful – they can actually help you with this during the interview itself. In addition to building a picture of their level of seniority and span of control, it is also very useful if you are interviewing a candidate from one of your competitors – you will gain a wealth of information.

THE QUESTION PLAN

In conjunction with the overall interview structure there is a need to formulate your own questioning plan within it. This gives further structure and purpose and will avoid overly long interviews as well as wasting unnecessary time on the wrong things. I have suggested an order below, which you can tailor to suit you. The important thing is to spend the most time on the questions that will establish a fit for the job and company.

The structure below not only ensures you will gain the best information in the early part of the interview, but it also gives you the opportunity to release the candidate at Stage 5 of the interview structure should they be unsuitable.

1 Present job
2 Personal qualities
3 Aspirations
4 Interests
5 Attitude to the company and job
   SAFETY STOP POINT!!!
6 Education
7 Previous jobs
8 Current circumstances
9 Sensitive issues
10 Rounding off

1. Present job

Questions on the present job, or most appropriate job to the one applied for, are very important and a priority. They should constitute around 50 per cent of your questioning time. Information from this will give you an insight into capabilities, responsibilities and ambitions at an early stage of the interview and you will know from the answers given to your different types of questions whether the applicant is likely to succeed with you. Time spent here is always worthwhile and will give you much of the information you identified as being needed following your systematic analysis of the application material.

It is also a good idea to concentrate the questioning on things like team playing, etc. rather than on things like which spreadsheet package they are familiar with. This is the time to ask the questions you cannot return to again on the phone. If you forget to ask about the spreadsheet package it is no big deal and if you need to know before the next stage you can always ring and ask. You cannot pick the phone up and say 'Oh by the way, I forgot to ask what kind of team player you are!' Use the time wisely.

2. Personal qualities

This is key to the new role and often left until far too late in the questioning. They will be evident at all stages of the interview process but a really good look at these is possible when talking in and around the present job.

3. Aspirations

Again much will reveal itself when discussing the present job. Notice how these three categories of questions work very well and very closely together.

4. Interests

Here you are finding more out about the 'person'. Remember to explore the motivation behind the interests as well.

5. Attitude to the company and job

This is where you need to tie in all of the above with the qualities you are looking for in the vacancy. Also, noting the level of enthusiasm for what they do and commitment to the work they do is useful at this point.

Safety stop point!!!

The idea of this question plan is to give you the information you require at the earliest opportunity to help you make up you mind quickly but effectively and fairly. It is person focused rather than purely task focused so you are matching the person to the job as well as the pure skills they have for it. This will increase the chances of their longevity with the company. Increasing your staff retention starts with good recruitment and selection skills.

By interviewing and questioning in this way you will avoid the interview time overrunning largely because you simply have the bulk of what you need to know about the person in the first part of the questioning. This would not be the case if you painstakingly work your way through the application material chronologically. This approach risks spending too much time on previous experience with less relevance to the role you wish to fill and you find yourself with only half of the vital information you need in the given time.

Once this most important part of the questioning plan has been completed you can then cover the nitty-gritty in the full knowledge that you already have the mainstay of your decision-making material in front of you. Also, once you have your questioning ability refined, the whole process of interviewing becomes even more enjoyable for you and less tiring – interviewing is a very tiring process.

6–8. Education, previous jobs, current circumstances

These three points are self-explanatory and represent the opportunity to cover the rest of the queries you noted down in your systematic analysis.

9. Sensitive issues

This section of questioning is used only if your interest in the candidate warrants further questioning. There has to be some flexibility here. You may decide to bring this forward. It obviously depends on the query.

10. Rounding off

This last stage is used to end the interview at the summing-up stage – at whichever stage of the interview plan you have chosen to do it. Your questions should reflect the content of what has already been said and direct the interview towards a summary and end.

A good structure for the overall interview and for the direction of questioning also helps avoid any bias. One may not deliberately set out to be biased but it can happen. Assumptions can be made about candidates based on class, religion, race or any group they may belong to, so sticking to good structure and question direction helps avoid this and ensures the individual is interviewed as just that – an individual with the potential to do the job. Also it is easy to slip into *positive assumption* or *negative assumption*. This is where the candidate displays one positive or one negative trait and the interviewer then presumes the rest without proper interrogation. Watch out for this. It can slip in more easily than you realise. Assumption is also dangerous during the offer stage.

OFFER MANAGEMENT AND COUNTER OFFERS

Following successful second and perhaps third interviews you will be in a position to send out an offer letter to the successful applicant. You will need to do this as quickly as possible and you will expect a speedy response from them in writing.

Most successful applicants will have to give notice to their current place of employment and this can prove an awkward time for both the applicant and the recruiter. It is worth talking about this at the interview and thinking carefully about keeping in touch and handling what is to come. Bear in mind the applicant is human and can and will be swayed by an offer of better circumstances in the place that they know. Also bear in mind that it is a very expensive and time consuming exercise for that current employer to try to recruit someone new for the post. The easier – as well as the cheaper – option under the pressure of an impending resignation is to offer the candidate more money and better working conditions to stay. This can be very flattering for the applicant at the time, although later they may realise it was not so flattering really and question why it took resignation to achieve the reward. As the new recruiter you need to keep one step ahead of the game. One idea is to bring up the possibility of this happening at your final interview with the applicant and ask them how they will handle it if it does. Keep in close contact with the applicant throughout the notice period. Remember it is harder to let you down if you are in good contact and welcoming them to your company.

Something along these lines at the interview may help:

> Now that you have informally accepted the offer we have made we are delighted and will set about making preparations for you to start with us. You now, however, have the unfortunate task of informing your current employer of your resignation. This is never easy and can be especially difficult if they, as many do, offer to improve your circumstances to stay with them. Of course it is not very flattering only to be offered such incentives on the threat of resignation but if you have any doubt about not being able to handle this please let me know and we will do all we can to help. How do you feel about this situation?

Not only does this educate the candidate, but it also ties them to you more in terms of loyalty. It is also useful to observe their reaction when you bring it up as it is a good test of whether a potential issue does lie ahead. At the very least if they do run a counter offer by you they will feel more guilty doing it!

It is a good idea to find out when they are going to hand their notice in so you can make a friendly call afterwards to see how it went. Ask them ahead for their permission.

Never make the assumption that once the offer is accepted it is plain sailing. People are complicated and capable of coming up with many disappointing surprises. It is not uncommon in a good job market for an applicant to accept a number of jobs at one time then choose their favourite at the eleventh hour, letting the others down. Such auctioning can be unsettling.

However good at recruitment you are, there are going to be times when you are let down, so being ready to deal with it is a good idea. If you happen to have interviewed a strong second candidate, play a little clever if it is possible. Do not inform the second candidate they have not got the job along with the other unsuccessful candidates. Leave it a bit longer if you can until you are aware of how things are going with your first choice. If your first choice lets you down you may be able to offer the post to the second candidate without them knowing they were the second choice. If it is not possible to do this it is still more flattering to be told you are being kept on a hold list than nothing. In any case think carefully before rejecting any close seconds. In all cases of unsuccessful candidates, they should be contacted in a courteous way which leaves them thinking well of the company. Polite and positive letters are easy to send out and make a difference in terms of professionalism.

As well as ensuring all candidates have the right impression of the company and that the successful candidate is followed up to help prevent counter offers, you should review your own interviewing performance regularly.

An interview check list is given here that may help you to assess your performance and your handling of the interview process. You can add other aspects to it yourself.

Interview check list		
	Strength	Area to improve
PREPARATION Systematically analysed applications Pinpointed sensitive issues		
INTERVIEW Created rapport Provided optimum environment Used open and probing questions Used good listening techniques Used an interview plan Used a question plan Used silence Observed body language Summed up Left the applicant with a good view of the company Written notes		
FOLLOW UP Recorded details on all forms Written offer and received reply Monitored resignation process Kept second applicant warm Informed all unsuccessful applicants		

APPRAISAL SKILLS

Appraisal skills are very similar to interviewing skills. The questioning techniques are the same, as are the listening skills, but the objectives this time are different. The objective of the appraisal is the development of the staff member. Notably, and this is often confused, the appraisal is a forward thinking, forward planning vehicle to develop and motivate the staff member resulting in their self actualisation and motivation. It is not necessarily and merely a performance review. Although some review of performance will inevitably be incorporated into an appraisal, this should not be the pivotal or key – or even the only – feature of one. This is a mistake made by many an inexperienced manager; such a mistake can contribute to a higher staff turnover. Valuable information about your staff can be gained during properly conducted appraisals and this may guide you to effective ways to keep good staff.

There are other components which may be included in the appraisal such as pay review, promotion, changing job duties, etc. but the emphasis should not be on 'review'. Often there is too much focus on the different types of review and not enough time devoted to thinking onwards and into the future for the development of the employee.

For this reason, and others, employees can be very sceptical about the whole appraisal process, so it must be approached with a professional attitude.

CROSS CULTURAL COMMENT

Be wise to the cultural requirements of your interviewees. Listen to any needs they highlight, such as Muslim prayer times, and incorporate these as well as you can. There is no need to make a big issue of this – often a private place to go is all that is needed and you can furnish this in a subtle way.

Summary

The importance of good preparation before interviewing a candidate is stressed and a detailed walk through the systematic analysis of the candidate's CV is given to strengthen this. The interview plan and question plan are offered as clear structures to work to through the interview process. These structures maximise the use of time and ensure the interviewer is the one in control, which is useful for recruitment and perhaps appraisal purposes.

The management of offer and counter offer are placed in this chapter to ensure a realistic look at recruitment in a busy market where the candidate has choice. A check list is provided so the reader can constantly monitor and refine his or her interviewing skills.

TASK 1

Fill in the check list for the last interview you did to recruit staff or, if you are interviewing for the first time, fill it in after that. What are your thoughts? Write a short reflective piece outlining what you would have done differently.

TASK 2

Using one of the group's CV, set up a panel interview and role play the event. Illustrate the use of the interview and question plans in your presentation.

TASK 3

Reflect on the last appraisal you had. Was it geared to your development or was it simply a review of your past performance. Review your reviewer/appraiser by listing things they could have changed to improve your appraisal experience.

References and further reading

Beardwell, I. and Holden, L. (2001) *Human Resource Management – a Contemporary Approach*, FT Prentice Hall.
Peel, M. and Dale, M. (2001) *Readymade Interview Questions*, London: Kogan Page.
Torrington, D. and Hall, L. (1998) *Human Resource Management*, Prentice Hall.
Wood, R. and Payne, T. (1998) *Competency-Based Recruitment & Selection: A Practical Guide (Strategic Human Resource Management)*, John Wiley & Sons Ltd.

Websites

www.rec.uk.com
www.reed.co.uk

CHAPTER 11
Questioning and listening skills

- To focus questioning in the right direction to suit the purpose
- To obtain the maximum information in the minimum time
- To attract the widest variety of information from which to choose a direction for discussion
- To control the direction of an interview or appraisal situation
- To look at listening from a different perspective
- To examine the depth to which we listen
- To emphasise the positive outcome of good listening

Having taken the time and trouble to prepare carefully for an interview or appraisal, you now need to acquire a deliberate and finer use of questioning skills which gain the information you require in the time allocated. Using certain types of question to get what you need is essential to maximise the use of time and to ensure that you are in the control as far as the direction of the interview process goes. The wrong types of question will miss the essential detail needed to make up your mind about the selection of or direction for your staff, or it will attract excessive detail which will blur the picture.

QUESTIONING SKILLS

A deliberate **funnelling process** is needed and this consists of the skilled and repeated use of the three basic types of question known to most:

1 open questions
2 probing questions
3 closed questions

The open question

This is your most important question. It is, as the name suggests, an open start and should give you a broad amount of information initially.

Phrases such as 'Tell me about . . .' are useful here as a number of key pivots will appear in the candidate's answer and you can begin ear marking which ones you will focus on. The basic 'Who', 'What', 'When', 'Where', 'How' and 'Why' question forms can be used here but be careful. The idea is to achieve several or more 'subjects' of conversation to choose from. For example 'Tell me about the main responsibilities in your current role' as a prompt may open subjects such as financial management, people management, administrative ability and team work. This gives four pivots and you can choose which one to focus on first according to which best suits the vacant post. You are then in control of the direction the interview takes.

The probing question

Once you have selected a subject from your open questioning, probing questions are used to *funnel the facts* in the direction you require. These are the questions that establish the detail about the chosen subject. For example, having chosen say 'team work' as a subject, you could ask 'Who do you work with in your team?' This may lead to another level of selection.

The closed question

Use closed questions as the final part of the funnel. This question will ascertain a single, specific fact about your chosen subject. Many interviewers use closed questions in the wrong way and expect the candidate to offer the information. This rarely happens and misuse of the closed question can lead to a stilted, difficult interview and of course poor selection resulting in a short-lived appointment.

TIP
Equally poor questioning at appraisal can result in overlooking staff needs.

These three types of question are the mainstay of your information collection process and the funnelling technique will ensure that you remain in control and that the interview proceeds as you want it to.

The illustration in Figure 11.1 shows how, once one funnel is completed, another subject unveiled by the open stage is pursued until the required amount of information is attained. It is also likely that rallies are made at the probe and closed stages until the relevant detail is achieved there. In any case, it is essential that the control is maintained by the interviewer and that the opportunity for the interviewee to talk is given within the set limits.

Further useful question types

There are two other very useful types of mainstay questions for the interviewer – the hypothetical and summary questions.

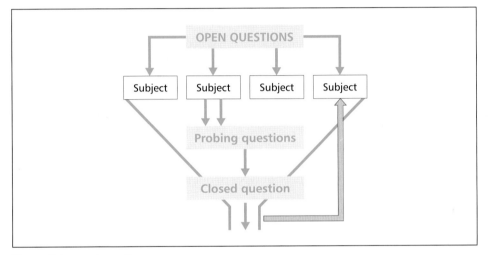

Figure 11.1 The funnelling process

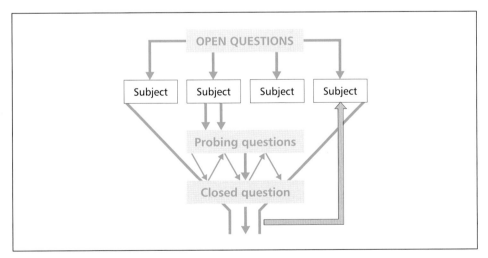

Figure 11.2 The funnelling process II

The hypothetical question

These are also known as *situational questions*. They take the form 'What would you do if . . .?' questions. You set a scenario and watch what the candidate does with the answer. How they work it out and how they prioritise their answer gives a clear indication of their default thinking because they are put on the spot.

TIP

Giving the same scenario to all candidates is a good technique: you can compare how the candidates deal with situations.

The summary question

These are the questions which pull back what has been said to check understanding – for both sides. For example 'Am I right in concluding that you have managed . . .?' This uses the skill of repeating back what has been said, but in the form of a question. It is a useful way to avoid future misunderstanding.

QUESTIONS TO AVOID

Having concentrated on a portfolio of question types to see you through the interview successfully, there are also a number of types of question to avoid.

Assumptive questions

Questions and statements that start with, for example, 'You probably . . .' will only result in the candidate defending or justifying something, so they are not productive in terms of time or the quality of the answer. You are prone to being wrong as well as on the point of being rude.

Leading questions

As the name suggests, this is a question which indicates the answer you are seeking. Use this type of question and you will invariably get the answer you want to hear. In no way does it actually help you to establish what the candidate or staff member's true feelings actually are. For example 'All our staff here are strong, confident characters: are you?' Are they really likely to say anything other than they are?

Self-opinionated questions

These show a marked lack of professionalism and are in the same category as leading questions – only worse. For example 'Don't you agree with me that the company is poorly equipped?' What choice has the candidate or member of staff got but to agree with you?

Multiple and ambiguous questions

Asking multiple or ambiguous questions is a very common mistake – especially from very new interviewers who just want to get the questions out quickly lest they forget what they need to say. These questions can confuse the candidate and therefore limit their answers. They are an indication of insufficient preparation.

> ### TIP
>
> Ask only one question at a time and funnel the facts to get the desired result. You will get more information by careful pacing and the candidate will not have to answer under the strain of worry that they will forget what you have asked them.

Questions which do not tie in with what has just been said

This shows poor listening skills and makes you look foolish. The very new interviewer may do this initially as they may be worried about their own input. However, with experience you should begin to ask questions that link directly with answers the candidate has given.

Emotive questions

This is where you arouse emotion on a subject, for example by using a word that may have a de-motivating effect, for example failure or weakness. You will not get full cooperation from the candidate if your questioning makes them sound quite inadequate. It is better to use motivating words.

Discriminating questions

It should be obvious that these questions should be avoided, but bear in mind it can happen without intention. Discrimination is covered by a range of laws – Equal Opportunities, Race Relations, Disability, etc. Strictly speaking it is not the question itself that is legal or illegal but how that information is used. If the candidate were to feel in any way that the answer to such a question would hurt their chances then they might have a legal case. Avoid age, family, marital questions, etc. in addition to those which focus on race, religion, culture, etc., unless this is being done in the context of equal opportunities screening.

Questions obviously answered on the paperwork

Again, this is obvious, but it is a clear indication of a busy manager who has grabbed the CV just before the interview. Always make time for preparation.

With this basic ammunition, it should be possible to increase the quality of your interviewing and any similar one to one communication.

> ### TIP
>
> Review yourself regularly to ensure you are constantly refining your questioning skills.

LISTENING SKILLS

Listening skills not only link with good interviewing and questioning as outlined in this and previous chapters but are also valuable in many aspects of working and private life. It is often the case that we all think we are good listeners while we are in fact lacking in this area. Ironically, it is also the area we most frequently accuse others of getting wrong.

This short section sets out to increase awareness of the subject so each reader can review their own quality of listening and endeavour to improve it at every opportunity.

One rule identified by Dale Carnegie in *How to Win Friends and Influence People* (1977, p. 105) is: 'Be a good listener. Encourage others to talk about themselves.' Alasdair White, in *Managing for Performance* (1995), outlines two different types of listening: active and passive.

Active listening requires effort. It requires you to show small signals that you have heard and understood, this demonstrates that you are paying attention. It is used with information on which you have to act – for example when you are being approached for advice. It is also used when you are obtaining information and you ask questions. You must listen actively to the answer. As a manager, you must use active listening when dealing with teams, colleagues and superiors.

Passive listening requires no response, for example attending lectures or presentations. It can be thought of as easy listening – even lazy listening! Consider which type of listening will lead to you gaining and retaining the most information from what you hear.

Listening is as much about visual activity as audio, for example good eye contact, body posture, etc. Alasdair White (1995, p. 75) says, 'Good listeners also make good communicators since they are in a position to ask the right questions and to supply the right responses.'

General Patton of the USA promoted an open door policy for good communication to promote good listening (Axelrod 1999, p. 216). Patton said 'If you cultivate an air of remoteness and unavailability, people will stop talking to you, and you will cheat yourself of the single most valuable commodity in any enterprise: information.'

Paul Taffinder, in *The Leadership Crash Course* (2000, p. 146), states: 'spending time listening to your people (and showing you are listening) can, both in the short term and over time, be immensely powerful in motivating individuals. In the short term it enables people to get out their frustrations and deal with underlying problems; in the longer term it builds trust and commitment.'

Stephen Covey, in *The Seven Habits of Highly Effective People* (1989, p. 235), outlines five different types of listening within his marketing of Habit Five: 'Seek first to understand, then to be understood':

- *Ignoring* – where we are not really listening at all
- *Pretending* – where we may say 'uh uh' without really having heard anything
- *Selective* – where we hear only parts of the conversation
- *Attentive* – where we pay attention and focus energy on the words being said
- *Empathic* – which is the highest level of listening with an absolute intent to understand – it is listening not just with your ears but with your eyes and your heart

Summary

This is a simple chapter dedicated to understanding the basics of good questioning and good listening. By defining the types of question the interviewer can use, it becomes clear how a wide variety of data can be collected and sorted and the interview steered in the required direction.

Funnelling the facts to maximise interview time is helpful for successful staff recruitment and retention and, as well as discussing the types of questions to use, the chapter also covers some of those which should be avoided.

Finally, there is consideration of different types of listening to complement the questioning skills.

TASK 1

Working in a small group, quickly put together a series of questions relevant to your work or study environment which demonstrate your use of all three types of funnelling question.

TASK 2

Following an interview or appraisal type situation, review the types of question you used during the time and reflect on how you could have improved the technique.

TASK 3

In the next few days pinpoint an example of each of Covey's five listening types in your working or study life.

References and further reading

Axelrod, A. (1999) *Patton on Leadership*, New Jersey, USA: Prentice Hall Press.
Carnegie, D. (1977) *How to Win Friends and Influence People*, Surrey: Cedar Publishing.
Covey, S. (1989) *The 7 Habits of Highly Effective People*, London: Simon & Schuster UK Ltd.
Rees, W. D. and Porter, C. *Skills of Management*, Thomson Learning, UK.
Taffinder, P. (2000) *The Leadership Crash Course*, London: Kogan Page.
White, A. (1995) *Managing for Performance*, London: BCA.

Websites

www.fno.org/nov97/toolkit.html
www.businesspotential.com/adquest.htm

CHAPTER 12
Body language and assertiveness

- To gain an overview of the effect of clusters of body language
- To observe body language traits in self and others
- To differentiate assertiveness from aggression and submission
- To develop the habit of assertiveness by knowing what to aim for

Introduction

Body language is an important part of an overall picture of competence in the successful student and manager. Although it is isolated so that it can be focused on in this chapter, it is important to note that it is part of a cocktail of other attributes which make up the overall person. Also, by defining assertiveness, an understanding is achieved of its effect on body language and managerial competence.

BODY LANGUAGE

> **TIP**
>
> It is essential to ensure body language is correct when actively listening.

Showing you are listening is part of encouraging others to talk more freely to you and is as important as using the correct questioning techniques. The wrong body language can make you look aggressive and stop people talking to you. Equally, we should be aware of our own body language and what it may give away about us. As much as it is good to learn to familiarise ourselves with different body language traits in others, it is good to learn to control our own and be aware of what we are saying without actually speaking.

This chapter does not claim to make you an expert in spotting certain moods, but it aims to help you appreciate the different ways in which information can be given and extracted. It is important to remember not to judge everything on the strength of one bit of body language. Clusters of body language indicators are more likely to give a better picture. The idea is to be aware of the body language associated with different attitudes, not to make judgements just because you think you have spotted one thing.

> **TIP**
>
> Always use the information you receive in this way along with other information. Do not jump to conclusions.

Let us look at a number of different clusters of body language which may tell us something.

- Openness
  - open hands
  - uncrossed legs and arms
  - moving closer
  - taking coat or jacket off
  - unbuttoning collar
- Enthusiasm/readiness
  - smile
  - good, upright posture
  - wide and alert eyes
  - lively and bouncy
  - leaning forward but openly
  - standing with hands on hips, feet slightly apart
- Defensiveness
  - body rigidity
  - crossed arms and or legs

- little eye contact/glances sideways
- closed/pursed lips
- head down towards chest
- closed hands/fists

- Anger
  - all of the above for defensiveness, plus
  - continued eye contact
  - narrowing of eyes
  - breathing more shallow
  - nostrils flaring

- Evaluation/critical evaluation
  - sitting on edge of chair, body drawn back
  - tilted head
  - hand to cheek – hand supporting head or one hand on cheek
  - stroking chin or pulling facial hair
  - chin in palm with index finger along face or nose and rest of hand under mouth

- Nervousness
  - clearing throat
  - touching face or mouth
  - covering mouth when speaking
  - little eye contact
  - twitching in face
  - fiddling
  - fig leafing (this is an unconscious covering of the genital area with the hands)

- Suspicion/secrecy
  - resisting eye contact
  - glancing sideways and turning body away slightly
  - rubbing nose
  - squinting or peering over glasses

- Doubt
  - touching nose
  - rubbing eyes
  - crossed limbs
  - raising eyebrow
  - rubbing hands or tugging ear

- Reassurance
  - pinching fleshy parts of hands
  - fiddling with jewellery

- Confidence/authority
  - steepling (hands together and pointed outwards and upwards)
  - raising feet toward or on desk
  - leaning back or tipping back chair
  - continued eye contact
  - upright posture

Body language is usually described as either open or closed and it is generally visible in clusters which can indicate mood or attitude. It is a form of non-verbal communication, which constitutes 60–70 per cent of communication. The actual words are only around 10 per cent and the tone of voice makes up 20–30 per cent.

Other considerations

In addition to the actions and posture of the body, the use of furniture or props can convey more information, for example fiddling with glasses, earrings, pens, etc., can give an indication of nerves. Holding things directly in front of the body or hiding behind furniture also has an effect on how we are seen and how confident we appear. In presentations for study or work it can be tempting to use such things for comfort. Think carefully about this before going ahead. More marks can be gained in presentation exams and more impact made through presentations at work if these barriers or temptations are removed at the preparation stage.

TIP

Ensure your handshake is up to scratch. The intensity of grip should match that of the other person and palms should be vertical (Pease and Pease 2004).

CROSS CULTURAL COMMENT

Also bear in mind cultural differences such as proximity and certain gestures which are acceptable in the UK but may not be in other cultures. Even things like nose blowing can be an issue between different cultures. The Japanese, for instance, regard nose blowing as a sanitary affair. Sensitivity to such things is necessary when in an intercultural environment.

TIP

It is best to check for cultural issues as part of the preparation process.

CASE STUDY 12.1

Giovanni enters the room for his interview. He is being interviewed by a team of four executives of the company who came from different continents and they are recruiting for the management team. The successful recruits will travel extensively and have bases in Tokyo, Rome, London and New York. Giovanni has made a big effort with his appearance and strides into the room. He meets the interviewers and shakes each of their hands. Not to be beaten, he immediately goes for the big hand over dive and squeezes very firmly.

(continued)

Mr Yuko Oko on the panel bows but this goes unnoticed. Giovanni takes the seat which is directly facing the panel and feeling like a rabbit in headlights crosses his arms and legs. As each asks a question Giovanni talks directly and intensively to the individual but occasionally rubs his nose and constantly clears his throat. He gets out a grubby hanky and gives his nose a good blow while talking and puts the hanky back in his pocket. One of the interviewers (Mr Yuko Oko) is quieter and resting his face in his hand, although the others are sitting forward and look keen.

As Giovanni gets up to go the interviewers keep talking to him – mainly about social things. As they do this he clasps his hands in front of him in footballer fashion. He finishes off with the pleasantries and leaves the room relieved.

- What do you think of Giovanni's body language? What traits did you notice from the description and how do you think they will help or hinder his case for getting onto the international management team?
- What do you think Mr Yuko Oko personally thinks of Giovanni's international prospects?

ASSERTIVENESS

Definition

Assertiveness is the balance between aggressive and submissive behaviour and it is commonly misunderstood as aggression. Getting your way or winning at the expense of someone else may momentarily feel good but that is aggression not assertiveness. The short feel-good factor can subsequently be diluted by the after effects of such behaviour. For instance, if you have used your position to put pressure on someone, they will probably do what you ask. However, you may have lost their loyalty and respect in the long term. We also often mistake aggressive behaviour as loud and angry but in fact aggression can come in many forms and identifying it is part of the key to succeeding in developing refined assertiveness skills.

Aggressive behaviour is best defined as getting your way, but at the expense of someone else. You may have done this politely and with a smile but you will still have been aggressive.

It follows, therefore, that *submissive behaviour* is the opposite. This is where you let someone else have their way at your expense. Being submissive may appear to lead to an easy life in the first instance but the cumulative effect can create problems in the long term. For example, not being able to say no to tasks not only overloads you but makes you feel bad about yourself. Being constantly submissive makes people respect you less and, what is worse, you respect yourself less.

Submissive and aggressive behaviour both arise from a feeling of lower self worth or fear and act to reinforce this feeling. They are self-perpetuating. Any gain from using them is short term. Submissiveness may reduce anxiety in the short term but will result in disappointment in the self and increase the inability to act assertively.

Assertive behaviour describes the 'middle' approach where no one is left feeling badly treated and all parties come out of the encounter feeling full of worth. Assertive behaviour makes you feel better at the time and makes it more likely that you will be assertive in the future as it is confidence building.

Behaviour	You	They
Assertive	WIN	WIN
Submissive	LOSE	WIN
Aggressive	WIN	LOSE

Figure 12.1 The Assertiveness Balance

Assertive people

- feel good about themselves
- protect their rights but, importantly, those of others too
- always achieve their goals without harming others

TIP

It sounds corny but it works: treat people the way you would wish to be treated – whoever they are and whatever their level.

How to be assertive

- Criticise the argument never the person!
- React positively to criticism
- Say no – nicely
- Learn to adopt confident body language
- Make your point but not an enemy!

CASE STUDY 12.2

Luke has charged into a meeting looking very hassled. As operations director he has found the group considerably under target for the quarter. He presses for each region to account for their part of the shortfall, especially as he will now not be getting his quarterly bonus. Each regional manager stands up to present their prepared figures and Luke hurls question after question at them, clearly indicating his disappointment.

The regional managers have been working very hard, during what they feel to be more difficult times. They do their best to relay this to Luke who merely sees it as an excuse. They feel very defeated and completely de-motivated after the meeting and agree that it is not worth trying to tell him the details at all. They agree to just take the rap and get on with it.

- Luke is obviously aggressive but what has he really won? Discuss.
- The regional managers have been very submissive but, apart from the immediate argument above, what else have they lost?
- Suggest ways in which both parties can reach more assertive ground.

CROSS CULTURAL COMMENT

Some cultures, particularly Chinese, have a submissive note to their greetings as a matter of general manners. It is important to accept these manners as a privilege and not to interpret this as a lack of assertion.

Summary

With an emphasis on looking at traits rather than individual pieces of body language, this chapter sets out to give an overview of the subject and deter the reader from being too judgemental. By listing some key types of body language clusters, the reader is also encouraged to think about their own physical presentation to others and what might be interpreted from the impression they give.

This chapter has left the reader in no doubt as to what assertiveness actually is. The reader should be able to practise this so it becomes normal behaviour.

TASK 1

Split into pairs. Each member of the pair observes the other for two hours and compiles a short report describing the different types of body language cluster observed. Report back as a group at the next seminar or meeting.

TASK 2

Get someone to take a video of you giving a presentation. Watch your own body language carefully.

TASK 3

Think back over the last week and write down an example of aggressive behaviour, assertive behaviour and submissive behaviour that you have seen in your fellow students or colleagues.

References and further reading

Pease, A. and Pease, B. (2004) *The Definitive Book of Body Language*, London: Orion.
Pedlar, M., Burgoyne, J. and Boydell, T. (2001) *A Manager's Guide to Self Development*, Berkshire: McGraw Hill.
Rees, W. and Porter, C. (1996) *Skills of Management*, London: Thomson.

Websites

www.tufts.edu/hr/tips/assert.html
www.alec.co.uk/interview/bodylang.htm
www.kevinhogan.com/bodylanguage1.htm

PART 4
ONE TO MANY COMMUNICATIONS

Part 4 moves onto those more complicated situations where many eyes are upon us and our intentions can be interpreted in so many more ways. With management advancement in mind, as well as key assessment skills for study, the part puts a big emphasis on the key communication areas of presentation skills and managing teams.

A good deal of time has been spent on presentations. Many assessments for the student are now presentations and most management jobs expect good presentation skills as a basic currency. Because many presentations in the study environment are group ones and with the intention of grooming leaders to get as much from their team as possible, a further focus in this part is on team dynamics and working in teams. It is as important to be able to work within a team as it is to successfully manage one. With an outcome focused approach towards synergy, a good understanding of how teams work and what to get out of them ensures the right choice of approach and attitude from the start. The basics are also written with the theme of tolerance in mind and encourage a spirit of appreciation of the differences in others. This is then linked not only to successful communication but to how that manifests itself in terms of business productivity through staff retention. By seeing how small local actions can make a big difference to an overall picture, a more sophisticated management attitude can be adopted.

By student request, this part also includes a consideration of good manners to round off the groomed package which provides another level of communication with those around us.

CHAPTER 13

Presentations

- To develop presentation skills
- To build confidence in ways of addressing others
- To predict and prevent mistakes and embarrassment
- To use up to date tools with confidence

Introduction

Presentations are such a key part of student and working life that they should be prepared for carefully and approached with respect. Presentations in student life are essential in helping us develop and gain a job after university. In working life presentation skills are key to personal success such as sales, training, reporting to superiors, etc.

Having ensured an awareness of a cocktail of skills such as body language, listening, questioning, etc. for one to one communication, it is important to use these and expand into the territory of one to many communication. One to many communication forums such as presentations magnify the need to focus on getting these skills right as many more people are watching and you are in an even more vulnerable position. In this chapter we will cover:

- the presentation structure
- who you are presenting to
- the content of the presentation
- checking
- practising with any equipment
- your appearance and stance
- any habits you may have
- your voice and speech
- notes or cards
- PowerPoint® presentations

TIP

As with reports, essays, etc. it is important to work to the trusted pattern of:

- tell them what you are going to say
- say it
- tell them you've said it

THE PRESENTATION STRUCTURE

Another way to look at the structure outlined in the tip box, is to say that your presentation should have a beginning, a middle and an end.

Beginning

This is your introduction of yourself and your topic and it should include a number of housekeeping points in addition to arousing interest from the start.

- Tell them what you are going to say

Attract attention and explain audience benefits Starting with a value statement for the audience is a clever move. Knowing what they are going to get out of the presentation gives them a sense of value to being there and increases their listening quality from the start. By outlining the benefits of the presentation, it is clear to the audience that it is tailored for them.

It is important in doing this to translate the benefits into their working life. A little research here will mean greater success. For example, a presentation on leadership is easily introduced but if it is broken down into the benefits of staff retention or higher productivity, greater interest and learning will occur.

This will in itself attract attention but you can also think carefully about using a visual aid or humour in the introduction to break the ice or to help outline the forthcoming material. Silence is a powerful tool – use it wisely. It can be used throughout the presentation but is particularly useful at the beginning. I have seen a number of good speakers take a moment to put themselves in order at the lectern or on stage and then look up and around the audience without saying anything. This attracts the attention well.

Outline the topic to be discussed, the duration, the stages and structure you will follow
This provides security for your audience. They like to know what you are going to cover exactly and when. It also advertises your high level of organisation showing your preparation and keeps you in control.

Also should you forget something or lose your concentration (as can happen when under stress), the logical order will ensure you quickly find your feet again. So it is a safety measure for you too.

Discuss the overall duration, but there is no need to break down the timings too pedantically.

Outline your question policy Now this is up to you. You need to do this but how you do it depends on your level of experience and confidence. It is common to indicate that questions will be taken at the end. However, it does invite the risk that no one asks any and you are left looking expectantly at the audience, feeling uncomfortable. You can put plants in the audience – colleagues who will ask something to help to get the questioning started.

It is also acceptable to invite questions as you go through each stage or section. However, you need to be confident that you can keep the presentation on track and not get diverted. If your chairing skills are strong and you can chair long points to the end, this is a good method as audience members feel more participative, ask while they remember things and it gives you the chance to tailor the presentation further as you speak, incorporating their points. There is nothing more flattering to an audience member than to have a point they have made referred to. Then, at the end, you can ask if there are any more questions. If none exist at that stage you can happily state that most were dealt with throughout the presentation and indeed helped the presentation.

Keep it simple and unhurried When you are nervous, and most people are when they presenting (however calm they look), it is easy to hurry through without realising it. A simple, easy to follow structure is important for you and will help you feel more secure, keeping the pace at a calm level. If presenting on a report for instance at university or work, working in the order of the report can often help keep things structured in this way.

Middle

- Say it

Pay attention to the timing Keeping the structure simple, as discussed above, will help with this. Practise the presentation through a number of times so you are aware of timings. You can time PowerPoint® slides if you wish but be sure to be able to stop when you need to if things get out of synchronisation. I tend not to programme timings in electronically as it allows for some audience spontaneity.

Watch the audience reaction and adjust timings if you think you are losing them at any point.

Allow time to absorb the information When standing at the front of the presentation, time has a habit of seeming to be much slower than reality. It is easy to rush through because of nerves. Bear in mind that the audience need time to digest the material you are putting before them, so use short silences here and there to allow for this as well as to emphasise certain points.

Put in memory retainers Earmark the presentation periodically with small memory retainers for the audience. This can be a short statement or a visual aid – just something that encapsulates what is being said and acts as an anchor.

Use appropriate media This is part of the preparation for your presentation but the middle part of the presentation will show up any bad choices more than any other.

Think carefully about how the content is displayed and whether you have used the right medium to get it across.

Also be careful about trying to be too adventurous and using too many different types of media because you think it will be more interesting. It is the content which should be of interest. Fussing with too many media shifts through the presentation will break concentration and lose the theme. It also increases the chance of something going wrong.

End

Summarise all main points

- Tell them you've said it

This not only serves to prove you have done what you promised at the beginning of the presentation but it also acts as a further memory retainer for the audience. It reminds them again of the value they have gained from the time and they are more likely to leave in a good frame of mind.

Finish on a high note, a key observation or very interesting fact As well as summarising as above, it is useful to leave on a high. Some presenters do this very well with humour, an anecdote or interesting fact. It's your choice – choose something to suit you.

I once went to a presentation where the presenter introduced herself to the audience in a cheerful manner and held up an odd piece of plastic. She asked the audience whether anyone knew what it was and then said she would discuss it with them at the end of the presentation. At the end she thanked everyone and then, in an 'oh yes' sort of way, picked up the plastic and asked again. When the audience stated they did not know she with a big smile on her face said neither did she – she had simply found it on the floor of her car. Odd, but it worked and she carried it off.

An another presentation the speaker, who had prepared carefully beforehand, ensured he was standing on a certain part of the stage. On the screen behind him the slides had thought bubbles which were strategically placed to appear from his head. As he was talking he clicked on and the bubbles, which contained light humour. The audience loved this.

Thank the audience and any helpers This would seem obvious but at the end of the presentation the temptation to get off the floor as quickly as possible can sometimes make us overlook the necessary politesse. Each member of the audience should leave feeling you have appreciated the time they have taken to listen to you. Also give credits to those who help set you up as the front line person.

With the above as an overview, it is now necessary to drill into more detail. There are a lot of elements which contribute to a good presentation and a number of considerations to avoid blunders. Not every presentation will go smoothly for you – it would be wrong to promise that. In fact one wonders if there is actually a presentation gremlin which hits like a bug every so often. It is best to presume the odd thing will go wrong and take it in your stride. There are a number of considerations you can make to reduce unsuccessful events, errors, etc. Let us work through these elements carefully.

WHO YOU ARE PRESENTING TO

Before you start consider your audience

Writing the presentation starts after this consideration and also affects your choice of media.

The size of the audience

This is easily established beforehand and handling it correctly can make the difference between success and failure. Audiences are too sophisticated now to accept an ill-tailored presentation. The size of the audience will also dictate the range of media used for presentation, for example the size of screens, etc. Ensure the seating arrangements are adequate and allow you to reach all members of the audience with your voice. If possible, it is good to occasionally walk down the aisles through the audience.

The type of the audience

Consider the working background of your audience to ensure you use the right language in the presentation. The overall intellectual level of your audience will dictate the theoretical, analytical level of the material. Other things such as the age range or range of hierarchical position in a company may make a difference to how you tailor your content.

The current knowledge/understanding of your audience

Do not make the mistake of oversimplifying the material. Establish the current understanding of your audience about the material so you can hit them at the right level. Bear in mind their level of understanding and give them time and techniques for the facts to sink in.

How are your audience seated, for how long and why are they there?

Aside from ensuring adequate seating for the size of the audience, it is essential to respect the amount of time they may be seated and allow for appropriate breaks. Changes in the way you present or even using different speakers can help ensure the delivery is interesting all the way through.

THE CONTENT OF THE PRESENTATION

Consider your content carefully. It must be written with the purpose in mind.

Keep to the purpose

Reiterate the purpose regularly throughout the presentation. This serves as a memory retainer and shows you are in control of the presentation rather than it being in control of you.

Make it varied and entertaining

Visual aids, different slide colours and fonts can help. Change the speed and tone of your voice as you speak. Work around the whole audience. Change speakers wherever possible.

Be careful of trying anything too clever or risky though. There is nothing more agonising than waiting for a video clip to load and nervously trying to small talk your way through the silence while you wait.

Encourage audience participation

You cannot do too much of this. Audiences like to be included. Throw questions out to the audience. If you are brave enough, try competitive games. Quizzes at the end of a presentation often work well. If you tell the audience you are going to do a quick quiz at the end, they are more likely to be attentive. Then do one and make it fun. One method I have seen that works well is to split the audience into say four and give each one has a particular noise they must make as they stand up to answer a question. So you build up the enthusiasm of the audience by getting them to test their group noises before you start the quiz. Not only is it a memory retentive technique but it is also good fun and you finish on a high.

Allow time for and control questions

Allow time at the end of certain sections for questions if you do not feel confident, as previously mentioned, to take them as they occur. Answer well but do not get caught up in a redirection of the presentation or even a debate.

Plants

You can consider putting colleagues in the audience to help with questions, reaction, etc. Audience members do tend to copy each other naturally so if someone with enthusiasm and a good reaction to your humour is there already, the chances are it will infect the rest of your audience.

CHECKING

Organisation of the event

Never make any presumptions that someone else has organised anything. Check, double check and check again. It pays to be pedantic at this point because it is you who will be standing in front of the audience when anything goes wrong. The audience will care very little about why something has gone wrong and you are the one who will be labelled with any failure. Don't do it to yourself. Standing there blaming others also looks bad so you can't win. They will complain to you or grade you down if any negative points occur.

Audiences are very unforgiving if their basic needs are not met and this will affect their reaction to you – however wonderful you are for your bit – as well as their impression of the company overall. Check all the details, such as whether each member has received appropriate instruction to get there, times, venue, car parking, etc. Then walk through the process of being an audience member, in addition to worrying about your bit. I use a 'meet, greet, seat and eat, coos, loos and shoos' as a quick mental check to see whether they are welcomed appropriately, have somewhere to sit and, importantly, are fed and watered. Always check arrangements for food and drink as these are the most likely to cause upset if they are not adequate or do not arrive. 'Coos' – are they all talking positively about what is happening and do they have somewhere to do that? Loos are obvious but again check the facilities. 'Shoos' relate to whether the audience is sent off on a high, possibly with something to take away. This kind of check can increase audience satisfaction and make a real difference. The checks can prevent potential problems ruining the whole event. Think of the hours of work it takes to produce a presentation – what a waste if something simple affects the audience in a negative way.

So keep your **WITS** about you:

W	walk
I	it
T	through
S	slowly

The room

Is the room size appropriate and do you need a microphone? If possible, try to get into the room beforehand so you can practise the presentation – not just in terms of content but also in terms of where you stand and where you can and cannot walk. Work out beforehand how to reach each part of the audience. Check any health and safety requirements and announcements you need to make at the start.

PRACTISING WITH ANY EQUIPMENT

Lighting

Know where the light switches are, as well as emergency exits. Set the mood and ensure you are lit in a flattering way. In bigger presentations for conferences this is worth checking, as the wrong lighting can make you look ill or like a rabbit in headlights. Check what can be seen by the audience right at the back by actually going and sitting there.

Sound

Check you can be heard and try the microphone beforehand if you have one. Then you can just get straight to talking and not do that 'testing, testing' thing which is annoying and makes you look nervous. Watch out for feedback noise which is very annoying.

Equipment

Check furniture for stability: you wouldn't want to lean on something and have it collapse underneath you. Lecterns need checking for height, so you do not look tiny behind them, and for position, so you can reach the whole audience.

Check all the aids work. The overhead projector should be ready to go, and the computer set up beforehand so there is no slow, clumsy wait for documents to load.

Whatever you are using, check the projection is clear and in focus. All of this should be done before the audience is in the room wherever possible. Do not stand in front of the projection when you are speaking – apart from detracting from the presentation and being very annoying, it makes you look absolutely dreadful. Try not to stand right over the light of an overhead projector – it shows all lines and gives the most unflattering vision, a bit like holding a torch under your chin to frighten people at Halloween.

Practise using the equipment beforehand. Know how to work your equipment and how to get out of scrapes. Nerves attract extra gremlins. If using a laptop for instance with one of those small 'nipples' to move the mouse, bear in mind how your hands work when they are nervous and whether on a big screen the audience will be able to see the arrow move all over the place and shake as you use it. Get used to holding remotes, etc. in a natural way so you look comfortable with everything you use. Sort out extensions, plugs, etc. early on and with the audience out of way so you can give a good first impression.

APPEARANCE, STANCE AND HABITS

Obviously you should dress smartly, as discussed in Chapter 9, but in particular:

- take care of wearing brand new clothes you are not used to
- in general classic dress works best with no particular attention drawn to any particular part of your body
- remember they can see all of you, so grooming is important

Remember that the lights will show up lint on dark clothes and dirt on shoes.

Practise a confident stance in front of the mirror at home, thinking about the position of your feet, etc. Beware of the following aspects:

- fiddling, pen clicking, etc. because of nerves
- overextravagant arm and hand movements
- fidgeting with your feet or prowling up and down
- make eye contact with the whole of audience but don't look like a nodding dog

Do not be tempted to hide behind props such as clip boards, pads, etc. Once you are up there at the front, there is a tendency to want to hide behind anything. No matter how hard you try and high you hold it up that marker pen will not protect you!

Tics

There are further habits which may put off your audience. Tics are a well-known habit which you may have to develop particular strategies to cope with. However, other habits that can be annoying for the audience include:

- fiddling with jewellery – don't wear it if you do this
- shaky hands – paper, OHPs or laptops show these up very well
- flushing
- flicking hair

Find out what you do – we all do something!

YOUR VOICE AND SPEECH

- Speak clearly to the audience – never turn your back on them
- Use short sentences – nerves affect the breathing
- Be careful when using microphones – all sniffs and deep breaths can be heard. If the mike is fixed don't move around too much as the sound will be loud one minute and low the next!
- Speak slowly and use silence when appropriate

Mechanics of speech

Bear in mind when you are nervous that basic speech can become more difficult. Some people slur their words or talk too quickly. Take a deep breath. There are three basic areas to focus on to improve your speech:

Articulation Slowing your speech down helps with articulation. Focus on the letters P, T, K and D and the beginning and end of words. Diction is important and the crisper the words are, the more clearly they will be heard at the back. You do not have to go too far, just allow time for one word to finish and another to start.

Resonance will carry the voice further Resonance relates to the echoing quality of your speech and the ability of the sound to carry to the back of your audience. The letters M and N and the NG sound are highly resonant, for example enemy, enemy, many men, enemy

Emphasis Consider the different meaning implied by the same sentence when the emphasis is changed:

- <u>John</u> walked down the High Street
- John <u>walked</u> down the High Street
- John walked <u>down</u> the High Street
- John walked down <u>the</u> High Street

Underline the words to emphasise on your notes or PowerPoint® slides. Emphasis can dramatically change the meaning of the delivery, so work out where you want the emphasis to be.

NOTES OR CARDS

Having some notes to prompt you is definitely recommended. Use small cards which you can easily hold in one hand as you walk about. Do not use note pads or anything A4 size. These look untidy and show every shake, as well as acting as a barrier.

- Number all the cards in order
- Underline emphasis, special points, etc.

- Put on smiley faces – when we are nervous we forget to smile
- Fix the cards together with a ring or tie, so that if you drop them they do not scatter

"This PowerPoint slide has a dynamic layout comparing reading scores throughout the district, which you would have seen if I remembered to bring a spare projection bulb."

© Aaron Bacall / Cartoonstock.com

POWERPOINT® PRESENTATIONS

The technical side of things can be difficult. In this chapter we will deal with a few pointers in the general use of the PowerPoint® presentation graphics program. The details of constructing a presentation on PowerPoint® slides are covered in Part 6. If you are not familiar with this package it is highly recommended that you become so, in terms of both student presentations and future/current career. The important thing in general terms for this chapter is to ensure you do not hide behind the technology but are familiar with it and use it to augment the presentation, not be the presentation itself.

We will look at a number of tips in three areas:

- design
- delivery
- dealing with disaster

Design tips

The same rules for the content of your presentation apply throughout, but also:

- Pick a clear design that can be read easily.
- Ensure the font size is large enough and do not have too many words on each slide. Use notes pages for detail where possible. You can then give handouts.
- Ensure the font colour stands out clearly from the background.
- Don't use complicated tables on the slides – translate them into clear graphs.
- Keep artwork appropriate and effects to a tasteful level. Many experienced managers have seen it all before. Also, too many bits of art can make for a big file which may not transport well on e-mail or disk.
- Keep sound effects to a minimum – the novelty of these wore off in the early 1990s.
- Ensure transition effects to slides and to text/artwork for smooth presentation.
- Beware of 'timed' presentations, if you get out of synchronisation, you could be in trouble.
- It is a good idea to keep 'corporate' in theme – especially for an interview. You can even scan in logos from the internet.
- Popping your name on the master slide is also a good idea.
- Keep a library of slides on disk as many diagrams, etc. can be adapted to save time.
- Copying short cuts is also useful.

Delivery tips

The same rules for venue checking, etc. are important here, but there is a greater emphasis on technical back up. You should double check on the delivery of any equipment, and try to do the following:

- Allow yourself time to set up beforehand. There is nothing worse than having a number of delegates view your back side as you prepare the laptop, etc. Crawling around on the floor for plugs is also not an image you want anyone to view. It depresses your diaphragm, so when you get up you are breathless. Get there beforehand or have the audience wait in a reception room until you are ready to greet them.
- Practise setting up before the day so you know which lead goes where. Never start your presentation with 'I am not sure how all this stuff works!'
- Use the remote control like a calm weather person not a Star Wars character or cowboy.
- Extension lead. Always have a spare.
- Function F5!! This is the key at the top of the keyboard with the screen on it, and it is the one to make the presentation project.
- Ensure the screen can be seen by all and that the projection is large and clear enough. Go to the back of the room to check. Do the same with any sound equipment.

- Work out where you can stand and walk during the presentation. Watch out for leads to trip over and do not stand in front of the projector – the light is not flattering. Watch out for puffing and sniffing over the microphone.
- Do not face the screen as you talk – address the audience. There is a tendency to hide behind the equipment. Be energetic and enthusiastic.

Dealing with disaster tips

You may be able to avoid disasters by always thinking belt and braces and then another belt. Plus, you can take the following advice:

- If the laptop or projector breaks down – spend only a limited time trying to put it right and quickly go to a back-up plan. You should have several.
- Acetates should be at the ready and are easy to have printed off beforehand. Order a back-up OHP.
- Failing that, your pre-printed delegates' notes can be used for reference and you can speak vividly around these.
- If your presentation is on a removable disk or CD, have two – just in case. Think about the 'package' you have saved the presentation in. It would be a shame to spend all that time on a wonderful PowerPoint® presentation on your new machine at home on Windows® XP and find that the company are still using Windows® 98 or Windows® 2000. It will not show or open and you will look a fool as you insert your disk. Save it in the version they have or, if in doubt, save it to a lower/older version. The newer ones will take the older ones but not the other way round. Alternatively save it in several versions to keep any effects.
- Don't rely on memory sticks – not everywhere has a USB dock for them.
- Even if you will be using a Smart board where you e-mail yourself and touch the screen open, still take a back up – just in case there are difficulties.
- Watch how you use equipment like Smart boards – do not touch the board for too long or you will see your presentation flash before your eyes at great speed. Equally do not bang the board with each move – it just takes a gentle touch.
- Don't just cover the potential PowerPoint® disasters – remember it is a tool and should only be a part of your whole presentation. All the other elements still need to be attended to, such as the venue, delegate checks, the meeting, greeting, seating, eating, etc.

CROSS CULTURAL COMMENT

When assessing content and its appropriateness for a specific audience, make a particular effort to screen for anything which may inadvertently cause offence to other cultures. Do this well ahead of the presentation. Equally consider the appeal of the presentation to all.

Summary

This chapter focuses on all the elements of a successful presentation. Considerations are made for the type of audience to be addressed as well as the appropriateness of content. With an emphasis on careful preparation, a number of checks are advised, as is practising with the equipment to be used. A look at many of the personal elements for successful presenting is made from appearance and stance through to habits and speech. There are a number of guidelines on speaking with confidence and clarity as well as numerous tips for presenting with PowerPoint® presentation graphics program.

- If you have presented before:

TASK 1

Take two of your previous presentations and list six things (or more) you could have done to make it even more successful.

- If you have not presented before:

TASK 2

Find an opportunity to present – even if it is short or as part of a group – in the next six weeks.

TASK 3

Watch several presenters and, as a group, compare the strengths and weaknesses of their presentation style.

References and further reading

Atkinson, C. (2005) *Beyond Bullet Points: Using Microsoft Powerpoint to Create Presentations That Inform, Motivate and Inspire*, Microsoft Press International

Atkinson, M. (2004) *Lend Me your Ears: All you need to know about making speeches and presentations*, Vermilion

Lashley, C. and Best, W. (2001) *12 Steps to Study Success*, London: Continuum.

Rees, W. D. and Porter, C. (2003) *Skills of Management*, London: Thomson Learning.

Websites

www.kumc.edu/SAH/OTEd/jradel/effective.html
mmu.ac.uk/academic/studserve/.../studyskills/**presentations**.html
www.support4learning.org.uk/jobsearch/interviews.htm
webster.commnet.edu/grammar/powerpoint.htm

CHAPTER 14
Working in teams

Learning objectives

- To understand how teams develop
- To cultivate synergy
- To appreciate differences in others and use those differences in the most effective way
- To reduce negative conflict and encourage wider thinking

Introduction

Working in teams, both at university and at work, can be one of the most rewarding experiences you have. It can also be one of the most upsetting and frustrating. In the student world successful teamwork has an impact on your final grade and at work it can affect whether you get the task completed to deadline or not. Love it or loathe it, team skills are a necessity. The management world is not very forgiving of individuals who moan about their fellow team members or blame them for failure. Loyalty as well as synergy is important and understanding how teams work is essential in order to adopt a healthy and perhaps more forgiving approach to the behaviour of others.

We have all worked with people who aggravate us to distraction and many have worked in teams where arguments have distressed us. By studying the team itself and by looking at individual differences, conflict can be managed into a constructive framework and a synergy achieved.

Most managers can take a team, of say four people, and achieve an output equivalent to four people. The contribution of each individual is a good probability anyway. However, it could be said that a bad manager would only get an output of three or less, as they allow conflict to interfere with the overall purpose and the energy destined for output is actually used up within the team. A good manager can get an output of five or six from the same four people simply because they understand how to manipulate the development of the team as a body and because they respect and value the differences and diversity within it.

TIP

Enter any teamwork situation with a positive attitude – especially towards counterparts. Start as you mean to go on by valuing their input, however different it is to your own.

From an organisational point of view, the search for the ideal employee is a difficult one. Indeed, does the ideal employee actually exist? It is conceivable that a successful team, working as a unit, could come close to being the ideal employee.

An article, by Jay (1980), 'No individual is perfect – but a team can be', outlined that while a single person might not possess all the skills, knowledge, experience and aptitude to do a job well, a team of people collectively might do so. This of course depends on whether the team is an effective one.

Whether you are an individual team member or a manager in charge of a team, it is important to view the team in three ways:

1. the way the team develops as an organism
2. the balance of the team focus
3. learning about and respecting the differences of the team members

TEAM DEVELOPMENT

One of the best known and classic theories of team development is the Tuckman (1965) model. It is useful but not definitive. It had been chosen to demonstrate the evolutionary nature of team development, and indeed it does this very well, but, as with all theories, it is a tool to enable us to view things further, and not the only way of doing so. Having said that, I have to comment that in over 20 years of management, I have found it to be true and found it a very useful template to follow and use to predict problems.

Tuckman (1965) held that teams follow four core stages. He did outline others but the pivotal four are:

1. forming
2. storming
3. norming
4. performing

Figure 14.1 shows the four pivotal stages as outlined by Tuckman. A look at each stage will assist our understanding of team development.

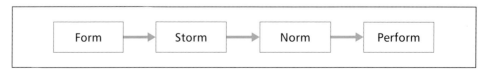

Figure 14.1 Tuckman team development

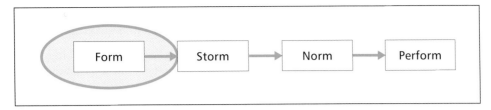

Figure 14.2

1 Forming

This is the introductory stage when the individual members of the team first get together. They are cautious, tending to be polite and guarded and spend their energy sizing up the other members. They behave very much as individuals in that they are still autonomous at this stage. They will be worried about fitting in and worried about being able to cope with the task. At this stage they will, understandably, be most concerned about themselves rather than the needs of other team members and even the task itself. The individuals will isolate areas of space to occupy while carefully observing other talent and potential competition.

TIP
As a manager you can help the forming process with ice breakers, social gatherings, friendly briefings, etc.

2 Storming

Having sounded the situation out, the individual will now start to claim their own territory. In doing this things can get lively. Hidden agendas may emerge and arguments may occur. Individuals may also compete for leadership of the team and this can sometimes be at the expense of the team achieving their goal. It is a selfish and indeed immature individual who puts their own needs ahead of the overall team goal. Storming can take the form of soft negotiation or all out argument. Handled correctly and channelled positively, this stage can be the most productive of the four as the team hammer out their objectives, methods and delegate tasks.

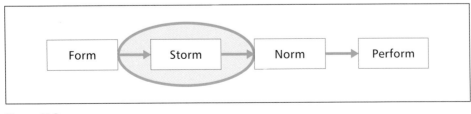

Figure 14.3

TIP

Warn teams that they may well argue as they form. This way they will not be surprised when an argument does occur and are more likely to handle it positively.

Ineffective teams can break up at this stage. Individuals can walk out of the team and feel isolated. Storming is a natural part of the evolution and should be approached constructively. Teams can get stuck in a storm from where they seem to be unable to move on, becoming a self-perpetuating tornado. This is where good management guidance is invaluable, taking away blame and moving towards cooperation.

Conflict is often assumed to be negative but, carefully and definitely managed, it can be positive. Having different and diverse opinion is healthy. The air can be cleared by conflict but it also assists with creativity making the team think more widely than they may have done on their own. This stops people leaping to assumptions and makes each individual question what they do. The wider exposure may lead to a more appropriate response than might have been gained had an autonomous route been taken.

This stage can help to cultivate the skills of diplomacy and a respect for the views of others. The right approach to seeing it through to the next stage is to have a healthy respect for all views as negotiations and compromises are made. The resulting co-operation then is of a much higher and informed level than would have been gained through a dictatorial and single minded approach. A shared environment is being developed as this happens if the storm stage is a healthy one.

3 Norming

At this stage the team members settle into their roles and share the way forward. Each individual has isolated their role within the team and how that contributes to the overall task. In some cases this will require compromise. For instance, where there are two clear leaders, it may be the decent thing to do for one of them to step back and allow space for one leader. This would probably be the more experienced of the two, as their ego requires the position to a lesser extent and their experience can be given in other ways to help the leader and the overall team purpose.

It is clear that the successful team is now in a position for synergy. A team of four can now be managed to achieve an output of five or six as all the energy is focused towards the team goals and not on each individual.

The team also develops their own set of agreed internal rules – their own 'norms' such as rules, task division, behaviour, etc.

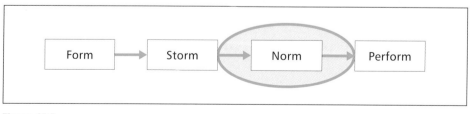

Figure 14.4

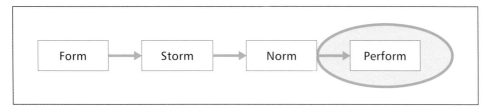

Figure 14.5

4 Performing

With all the rules and roles sorted, the team is now able to complete its task. The members work together in cohesive manner and for the overall good of the team and the company/purpose. This is the ideal and indeed, it is highly achievable with the correct management and participation.

CASE STUDY 14.1

Charlotte, Claire, Rob and Ben have to give a group presentation for their business module. They must do an external and internal audit on a company of their choice and comment on its existing strategic direction and make recommendations to change. The presentation must also be followed by a group report of 3,000 words. They have been put together randomly in the seminar and know little about each other. With five weeks to complete the task they meet casually for the first time.

Everyone has a coffee and they sit down to discuss issues. Everyone introduces themselves. No problems so far. A list of tasks is drawn up after they decide on which company to study and they all agree to meet at the same time the following week.

Charlotte and Rob sit talking in the library the following week. The others haven't shown up. Claire hasn't been to lectures or seminars and Ben has phoned in saying he hasn't got round to doing his task but it is in hand. Another meeting is set for the following week.

All four turn up this time. There are three weeks to go. Claire hasn't been in and so is behind with everything and Ben says he has been so caught up with other assignments that he hasn't got round to this as there is still plenty of time for it. Charlotte is getting

frantic. She has all her work done on time and is meticulous about keeping to deadlines. Rob has dutifully completed his part and is happy to go with the flow. Charlotte speaks her mind and says they should all pull their weight. The lists are made to catch up and include everyone starting their PowerPoint® slides relating to the bit they are doing.

Next week Claire does not show up again. Ben shows up and has done half of his list. Rob has completed his part with Charlotte, who is now in a foul mood. She has a moan at Ben who says something rude and walks off and she leaves a message on Claire's mobile telling her she has let the side down and they are all very disappointed with her.

A week to go and the next meeting is tense. Ben has turned up but is distant every time Charlotte makes a suggestion. Claire charges in and says she is going to see the tutor as she finds it impossible to work in this team. The three remaining members of the team have a set of slides each and a contribution for the report, but only Rob and Charlotte have read each other's work.

The tutor has advised Claire to go back to the team and discuss their issues which she does. By the day before the presentation she cobbles together her bit and then adds it in on the day. Ben has

(continued)

already added his and stated that he just wants to do his bit and for Charlotte to hand over to him in the presentation for that. She and Rob are not exactly sure what he is going to say and are completely unaware of what Claire has produced.

The presentation day arrives and the four nervously set up the system to start. With more than a touch of cynicism, Charlotte heads straight into the presentation without proper introductions to the team or the content. She presents her bit superbly and with great confidence and feeling smug hands over to Rob who does a fine job. Claire and Ben, however, are less confident and their material is not quite what was asked for in the assignment brief. This is reflected in the report and the whole thing gets a D grade mainly because of its disjointed structure and not answering all the issues set. Charlotte is furious about being brought down by the rest of the team.

- Is Charlotte right to be angry with the rest of the team?
- Consider each stage of Tuckman's model given in the chapter and describe how Charlotte, Rob, Claire and Ben moved through them.
- What would you advise the team to do to improve the quality of their output and get a better mark for the module assignment?

SELF-PERPETUATION

As well as sharing task decisions and outcome, the successful team also operate at another level having worked together well. They become interested and sometimes very much devoted to the cause of self perpetuation. They maintain their existence. Successful teams replace members as they leave and, on joining, new members often have a probationary level before they fit in fully.

The successful working pattern is therefore safe guarded and the team re-created in the same way. However, this can be worrying. If the team maintains itself in this way then new views and fresh creativity must start to be stifled. Fitting in with the existing practice becomes more important than finding the best practice.

The team may continue to maintain its loyalty long after the task is over. Loyalty and commitment can be such that individual team members find it difficult to make a commitment to a new team and start afresh. In matrix structures where project work is common, individual team members can find it difficult to return to their original functional departments.

Tuckman recognises this in a fifth stage of – 'mourning' – where termination of the task and team is recognised through an event or ceremony.

DECISION-MAKING

With all of the stages above, it is fair to conclude that team decisions will take longer than those made at individual level. Time should be allowed for the necessary discussion. If considered an investment, this time furnishes the possibility of a more appropriate and informed decision.

It is also useful to look in the other direction too. It is possible that a team decision may well be a more risky one. As a body there may be no individual accountability, so each member is able to take a bigger risk than they might on their own.

GROUPTHINK

On the same lines as greater risk taking, Janis (1972) pointed out another particular aspect of negative team behaviour which may actually result from a successful team formation: groupthink. This is where the team have become so cohesive that it is a victim of its own success. The team are so together in their thinking that fresh and opposite views are ignored and this decreases the material from which it makes the decision.

Equally, one could interpret groupthink as a pressure condition. If an individual actually has an opposing opinion but is too worried about their status or likeability in the team to actually voice it, the team is further deprived of a fresh look at a situation as self-preservation wins the day.

The team then collectively rationalises its response while sharing a stereotypical view. It is under the impression that it has greater power than it actually has and can convince itself that the decision it has made is a moral one. Such justification comes under the guise of the perceived unanimity.

TIP

Regularly add fresh opinion and team members to your teams.

EFFECTIVE TEAMS

The successful team operates at several levels. Synergy is achieved by a balance of individual satisfaction, the team itself in terms of its inter-relationships and of course the task itself.

In the same way that Adair (1986) introduced the concept of effective management or leadership consisting of three things, team work consists of a similar balance – see Figure 14.6. Indeed management and leadership are about effective teamwork and this is covered in more detail later in this book.

Keeping the balance of the three elements identified by Adair keeps the team in check. It is important that the task is achieved but not at the expense of anything. As the team evolves, it is important that individual satisfaction is still retained while developing and establishing a team relationship. The relationships should also continue in a way which allows fresh and individual opinion to be heard over time, so there is no danger of group think or staleness. Just as a three-legged stool will not stand if one of the legs is short, so a three-legged team will not achieve its goal. The team will not last or be at its most effective if one of the triad of elements is neglected.

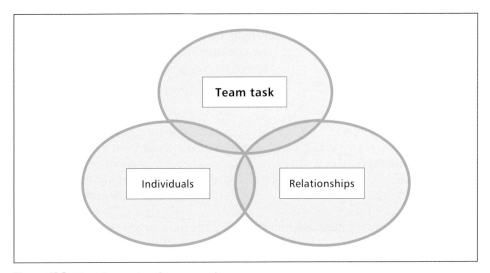

Figure 14.6 The elements of teamwork

Source: Adapted from Adair (1986)

TEAM ROLES

Now to the individuals who make up the team. The emphasis is on the individual in terms of valuing their differences and the way in which they contribute using those different strengths. Not appreciating these differences can waste valuable talent and perspective and make individuals feel excluded. It can ultimately lead to failure.

One of the most famous models of team role classification is that of Meredith Belbin (1981). He originally devised eight team roles and later added a ninth. This is one management tool used to view the differences in order to appreciate them. It is not definitive and there are many others. As a well-respected classic it is used in this chapter to outline the amount of diversity that team members and managers needs to be aware of and capture. However, beware of pigeon holing or labelling people.

The nine roles are as follows:

- company worker (or implementer)
- chair (or coordinator)
- shaper
- innovator (or plant)
- resource investigator
- monitor-evaluator
- team worker
- completer-finisher
- expert (or specialist)

By quickly looking at each of these roles in turn, we can begin to get an idea of the range of skills to value in others, as well as the self of course. You can complete your own questionnaire to learn your own particular tendencies: websites are given at the end of the chapter. However, although I would encourage you to do it, it is important to approach it with the same attitude that is contained within this chapter, the appreciation of self and others, rather than a direct categorization which then becomes a label. Belbin is but one of many very good methods of achieving this and it is important to have a rounded opinion and an open mind.

Company worker (or implementer)

This personality is a doer. They will work hard on what needs doing to complete the task and like specific instructions to take away and allow them to contribute. They also tie their contribution, and that of others, to the overall task and the company.

Chair (or coordinator)

As the name suggests, this personality chairs the activities and contributions of all. They ensure that all have a fair chance to contribute and that all views are considered as well as direct the whole thing towards the overall goal. They are neutral and pull in all the others.

Shaper

A shaper shapes events and has a major influence on the direction the team takes and especially in the decisions made. It is another leader type role but, this time, it is fuelled more by emotion and a desire to get things done. They are likely to have a 'let's stop talking and just get things done' type approach.

Innovator (or plant)

This personality is creative and wide thinking. Their contribution will be to think more laterally and come up with different ideas and approaches to the situation. Some of the ideas may even seem unrealistic.

TIP

Never pass over an idea just because you think it too 'whacky'. Adopt a 'catwalk' approach – we may not necessarily wear something as it is presented on the catwalk but we do accept a diluted or derivative of that image – it is the same with ideas. Some of the most outlandish ideas can contain useful suggestions we can actually use or even inspire other ideas which are more realistic. All ideas are good.

The plant can also come in many different guises, possibly with a more unconventional appearance. The key is not to judge before you drill into their particular source of talent. They are also held to be very intelligent.

Resource investigator

A confident personality who is not afraid to go out and get the tools for the job that the group needs. They will source things from outside and quite happily contact people they do not know in order to help the team.

Monitor-evaluator

This personality is the auditor of the team. They are realistic and like the facts. They will cost up exercises carefully and check that the resources actually do exist to complete the task. The will measure the actual picture against the predicted one and keep the team on an achievable track.

Team worker

This member is the social secretary and social worker of the team. They care about the overall welfare of the team and include everyone in a social sense. They are the ones most likely to say, 'right that is enough for now, let's go to the pub!'

Completer-finisher

As it says on the tin – this is the personality who ties up the loose ends. They ensure things get finished to deadline and keep the team posted of the time stages of the project necessary to successfully see it through. They will also plan the team's time well and carefully.

Expert (or specialist)

This is a 'visiting' member of the team who has a specific expertise which the team requires to be brought in. For example, if implanting new IT systems, a particular specialist will be needed.

Each role has its strengths and there are also what Belbin calls 'allowable weaknesses':

Company worker	indecision
Chair	dispassion
Shaper	intolerance and insensitivity
Innovator	does not like details and may be unrealistic
Resource investigator	over-optimistic and gets bored easily
Monitor-evaluator	can be overly critical
Team worker	sometimes easily influenced
Completer-finisher	poor delegator, inclined to nit-pick
Expert	too focused and overlooks the big picture

By looking at these traits or strengths and weaknesses, we have achieved a rounded view of the talents within the teams we work in and perhaps formerly took for granted or even found irritating. Now we have seen how synergy can be achieved by encapsulating the differences we can go forward and value them.

It should be remembered that no one role mentioned here is better than any other: each should be valued equally. Also, there are many personality questionnaires available; Belbin is used here for demonstration.

Summary

An emphasis is given in this chapter on remembering that all members of a team are equally important. A look at different personalities outlines the value they bring to the team and the workplace. In addition to individual dynamics, the whole dynamic of the team as a unit is outlined from formation. An understanding of how a team starts and develops also helps with the future management of teams as well as participation in them.

TASK 1

Think of the last time you worked in a team and retrospectively analyse the team members within it. What particular talents did they have? What did you contribute? With hindsight and having read this chapter do you think you may have judged anyone unfairly or handled anything better?

CROSS CULTURAL COMMENT

All of the points made throughout this chapter regarding the diversity of contribution and personality also apply to diversity of culture. It is important to allow room for cultural diversity and indeed it is often very enriching to do so.

References and further reading

Adair, J. (1986) *Effective Teambuilding*, Gower.
Belbin, R. M. (1981) *Management Teams: Why they Succeed or Fail*, Reed Elsevier, UK.
Janis, J. (1972) *Victims of Groupthink*, Houghton Mifflin.
Jay, A. (1980) 'Nobody's Perfect – But a Team Can Be', p. 26, April 1980, *Observer* Magazine.
Tuckman, B. W. (1965) 'Development Sequence in Small Groups', pp. 384–99, Vol. 63, *Psychological Bulletin*.

Websites

www.seanet.com/~claveg.teams.htm
www.hrzone.com/articles/teams.htlm
www.teams.org.uk/roles.htm

CHAPTER 15
Leading and managing meetings

Learning objectives

- To effectively prepare and organise a meeting, whether you are holding or participating in it
- To achieve the meeting's purpose during the event
- To save company time
- To be aware of all delegates and encourage their full input
- To refine own chairing skills for the future

Introduction

Meeting skills are pivotal to success whether you are a delegate at a meeting or whether you are chairing it. From the start of your career, it is a good idea to get involved with chairing meetings as these skills need refining over time and it is only by doing it that you feel the weight of the event and season yourself to coping with bigger and better ones.

Successful meetings are not just a matter of good organisation, although, as we see here, that is important too, but success is a matter of including others and of getting the most out of the time and the people present.

In this chapter we break up the components of the process and the people involved in the meeting for more detailed consideration. Ticklists are provided to help efficiency and tips are given to effectively gain as much from that process and the people as possible. We concentrate on the formal meeting but much of the discussion can be diluted accordingly for informal meetings and ad hoc meetings.

THE PROCESS

Purpose

Meetings, whether formal, informal or ad hoc, can serve many purposes:

- bring together a range of experience
- give or gather information
- make decisions
- influence policies – useful contribution important
- problem solve
- develop cooperation, get commitment or give ownership
- encourage good communication
- evaluation
- air grievances
- moot and explore points, e.g. effects of change
- give positive feedback and gain self affirmation

The purpose of the meeting should be clear from the outset. The purpose should be achieved and the meeting has failed if this is not the case.

TIP
Never go into a meeting without an objective.

Preparation

Good basic organisation is essential for a successful meeting. Many meetings are ruined because of simple things such as venue, food, etc. Do not underestimate the effect an item of meeting housekeeping can have on the whole event should it go wrong. Clean efficiency is good and everything should be checked carefully before the start. In the same vein as for presentations, the chair should take responsibility for checking all is in order before the event. This practice also ensures that the chair remains calm as delegates come into the room. Running around trying to fix things at the last minute makes the chair look flustered and takes away a certain degree of command and capability. Check out the meeting venue and details as below.

Place Choose your meeting venue carefully, considering the following aspects:

- does it have a suitable room?
- equipment check – what is available and does it work? (Remember to bring back-up slides/notes in case technical disaster occurs)
- facilities – car parking, loos, etc.
- food and water – very important!
- waiting area for part-time attendees

All of this should be straightforward. However, these are the things which often go wrong because people tend to think someone else has dealt with them – basically communication has failed. Treat any meeting as if you are preparing for a presentation and you should not go too far wrong. If you have part-time attendees coming, make sure you know exactly what time they will arrive and ensure someone is available to greet and seat them. Chair your meeting to respect their agreed arrival time – not your discussion time on other things. It is really bad form to have your part-time guest waiting while you finish off points. Arrest the point and resume later if necessary and classily introduce your guest as planned. This also applies to visitors from within the company. They should be treated with the same respect so as not to waste company time.

Plan Your plan should encompass the:

- formal agenda
- hidden agenda

Planning starts here and the way these agendas are handled can affect the process of the meeting and of course what you ultimately get out of it.

The formal agenda If you are calling a formal meeting, it is your responsibility to ensure that an appropriate agenda is drawn up and preferably circulated in advance. About a week is right as it is not too far away to be forgotten and not too close to be too late for the delegates to prepare. Wherever possible, you should also provide the opportunity for participants to contribute to the agenda. Make yourself approachable and encourage people to own an agenda point at your meeting. If you haven't chaired meetings before, this is also a good way to start building up your own confidence: own an agenda point at a meeting and see how it feels to run the discussion.

As a delegate make sure you prepare for any agenda items concerning you or your staff or where you feel you can make a useful contribution. Put points on the agenda so they get quality time rather than timidly squeeze your point in at the end under Any Other Business (AOB). Not only is the latter inefficient and frustrating, it is cowardly. Where you do have to use AOB, try to warn the chair at the start of the meeting so they can plan the time properly.

The essential components of a well-planned formal agenda are:

1 Clear purpose.
2 Clear location, date and time.
3 The subjects to be discussed are in a logical order:
   a. place routine or easy items in the first third of the meeting
   b. introduce difficult items in the middle
   c. place discussion or consensus items in the last third of the meeting to end on a high.
4 Enough detail for delegates to prepare in advance.
5 A list of the agenda recipients for all to view – people like to know who will be there, especially if superiors are likely to be present.
6 Anything the delegates need to bring is clearly listed.
7 Continuity – any outstanding issues form previous meetings are identified. Previous minutes can be circulated where necessary, as can ACTION lists.

8   Items are numbered and time allocated according to the importance of the topic and not the importance of the speaker. In fact, as a rule, the more senior the speaker the more flexible they can be if necessary. More junior members of staff should be given more time and patience as they learn their skills in the meeting room.

9   Items requiring discussion and a decision are kept separate.

10   The duration of the meeting is stated with a view to keeping it or finishing before the time stated – not after it.

The chair can change the order of the items as the meeting progresses if necessary to reflect the input from the delegates.

The hidden agenda   As the name suggests, this is the personal agenda that each delegate brings to the meeting. They can be quite difficult to spot, but it is a duty of the chair to try. A formal agenda is transparent and all participants know it in advance. A hidden agenda is opaque and is different for every single member of the meeting, although there may sometimes be a shared hidden agenda among members with a common interest. The underlying influences can often be traced to organisational politics with individual members trying to do their best for their department or sometimes simply for themselves.

The importance of recognising hidden agendas cannot be overstressed. They can explain many of the subtle behaviours that appear to have little to do with the topic under discussion. Through skilful manipulation of the group, hidden agendas may lead or dominate discussion if the chair is not careful and unless they are recognised potentially effective meetings can be sabotaged or undermined.

Prepare to chair

Effective meetings rarely occur by accident. As a chairperson, you have the major responsibilities:

- managing the process
- managing the people

Within the management of the process, there is also the key element of managing the time.

Managing the time   The basic requirement of time management in a meeting is that it should start on time. You will have allocated enough time to each point on the agenda. Many meetings are ineffective because too much time is devoted to minor issues, and important decisions are made too hastily or have to be postponed.

One of the chairperson's key roles is, therefore, to control the meeting by discouraging unhelpful arguments or digressions and to keep to schedule. Unless unexpected problems arise, a meeting should finish on time.

TIP

State the finish time of the meeting and always finish five minutes early.

TIP
Never take the minutes when you are chairing.

Firm leadership One of the prime skills demanded of an effective chairperson is to steer the discussion towards the achievement of the meeting's objectives. This involves making a clear statement about its purpose as well as what is to be covered and then leading the discussion in a systematic and fair way.

With active listening and purposeful questioning you will:

- Remain neutral, objective and focus on facts whilst acknowledging the input from everyone fairly.
- Focus on solutions rather than the causes of problems.
- Do not allow individuals to dominate the meeting.
- Do not show favouritism in any way.
- Make sure that everybody has the opportunity to contribute and that they are listened to attentively.
- Acknowledge positive and discourage negative contributions.
- Periodically summarise the points that have been made.
- Record and re-state decisions for clarity and note agreed actions.
- Thank participants for their involvement.

MEETINGS CHECK LIST

1 Invite only the appropriate people to the meeting
2 Give advance notice of the time, place and purpose
3 Give participants the opportunity to contribute to the agenda
4 Prepare and circulate the agenda well in advance, along with any minutes of the previous meeting
5 Chose an appropriate venue for the meeting
6 Check all equipment
7 Provide timely and appropriate refreshments
8 Adhere to start and finish times
9 Discourage digressions from the agenda
10 Do not allow one person to dominate the discussion
11 Give all delegates an equal opportunity to express their views
12 Encourage listening etiquette and do not tolerate side conversations
13 As chair, watch the audience reaction, not the speaker
14 Allow all delegates a voice in any decision making

15   Give periodic summaries throughout the meeting

16   Note agreed deadlines for actions

17   Conclude the meeting with a summary of what has been achieved in the meeting

18   Follow up any action agreed after the meeting

19   Make sure the minutes follow the meeting as quickly as possible

20   Make the meeting as enjoyable as possible

TIP

Where does the chair stare??
At the audience!

In addition to actual chairing skills, it is as important to be a good delegate or participant at a meeting. Remember, it is easy to get yourself noticed at meetings, but make sure it is for the right reasons.

As a delegate:

- sit back and listen to others, then offer your view
- refer to your colleagues as you express your opinion to show generosity and listening skills
- be supportive – e.g. 'That sounds like a good idea.'
- confront issues tactfully
- question anything you are not sure of
- avoid pencil tapping or fiddling or reading other things
- *do not* have a side conversation with your neighbour!!!
- if there is a rotating chair on offer – take it

On this last point, many meetings have a different chair each time and offer the chance to staff to take turns – be brave and have a go.

THE PEOPLE

Having already looked at the differences in people in the previous chapter and begun to value their various inputs, we can transfer this to the meeting forum. A meeting is team work with an objective and should be treated as such. All inputs are important and synergy is possible with the correct attitude towards valuing diversity.

In addition to making the most of the personalities, there may be occasions when negative behaviour has to be corrected in a sophisticated way. Delegates can ramble, dominate, go quiet, have a clash with other members, moan about the company and indeed talk through your meeting, if you are not in control. These traits must be dealt with effectively.

Summary

This chapter provides a clear brief on how to run meetings, not only in terms of the housekeeping details necessary for things to run smoothly but also in terms of managing the people, time and process to maximise the effectiveness of the event for the chair and for the company as well as for those who attend.

TASK 1

In groups work out how you would deal with each of the issues outlined in the Summary above at a meeting.

TASK 2

Chair a meeting as soon as you can – any meeting, informal, ad hoc etc. – subject to your situation and experience. Reflect on your level of control and order.

TASK 3

Review the last formal meeting you chaired in fine detail using the check lists and comments in this chapter. Write 500 words, including what you did well and how you could improve for the next one.

CROSS CULTURAL COMMENT

Different cultures have different practices, so be prepared to set out your rules for your meetings. For instance, in some cultures it is accepted practice to talk on a mobile phone during a meeting. Set out your own expectations at the beginning of the meeting in a polite way and then no one can be accidentally embarrassed.

References and further reading

Forsyth, P. (2004) *The Meetings Pocketbook*, Management Pocketbooks.
Goodale, M. (1987) *The Language of Meetings*, Language Teaching Publications.
Pincus, M. and Miller, R. (2004) *Running a Meeting that Works*, Barron's Educational Series.
Rees, W. D. and Porter, C. (2003) *Skills of Management*, London: Thomson Learning.

CHAPTER 16
Manners

- To promote an interest in appropriate manners in the business world
- To ensure positive communication through good manners

Learning objectives

Our manners form another mode of communication with the outside world. Getting them right is actually very easy and, when you think of the adverse effect of getting them wrong in terms of offending others, you can wonder why they are sometimes overlooked so casually. Manners form a code of basic respect. It is not just a question of etiquette or the right form. It is a question of flattering and showing you value other people around you.

This short chapter does not set out to teach all the manners appropriate for every situation: there are special texts for that. It does, however, fulfil a communications obligation in that it will list some useful tips so our business conduct is smooth, polite and acceptable.

Introduction

TALKING

We have already seen that good body language and listening skills make a manager and potential manager more effective. It is also basic politeness to look at someone who is talking to you and not be diverted in any way. Your *quality of attention* is the measure of the *quality of your manners.* This includes eliminating the temptation to glance at incoming e-mails and avoid taking phone calls when in conversations where possible.

When you are talking to others, it is also good manners to ensure you speak clearly and do not put things over your mouth. Good diction is important anyway but, bearing in mind that as according to the RNID one in seven people have a hearing difficulty, it pays to speak clearly.

TIP

When speaking to a deaf person, do not speak to them loudly and as if they are an idiot. Clear, normal speech with a view of your lips is often all that is required. You do not need to be overly demonstrative. Also, it is just as bad to drown someone with sympathy and be overly demonstrative about the fact that you are helping them. Not only does this highlight the problem to all others – which the person will not want – but it also asks the question, why are you doing it – to actually help them or to look good yourself?

In general and regardless of recipient hearing levels, always face a person when talking to them and do not say things as you walk away.

People also have different terms for things. Whilst there are considered to be words that are more correct than others in the world of classical etiquette, modern etiquette holds that it is not polite to correct people in public and it is good manners to mirror their own terms. Therefore, classical etiquette informs us that 'lounges' only exist in airports and 'sitting room' may be more appropriate; modern etiquette would have us adopt the language used by our hosts in order not to offend. It is a fine line, but in more recent times there is an almost inverted snobbery about such things.

Not talking to people at a gathering is socially rude. It is very easy to stay safe and keep with known friends at business and social gatherings. This is fine if it does not exclude others. If there is a person who is isolated in any way, it is bad manners not to include them in the conversation. It is equally bad manners to keep your back to an approaching person. They can find it hard to enter a group of people and join in the talk because ill mannered people do not move to make room for them or ignore their presence. Presences should be acknowledged and conversations should not continue as if they were not there.

If you are hosting an event then it is a 'responsibility' to ensure people are introduced to each other and that they are mixed as well as possible.

As a host, hosting team or even as a recipient of hospitality, it is important to circulate. It is considered rude not to make the effort to talk to a range of people at any gathering. 'Cop out in the kitchen' is a common way of avoiding the initial nerves about talking to others. You can convince yourself you are very busy indeed in a kitchen, fiddling around with food or drink. Avoid this and get out there and circulate – with the food and wine if you like – but just get out there.

TELEPHONING

- Taking calls for others can be good manners but ensure the quality of the gesture is maintained by gaining detail about the caller so your colleague can call back fully prepared.
- Put phones on DND (do not disturb) when in meetings.
- Turn off mobile phones in restaurants/meetings, etc. In meetings, it is considered bad management to have a number of calls from your department as it shows you cannot delegate.
- You should never answer your mobile at a restaurant table. If you have to have it on, you must excuse yourself and make an exit to a convenient place which does not disturb others. Even this, however, is very rude if it is not a necessary call such as a babysitter calling or an emergency from the office.
- Constant use of your mobile in public company actually makes you look insecure.

CASE STUDY 16.1

It is the office party and Jo, Jane, Julie and Jeannie have glammed up and made a big entrance. They grab some bubbly and join Jack, John and Julius who are gathered together at the back of the room. They all start screeching and laughing about memories of the office party last year. Newcomer to the group Alice arrives on her own. She wasn't kept in the girls' internal loop for transport arrangements. Drink in hand, she approaches the group through the crowd and attempts to find a space to fit in to talk to them. Julie and Jeannie know she is there but keep their backs to her as they laugh along with the others. Alice looks around nervously but sees no one else she knows. Finally, Alice catches Jack's eye and he beckons her over to join him the other side of the noisy circle. He includes her in the conversation. Alice has a hearing impairment and finds it is accentuated more when in noisy environments. All sound merges and she cannot always hear. The girls know this but talk to each other behind cupped hands and facing away from Alice. Jane fancies Jack like mad

and notices the attention he is giving Alice. Jane then crosses the group to join Jack and Alice and specifically asks Alice about her hearing in a very loud and slow voice. She also then takes it upon herself to translate everything to Alice in an obvious way just as two Board members of the company approach.

The Board members make introductions and a more formal chat emerges about the company so everyone is on their best behaviour and very polite back. Jo's mobile goes off and she takes the call where she is, shouting above the existing conversation. The Board members frown and invite the group over to eat at the buffet and continue conversations with the group as they eat. Julius manages to get mayonnaise on his chin but is completely unaware of it. Two of the girls snigger and no one tells him it is there so he spends all evening circulating with it as company.

Nilesh from Accounts comes over to join several of them. He is on secondment from the company's

(continued)

Indian call centre. The group members say a quick hello and then proceed to continue their banter without including him. Nilesh is not put off and introduces himself as well as making polite conversation about how nice the champagne was. However, he mispronounces the brand name. Jeannie titters and puts him right about the correct way of saying it.

- Use the tips in the chapter to isolate the bad manners.
- What would you do regarding the mayonnaise?
- What do you think of Jeannie correcting Nilesh?

E-MAILING

This medium can cause the most confusion. One difficulty is that we tend to treat it as speech in the main. We talk to each other, but electronically. However, as good as this feels, the law and organisations treat e-mails as letters, so be careful about what you write. Many people have learnt this the hard way as e-culture has evolved. The point to realise is that the law acts on what it sees as evidence and does not necessarily contextualise things. You may think you can trust your recipient and that you are having a 'fair', two-way and private communication about, for instance, a dispute. However, if your 'opponent' does not have the ability to sort things out with you individually or in fair forum, they can covertly store up evidence, entrap you and have you brought to account with black and white evidence. Exercise caution – particularly as a fresh, talented, up and coming employee who may be inadvertently 'threatening' a less well-equipped superior.

When writing by e-mail, avoid using only capitals, as this looks rude and aggressive. Also try to maintain a letter-level of politeness in terms of still saluting and signing off. It is very rude to go straight into the text.

Avoid including too many people and take care to screen the delivery list so no offence is caused accidentally.

The quantity of e-mails is a real problem in the workplace now, so avoid general group or whole company ones if you can. In fact unless you really need to send an e-mail – don't.

Avoid marking e-mails high priority unless they actually are to avoid the 'cry wolf' syndrome. People can become seasoned to ignoring the urgency of anything that is marked urgent.

When you know the recipient is a high volume e-mail user – for example lecturers – ensure you put clear information in the subject line. This helps with sorting out priorities. Also do not just put your student number. Lecturers cannot memorise all the numbers for each student and they will have to go and look you up, which involves a further transaction. Ensure your name is clear and also that the course you are on is there to save the recipient time. These simple rules are relevant to all e-mail correspondence.

Consider carefully whether e-mail is the correct medium to use. For instance, if the e-mail is to a colleague sitting at the desk opposite, might it be a bit more polite to actually get up and go over and talk to them?

Do not use e-mail to relay bad news. Companies have been known to make staff redundant using this medium!

TEXTING

The guidance for text messages is much the same as for e-mail. Choose your audience carefully when texting. It can be seen as a medium more appropriate for the younger generation. Some older parties regard it as a more down-market method of communication which overlooks the manners of grammar.

Do not send text messages while you are speaking to people, however competent and fast you are at doing so.

TABLE MANNERS

Eating out can cause the most worry about one's own manners and as entertaining is very popular in the business world it can be difficult to avoid. I have been asked to include some basics here to help with seeing a client lunch through, for instance, or if eating out properly for the first time.

- Hold doors open for both sexes.
- For men: do pull out a chair for any female guests and help seat them.
- If you are trying to impress, order simple dishes you know you will like and avoid being 'clever' by ordering the frog's legs or the hottest curry. This is not the time to battle with a lobster if you are not used to it.
- Cutlery is straightforward: you simply work from the outside in. Everything will be in this order except for your butter knife which may be on the very outside or on or by the side plate. Dessert cutlery in very good restaurants will be that nearest your plate, although some restaurants place it in what is known as 'nursery' fashion at the top of the plate. If you order steak or fish you will be given appropriate cutlery for the dish.
- If there are three glasses on the table, the largest is the water goblet, the middle one is for red wine and the smallest is the white wine glass. The water goblet may also be a single coloured glass.
- Bread rolls go on the left and you should never slice or cut it. Break it elegantly with your hands, place some butter on your side plate and put a little butter on a small piece of bread before placing it in your mouth.
- Do not shake out your napkin like a piece of laundry and do not crumple it at the end and throw it on your plate. This looks arrogant and 'affected'. Place the napkin on your knee and when finished place it on the table. Do not refold it! Also it is more appropriate to call it a napkin in good company – not a 'serviette'. If entertaining yourself, do not put napkins in glasses, however prettily folded.
- Do taste the wine if offered to you as the host or hostess of the table. Hostesses: it is up to you if you wish to pass over this duty but it is more than acceptable for you to taste the wine nowadays.
- Eat soup with the most rounded spoon and push the spoon away from you in the bowl. To get the last of it from the bowl, gently tip the bowl away from you and then scoop the spoon away from you.
- Do not start eating until all the people at the table have their food.

- Do not use your fork to scoop – press all food onto its back.
- When finished close your cutlery. If you are talking and not finished eating, leave your cutlery open at 'twenty to four' on the plate clock.
- Do use a fork and spoon for dessert.
- In a French restaurant, the cheeses come before the dessert.

There are many different things to think about with different foods, so the list above is a basic one for reassurance. If you are in any doubt – ask. It is better to ask confidently how to do something if you are not sure than 'fake' it and make a fool of yourself.

CROSS CULTURAL COMMENT

Remember that manners vary in different cultures. It is best to look these up if you are any doubt. There are too many variations to mention so it is best to check beforehand. Indeed it would be considered bad manners not to have done some homework when entertaining guests from any background. There are also certain foods which some cultures or religions may find offensive, for example pork/bacon or alcohol. Check first.

Summary

This chapter provides a brief look at basic manners for reassurance. It is designed to provoke the reader's own thoughts and encourage them to develop their own social skills further.

TASK 1

Think of the last time you went out to a decent restaurant. What would you now do differently? Was there anything you were not sure about? If so and it is not covered here, go and look up the etiquette for it now.

References and further reading

Bremner, M. (1992) *Modern Etiquette*, Chancellor Press, UK.
Hawthorne, R. (1997) *Do's and Don'ts, An Anthology of Forgotten Manners*, Pavilion Books, UK.
Morgan, J. (1996) *Debrett's New Guide to Etiquette and Modern Manners*, London: BCA.

Websites

www.holidaycook.com/table-manners/index.shtml
members.aol.com/rutheruthe/myhomepage

PART 5
ORGANISATIONAL AND MOTIVATIONAL COMMUNICATIONS

In the spirit of further grooming for employment, promotion or just a more organised student life or work–life balance, this section starts to widen the pathway towards independence further. The basic organisation of time is the starting block. This is a key communication skill with a high impact, which not only affects the self but those around us. More control in this area makes for a less stressful existence. Stress itself is then considered in order to limit its effect on the self and others too.

After this the part deliberately lifts the focus towards our own direct effect on the workplace environment we create for our staff. The idea is to set a scene of accepting responsibility and to encourage a more lateral vision when analysing situations. The final chapter of this part looks at management and leadership directly. Its purpose is to pull the two skill sets together and encourage an interest in how different management and leadership styles will be appropriate in effective communication with different individuals. This lifts communication from the personal levels of effectiveness to its effect on corporate effectiveness.

CHAPTER 17

Time management

- To analyse current use of time and identify the strengths and weaknesses of time management practices
- To recognise the implications of the use of time on subordinates and colleagues
- To identify priorities
- To plan ahead and anticipate time needs
- To adopt behaviours essential for effective time management: assertiveness, prioritisation, saying 'no', dealing with interruptions, getting out of meetings, ending conversations, dealing with the phone and e-mails

Time management is really a misnomer, because we all have exactly the same amount of time, although some accomplish several times as much as others do with their time. Self management is a better term, because it implies that we manage ourselves in the time allotted us. Most people manage their lives by crises; they are driven by external events, circumstances, and problems. They become problem minded, and the only priority setting they do is between one problem and another. Effective time managers are opportunity minded. They don't deny or ignore problems, but they try to prevent them. They occasionally have to deal with acute problems or crises, but in the main they prevent them from reaching this level of concern through careful analysis into the nature of the problems and through long range planning. (Covey 1999, p. 137)

Introduction

It is true – we do all have exactly the same amount of time so why do we spend such a lot of time talking about not having enough of it and trying to 'out busy' the person next to us? Time is perishable, so once it is spent it is natural to justify to ourselves that we have spent it wisely and we may go to great pains to do this. The truth is, we may not have spent it wisely or planned ahead properly so our reactivity makes us look very busy while in reality we are not using the time to full effect. Running around like a headless chicken is neither flattering nor professional, yet so many people think this busyness is the answer. True time, or rather self, management involves a real grasp of how we use the time. Being aware of impending situations and being proactive not just in terms of the time used but in terms of the nature of the tasks in that time is key to more effective time usage. A calm, measured and more scientific approach to time use is not exactly the most exciting thing to undertake but it could be one of the most revealing and useful things you are likely to do as a manager or potential manager. Don't forget, how you use your time has an impact on many other people too and small changes in this case can make all the difference.

In this chapter, rather than ask you to look at a case study, you will be asked to undertake two time studies. The first is a simple overview of time use in a week, which will serve as a warm up and set the right psychology towards time science in place. The second is a more detailed time log to be kept over at least two weeks, which will act as a solid collection of primary data on which to comment. You will not thank me initially, in fact you may well be cursing me when you are keeping the log as, frankly, it is a boring task, but when you have analysed the findings you will be surprised at what you find and how many areas there are for you to start working on for greater effectiveness.

TIME USE OVERVIEW

TIME STUDY 1

There are 168 hours in a week! How do you spend them? Work it out . . .

- Employment hours per week =
- Nightly sleep hours $\times$ 7 =
- Daily grooming hours $\times$ 7 =
- Meals including cooking hours $\times$ 7 =
- Travel in week $\times$ 5 =
- Travel at weekend in total =
- Regular clubs, associations, etc. hours per week =
- Housework, shopping, gardening, errands, etc. hours $\times$ 7 =
- Class attendance hours per week =
- Social hours per week =
- Study hours per week =

Add up all the totals =
Subtract from 168
What are you left with? TIME BALANCE =

If something you do in the week is not covered in the list then simply incorporate that into your calculation.

Think about your time balance
Is your time balance over 35 hours per week? If so you have a whole working week there which is unaccounted for. Where has it gone and how have you spent it? If someone said to you 'Here is a whole working week, spend it as you wish' what would you do with it? Be proactive and engineer the time in the way you want it to go.

Is your time balance in single hours or even in the negative? What does this mean? Are you lacking control on how you spend the time? If someone said to you 'Here is a whole working week, I will tell you how to spend it' how would you feel? Why are you not in control of your time?

There is no correct answer to this study. The idea is for you to interpret it individually and according to your personal circumstances.

I have deliberately used the terms 'spend' and 'balance'. Time is money and starting with this simple study gets us into the right frame of mind to tackle time use. In the same way that we reconcile our bank balances to ensure good fluidity, we should reconcile our use of time regularly. We have 168 hours going into the account every week and we should be aware of how we spend them. We can do even better than that for further effectiveness. Rather than account for hourly units, breaking up the use of each hour can be revealing and using it with this mentality can increase our output.

TIME STUDY 2

Keep a time log for at least two weeks. It is your choice whether it includes your private life if you are working. Log at least at 30-minute intervals through the day, 15-minute if you like.

The following website has a number of log sheets for your use

http://www.brefigroup.co.uk/resources/
timetools.html

Now sit down and analyse your log thoroughly.

What kind of tasks do you do in the main? Can you group tasks into certain categories? Can you see a trend where time may be wasted? Can you trim certain events to save daily minutes which have a knock on effect all year. How much of your time is reactive time and how much is proactive?

Prepare a pie chart or graph to show the divisions in your time. What does it say to you?

Task

- Find a 30-minute time trimming in your day

Translating time into money is also a good exercise. As managers and potential managers your worth to the company is great. You should also think of this in terms of self worth in how you spend your private time. For the sake of convenience, let's imagine that each minute of your time is worth around £1.00. So for every five minutes of deliberation you are throwing away a fiver. Imagine it floating out of the window. Bear this in mind when attending meetings, etc. If ten people attend a meeting and it is prolonged unnecessarily by 15 minutes then that is £150.00 floating out of the window that day. If that is a weekly meeting then £7,800-worth of time has been wasted in a year. If that meeting is reflected in ten different departments of the same company then £78,000 per year is being wasted during one simple communication exercise. And so it could go on. (It can now be seen why good chairing skills are necessary.) By 'time trimming' certain activities or giving them a time limit, a small amount is saved at local level. The impact this has at a higher level can be seen from the simple demonstration above.

Towards time triage

Having looked at time scientifically in the retrospective, it is time to think about how to proactively use time for the present and the future. This entails being able to prioritise the time at source and plan time ahead.

The triage system dates from the Napoleonic Wars. Injured soldiers were so great in number and beyond the coping abilities of the medical teams present that a system was put in place to prioritise and appropriately direct the care. Placed in tents according to injury level, the medical team could manage their precious time in the best possible way. The same system is in place in our casualty departments today usually in the form of a colour allocation – red, amber, green, etc. and with the presence of a triage nurse. This and other planning forms the basis of taking control over future time use and helps to prevent us getting swept up in chaos.

Best times

Work out your best times in the day – the times when you feel at your best to tackle things. This will help you perform better and more time efficiently. For instance are you a lark or an owl? Knowing you are not so good first thing in the morning and working around that means people get you in a better state. Wherever possible, plan to cater for this. It is very easy to allow other people to dictate the timing of things. On some occasions, this cannot be helped but there are probably a number of occasions when you have reacted to their schedule instantly and not fully considered the implications for your own. Take more control and use phrases such as: 'that's great but it would work out even better for me that day if we could make it at (time).' This is relatively easy to say and a high percentage of the time you will get your way. Also, even if it cannot be changed to suit you, you will still feel better for having asked and less like you have been time managed by someone else – which is a hollow feeling.

TIP

Highlight the best times in your diary and put the appropriate tasks in these sections first.

GENERAL ORGANISATION

For the purpose of order, I have divided up the path towards and including time triage into the following headings:

- timetabling – study schedule/project planning
- diary and daily to do list
- combinations
- refusal
- prioritisation – time triage
- review

Timetabling – study schedule/project planning

Whether studying or working there are times when a good old timetable serves the situation best. They come in many forms but essentially do the same thing – they help you plan. As a student, create order and plan your study carefully. Assignments seem to have a nasty way of coming in at once – or do they? Well to be fair, even where attempts are made to pace assessment, inevitably much of the assessment will take place following the delivery of the material you need to do it and as the assessment is a demonstration of your understanding of the subject some of it is likely to be at the end of the module. You will then have several assignments/presentations due around the same time. You will have the dates for these up front so rather than leave it all to the end of the term, plan in carefully work that you can do beforehand and plan how you will use the time when the pressure gets greater. A study timetable is also useful, as is a revision timetable in exam time. Don't just talk about doing one – do it.

TIP

Post your study timetable up on your door or on a notice board for others to see. This politely helps them manage your time the way you want them to.

In business much the same rules apply and the study plan is replaced by the project planner. Using charts and planners carefully can save a lot of time and money. Staff can easily see what is happening, when it is happening and who is doing what. This saves your staff asking a lot of questions and helps them prepare for anything they need to do. This system need not necessarily be just for projects. This mentality can apply to many operational aspects of business. For instance publishing a whereabouts sheet on e-mail to staff can save a lot of chasing remote managers around the country by phone. Not only does it save chase time, it also saves on the phone bill. Many examples like this exist in a company day but the main theme would seem to be transparency in terms of keeping people informed and included.

Wherever you are, at university or at work, these are then translated into your diary system.

Diary and daily to do list

Book the time Enter all key deadlines in your diary immediately. That is the easy bit, but don't forget the following points.

Backtrack Put in the preparation leading up to each diary entry as a matter of habit. Apply the baker's dozen principle to the entry; this principle essentially incorporates a 'more than you are asked for' attitude. Allow more time than you think you need in case of emergencies and to give you the chance to produce more than you are asked for. You are more likely to be promoted with this attitude. Be a 'clearly there' person not a 'nearly there' person.

Balance the entries with other items in your diary Take a moment to see how all the items fit together. Will it mean rushing from one thing to another or take you to different parts of the building, or country for that matter? You can avoid a lot of rushing around and time wasting if you take a few moments at this stage to think through the logistics. Also is there an impending task which could be usefully placed with your entry to save time later?

Batch any like tasks together Whether it is by geography or type, it pays to do tasks in batches of similar kinds. This may reduce the amount of travelling you do, but it may also mean less travelling for work colleagues who have to come to you.

Along with diary management also do a daily 'to do' list for the following day. This serves to help you plan and think ahead, but it is also useful if you are delayed or off work ill so that others can step in and do your work for you. Customers are not put off until your return as someone else can help them. It is also a good psychological cleanse at the end of each day to 'dump' the business pressures on to a piece of paper or electronic list so you can go home with peace of mind.

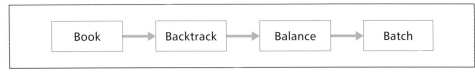

Figure 17.1 The diary entry process

Combinations

Combining tasks or multitasking is a great way of saving time. Take a good look at your time log and seek out tasks which can be batched as before, but this time think proactively ahead of them happening. What kind of things in your study, business or private life could you combine?

For example, could you listen to study tapes while travelling or dropping the children off at ballet or football? These can be tapes/CDs you have recorded yourself. Can any documents you are compiling at work be used elsewhere in the company to save someone else time? If you set off a culture of sharing and favours, you may be surprised what favours come back to you. How can a report for academic study be adapted for use in the business world to help you create a favourable impression?

Also start timing procrastination – how long does it actually take for you to sit down to a task you find unpleasant. Start when you say you will and resist the temptation to justify to yourself that something mundane needs doing instead.

Refusal

- Learn to say no nicely!
- It is better to do fewer things well than attempt lots of things which never get done

Try something like this:

> That sounds really interesting and I would so like to be involved but unfortunately I have made promises to others on particular deadlines which means I cannot help right now. I like to keep to all the promises I make so I have to be ruthless, but how about we look at how I can help in the future when I have delivered on my current projects?

This type of approach is worth working on. Saying no is not as hard as you think. Have you ever walked down a set of stairs or out of a building feeling put upon because you simply could not say no? Most of us have agreed to do things and then regretted our lack of assertion. Control at the point of entry of tasks is important and the very first step towards time triage.

Prioritisation – time triage

- Categorize your tasks.

It does not actually matter what triage system you use as long as you use one: 123, ABC, 'Must, should could', 'now, later, never' etc., it is up to you.

For our purposes let's stick to a colour code:

- Go for it now – essential

- Wait for the right time – important but can delay

- Stop yourself from doing this immediately – low priority

- ★ Interruption

- ★ Go for it now – essential

- ★ Wait for the right time – important but can delay

- ★ Stop yourself from doing this immediately – low priority

Interruptions should then be triaged as they happen in their own right as above. Often we treat interruptions as urgent because they feel urgent having arrived unexpectedly. In fact, they are often non-urgent and easily categorised.

You can apply this code or your own triage code to the tasks on your to do list or as they come in. The important thing is to develop the habit of thinking the priority through in your mind each time.

For example, your secretary runs into the office upset, having been dumped by her boyfriend. It is easy to stop everything and console her and in error treat her as a ★. In actual fact she is a ★.

Obviously you are not going to let on that this is what you are thinking and will appear to be most sympathetic, but in your mind you must think about the business day and what is right for it and you and channel your sympathy into a more appropriate time with clever ease:

> What awful news for you, I think cake is in order. I'll pick up some at lunch when I go out and how about we meet at 2.00pm for a proper and longer talk to make sure you are OK. Now, is there anything you need to get on with your work in the mean time?

This is an example of how it is possible to down categorise someone without making them feel bad; in fact they may feel better. Your secretary will feel much better for quality time with you which is hers and more special because you have made the effort. Of course the business and you have continued to go on.

In a similar vein, the results of your time log can be analysed and channelled through a system such as the Covey matrix which divides tasks into important and non-important, urgent and non-urgent. Available via the website given at the end of this chapter, this is a good approach for turning your analysis forward and planning for effectiveness.

Review

Look back on chunks of time regularly as a matter of course to see how you have spent them. This will isolate areas of procrastination, bad management and of course good management which can be repeated.

Time templating is also useful – where something has succeeded and you have achieved well, apply the same template to future work.

SOME TIPS FOR TIME EFFICIENCY

Time tips

- Build breaks and social life into your planning. Rest is important and so is having a life outside of work and study.
- Know your limits.
- Stand up when you are on the telephone if you want to cut the call short – body language can be 'heard' on the phone.
- Screen calls: have colleagues take clear messages for you so you can call back fully informed.
- Clear your desk. Just use the desk space for what you are currently working on. Cluttered desks suggest a cluttered mind. Even if it is just for show, clear your desk regularly. You will look more in control.
- Have an 'In to Out' system on your desk – all things should have a shelf life.
- Eat! This sounds silly but the 'lunch is for wimps' culture is very out of date. The simple biology is that if you have low blood sugar, you will not perform as well and things may take longer or you may make more mistakes which all cost time.
- Start when you say you will – be ready to start at that time.
- Handle memos, e-mails, etc. once. It is tempting to read through things several times before acting on them but time can be wasted if action is not taken on the correspondence directly.
- Break bigger projects up into smaller chunks.
- Time triage tasks according to their importance, not according to how much you like doing things.
- Delegate – up and down. There is nothing wrong with asking the boss for ideas and help, in fact being asked if you can pick their brains is actually quite flattering. Also with subordinates don't just delegate the boring tasks, delegate tasks which also develop them. Not only will this be time efficient, but it shows you trust them which helps your relationship. You will also be saving future time, as your delegation is part of that person's development and training.
- Always set deadlines for working on each task. Make sure the deadlines are realistic and that you stick to them as much as possible.
- If you cannot meet a deadline – and with the best will in the world this will sometimes happen – confess early and manage the time. Owning up or just being realistic will court any help you need or encourage your boss to eradicate any less important items for you to help.
- Have objectives before going into all meetings.
- Use the waste bin or delete key.
- Say no. Get used to asking 'Am I the right person for the job?'.

- Make time for proactive tasks. Planning for the future is important and a percentage of your working week should contain planning time. You can allocate 'protected' time for important longer term work.
- Schedule activities to match your preferred or best times, for example if you think better in the morning then schedule thinking time then.
- *Time tranching* – structure your time into blocks/tranches and allocate each to a different activity. Establish fixed daily routines, scheduling definite time for routine matters. Use definite times/meetings for discussing routine matters with colleagues.
- Do not be late for things. If you are ten minutes late for a meeting you are actually at least twenty minutes late for yourself and have let yourself down. It takes time to settle and catch up with what is going on so you have robbed yourself of essential information collection and time will be wasted – yours and the chair's, as they may have to repeat themselves for your benefit.
- Establish realistic work goals. Time consuming stress and fatigue are not caused by the things you have managed to do, but by thinking about those you didn't do.
- Plan your telephone calls and batch where you can.
- Make it a regular rule to check your use of time to see if you could have used it better and how.
- Manage in tasks which work towards your life goals and from your action plans following your SWOTPLOT self audit.
- Make some time every day to manage your time: five or ten minutes spent doing this can really help.
- Examine the types of task you do – are you doing the work of others?
- Manage your manager – ensure clear instructions are received and that a two way agreement exists regarding what you take on.
- Watch out for bad time management in others. Don't let them spend your life for you – that's your job!

Telephone tips

- Making calls:
  - handle in A B C time as appropriate
  - batch
  - avoid hold
  - control and be specific
- Taking calls:
  - establish priority
  - ask when you can ring back where possible to save chasing

TIME THIEVES

From your time logs and analysis, you will be able to identify the main time wasters in your life. The first thief is yourself, the second other people and environmental pressures and the third a lack of proper planning to control the time.

Yourself

Your confidence level will be key here and any inability to say no will make a difference. Have you a lack of time urgency or a lack of belief you can do things? Deliberation costs money. Do you talk about things rather than action them? Do you fail to delegate or just take on too much? Are you a perfectionist?

Others and your environment

Your reactivity levels will be telling here. How in control of events are you? Do you allow drop in visitors and telephone interruptions? Are your meetings all necessary? Are there foggy areas of responsibility? Are you over-managed by your superior?

Lack of planning

Have you failed to record your goals? Have you taken on too much? Have you failed to break a big project up into more manageable parts? Are your time estimates unrealistic? Have you forgotten to put check points into your planning?

CROSS CULTURAL COMMENT

When managing corporate time and arranging events it is a good idea to be aware of religious festivals, etc. for different cultures. Where one has a choice of where to position events, it is considerate to allow for busy times of year for other cultures. Divali for instance is an extremely busy time for the Asian community. In the same way that the Western Christmas breaks are catered for in time management, a similar respect can be held for this important event and those of other cultures such as Eid.

Summary

From *time tracking* and *totalling* you have *time trimmed*. Then with *time triage* and *time tips* you have progressed to *time tranching* and *time templating* and achieved *time triumph* – well done.

Time/self-management is about transparency and awareness. The approach in the chapter sets you about highlighting your own issues by making you look at them carefully.

TASK 1

In pairs, write a short script which demonstrates being asked a question to do something and one of you saying 'no' nicely. Role play these out in the group.

TASK 2

Working in groups, write down a list of routine tasks for a typical day. Follow this with a list of at least ten likely interruptions. Be as creative as you can be. Now time triage these events and be prepared to justify your decisions.

References and further reading

Covey, S. (1989) *The 7 Habits of Highly Effective People*, London: Franklin Covey

Covey, S. (1999) *Principle Centred Leadership*, London: Franklin Covey

Lashley, C. and Best, W. (2001) *12 Steps to Study Success*, London: Continuum.

Pedlar, M., Burgoyne, J. and Boydell, T. (2001) *A Manager's Guide to Self Development*, Berkshire: McGraw Hill

Rees, W. and Porter, C. (1996) *Skills of Management*, London: Thomson.

Websites

http://www.brefigroup.co.uk/resources/timetools.html

http://www.psychwww.com/mtsite/page5.html

CHAPTER 18
Stress management

- To define and recognise the symptoms of stress in self and others
- To isolate the causes of stress
- To cope with and minimise stress in everyday life

Stress is not just for the high powered executive. Each person has their own perception of events – some cope better than others.

Personal thresholds to stress vary and that is true of boredom thresholds too! Boredom causes stress. This makes stress very difficult to define, because it manifests itself in many different ways too. It is difficult to accurately pinpoint.

COMFORT ZONES

Any definition of stress must acknowledge the perception of the individual concerned. A discomfort occurs when they feel out of control in some way. This point of discomfort will vary from person to person but it is that point of discomfort which is constant in all – the point at which biological 'distress' takes hold. The signs of stress can be biological and cognitive and are linked to the inbuilt 'flight and fight' mechanisms our body has for survival. These signs are triggered by our level of mental discomfort so if we perceive that something is out of our capability we feel uncomfortable about it and worry. So stress is something which is in the eye of the beholder, that is in how they see what is before them and how they feel they can cope with it. If an individual does not believe they have the ability to do a task and the task arises, then stress will occur. The individual may be more than capable of achieving the task but their perception stands in the way.

Comfort zones, therefore, are individual and form the baseline from which to self-assess. It is all too easy to stay within a comfort zone but the problem with that is that the perception of events remains the same. Individuals can season themselves to withstand greater things if they do push themselves a little into a stretch zone (Figure 18.1). Equally, an individual continually exposes themselves to stress if they do not learn about their abilities by stretching themselves. Perhaps, then, it is wiser to slowly season oneself towards a little natural stress in a controlled way than wait for it to dictate the situation and put one under pressure.

Having pinpointed individual perception as key to the degree, and definition, of stress, we will now consider external sources of stress and particularly those prevalent in the world of work and study. Personal sources will always be there and some are out of our control. From moving house, to divorces and deaths in the family, situations will push us out of our comfort zone further than we would wish. This chapter does not set out to analyse the effects of personal sources of stress as it gears itself more to preparing for you or improving your career opportunities. By isolating the different areas likely to cause stress from in the world of work and study, we can learn to manage and even anticipate it, and therefore cope with it.

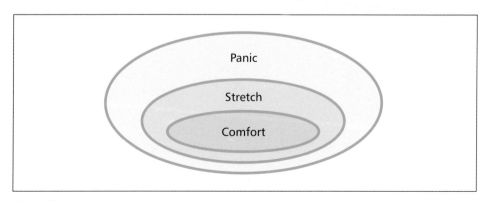

Figure 18.1 Comfort zones

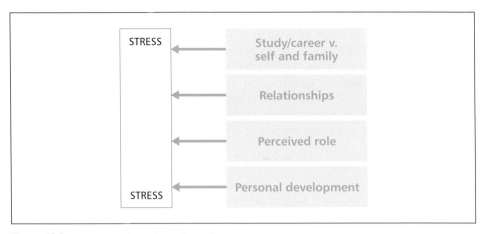

Figure 18.2 Sources of work and study stress

SOURCES OF EXTERNAL STRESS

Study or career versus self and family

An individual's own interests may not be in parallel with the job they do or the company they work for. If a member of staff does not truly believe in the company they work for, this can cause demotivation, dissatisfaction and, of course, can be stressful. This is also true in the world of study, in terms of believing in the institution and whether the course is the most appropriate one.

Career and study commitments may not fit in with family life. Finding the right balance of working and studying and maintaining family obligations is very stressful. Whether it is caring for relatives or having to fit school runs and domestic commitments alongside study or work, situations will occur which will cause stress. However well-organised a person is, clashes will occur. The secret is to manage these in order to minimise stress but accept that it is likely to occur and so season ourselves for it.

Relationships

The different relationships we have at work and university can cause us stress. At university, being part of a dysfunctional group preparing for a presentation has its own brand of stress. At work, a poor relationship with a boss can cause an enormous amount of stress and all of us at some point will encounter this.

Equally, poor relations with colleagues and subordinates can make us feel isolated and therefore stressed. We all like to be liked and the worry caused by difficult relationships should not be underestimated.

Perceived role

How we see ourselves in the role we occupy is also key to whether we court extra stress. Time pressures are there for the student and manager at work. There are a number of occasions in both worlds where it seems there is just too much to do in the time. Feeling overloaded is common. Equally, how we feel we can cope with the role will affect the levels of stress we have as will feeling we have an input. Stress can be caused by feeling that there is a lack of participation in the decision-making process and having no control over events, for instance. A role with responsibility for others will have its own stresses. We could occupy a role where we do not feel up to the challenge. The 'Peter Principle' can occur: this is when an over promotion has taken place and the individual is out of their depth. At university if a student believes they do not understand a particular subject and they feel out of their depth, then stress will occur.

Personal development

Our personal development is important. If our ambitions are thwarted in any way we are as likely to be stressed as if we were out of our depth. Under-promotion can be as stressful as over-promotion because boredom and a feeling of not being recognised can also cause stress. If we are groomed as individuals at university and at work we are more likely to feel we are progressing. Companies and institutions need to ensure that students and employees are developed as a whole person rather than just training in a set of skills for a particular job or studying for pure academic outcome.

RECOGNISING STRESS

There are many signs and symptoms of *stress* and these essentially originate from our biological reaction to *distress.*

Distress and the 'fight or flight' mechanisms in our body are indicated by adrenalin levels which cause raised heart and breathing rates, an increased blood flow to muscles, the stomach contents to become more acidic and nerve endings to become less sensitive to pain; they also make us less able to make more complex decisions.

The signs and symptoms of stress fall into two categories: physical and cognitive.

Physical

Nausea	Feeling faint	Holding breath
Tense neck	Back pain	Palpitations
Dry mouth	Butterflies	Skin rashes
Visual disturbances	Headaches	Chest pain
Sweating	Flushing	Shivering
Asthma	Diarrhoea	Stomach ulcers
Exhaustion	Indigestion	Twitching

Cognitive

Low satisfaction	Apathetic	Crying
Depression	Fearful	Low self-esteem
Withdrawn	Negative	Forgetful
Unable to concentrate	Difficulty making decisions	Putting things off
Lonely	Late for things	Excessive drinking
Excessive smoking	Nightmares	Rushing around
Insecurity	Impulsive	Over-reacting

Exercise caution when reading this list: just like reading a medical dictionary, it is easy to fit yourself too readily to symptoms. However, the list is useful for spotting signs in yourself and others. This is important as long-term exposure to stress can lead to migraine, ulcers, heart attacks, hypertension and mental illness and even suicide. It is also a factor in cancer, strokes and bowel disorders.

How many sick days are actually attributable to stress? As a manager or future manager, this is a consideration. Not all staff will ring in and say they are stressed and are therefore taking some time off – in fact very few will actually admit it. It is more likely that they will register a physical ailment as cover – they may even believe in this physical ailment themselves if their stress is unrecognised. This makes it hard to accurately record the number of days staff may have off because they are stressed. It is important to look out for changes in behaviour and look at the trend of absences a person may have.

> **TIP**
>
> Remember, stress as a condition itself is infectious!!

Having run through the ways in which stress manifests itself and the potential causes, we are moving towards helping ourselves to cope with it. Looking out for the signs is a healthy occupation as is analysing where most of the stress we suffer comes from. With this information, it is possible to tailor life to reduce stress more and even anticipate events so we can prepare more readily for them. Such preparation helps build up our stamina and ability to cope with stress.

HOW DO YOU COPE WITH STRESS?

The ten Rs of stress management

- *Recognise* – not just the symptoms but the cause.
- *Realise* – that it is a fact of life and some challenge is necessary for better performance.
- *Reorganise* – towards minimising stress. Use tactical and strategic measures to reduce the amount of stress in your life.
- *Regulate* – the excesses in your life.
- *Reality check* – regularly weigh up the important things in your life.
- *Return* – the stress back to where it came from.
- *Refuse* – to do things: say NO!
- *Redirect* – the stress to someone else: delegate.
- *Reflect* – on your achievements.
- *Relax* – you deserve it!

Recognise As well as the other factors mentioned in this chapter, don't forget that there are a number of life events outside of work and study which will heavily influence your stress levels. For example:

- death of a loved one
- divorce
- marriage
- pregnancy
- finances
- moving house.

TIP

Assess the main culprits in your working/studying life and prepare yourself for them. Look out for the symptoms and recognise the signs of stress in yourself and others, but think back to what may be the cause of it in the first place. Understanding the cause goes a long way to being able to cope with the stress.

Realise Learn that there are just some things that are outside of your control. There is little sense in worrying about something you cannot do anything about. Put your energy into positively solving the problem and go forward. Also learn to put things behind you on occasions.

Reorganise Go back and look at the area in which you work/study. Is it conducive to effectiveness and enjoyment? Think about aspects such as heating, lighting, clutter.

Find time to exercise. Research has always shown that those who exercise regularly feel more energetic. The increased oxygenation enhances alertness for up to four hours. Endomorphins are released (happy hormones).

The following tips suggest some small changes that can make a big difference:

- Posture – walk and sit properly to aid breathing and so oxygenation.
- Eat breakfast and ensure a balanced diet. Do not eat too late in the evening.
- Take lunch breaks – use the time to stretch your legs.
- Set sensible performance goals.
- Take time to listen to others – this may save you time and errors.
- Drive in the slow lane.
- Fill the car up with petrol before the needle reaches the red.
- Let other motorists in front of you.
- Practise smiling and 'stroke' others. Thank people.
- Avoid queues and tailbacks. No last minute rushes.
- Admit when you are wrong.
- Use positive language – avoid don'ts.
- Manage your time effectively.

Regulate We all have things in our life which we may do to excess. We can lower stress levels if we admit these excesses and take control of them. For example:

- Cut down on coffee – the stimulating effects only last for 30–60 minutes and coffee raises stress hormones in the bloodstream. It also has a half life of up to five hours, reducing energy and causing fatigue.
- Cut down or cut out cigarettes.
- Moderate alcohol consumption – it is a depressant.
- Eat regular meals.
- Ensure you get enough sleep – you need more sleep when you are stressed.

Reality check Remind yourself what is good about your life. Too many people talk about what they haven't got or haven't done. Think of what you *have* achieved and what you *do* have and appreciate it. This optimistic or 'glass half full' approach makes a big difference to the perspective of any problem. It puts things into context and positively affects your perception. Remember stress is often about a distorted perception.

Return Rally back some issues. Get staff to come to you with answers not problems. This also serves to create a more positive culture made up of constructive ways forward rather than moans. It also helps to solve issues for you which in turn reduces the stress.

If your boss has asked you to do something and you are not really sure – ask. There is no shame is asking to pick the brains of someone so you can get started, in fact this can be quite flattering for the person you ask. It is not an admission of not being able to cope, it is a common sense approach and reduces the stress from the word go.

With assignments at university, do not be afraid to ask lecturers for guidance if you do not understand something. Why spend weeks worrying about something when a few minutes further explanation can help you get on the right track.

Refuse Sometimes, you should just say NO!

You can say no nicely by explaining that you would rather not tackle a task half heartedly and only accept what you feel you can do full justice to. Be honest, it is better to say no than to say yes and then fail to deliver.

Redirect Give others the benefit of the doubt. Delegate more than you think they can do and you will be pleasantly surprised 90 per cent of the time. By delegating more than just the tedious tasks, you are also helping develop others to assist you more in the future so creating a virtuous circle of stress reducing assistance in the future.

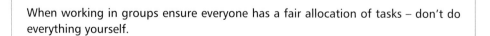

TIP

When working in groups ensure everyone has a fair allocation of tasks – don't do everything yourself.

Reflect Make time to consider what you have achieved:

- Pat yourself on the back.
- Count your blessings.
- Open your eyes and see just how capable you really are.
- Pat others on the back – you will feel better by praising others and they will praise you.

Relax Make sure you make time for fun and relaxation. Do not feel guilty about relaxing – enjoy it.

If you can adapt the ten Rs of stress management, you will be more organised, nicer to be with and you will live longer! You have travelled from *distress* to *de-stress*.

CASE STUDY 18.1

Barbara has hit a hard time at work. She has been with a national company for five years and enjoyed a high profile, dynamic role. The operations director under whom she has positively thrived and been well cared for all this time has suddenly resigned and been replaced by a peer of hers who has always made it clear she found Barbara competition for her. Sharon, the new operations director, starts as she means to go on. She reduces Barbara's standing in the workplace by minimising all of her contributions and recruits friends on to her new team who wholeheartedly follow her lead without question. Barbara is very intelligent and creative with lots of new ideas and tries to penetrate the new regime of robotic duty with her usual energy and enthusiasm despite the harassment. Barbara also brings some of her academic study material to the meetings for use in discussion. Sharon dismisses the new thoughts and references to books, although oddly some of them appear via the Board some weeks later as ideas from Sharon herself who is praised for her ingenuity and commitment to keeping up to date with business texts. Sharon does not acknowledge the input from Barbara. Barbara approaches Sharon about it privately and is told there is nothing she can do and if she doesn't like things the way they are she can always leave – in fact she is invited to leave by Sharon who says she wil! deny it if Barbara says anything to the Board. Barbara does try to take things further

but ranks are closed and all support is for their new senior recruit.

Barbara starts getting migraines and is off sick from work for the first time in years. Where she used to be lively and energetic at meetings, she is now quiet. She is given tasks well beneath her ability and treated as much lower in standing than she was before at the company. Barbara can no longer be bothered to contribute ideas and just does her job – no more, no less. Sharon continues the relentless harassment, particularly at meetings where Sharon has her support team in place. Barbara feels outnumbered and under great pressure and finally loses her temper. This has never happened before. She is physically sick and feels faint. She doesn't really want to leave the company as she believes in what they do even if they have let her down at the moment and cannot see what is happening. She goes home to bed depressed.

Barbara opens her mail on Saturday morning to find she has been summoned for a disciplinary hearing for gross misconduct involving insubordination. Physically sick, she tries to contact Sharon and ask why no direct communication was made regarding the matter to sort it out in a less stressful way for all and in a less expensive and time consuming one for the company. Barbara is too ill to fight the system – although she tries – and is hammered at the hearing and given a final written warning. She is off ill again and finally tenders her resignation which Sharon eagerly accepts.

- Discuss the actual sources of Barbara's stress – not the symptoms.

- What do you think of Sharon's handling of the matter?

- What are the different losses to the company now this situation has been allowed to happen?

- What would you have done differently as Sharon's boss?

CROSS CULTURAL COMMENT

Different cultures have ways of showing stress/upset, etc. Some cultures express emotion very readily and demonstrably and others hide it. It is important to allow for these differences and not to make judgements based purely on the way you deal with stress. It may be that those dealing with it in an outward way according to their cultural norm are actually dealing with their stress more effectively than someone who thinks they need to hide it.

Summary

By defining and recognising stress in self and others the journey to coping with it was half achieved. This was then complemented by a ten Rs rule to cope with stress in general.

TASK 1

Draw a diagram that shows all the sources of your stress at work, home and study.

TASK 2

Devise a stress management plan which is supported by your time management plan. Incorporate all the big events you are able to predict and set out some actions which make tasks more manageable.

References and further reading

Brewer, C. (1997) *Managing Stress*, USA: American Media Publishing.

Mullins, L. (2002) *Management and Organisational Behaviour*, Harlow: FT Prentice Hall.

Pedlar, M., Burgoyne, J. and Boydell, T. (2001) *A Manager's Guide to Self Development*, Berkshire: McGraw Hill.

Turkington, C. (1998) *Stress Management for Busy People*, New York: McGraw Hill.

White, A. (1995) *Managing for Performance*, London: BCA.

CHAPTER 19
Workplace attitude

- To recognise the importance of workplace attitude in workplace communications and performance
- To appreciate what individuals need in the workplace environment to work at their best
- To examine the workplace in terms of its physical and psychological environment

Introduction

This chapter will not provide you with definite answers but it is designed to make you think about your current or future workplace with a view to appreciating how staff need a positive working environment in which to thrive. In addition, the chapter will reinforce that this does not happen by accident.

This chapter will ask you questions to make you look at the workplace and yourself either with renewed vigour as a current manager or with a view to future management skills as a potential manager.

As well as looking at the work itself, we will examine the physical and psychological environment with a view to assessing our own impact on it and the performance which ensues.

THE PHYSICAL WORKPLACE

The area or physical space in which we work can have a great impact on output and performance – more than you might imagine. As a manager you must assess the needs of your team in terms of space, equipment, etc. This will take into account health and safety laws defining ergonomics which outline the heights and distances of equipment in terms of posture, eyesight, etc. Your job is to ask yourself: 'Is the place in which we work conducive to a good attitude and therefore maximum productivity?' Look at physical aspects such as furniture, light, thoroughfares, access to others, access to information, music, noise, proximity to others, comfort, barriers and so on. What you do will vary within different office and work settings but it is one of the easiest things to change to help achieve the right attitude.

THE WORK ITSELF

In terms of the work undertaken, it is useful to ask yourself a number of questions:

- Is the workload too great for the individual? This will disturb the balance necessary for enjoyment. Stress does not contribute well to a good workplace attitude.
- Is the workload too little for the individual? Bored people are not happy people. Their work needs to be rewarding.

A sense of achievement is imperative:

- Do our staff have an idea of how important their task is in the overall picture?
- Indeed – do they know what the overall picture is?

The work itself must have a value to your member of staff as well as a direction. Recognise that value and thank them. Keep them informed and do not treat them like mushrooms, which are fed a load of manure and kept in the dark!

Here are a few more questions for the competent manager/leader to consider:

- Have you, as the manager, given your subordinate a varied workload which will stimulate them?
- Have you, as the manager, taken into account the actual ability of your subordinate? Are you stretching them enough or are you overstretching them?
- Is the work monotonous? How can you as the manager make it more rewarding? Targets, incentives, workbursting, synergy, fun, reward and so can aid *satisfaction*.

THE PSYCHOLOGICAL WORKPLACE

Alasdair White, in *Managing for Performance* (1995, p. 185), states:

Environment impact goes beyond the purely physical – you have to be aware of the impact of the psychological environment which is generated whenever people have to work together. You have to be sensitive to the 'perceptions' that your team has about such things as each other, the goals, the company itself, internal politics, and the market in which they work. Perceptions are very powerful, they are difficult to define and even more difficult to change.

He goes on to indicate that these, 'perceptions translate into an issue of "morale".' To help understand the environment in which we work, or will work, we will consider definitions of 'attitude'. According to *Collins English Dictionary*, 'attitude' is:

1 the way a person views something or tends to behave towards it, often in an evaluative way
2 a theatrical pose created for effect
3 a position of the body indicating mood or emotion
4 the orientation of an aircraft's axes in relation to some plane
5 the orientation of a spacecraft in relation to its direction of motion

Attitude definition 1

The way a person views something or tends to behave towards it, often in an evaluative way Studies into this meaning of 'attitude' were fashionable in the USA in the 1960s when an interest developed in 'why people do things'. One could generalise the research by saying that 'people only do something if they obtain a psychological or material benefit from doing it' (White 1995, p. 9). For example:

- material (extrinsic) benefits such as money have their place but cannot be relied upon alone
- intrinsic motivation is believed to be more effective
- if we are to analyse the way a person 'views' something or 'behaves', then it could be argued that some of that depends on what they themselves are like in the first place. Let me tell you about the 'Marshmallow Test!'

Walter Mischel, a psychologist at Stanford University in the 1960s, conducted this study on a group of four year olds. Designed to test the soul of any four year old, the study offered a quick reading in the days before IQ tests not just of character, but, it was suggested, of the direction that the child would probably take through life. Bear in mind that it was one type of test and was used over 40 years ago. We consider it here to widen our own thinking, not necessarily to agree with everything it suggests. The test worked like this: A four year old child was given a proposal thus:

- If you wait until after I run an errand I will give you two marshmallows.
- If you cannot wait, you can only have one – but you can have it right now!

The child was then left in the room with that one marshmallow . . . Think about what you would have done.

Daniel Goleman, in *Emotional Intelligence* (1996, p. 81), states: 'The emotional and social difference between the grab-the-marshmallow preschoolers and their gratification delaying peers was dramatic. Those who had resisted temptation at four were now, as adolescents, more socially competent: personally effective, self assertive, and better able to cope with the frustrations of life.' He continues: 'The third or so who grabbed for the marshmallow, however, tended to have fewer of these qualities, and shared instead a relatively more troubled psychological portrait.'

Apparently, when the same group were tested later at high school, those who grabbed the marshmallow scored considerably less in their exams!

You may have heard about theories of nature versus nurture in relation to child development. The same theories can be applied to the development of staff and accommodating the differences in people that nature presents us with while also nurturing staff to see tasks in a certain way. Perception may be affected by their nature but our influence as managers and leaders can nurture a positive view.

This echoes the comments made above about the work itself:

- What are your staff getting out of it personally?
- Could you, as the manager, influence their view by further education, motivation, explanation, etc.?

Martin Seligman, psychologist at the University of Pennsylvania, looked at optimism. Goleman (1996, p. 88) says: 'Seligman defines optimism in terms of how people explain to themselves their successes and failures. People who are optimistic see a failure as due to something that can be changed so that they can succeed next time around, while pessimists take the blame for the failure, ascribing it to some lasting characteristic they are helpless to change.' Optimists are sometimes described as those people who see a glass half filled with liquid as being half full, while pessimists see it as being half empty. In life there are always going to exist 'glass half full' and 'glass half empty' people. Can we, as existing and future managers and leaders, paint a positive 'half full' picture as a way of capturing the best from our staff?

Walter Goldsmith and David Clutterbuck, in *The Winning Streak Mark II* (1997, p. 51), say: 'how important it is to maintain the right balance between keeping people in check and harnessing their energy and enthusiasm. Get it wrong and people look for their excitement and fulfilment outside the job; get it right and you capture not only their minds but their very essence as well.'

It is clear that as well as physical environment, attitude is affected by psychological environment and this can be affected not just by team members by also by the attitude of the manager/leader themselves. It can also be affected, as we have seen by what lies within the individual already.

Peter Singer (1994) highlights Albert Camus' (1969) view on the myth of Sisyphus. Sisyphus is condemned to roll a rock up a mountain only to have it roll back again for all time. Camus' argument is that Sisyphus himself finds motivation from within and from the task he creates purpose and satisfaction.

Other definitions of attitude highlight the leader's responsibility further.

Attitude definitions 2 & 3

A theatrical pose created for effect

A position of the body indicating mood or emotion Daniel Goleman (1996, p. 85) says:

Even mild mood changes can sway thinking. In making plans or decisions people in good moods have a perceptual bias that leads them to be more expansive and positive in their thinking. This is partly because memory is state specific, so that while in a good mood we remember more positive events; as we think over the pros and cons of a course of action while feeling pleasant, memory biases our weighing of evidence in a positive direction, making us more likely to do something slightly adventurous or risky, for example.

Goldsmith and Clutterbuck in *The Winning Streak Mark II* say, 'High performance companies do extract extraordinary performance out of ordinary people. They often do so by challenging these people to become extraordinary. The right people, with the right attitudes and behaviours in the right environment.' (1997, p. 198)

So here we become aware of our responsibility to create the right mood or emotion for the benefit of our staff and the organisation. Staff will react to our moods, so ensuring we are positive becomes a key requirement of any leading role. Helping staff enjoy their work will create a virtuous cycle of further positivity.

TIP

Start now wherever you are. If you are at university, start by being a positive force when working in a group.

In addition to creating the right positive atmosphere to boost the working environment, the last quote also gets us thinking about being positive towards the staff in terms of believing in them and their abilities.

The *Harvard Business Review* (HBR) *on Managing People* (1998) contains two articles which outline the effect of positive and negative influences on staff.

J. Sterling Livingston introduced the more holistic concept of 'Pygmalion in Management' in the late 1960s. The name Pygmalion is derived from Greek mythology where a King of Greece wished so hard for a beautiful statue of a woman to become his wife and bear him a son that it happened; it was reworked in the play 'Pygmalion' and its musical version 'My Fair Lady' where a professor believes he can turn a street flower seller into a lady and does. Livingston's research revealed 'What managers expect of their subordinates and the way they treat them largely determine their performance and career progress.' (p. 45)

The opposite of positive Pygmalion is mentioned in Livingston's article but most focus is on the positive. He called negative Pygmalion the 'dark side' and gave us the thought that, 'The difference between employees who perform well and those who perform poorly is not how they are paid but how they are treated.'

In a second article in the *Harvard Business Review on Managing People*, Jean-Francois Manzoni and Jean-Louis Barsoux introduce us to 'The Set-Up-To-Fail-Syndrome' in 1998. They suggest that bosses can even accidently have an 'in group' and an 'out group' and that this has a dramatic effect on performance and happiness in the job.

Attitude definition 4

The orientation of an aircraft's axes in relation to some plane With all this food for thought, what does this definition suggest?

- Are you the aircraft taking staff in the right direction?
- Are you on the same plane as your staff?
- Are you on the same aircraft as your staff?
- Do you really understand the physical and psychological needs of your staff?

Attitude definition 5

The orientation of a spacecraft in relation to its direction of motion

- So if you are the spacecraft – are you leading your staff in the right direction?
- Do the goals of the staff follow the same direction as the corporate goals?
- Do yours?

These last two definitions introduce us to the prospect of leadership in a wider form. Not only are we then responsible for the physical workplace and the personal psychological one, but we are responsible for linking that to the overall vision and purpose of the company. As leaders and managers we are the link between staff and organisation.

As we develop, or even refine, our work and study skills it is worth assessing the overall destination for them in the workplace. Each thing we learn or improve then has a definite purpose.

CROSS CULTURAL COMMENT

A healthy respect for different cultures is essential in creating a positive working environment. The 'nurture' of culture will have an effect on understanding and attitude in the workplace and the accommodation of this diversity is as important as the accommodation of the diversity of personalities alluded to.

Summary

This chapter has directed learning towards the workplace further. It outlines the responsibilities which exist and await us in the management world with a view to giving purpose to the skills we develop at university either in full- or part-time study alongside a current management role.

By illustrating the impact one person can have on environment and job satisfaction for others, it highlights the importance of good, positive communication and the appreciation of differences in others. Also clear is the prospect that personal development is ongoing. Acquiring a culture of ongoing improvement is therefore important now.

TASK 1

Working as a group, review your work experiences and isolate examples of how work, physical environment, the attitude of the boss and corporate vision affected your enjoyment and motivation – not to mention your productivity!

TASK 2

Talk to friends and colleagues who have worked in other countries and compare notes.

References and further reading

Camus, A. (1969) *The Myth of Sisyphus and other Essays*, trans. Justin O'Brien, New York: Alfred Knopf.

Covey, S. (1989) *The Seven Habits of Highly Effective People*, London: Franklin Covey.

Goldsmith, W. and Clutterbuck, D. (1997) *The Winning Streak Mark II*, London: Orion Business Books.

Goleman, D. (1996) *Emotional Intelligence*, London: Bloomsbury.

Livingston, J. S. (1998) 'Pygmalion in Management', *Harvard Business Review on Managing People*, pp. 45–72, Boston: Harvard Business School Publishing.

Manzoni, J.-F. and Barsoux, J.-L. (1998) 'The set-up-to-fail syndrome', *Harvard Business Review on Managing People*, pp. 197–226, Boston: Harvard Business School Publishing.

Singer, P. (1994) *Ethics*, Oxford: Oxford University Press.

White, A. (1995) *Managing for Performance*, London: BCA.

CHAPTER 20
Management and leadership

Learning objectives

- To define the concepts of management and leadership
- To differentiate between the two sets of skills with a view to using study to develop skills for a future role or refine skills in an existing one
- To appreciate the importance and impact of management and leadership styles and skills on the workplace

Introduction

Having outlined a number of work and study skills, with a view to enhancing your success in the workplace, this chapter attempts to put the use of them into context. The last chapter gave you a flavour of the workplace itself and the attitude of staff. We will now take a closer look at the skills required in the type of role that you are likely to be in now or apply for in the future.

Your successful personal development in whatever field you choose is likely to put you in a position of responsibility and authority. Along with that goes duty and this last chapter in this section is designed to make you think about your personal impact on others as you lead and manage them and, yes, now is the time to start thinking about it. Your attitude towards this needs attention as early as possible. This power is a privilege and your use of it, or abuse of it, can make all the difference to you, your staff and your company.

"I used to lead by example, but it was too much work."

© Mike Shapiro / Cartoonstock.com

Productivity and quality of service will not be the only criteria on which you will be judged as a good manager or leader in the workplace. Just as important nowadays is your ability to motivate and keep your staff – while still making money or providing a good service of course! Staff turnover figures are high up in the priorities of the directorate in any company and indeed have a direct impact on profits – their other key interest. How you use your power is key here.

MANAGEMENT POWER

'New Manager Syndrome' is an irritating condition in the workplace. The symptoms clearly indicate a discomfort in how to wear or use power appropriately. One can actually still spot some older managers with the condition who never grew out of it! 'New Manager Syndrome' is an over-demonstration of position and power and sufferers aggressively sport the new power in a clumsy and obvious way. It shows an insecurity within and is an over-compensation for feeling out of one's depth.

Real power is calm and almost invisible. It is classily worn and gently demonstrated. Admittedly it changes with different situations but it is carefully used and appropriately distributed. More experienced, good managers or leaders are at ease with their power and respect it along with their staff. This motivates staff to work for you because they want to – not because they have to. What good manager or leader would want the latter?

French and Raven (1959, in Yukl, G., 2002) identified five main sources of power:

- reward
- coercive
- legitimate
- referent
- expert

Reward

The member of staff believes the leader has the ability to influence, in a positive way, their pay, work content and progress in the organisation. Sensibly used this is a power which motivates the staff to perform well.

Coercive

The power derived from coercion is essentially based on fear or punishment and it is the opposite of reward power. The member of staff believes the leader has the ability to withhold or remove all of the rewards listed above, in addition to having an influence on the staff member staying in the actual job itself. This is often over-used and abused. Most of us can think of a particular manager whose intelligence levels never got them out of this groove.

Legitimate

In this case the member of staff believes the leader has a right to exercise influence because of their position in the company. So the power is based on authority and position rather than personal relationships. This is an inherited power derived through position or a privilege and must be worn with care and grace. This ensures a healthy respect for the person and position and should not require any peacock strutting to sport it in anyway.

Referent

Referent power is based on the member of staff's actual relationship with and identification with the manager or leader. This is power derived through character and respect for the actual leading individual. This is the type of power that really makes a staff member want to work for the leader.

Expert

Experts have specific knowledge of a subject, so followers believe the leader knows best based on that particular knowledge.

Further possible sources of power

Gary Yukl (2002) suggests two others sources of power:

- knowledge
- environment

Knowledge Knowledge here is used in a different sense to that mentioned under expert power. It means how we use knowledge or information in the company, for instance having control of certain facts, figures, etc. How these are used and how transparent they are is a form of power, which like other forms of power can be abused. There always exists the manager who doesn't like to share certain things because they feel 'special or powerful' knowing them. It makes them feel important to withhold information. Obviously some things are confidential and subject to a hierarchical order.

Environment The environment in which the member of staff works can be directly affected by the manager or leader, much as we covered in the previous chapter. Realising this is a power is half the battle.

By realising the impact we have on our current and future organisation's success through our use or abuse of power, we can start planning how to develop as a manager and/or leader.

To further that development a definition of the two skill sets will get us thinking of areas to start. We can use the strengths and weaknesses we pinpointed in Chapter 1 to make action plans for future personal success, but there is little point in this if it is not put into the direct context of the real working environment.

MANAGEMENT

Management theory has itself developed dramatically over fairly recent times. Mullins (2002) helps us trace the history. Definitions and interest in management as a concept really evolved during the nineteenth century. Starting with Max Weber's 'Bureaucracy', a structure of his principles formed the backbone and theory of management. These were:

- specialisation
- formalised rules and procedures
- clear hierarchy
- promotion on merit
- rewards and sanctions
- career tenure.

Henri Fayol was a practical and hands-on manager and his ideas contributed to the 'Classical' school of thought on management.

This approach saw managing as a profession in its own right. Fayol offered back principles of his own:

- division of work
- authority and responsibility
- discipline
- unity of command
- unity of direction
- individual subordination
- fair rewards
- centralisation
- a scalar chain
- order
- equity
- stability of tenure
- initiative
- esprit de corps

Henri Fayol's view was that managing is about:

- forecasting
- planning
- organising
- commanding
- coordinating
- controlling

Up to this point the history of management theory was more about organisational order but how it developed from there starts us thinking about the skills we use in the workplace today.

At the start of the twentieth century, Frederick Winslow Taylor devised an approach to managing organisations that he said was logical and rational and which he called 'scientific management'. Scientific management aimed at improving productivity and focused on the actual tasks.

Taylor used real examples of workers and demonstrated that, by controlling and measuring the tasks they do, a higher productivity would result. Control and measurement of tasks would be part of any management role today.

Taylor put forward four main principles of management of his own:

- A scientific selection of employees, based on fitness, strength, etc.
- A detailed and logical analysis of tasks, using 'time study' methods.
- A determining of not just what workers do, but how they do it – standardised methods.
- Breaking large and complex tasks down into a series of linked, simple jobs.

Henry Ford successfully picked up and used Taylor's methods and created the assembly line operation for his famous car. While we may not agree with all Taylor's principles – especially the first one – for every situation, it is clear that control over and study of the tasks makes a difference to greater productivity and such measured management has a place in a profitable and successful enterprise.

Management theory was evolving during this period but along task and production lines – literally by this point. A greater focus on the actual member of staff was the next stage in the management evolution.

Elton Mayo with his team did some ground-breaking work in the 'Hawthorne Experiments'. *Human relations management*, as the name suggests, started taking into account what the human doing the task needed to work well, not just in terms of environment but in terms of social needs and self-development. History teaches us here that it is as important to look after the individual as it is to look after the task.

Peter Drucker's Management Roles (Drucker 1997) would start to indicate an inclusion of this human element:

- setting objectives
- organising
- motivating
- measuring
- developing people

Neo-human relations management took this a step further and linked the human back to the organisation more closely, as did the *systems approach* to management, which took on board the views of the individuals working there as well as the internal and external environment in which they and the organisation worked. Management theory, therefore, has evolved to take in more of the picture and has today arrived at the *contingency approach*, which essentially states that there is no one way to manage – every situation is different and so different styles must be used at different times. Also clear from the history of management theory is that management is more about the short-term picture. Overall, however, it is clear from the history that a number of aspects must be taken into consideration when managing and clearly there is a balance to be found between people versus profit.

Blake and Mouton outlined the people profit emphasis (in Smith 1998). According to them true 'team management' is achieved only when concern for production and people is both balanced and high. Their theory pulls together the history of management theory well and focuses our minds on what may be necessary for the future. We can probably all name an Authority Compliant Manager and it would be interesting to link their staff retention figures with their particular autocratic style. Interestingly, the Blake and Mouton grid also sports the message of not taking your eye off the bottom line and that you can be too nice. The Country Club Manager will have let the staff down just as much as the Authority Compliant one, only this time the staff leave because a job no longer exists for them when the company goes bust.

LEADERSHIP

Leadership theories have evolved in much the same way, although over a later period and largely from the post World War II period in the last century. As with management theories, they have focused on different aspects – the leader themselves, the follower, the situation they are in, etc.

The starting place was with the leaders themselves and the concept that they had certain characteristics which made them successful leaders. The *trait approach* took no account of environment or followers and focused on the 'Hero' as already having the qualities within. This evolved to a *functional approach* which moved from the character of the leader and *who* they were to *what* they actually did in terms of the task needing to be done and the staff doing it. In the same way that Blake and Mouton suggested that a balance of functions was necessary for managerial success, John Adair (1983) suggested the same for his action-centred leadership. He specified that three things must be in balance – the task, the team and the individual – in order to achieve success. Stressing that it was still important to achieve the task outcome, Adair's balance was largely people led suggesting that this was a big 'what' to concentrate on. Like a three legged stool, if one of these legs was short, it simply would not stand.

Later approaches looked into the *style and behaviour* of the leaders themselves. Rather than look at who they were and what they did, these approaches focused on the *way* in which they did things and behaved towards their followers.

Many theorists devised models which encapsulate such styles and behaviour. Each of these theories outlines different levels of consulting and participation by the leader. From none at all and telling the follower what to do without consultation, to selling an idea with some respect for the feelings of the follower, to asking the follower for their opinions and incorporating them in the final picture, to getting the follower to make the decisions. This chapter is not designed to go fully into these different theories but I do recommend a 'deeper' read on these ideas in a good organisational behaviour text book.

From here a *contingency approach* emerged, much as with management theory – where again it was felt that there was no one way of leading that was appropriate to all situations and that the leader should react to the situation. *Situational approaches* brought in the concept of the follower and how their level of ability and readiness would affect the style of leadership used too.

Bernard Bass (1985) built on many of these concepts by introducing *transactional* and *transformational* aspects to leadership theory.

The transactional elements of leadership could be held as the task led ones and the transformational element would appear to be the holistic element of the individual and team if linked to the theories of John Adair.

Is leadership a mix of management and leadership skills or are the two distinctly different but both necessary?

Gary Yukl (2002) outlines that definitions of leadership differ in many respects in terms of influence and how it is exerted, by whom, the purpose and the outcome. He says: 'Most definitions of leadership reflect the assumption that it involves a process whereby intentional influence is exerted by one person over people to guide, structure, and facilitate activities and relationships in a group or organisation.' (p. 3.)

Evolving definitions

Yukl also gives a number of definitions from over half a century of leadership theory:

- 'the behavior of an individual . . . directing the activities of a group toward a shared goal.' (Hemphill and Coons 1957, in Yukl 2002, p. 7)
- 'the influential increment over and above mechanical compliance with the routine directives of the organisation.' (D. Katz & Kahn 1978, in Yukl 2002, p. 528)

- 'Leadership is a process of giving purpose (meaningful direction) to collective effort, and causing willing effort to be expended to achieve purpose.' (Jacobs and Jaques 1990, in Yukl 2002, p. 281)
- 'the ability to step outside the culture . . . to start evolutionary change processes that are more adaptive.' (E. H. Schein 1992, in Yukl 2002, p. 2)
- 'Leadership is the process of making sense of what people are doing together so that people will understand and be committed' (Drath and Palus 1994, in Yukl 2002, p. 4)

Where and how has this evolved? Note how the willingness of the follower increases over time as does the ability of the leader to relate the direction to the outside environment. Also note that leadership is seen to be in excess of management and to be more oriented towards the long term.

In all, leadership qualities include:

- The interpretation of external events by members
- The choice of objectives and strategies to pursue
- The motivation of members to achieve the objectives
- The mutual trust and co-operation of members
- The organisation of work activities
- The development of member skills and confidence
- The learning and Sharing of new knowledge by members
- The enlistment of support and co-operation from outsiders (Yukl 2002)

Whatever the leader does has an effect on the business, whether this be positive or indeed negative.

We will now go on to consider whether leaders and managers themselves are the same or different.

LEADERSHIP VERSUS MANAGEMENT

Warren Bennis (1989) initially promoted leadership at the expense of management. He listed these thoughts at the time, although his more recent writings favour a balance of the two skills sets.

- The manager administers; the leader innovates.
- The manager is a copy; the leader is an original.
- The manager maintains; the leader develops.
- The manager focuses on systems and structure; the leader focuses on people.
- The manager relies on control; the leader inspires trust.
- The manager has a short-range view; the leader has a long-range perspective.
- The manager asks how and when; the leader asks what and why.
- The manager has his eye on the bottom line; the leader has his eye on the horizon.
- The manager imitates; the leader originates.
- The manager accepts the status quo; the leader challenges it.

- The manager is a good soldier; the leader is his own person.
- The manager does things right; the leader does the right thing.

Bennis was not the only writer at this time to think this way. Leadership became the fashionable grail of the 1980s. Although it is put brusquely, here there is a more than definite split between what is leadership and what is management. Even more than hailing leadership as the better of the two, Bennis makes management appear markedly inferior.

Although this 1980s differentiated definition seems a bit insulting now, it does go some way to encouraging deeper thought about what a leader is, what a manager is and what it takes to contribute to high performance. Reading provocative material like this can really help us explore things more.

The BT Global Challenge – a very competitive round the world yacht race – was used recently to investigate what skills balance was necessary for success. The 14 skippers were interviewed as much for their people skills as their task management and the particular traits of the podium winners put forward as the key leadership/management traits necessary for success.

A detailed breakdown of personal attributes, management skills and leadership attributes were measured and compared with the position of the skippers in the race.

This study values both management and leadership, and emphasizes the value of both in the winners. It promotes the theory that a balance of personal, management and leadership qualities result in good performance.

This has been followed through by Stephen Covey (1989), who emphasises the importance of self, the individual and the team in good leadership. He uses Aesop's golden goose fable and stresses how important it is to look after the goose laying the golden egg rather than maintain a pure focus on the golden egg itself.

Daniel Goleman (1996) evolved positive self traits for understanding the emotions of others as well as self and drew them into the concept of emotional intelligence (EQ) in leadership. In more recent times there has been a fashionable focus on this softer side of leadership.

Goldsmith and Clutterbuck (1997) note that the original differentiation of leadership and management was well intentioned at the time but that it may have done companies a great disservice in making the two appear to be opposites. They suggest that generations of managers could have striven to be good leaders in the belief that managers are second class citizens. They do not think the two skills sets should be separated and that both are key to individual and corporate success.

Bob Garratt (1996) thinks that 'the fish rots from the head' and calls leadership 'directing'. He too thinks a balance of the two is crucial to success and introduces us to 'malicious obedience' where followers do as they are directed but that if they do it reluctantly they are not as productive as they would be if they owned the situation or actually wanted to do the task voluntarily.

Alan Hooper and John Potter (2000) split up the leadership traits and the management traits but come to the conclusion, like many above, that 'For organisations to be successful in today's environment of constant change it is necessary to have some people who are good at both. Whilst many organisations are well administered and well controlled, few have the appropriate vision, innovation and original thinking.'

From transactional and transformational leadership, Hooper and Potter believe that 'intelligent leadership' is actually *transcendent leadership* which is the act of engaging the emotional support of the followers.

One thing that does seem to be clear, and is agreed by most in the varied approaches, is the allocation of particular skills to the leader or manager. Management skills of an organisational nature and leadership skills of a directional/visionary nature seem to be largely agreed. The argument beyond that is which set is the better of the two or what actual balance of the two sets is key to success.

We here offer a mnemonic listing of the different management and leadership skills applied to a service business. Consider these as guidelines for more rounded best practice.

Management	
M	**M**onitor all staff activity. Do you know each individual's activity for the day/week etc.? Do you have an activity formula to work to, and do you follow it up?
A	**A**spire to be the best. Who do you want to emulate? Talk to the best managers and replicate their best actions.
N	**N**urture the colleague relationship. Work on and maintain your relationship with staff. Encourage their good relationship with each other.
A	**A**dhere to company procedures, systems and structures. Set best practice working patterns. Train staff on best use of procedures, systems, etc.
G	**G**rab the reins and control by direction. Let your staff see you are in control – they will feel secure. Constructively let them know the boundaries. Help structure their day efficiently.
E	**E**valuate your tactics for the short term. What measures for growth have you got in the next week? Are your short-term campaigns bringing results now?
M	**M**easure your performance. Are you performing to budget? Are you behind and how are you going to make it up?
E	**E**scalate. Speed up now to make up for poorer months. Use competitions to drive your team towards synergy. Create deadlines with a challenge!
N	**N**ourish your team now! Never take them for granted. What training and drive do they need now? Pinpoint areas for improvement and do something now! Make their more laborious tasks more interesting.
T	**T**ime manage effectively. Time is expensive, are you devoting it to the right things? Thank your staff regularly.

Leadership

L	**L**ead by example in your client/customer relationships. Do you set the pace and the standards?
E	**E**xplain yourself. Explain why things are necessary. Explain how the work/activity fits into the overall picture. Explain where you are going.
A	**A**dd your personality to what you do. Your individuality is precious and so is that of your staff. Allow room for creativity.
D	**D**evelop your staff and your relationship with them. Assess their career needs and help them achieve them. Allocate tasks which stretch your staff.
E	**E**valuate your strategy for the long term. What measures for growth have you got in the next year? Keep your eye on the horizon but remember to break down the trip there into manageable chunks.
R	**R**espond well to change with a positive attitude. Your staff will usually respond to things the way you do. Relay changes in a positive way to increase acceptance.
S	**S**how your trust. Allow the reins to relax a little and let your staff think. Flatter your staff by leaving important tasks with them.
H	**H**ave time for the person. Keep up with the emotional needs of the individual. Measure whether the personal needs of the individual are in line with those of the company.
I	**I**nspire your staff. Infect your staff with enthusiasm for their work. Give them fresh new ideas and empower them!
P	**P**assion. Lots of it. Believe in what you do and get your staff to. Put meaning into the making of money.

Summary

This chapter has introduced a balanced view of management and leadership with a view to encouraging the reader to check their own management/leadership potential or practice. By showing the evolution of thought, a range of ideas should provoke proactive thinking for the workplace. An open mind is encouraged and a wide range of reading is listed to encourage further personal development. With the clear theme of a high respect for others and their differences, the content encourages a considered approach for those entering the management workplace for the first time – not to mention being better prepared for an interview for just such a position – and encourages those in a position of authority already to question and examine their methods.

Divide your group of students/delegates into two. Have one half as managers and the other half as leaders. Set the room up for a lively debate and tackle the issue below.

MANAGER

v

LEADER

Debate Motion

This House believes leadership alone is the way forward

Alternatively take six of the Bennis points in the chapter and use these for active debate.

Adapt the mnemonics for best practice above to suit your working world. Print out on both sides of an A4 sheet and laminate. This can then be put in a desk drawer for reference.

Choose six texts from the list at the end of this chapter and comment on how each have tackled management and leadership. As a group compare ideas about the same texts.

CROSS CULTURAL COMMENT

In addition to incorporating the development needs of followers, it also follows that their cultural needs should be part of this process. How followers understand their part in the business and how much freedom they have to make decisions can be influenced by cultural background. Some cultures have a linear and unquestioning respect for a leader/manager and will need to be encouraged to enjoy the process of debate and to express their opinion. Other cultures will have a natural inclination to question.

References and further reading

Note: I have deliberately provided a large and wide list of reading covering classic and modern texts and different views. These are for you to choose from but the list is by no means a definitive one – add to it yourself with books you discover. My list is designed to merely start you off and to encourage you to read more widely on the subject which will help your future development. Happy reading.

(1998) *Harvard Business Review on Change*, Harvard Business School Publishing, Boston.

(1998) *Harvard Business Review on Leadership*, Harvard Business School Publishing, Boston.

(1998) *Harvard Business Review on Managing People*, Harvard Business School Publishing, Boston.

Adair, J. (1983) *Effective Leadership*, Gower.

Axelrod, A. (1999) *Patton on Leadership, Strategic Lessons for Corporate Warfare*, USA: Prentice Hall Press.

Bass, B. M. (1985) *Leadership and Performance Beyond Expectations*, New York: Free Press.

Beatty, J. (1998) *The World According to Drucker*, London: Orion Business Books.

Bennis, W. (1989) *On Becoming a Leader*, USA: Arrow.

Bennis, W. and Nanus, B. (1985) *Leaders*, New York: Harper & Row.

Benton, D. A. (2000) *How to Act like a CEO*, New York: McGraw Hill.

Boddy, D. and Buchanan, D. (1992) *Take the Lead*, London: Prentice Hall International (UK) Ltd.

Camus, A. (1969) *The Myth of Sisyphus and other Essays*, trans. Justin O'Brien, New York: Alfred Knopf.

Carnegie, D. (1953) *How to Win Friends and Influence People*, New York: Cedar World, Works Ltd.

Cooper, R. and Sawaf, A. (1998) *Executive EQ*, London: Texere.

Coulson-Thomas (1990) *Marketing Communications*, London: Heinnman Professional.

Covey, S. (1989) *The Seven Habits of Highly Effective People*, London: Franklin Covey.

Cranwell-Ward, J., Bacon, A. and Mackie, R. (2002) *Inspiring Leadership – Staying Afloat in Turbulent Times*. London: Thomson.

Dalai Lama, His Holiness the (1999) *Ancient Wisdom, Modern World*, Little, Brown & Company (UK).

Drucker, P. F. (1977) *People and Performance,* p. 28, Heineman.

Garratt, B. (1996) *The Fish Rots from the Head*, London: Harper Collins.

Gates, W. (1999) *Business @ The Speed of Thought,* Harmondsworth: Penguin Books.

Goldsmith, W. and Clutterbuck, D. (1997) *The Winning Streak Mark II*, London: Orion Business Books.

Goleman, D. (1996) *Emotional Intelligence*, London: Bloomsbury.

Hamel, G. and Prahalad, C. K. (1994) *Competing for the Future*, USA: Harvard Business School Press.

Handy, C. (1994) *The Empty Raincoat*, London: Arrow.

Handy, C. (1998) *The Hungry Spirit*, UK: Arrow Books.

Handy, C. (1999) *The New Alchemists*, London: Hutchinson Press.

Handy, C. (1999) *Understanding Organisations*, London: Penguin Business Management.

Hooper, A. and Potter, J. (2000) *Intelligent Leadership – Creating a Passion for Change*, Foreward by Warren Bennis, Random House Business Books.

Kakabadse, A. and Kakabadse, N. (1999) *Essence of Leadership*, London: Thomson Business Press.

Mullins, L. (2002) *Management and Organisational Behaviour*, Harlow: FT Prentice Hall.

Ohmae, K. (1982) *The Mind of the Strategist*, New York: McGraw Hill.

Porter, M. E. (1985) *Competitive Advantage: Creating and sustaining superior performance*, New York: The Free Press.

Reed, A. (2001) *Innovation in Human Resource Management*, UK: CIPD.

Ridderstrale, J. and Nordstrom, K. (2000) *Funky Business*, London: Bookhouse Publishing.

Singer, P. (1994) *Ethics*, Oxford: Oxford University Press.

Smith, D. (1998) *Developing People and Organisations*, London: CIMA Publishing.

Taffinder, P. (2000) *The Leadership Crash Course*, London: Kogan Page.

Tzu, S. (1991) *The Art of War*, Boston & London: Shambhala.

White, A. (1995) *Managing for Performance*, London: BCA.

Yukl, G. (2002) *Leadership in Organisations,* USA: Prentice Hall.

PART 6
IT SKILLS

At home as well as in the workplace, the use of information technology (IT) and information systems (IS) is universal. Software such as Microsoft® Office is a common and essential tool. The IT skills section will explain the main principles underlying IT and IS, and the basic concepts and techniques behind Microsoft® Office and related software. It will provide common sense advice and a range of techniques to support your learning.

In each chapter you will find tips throughout the text and exercises at the end of each section. The highlighting and reinforcing of these key items will act as an aide-memoire as you practise your skills and familiarise yourself with the jargon. In addition the companion website contains a glossary of terms and extra material to enhance this IT skills section. The attainment of these skills will support you throughout your life and career, and prepare you for an ever changing workplace. These techniques are the key to adaptability in lifelong learning and flexible working. You can dip in and out of the chapters and the website, and use each section to develop initial skills in a particular area.

The main aims of the IT skills section is that you should be able to:

- understand the basic principles and terms used in IT and IS
- undertake straightforward exercises in Microsoft® Office programs and related software.
- acquire the key skills needed in today's working and learning environments.

This section will support new students come from a range of backgrounds:

- school leavers
- those who work in industry and commerce
- those who have been away from the workplace for some time
- mature students

Whenever you embark on something new and different, you relate it to something you already know. You move from 'known' to 'unknown'. Working with Microsoft® Office or any other suite of programs requires tactics, especially if you are a new user. This section will enable you to take small steps using illustrated examples.

The chapters here allow you to experiment without getting bogged down with too much technical detail. They are suitable for all ages. Education is now a lifelong pursuit open to all.

Realistically it is not possible to learn word processing, spreadsheet techniques, presentation and database skills prior to enrolling onto a new course. What your tutor needs from you may be smartly presented documents and crisp presentations. In addition you may be required to get your head around figures and formulae, graphs and charts, and you may also be involved with the manipulation of data and databases. Therefore you need a starting point so that you can cope with the requirements of your course, whilst building up confidence to try something new. That is the way in which these chapters are designed.

Chapter 21 deals with making the best use of the electronic (e-) support mechanisms that exist within further and higher education, including on-line facilities and e-mail. Chapter 22 helps you to produce smart documents using Microsoft® Word. The next three chapters consider Microsoft® Excel, first in Chapter 23 as a data management tool, in Chapter 24 as a facilitator of graph and chart creation and in Chapter 25 as a manipulator of facts, figures, formulae and statistics. Chapter 26 looks at data capture and databases using Microsoft® Access, whilst finally Chapter 27 is concerned with producing simple but effective presentations using Microsoft® PowerPoint. Throughout the text, the key words used to manipulate data and found on toolbars will be shown in bold and underlined in the appropriate place, e.g. **Tools**.

A final point is to encourage you to always take advantage of free or low cost courses that are available to you at your college, university or through your workplace. Practice makes perfect and *you* 'can make a difference' to your life by enhancing your capabilities and enriching your experience. The ball is in your court!

Susan Bailey

CHAPTER 21
Electronic organisation

Learning objectives

- To understand how to have access to and engage with electronic support materials
- To create an independent e-mail address and deal with electronic forms
- To maximise the use of on-line facilities and the Internet
- To facilitate the organisation of electronic files

Introduction

The advance in the use of electronic support can affect you in two ways. If you are confident with technology you will explore every e-avenue and fully utilise all of the facilities available. However, if you are a more novice user you may look blankly at the computer screen and panic!

Much of a student's life is punctuated by panic! This becomes particularly acute when deadlines are looming. If you are well organised from the start, it will leave you room and time to concentrate on assignment deadlines. This chapter will help to support you through your initial encounters with electronic support materials and e-mail.

The start of a new course can be very daunting; a new regime, new experiences, new friends and for many of you, a complete change of environment. All schools have an information technology (IT) suite and most people have the use of a personal computer (PC) at home, but the move into the further or higher educational environment shifts the responsibility of engaging and using the facilities provided, firmly into your own hands. One of the most important yet often marginalised activities at the beginning of your course is the induction process. The amount of information delivered at induction can be overwhelming. However, take full advantage of the sessions offered and be prepared to revisit the induction topics over the first few months, as they offer valuable techniques and information that will support you throughout your course.

> **TIP**
>
> Do not miss any of the induction topics offered and always note the contact details of the key tutors.

FIRST STEPS FIRST – E-MAIL

Your success depends in part on being able to access and use electronic facilities. The key to opening this more specialised 'electronic environment' is usually via a user name and password, although not all areas need this. Your user name and password will usually be allocated to you in the first week; once you have these details try to enter and use the on-line facilities as soon as possible. Set aside time at the very beginning of the course to ensure you are able to access the course materials, learning resources and e-mail. Also be sure to understand how your tutor will contact you outside the normal class times and how you can contact them. A wise hour or two spent finding your way around the virtual world early on will prevent days of anguish as course work and exam dates loom.

> **TIP**
>
> Remember that the accurate spelling of e-mail addresses is essential or they will 'bounce back' undelivered.

If you do not have access to a PC at home or work, you will need to use a local library or the campus facilities. Handwritten assignments, assessments and reports are rarely acceptable these days. So *you* need to get access to a computer at the critical times, that is when work is due to be researched or handed in for assessment. Also practise your typing because this simple skill is essential and it will hold back your creativity if you spend ages looking for the keys. Do not let the technology stand in the way of the wealth of thoughts and ideas you want to commit to 'electronic paper'.

Many institutes insist that you submit a soft copy of your work (e.g. on a disc or data pen). Sometimes you will be able to submit work directly to your tutor electronically. So from the beginning of your course you need to have an e-mail address and the skill to produce and deliver electronic copies.

> **TIP**
>
> Make sure your user name and password for your e-mail work from the start. Get help straight away if you have a problem.

A college e-mail address and password may be directly linked to your student number and other unique details. Once allocated it ensures you can be contacted quickly and that you can communicate. If your institute does not allocate e-mail addresses you need to sign up to a facility like MSN® Hotmail and create an e-mail address for yourself.

E-mail addresses

Your e-mail address and mobile phone will be essential contact points during your time as a student.

- Make sure your own e-mail address is meaningful
- Be aware that your preferred e-mail name is probably in use already
- Be ready with an alternative e-mail address for yourself, perhaps linked to your course or university to give a more unusual mix. E.g. beckituon@hotmail.com
- Alternatively use special characters like underscore (becki_elliott) in the name becki_elliott@hotmail.com
- Avoid e-mail addresses such as 'Sexylegs' or 'little diamond' which are not appropriate in either an educational or work based environment
- Think of a password you will remember, but that is not too obvious
- If you are given a mobile phone as a contact number do not text phrases such as 'it's me here!'; if you do not leave your name do not expect an answer
- Immediately inform the student office of changes to your telephone number or address

---

TIP

Ensure your e-mail address is meaningful and not too long. Choose a password you can remember and remember that it is usually case sensitive.

Signing up to e-mail and using forms in general

There are many providers of e-mail addresses. You can use one you know or you can try MSN® Hotmail. To sign up type the address www.hotmail.co.uk into the box labelled Address and the following will appear, when you request an e-mail account.

After deciding to sign up (Figure 21.1) you will be requested to choose an e-mail service. Some are free and some are not, so read the small print before choosing your option (Figure 21.2). Normally a simple free service is all you will need to start with.

The next step will be to fill in a number of registration boxes.

TIP

Make sure you click into the box before you begin to type in your details. It is disappointing to look up and find nothing in the box!

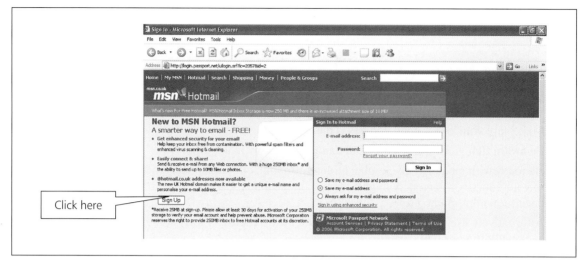

Figure 21.1

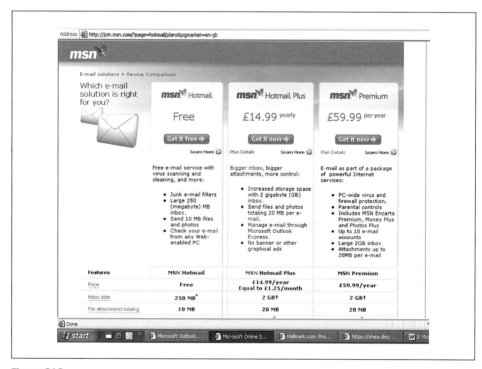

Figure 21.2

On-line registration forms often have compulsory boxes that need to be filled in with first name, surname, etc. (Figure 21.3). If you submit the form and you have missed compulsory items out, the form will come back to the screen with an error message to show the details you have missed.

Figure 21.3

TIP
If you see an asterisk * next to a box on a form it usually denotes a compulsory entry at this point.

Forms often have drop down boxes to give a choice, e.g. the box **Country/Region** shown in Figure 21.3. However, if you fill in a box and then immediately scroll down the page, the box can roll over to another choice.

A friend who booked her flights on-line ended up going to Almerai instead of Alicante. The reason was that she accidentally scrolled down the page using her mouse and this caused the destination to roll to the next option. She did not notice the mistake until after she had paid!! Consequently she flew to the new destination for a holiday with her family, as it was cheaper than changing the booking!

TIP
Beware the scrolling mouse.

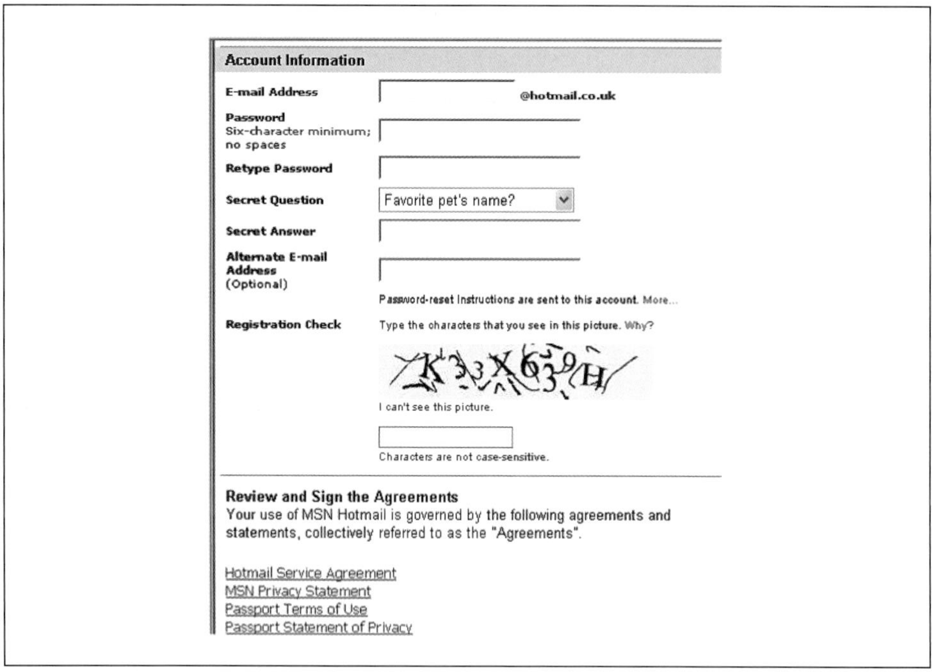

Figure 21.4

At one point in setting up an e-mail address you will be asked to think up a password (Figure 21.4). Remember that passwords are sometimes case sensitive, so when typing them in be aware of this. They are also notoriously difficult to remember, you almost need a theme!

TIP

To keep passwords simple, one idea is to choose an obscure but memorable word, then add a date format to it e.g. paris0505. The date reflects when it was created. The word in this case paris can then be used over and over again with different dates and as a reminder you note down p0505.

With the emphasis on security, questions are now asked to ascertain that on-line facilities are being accessed by the correct person. To do this specific questions are asked when an account is set up, the answers to which should only be known by the user. The question that used to be asked was 'What was your mother's maiden name?', but now you are more likely to be asked to supply a favourite town or a pet's name. These questions will be referred to when you try and gain access online to make sure you are the right person. On the form shown in Figure 21.4 (as part of a registration check) you are asked to type in random figures as seen on the screen. This is a new type of request that is a security measure to make sure the form is being filled in by a human and not electronically!

The final part of this type of registration is the agreement section, which should be read carefully before clicking on 'I agree'. It is well worth printing out the agreement in case you need to refer to it later.

Using e-mail – a few tricks worth noting

Shortcut keys E-mail provides a fast and efficient way of communicating with friends, relatives, work colleagues and fellow students. Microsoft® Outlook is a popular platform for reading and replying to e-mails and provides many of the facilities that are available in Word for manipulating the text. However, it is not the only platform you will come across when using e-mails. Other platforms will allow you to send and receive e-mails, build up a list of contacts and attach files to your messages, but may not have all of the sophistication that Microsoft® Outlook offers.

To help manage your text on e-mail in a more limited environment, it is worth noting that keyboard commands can be used instead. There is a whole range of these commands known as shortcut keys and they can speed up many operations. To find them, click on **Help** and type in 'shortcut keys'. For example by highlighting the text you want to copy, paste or cut, you can use the following shortcuts (Figure 21.5) to manipulate your text:

Action	Keyboard command
Cut	Ctrl X
Copy	Ctrl C
Paste	Ctrl V
Select All	Ctrl A
Undo	Ctrl Z

Figure 21.5

Opening attachments When you receive attachments by e-mail you can click on them with the right hand mouse button. This will give you a number of options including **Open**, **Print** and **Save As** (Figure 21.6). If you use these options, the file can be manipulated as needed. In most environments it is quicker and more straightforward if you save the file first, that is **Save As** and then **Open** afterwards.

TIP

Some files such as pictures and documents with clip art can take quite a while to upload or download, so be patient.

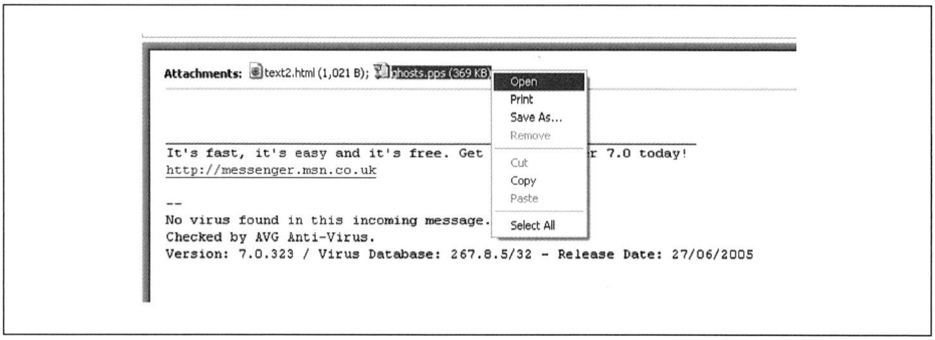

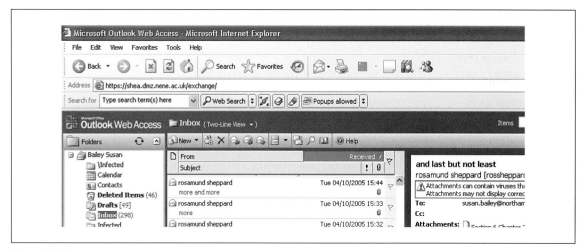

Figure 21.6

Figure 21.7

Finding specific messages The e-mail layout in Figure 21.7 uses Microsoft® Outlook Web Access. At the top of the messages are the words **From**, **Subject** and **Received**; if you want to find e-mails from one particular person you can highlight one e-mail from that person and click **From** and all the e-mails from them will be displayed (Figure 21.7). This also has the effect of putting the emails in alphabetic order. Similarly if you are looking for e-mails received on a certain date, click on an e-mail with that date and click **Received**. This has the effect of putting all the e-mails in date order.

There are numerous facilities available in an e-mail environment and it is well worth investigating some of the basic ones, like search facilities and spell checkers, as they will help you to work smartly with e-mail. If you see an icon and you are not sure what it does, hovering over it with the cursor will give you a clue, for example **Spelling** as shown in Figure 21.8.

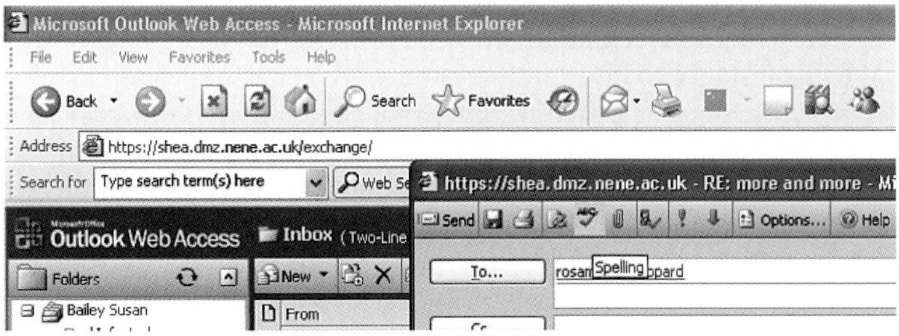

Figure 21.8

In addition there are a range of other options, for example:

- adding an e-mail address to a **Contact** list
- putting e-mails into **Folders**
- setting up colour ways to show the source of the e-mail
- prioritising e-mails that you send, e.g. private, confidential
- deleting an e-mail
- searching through e-mails for a particular keyword
- adding dates to the **Calendar**
- withdrawing an e-mail

The facilities and options will be different according to how and where you are accessing your e-mails. Once you have mastered the initial sending and receiving options, investigate these other options at your leisure. There will probably be a short course available at your college or university which will go over the most useful techniques.

INTERNET

The internet offers millions of sites for you to explore and search through. When you are on the internet you will probably be using Internet Explorer© although other platforms exist like Mozilla Firefox©. These platforms interpret how the website will look and then display it on the screen. Accordingly there are different icons at the top of the page to help navigate the websites. The key ones are the green **Back** arrow, which takes you back to where you came from and the red cross which will stop the search.

TIP
Position the cursor over all of the icons to find out what facilities they offer.

Searching for websites

There are many tricks and techniques involved in effectively searching for websites. It is best in the first instance to find a well-trusted search engine such as Google, Yahoo! Ask or MSN, which all offer search facilities that cover millions of websites.

The search engine name may have different endings (e.g. .co.uk; .com) and home pages that have a different flavour according to the country e.g. www.yahoo.co.uk for the UK and Ireland (Figure 21.9) and www.yahoo.com for the US version. The web address that locates the website is also known as the Universal Resource Locator (URL). By using a website, millions of web pages and images can be found from all over the web or just from the UK. You can make a choice of **Web** or **Image**, **the Web** or **in UK** (Figure 21.9) before you begin the search, and this then limits the selection.

Even more important is to pinpoint what it is you are really looking for. For instance, if I were looking for myself on the net and were to put in Susan Bailey Northampton everything with the words Susan, Bailey and Northampton would come up. Some 4,000,000 sites! Most of them not related to me.

If the search is narrowed down to the UK only, then there are 4310 sites and the top seven all relate to me! (Figure 21.10.)

But if the search is as a string in inverted commas (Figure 21.11) 'Susan Bailey Northampton' then only nine matches come up. All are connected to me, however some important ones have been left out, because the search is looking for the whole string within the website, not just the odd words. There are other more sophisticated techniques to try and these can be explored as you become more skilled at searching.

It is also interesting to note the spelling of certain words. If you are searching for a coloured glass panel from America, then do not forget to use the word 'color' as the word colour may limit your choice to UK suppliers only.

Another important facility is the **Favourites**. Once you find a website you like, use **Add to Favorites** and then you can always find it: Figure 21.12.

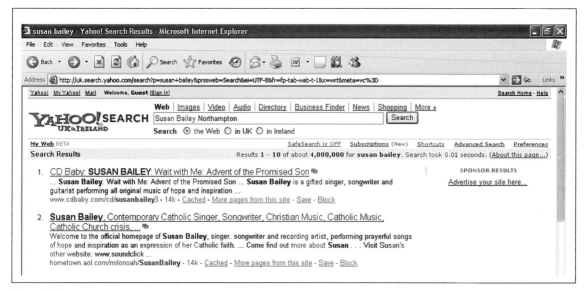

Figure 21.9

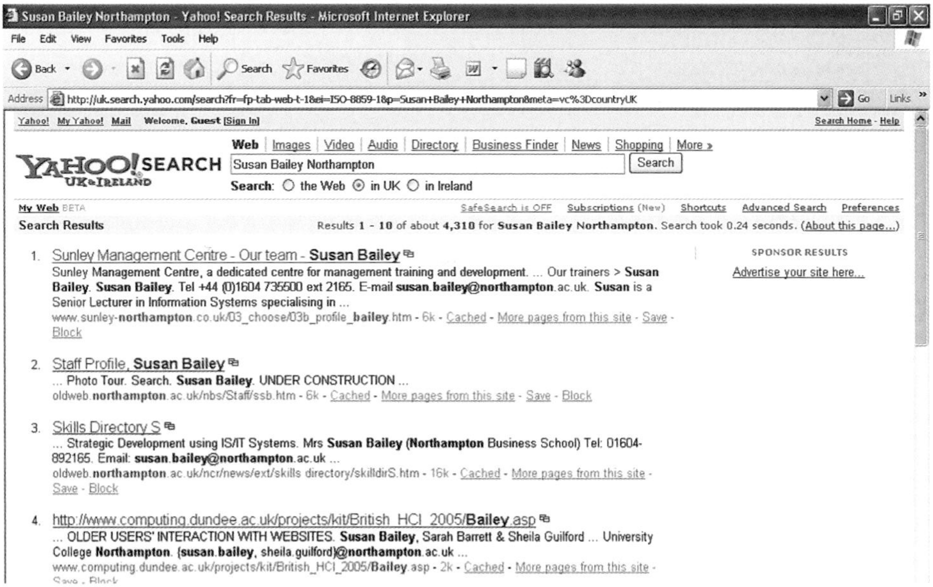

Figure 21.10

Figure 21.11

Finally, when you get round to using the Web to support your work, remember to reference the source. If you note it down straight away you will not have to access it again or remember where you found it.

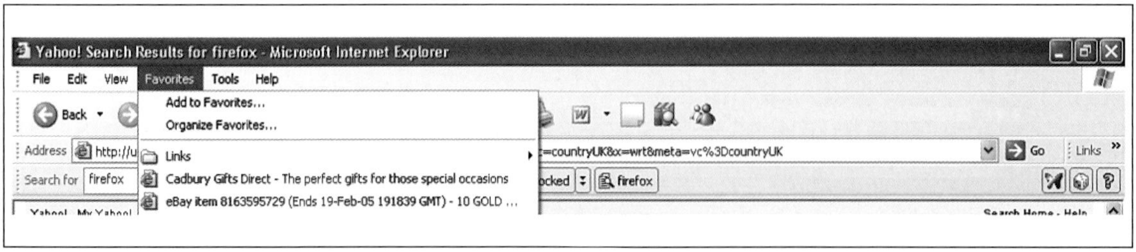

Figure 21.12

> **TIP**
>
> When using websites ask yourself: Is this a trustworthy site to use? Is it genuine, accurate and reputable?

To reference a website using the Harvard referencing system, do so in the following way: *Title of website* (year as appearing on site) [online]. [Date accessed]. Available from World Wide Web : <url of site>

WEBSITE AND LEARNING SUPPORT

College or university website

Explore and access the website of your institute and investigate the material and links available to you via the 'student portal' (Figure 21.13). This portal is 'a website that provides links to information and other websites' (Encarta dictionary ND) and can be a real boon once you become familiar with the contents.

Support can include:

- Student Support Services
- IT facility details and leaflets
- Course material links
- Timetables, events and exam calendars
- Maps and places to go

There will be numerous links, but some more specialised links may require a user name and password. Early on investigate the learning resources; there may be on-line facilities (e-books, journals), books, CDs and other support for your course easily available either on campus or from home.

Making the best use of your Student Portal or website

Your main priority as a student is to remain sane and unstressed for as long as possible. So why traipse into your institute when you could probably do the great majority of your communication, course access, 'housekeeping' and research from your home or local library PC? There is a list of questions at the end of the chapter for you to ask

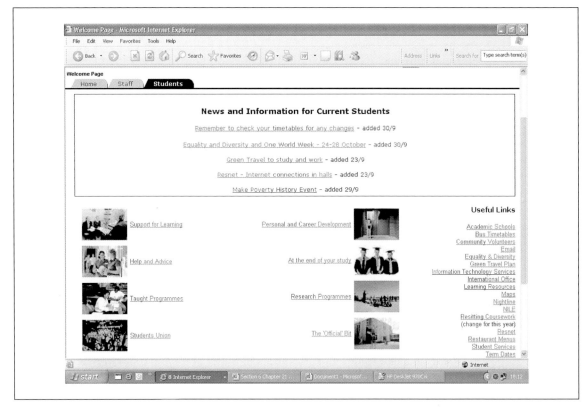

Figure 21.13 Student portal

Source: www.northampton.ac.uk

your course leader or information technology (IT) help desk once you have enrolled. You may find many of these are answered during Induction Week, but with so much to take in it is important to go through the check list before your course starts.

TIP
Do not be afraid to ask for help and advice.

HOUSEKEEPING – FILES AND FOLDERS

Manual filing

From the beginning of your course, there will be a wealth of new material presented to you! You will have lectures and seminars and to support these there will be handouts, suggested reading and electronic notes, for you to absorb and to collate. Some of these materials will be used in the classroom, some will form the basis of an assessment and some will be needed for exams.

Universities and colleges now give students access to information technology (IT) and information systems (IS) via a range of outlets, for example specialised computer rooms, suites of campus PCs and home access. As a new student you will usually be given an introductory lesson and instructions on how to access the facilities and the materials – take full advantage of these courses.

Managing such a wealth of material can be a real challenge. To minimise distress it is wise to draw up a plan detailing how you will file it and then keep to it. In terms of organisation it is very much like project management, with the main aim being to *successfully complete the course by the end of the academic timeframe*. From this viewpoint, colour coding each element of the course and labelling the course materials with the date can be a good first step. A red file for twentieth century history and a blue file for the Roman Conquest can help you to locate items quickly. However, the main concern of this section is to 'file' and access electronic material.

Electronic filing

In electronic filing, a folder is denoted by a yellow icon as shown in Figure 21.14. It can hold numerous files, for example Microsoft® Word documents, websites, Microsoft® Excel documents. You may not yet be familiar with these types of file names. Figure 21.14 shows the most popular types; here they are displayed as tiles. In other formats they will have an extension added to them like .ppt or .xls which also defines the type of file and therefore its contents.

To create a new folder look for the small folder at the top that looks as if the sun is rising behind it and click on it.

When you select the option to create a **New Office Document** make sure that you save it in a relevant folder with a meaningful **File <u>n</u>ame**. For example if you are doing history you could have a folder dedicated to *Roman History* and another dedicated to *Women in the 20th Century*, you can then file the relevant documents in separate folders, for example *Lesson Plan*, *Seminar Notes*.

TIP

After opening a new document save it straightaway with a meaningful file name in a relevant folder

---

If you want to use an old document and make changes to it, but keep the original, then use the **Save <u>A</u>s** option that is available under **<u>F</u>ile** (Figure 21.15).

Eventually you will build up a number of different folders and subfolders and these can be viewed in various ways.

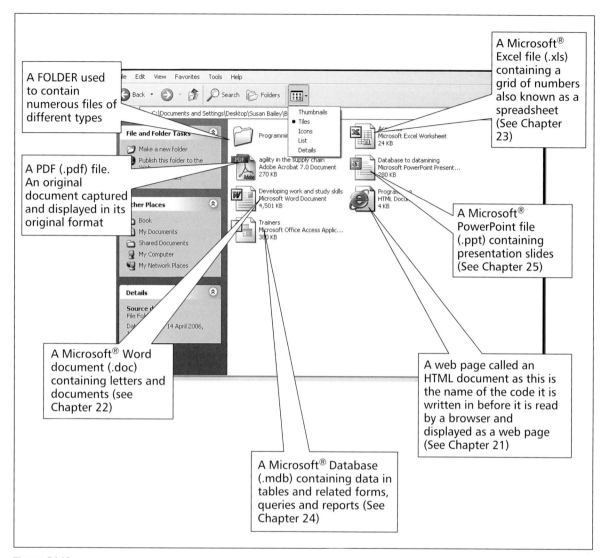

A FOLDER used to contain numerous files of different types

A PDF (.pdf) file. An original document captured and displayed in its original format

A Microsoft® Excel file (.xls) containing a grid of numbers also known as a spreadsheet (See Chapter 23)

A Microsoft® PowerPoint file (.ppt) containing presentation slides (See Chapter 25)

A Microsoft® Word document (.doc) containing letters and documents (see Chapter 22)

A web page called an HTML document as this is the name of the code it is written in before it is read by a browser and displayed as a web page (See Chapter 21)

A Microsoft® Database (.mdb) containing data in tables and related forms, queries and reports (See Chapter 24)

Figure 21.14

If you have the Microsoft® Windows Explorer option the folders will be displayed as in Figure 21.16.

From the main folder the + and − signs indicate whether the subfolders are open or closed. You can open or close the folders by clicking on folders. The term 'expanded' is used if they are open (−) and 'collapsed' if they are closed (+) (see Figure 21.16).

You can view the files in other ways. To change the view, select one of the options as shown in Figure 21.17.

For example, selecting **Details** will show the file name, size, type and date modified (Figure 21.18).

Because it is possible to create different types of files, for example Microsoft® Word, Microsoft® Excel, Microsoft® PowerPoint, etc; you should make sure you are

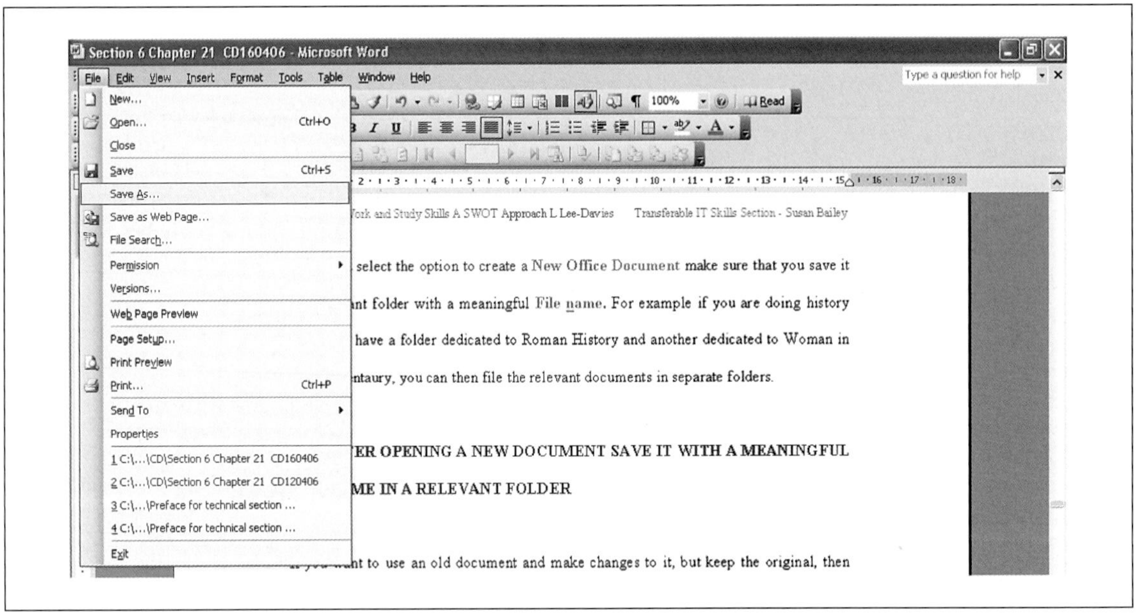

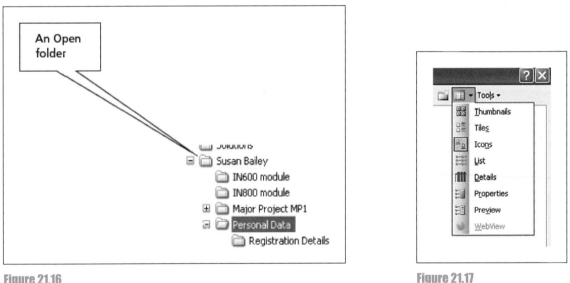

Figure 21.15

Figure 21.16

Figure 21.17

viewing the file in the right environment when retrieving them. For example if you try to open a Microsoft® PowerPoint document when you are in Microsoft® Word then the Microsoft® PowerPoint document will not display correctly.

Make sure that you select **All files** (Figure 21.19), when looking for files in general, but use the drop down option if looking for a specific type of file e.g. **All PowerPoint Presentations**. When you have located the document click on it and it will open.

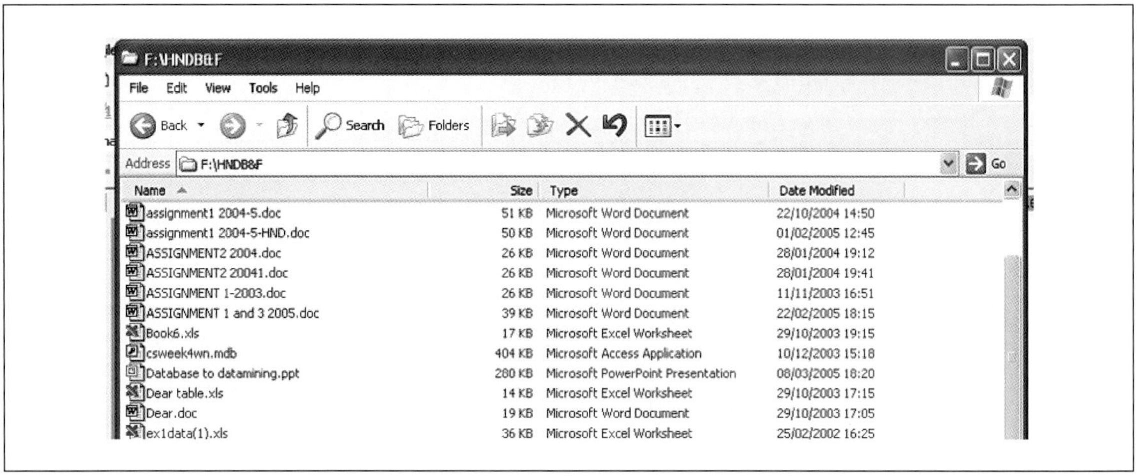

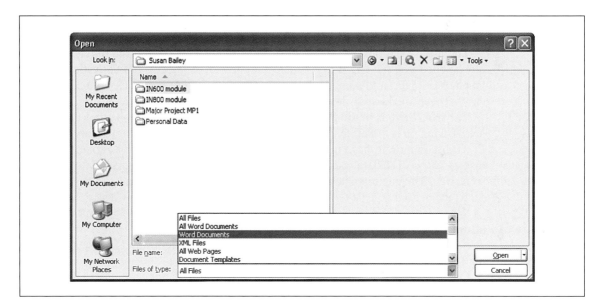

Figure 21.18

Figure 21.19

TIP

When you are working on a specific document, for instance a Microsoft® Word document, you may try to open another file at the same time, but remember if the file you want to open is not a Microsoft® Word document you will get a strange result.

Folders and files can exist in all sorts of locations, inside the computer, on floppy disks, on the network, on CDs, etc. When selecting the **My Computer** option from the **Start** menu the various locations are displayed (Figure 21.20).

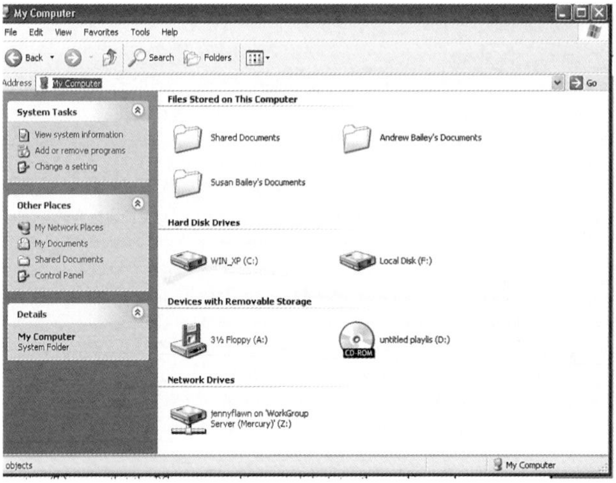

Figure 21.20

The usual locations are: the floppy disk (usually labelled A:), the hard drive (usually labelled C:), the CD drive (usually labelled D: as above), the data stick (usually labelled E: or F:) and sometimes a networked server (Z: in this case but letters can vary). These are all areas where documents can be written to or read from.

The hard drive is in the PC itself; the network option (Z:) means that the PC you are working on is linked to other machines and storage areas, remote from your own PC. It is common to have networked systems in universities and workplaces. Floppy disks, CDs, DVDs, data sticks and cameras can be attached or inserted into the PC in some way. The memory stick (F:) is a particularly handy device and was developed by Sony; it can hold at least ten times more information than a floppy disk.

When you are looking for a data stick, buy the one with the largest memory you can afford and for security wear it round your neck. That is what the string is for. You can also rename or adapt a stick or pen by clicking with the right-hand mouse and selecting **Rename**.

On newer PCs the memory stick (Figure 21.21) can be plugged into a USB port at the front of the machine (Figure 21.22). Otherwise the memory stick can be connected through the USB port at the back of the PC via a cable (Figure 21.23).

Security of your work

When working on a *major* piece of work remember the following:

1 Make two copies of your work, preferably in two different places

2 Save the modified version with a date and time indicator on the file name and keep at least two versions perhaps even three when you write your dissertation.

3 Back up all of your key files onto a CD or memory stick regularly and store away from your PC. This allows you to restore your files in case of loss, robbery or a major fire.

4 Clear out your files when the work is complete.

©iStockphoto.com/Richard Lister

Figure 21.21

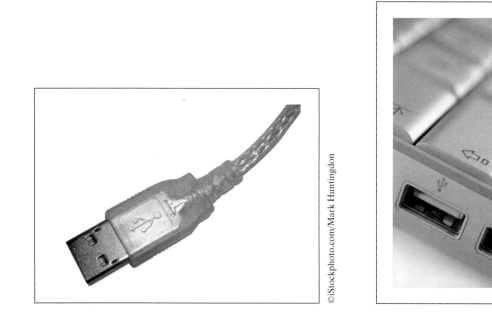

©iStockphoto.com/Mark Huntingdon

Figure 21.22 USB cable

©iStockphoto.com/Liv Friis-Larsen

Figure 21.23 Slot

TIP

If after all this clever filing you still cannot find your work, use the search option by selecting search from the start menu. Then look for a key word in the document! (Figure 21.24)

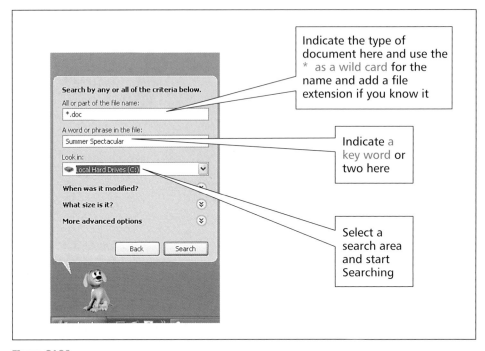

Figure 21.24

Summary

Set aside time at the very beginning of the course to ensure you are able to access the course materials, learning resources and e-mail. An hour or two spent at the outset will prevent days of anguish as course work and exam dates loom. The key to opening 'the electronic world' is a user name and password. Ascertain the e-mail address and password allocated to you by your institute and if one is not available set up your own e-mail.

If you do not have access to a personal computer (PC) at home or work, you will need to use a local library or the campus facilities. Investigate how to get the best out of e-mail and the web, so that you can use them to support your studies and your social life.

To prevent panic, facilitate the organisation of your electronic files and maximise the use of on-line facilities. Always investigate the learning resources that are available and be aware of the on-line facilities and the CDs/DVDs that support your course. Access the website of your institute and investigate the material and support available to you via the 'student portal' or university website.

The university and college world is changing. Sometimes you feel very much alone in a virtual world, but consider it to be your passport to success. Achieve a work–life balance as a student and have fun!

Check out which of these facilities are available **on-line** and how you can gain access. If they are not on-line, find out where can they be obtained.

1 Section 1 – Personal information
   a. student handbook
   b. personal e-mail address and how it is accessed
   c. course details and documents
   d. course notes
   e. personal timetable
   f. location of assessment results
   g. exam timetables
   h. location of exam results
   i. personal development portfolio

2 Section 2 – Discover details about
   a. Student Union
   b. skills workshops and lectures in addition to my course
   c. IT courses
   d. volunteering
   e. the local area and events
   f. campus activities

3 Section 3 – Find out how to get access on-line to
   a. disability support
   b. personal and financial advice
   c. advice and contact points when the unexpected happens and studying and coping with the workload become difficult

4 Section 4 – Check out the learning resources available on-line
   a. can I renew my library books or order a book remotely?
   b. where do I have access to on-line research materials, journals, papers, etc.?
   c. what other formats of research material are available – CD, DVD?
   d. Are the lectures recorded or available remotely by videoconferencing?
   e. Do electronic book lists exist and is their an e-book library?

Set up an independent e-mail address, send an e-mail and access the reply.

Create a contact list and add items to your calendar.

Carry out a search on a search engine e.g. Yahoo! for your own name. Narrow down the search so that you have a manageable number of hits to look through. Investigate other features such as **Advanced Search** and **Shortcuts** (see Figures 21.9 to 21.11).

TASK 5

Create a new document on Microsoft® Word with your contact details on it. Save it with the name *Contact details* in a folder called *Personal.*

TASK 6

Look at file formats and check how they are displayed as thumbnails, tiles, icons, lists, details, properties and with a preview (see Figure 21.17).

TASK 7

Invest in a data pen and plug it into the USB port of a computer that has the Windows XP® Operating System software installed on it. Save your document on the data pen with same file and folder name as above.

Reference

MSN Encarta Encyclopedia [online] [Accessed 7 September 2005] htttp://encarta.msn.com/

CHAPTER 22
Dynamic documents

- To establish a working environment supportive of efficient and effective document production
- To select a range of techniques to enhance report documents
- To create a table of contents for a report

Learning objectives

Each new generation of Microsoft® Word increases the desktop capabilities of the user and also serves to pre-empt or 'wizard' in a new set of options. This often overwhelms the user and there is probably no one user who has explored all of the available capabilities. The emphasis of this section will be the manipulation and presentation of data using Microsoft® Word as the tool.

Introduction

This chapter will support you by providing the skills needed to produce dynamic documents with the minimum of effort. It does not aim to take you through word processing techniques in detail, more to offer a starting point for further work.

There are numerous publications and a wealth of courses that can provide in-depth skills and enhanced learning; however, as a student, time is short and deadlines loom. Increasingly the manager of today has to cope with the complexities of word processing and spreadsheet management whilst still managing. The key to smart delivery is to increase awareness of the capabilities of the software programs and to produce meaningful outputs at the right level.

Your emphasis and priority are to provide assignments, reports and presentations in a way that gives maximum impact. These skills can and will be further developed over time, but taking the plunge is the key.

Until you reach the dissertation or final report stage of your course, the normal expectation would be the production of a number of pieces of work of around 3000 words. It is easy to get bogged down with layout and presentation, sometimes at the expense of the main document, so the best practice is to set up your document at the beginning, then saving it and printing it out at the end becomes more straightforward.

TIP

Set up your document and save it straight away with a meaningful file name before you begin.

DOCUMENT SET UP

New document

Having selected an option to create a new blank document, you should have a page similar to the one in Figure 22.1. It is important that you have the option to use the toolbars shown. These toolbars may not be present at the start and should be added in at an early stage.

The screens shown in this chapter are for the Microsoft® Office Word package and the version is Microsoft® Word 2003. The word processing software or version that is available to you at college, university or at home may be slightly different and you will have to experiment and use the **Help** facility to establish whether you can activate the same facilities.

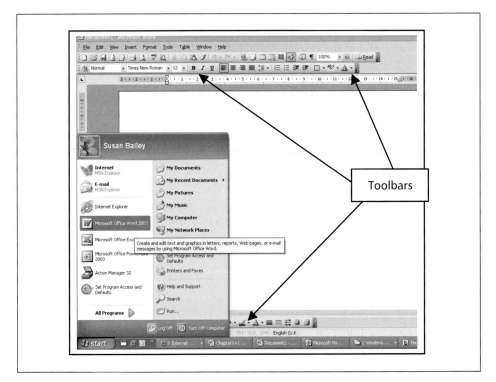

Figure 22.1

Key points

The most important points to consider when producing a document are to:

- Allow background saves and AutoRecovery.
- Make sure the words are spelt correctly
- Activate the Spell Checker to the UK English and not the American version
- Effectively enhance and improve the text content and appearance
- Insert page breaks
- Set quotes in *italics*
- Produce even text, correctly double or 1.5 spaced
- Create distinctive heading and side headings
- Insert a contents page
- Insert page numbers, headers and footers on each page
- Add in symbols, pictures, diagrams and screen shots as appropriate
- Give the report a distinctive front page
- Check and insert the word count

SETTING UP THE BASICS

Toolbars

At this point the document is open and you are ready to go. The three toolbars high-lighted in Figure 22.1 will allow you to create very smart documents. To set these up:

- Go to **View**, **Toolbars** and then select the ones shown on the list in Figure 22.2. As you click on each one, they will appear around your document.
- Tick the Ruler which runs along the top and the side of the page.

Autorecovery

Ensure that your AutoRecover facility and the background saves options are enabled (Figure 22.3):

- Go to **Tools** and then to **Options** and select the tab **Save**.
- '**Save AutoRecovery every**' appears. This is an option which allows the data to be saved every few minutes. Select the appropriate number of minutes between automatic saves.
- **Allow background saves** should also be ticked.

Manipulation and enhancement of the document content

The task now begins in earnest. One important consideration at the beginning is the naming and saving of your document (see Chapter 21). When you click on **File** the

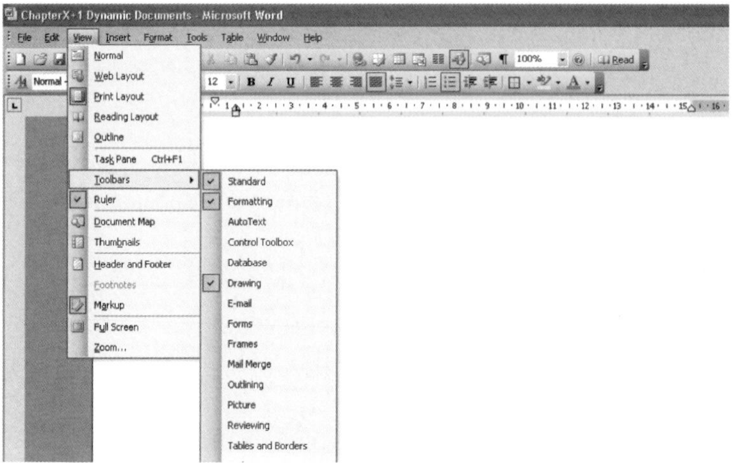

Figure 22.2

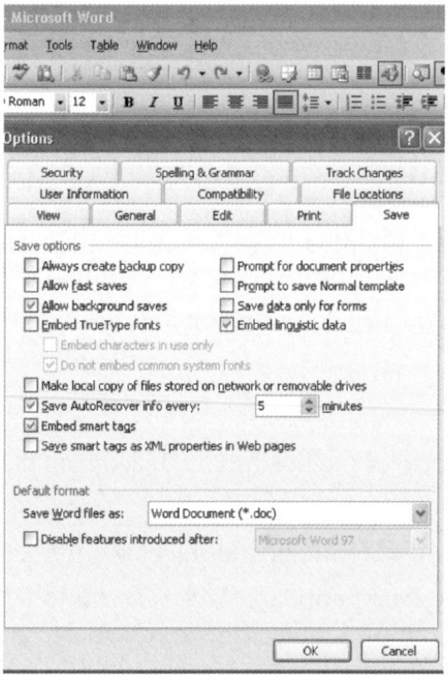

Figure 22.3

option to **Save** and **Save As** are shown. Create a meaningful title for your document and **Save** it in a **Folder** of similar work. After that click **Save** or press **Ctrl** and **S** on a regular basis to make sure you keep up to date with the changes. Do not rely wholly on AutoSave.

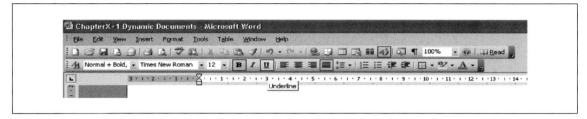

Figure 22.4

Manipulation techniques and the use of icons

We will now detail and explain the techniques for text manipulation and the use of the main icons on the toolbar. Note that some icons look grey (as in Figure 22.4) when you see them on the toolbar, for example the scissors used to indicate cut text. The reason for is that this facility is not available at this point. In this case, you cannot cut text unless you have highlighted it, which is why it is currently not available.

> **TIP**
>
> If you position your cursor over the icons on the toolbar a word or phrase will appear that indicates the function provided, e.g. Underline (Figure 22.4).

On the formatting toolbar (Figure 22.4) the **B will make the text Bold**, *I will Italicise the text and* <u>U will Underline it</u>. These are important when setting up a document. For instance, within the text you may have used quotes, using italics and quotation marks help to emphasis the detail of the quote. Whenever you need to highlight text:

- position the cursor over the beginning of the text
- hold the left hand button of the mouse down
- drag along the text highlighting it.

Once highlighted, the change (e.g. setting to bold) can be activated. If you find dragging the cursor along the text is not accurate enough (i.e. when you want to highlight the middle of a word) then position the cursor at the beginning of the section, hold down the up arrow ⇧ on the keyboard (**Shift** key) and then click along the text using the right arrow → or the left arrow ← to select the letters, until the section is highlighted. Similarly the upward ↑ and downward ↓ arrows can select text sentence by sentence, up and down the document.

Text colour, highlighting and display size

Also on the formatting toolbar (Figure 22.4) you can select icons that change the size of the text on the screen, change text colour and allow highlighting. Experiment with these as appropriate.

Symbols

Also investigate the insertion of a symbol. It is often useful to have access to symbols, for example a $\frac{1}{2}$ or a © sign or € (euro). If you require a symbol, go to **Insert**, **Symbol** and then choose from the range offered.

Bullets and numbering

To give further clarity to a document, bullets or numbers can be added as appropriate. To add these to a document select the relevant icon from the formatting toolbar.

To remove them click on the icon again and they will disappear. Individual bullets and numbers are offered in a variety of formats and by clicking on the bullet or number with the right-hand mouse button and selecting **Bullets and Numbering**, a number of different versions will be displayed and can be inserted. You can use the **Customize** option to make further modifications, for example a different colour button.

Spelling and grammar

When you begin to type your document, it is very useful to know if the spelling and grammar is correct. To set up an automatic check (Figure 22.5):

- Click on **Tools** and **Options** from the menu.
- Choose the tab which refers to **Spelling & Grammar** and make sure the essential options are ticked (Figure 22.6), e.g.
  - **Check spelling as you type**
  - **Always suggest corrections**
- In this example **Ignore words in UPPERCASE** has been ticked. Click in the box to remove the tick as it should not be set. This is because many documents use uppercase letters in the text and it is often these words that slip through misspelt.

There is a wealth of options to choose from in this section, so as you gain confidence check them out and make changes as necessary.

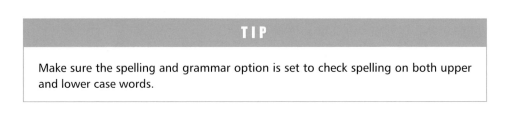

TIP

Make sure the spelling and grammar option is set to check spelling on both upper and lower case words.

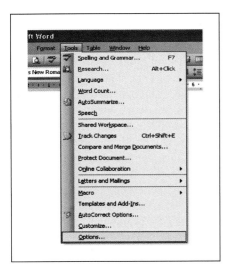

Figure 22.5

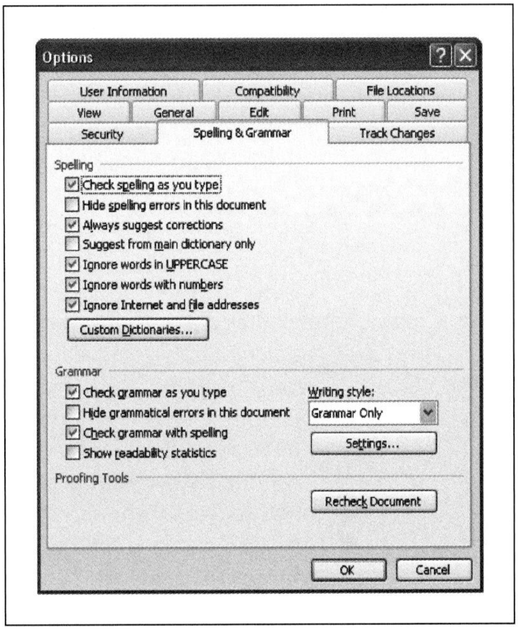

Figure 22.6

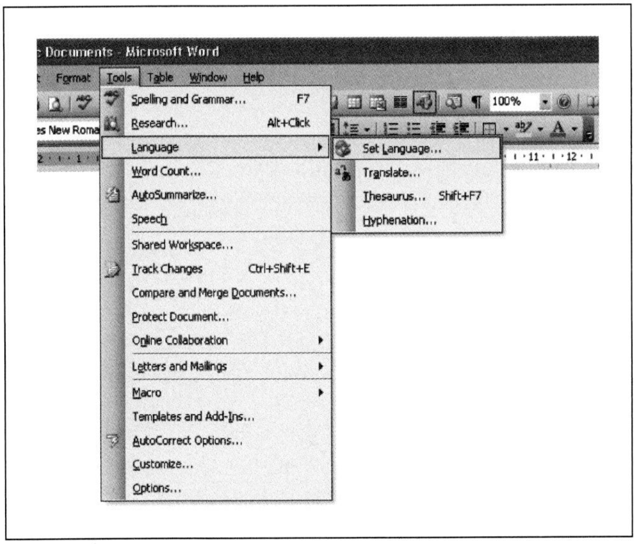

Figure 22.7

Figure 22.8

To set the language to English UK (Figures 22.7 and 22.8):

- Click on **Tools** and select **Language**
- Click on **Set Language** and choose English (UK).

Misspelt words and grammatical errors

As you type you should notice a red squiggly line appears under the text and some-times a green one. The red line indicates a misspelt word; the green one indicates gaps in the text, grammatical errors or fragmented sentences.

When you come across text underlined with a squiggly red line, position the cursor over the word and press the right-hand button of the mouse. As you do so, a spelling suggestion/s will be offered and you will have the option of choosing from the list by clicking on the word that fits (Figure 22.9). However, not all the suggestions are as you expect so, if you have checked the spelling in a dictionary and it is correct, you can se-lect the **Add to Dictionary** option. The next time you use this word it will automatically be deemed correct. Sometimes text is underlined in red because you have typed two words together or you have used a full stop but no gap. The Spell Checker sees this as one long word that it does not have in its dictionary. Once you put the gap in, the red line usually disappears.

Similarly by clicking the cursor over the green squiggly line and pressing the right-hand button of the mouse, a suggested change to the text will be offered. Again you may choose to ignore the suggestion or if it is deemed a **Fragment** to rewrite it or **Ignore Once** (Figure 22.10).

The green squiggly line also appears when gaps are present in the text (Fig-ure 22.11). The suggestion will show the text with the gap closed, which can be selected. The grammar check may suggest completely restructuring the sentence (Figure 22.12). Again, this can be used at your discretion.

> ### TIP
>
> Before saving and printing out the document scan through once more from the top to make sure you have made all of the necessary corrections.

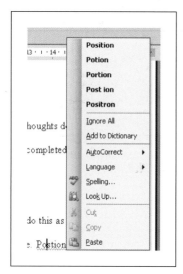

Figure 22.9

Figure 22.10

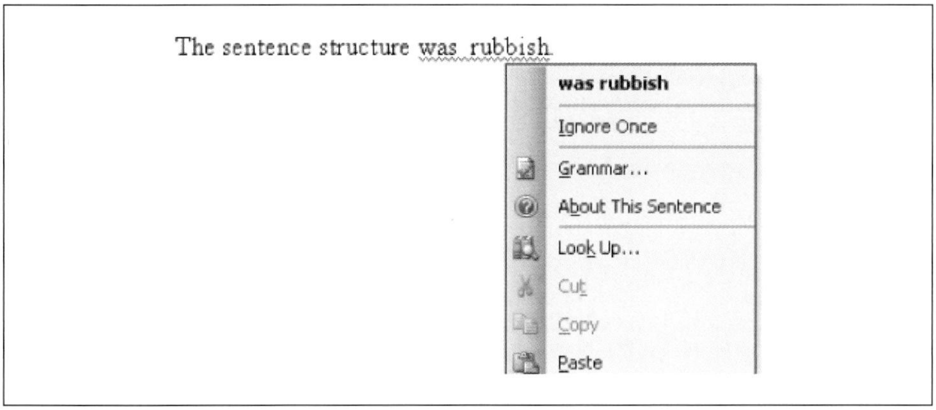

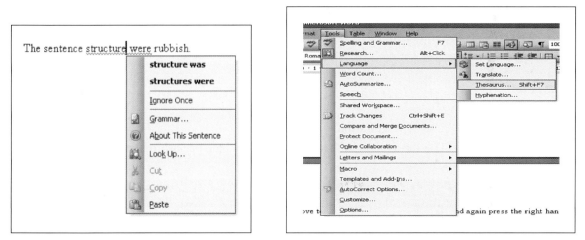

Figure 22.11

Figure 22.12   **Figure 22.13**

Thesaurus

Sometimes when writing a document you struggle to find the right word. Do not despair. Put a word in the text which is similar to the one you want to use and then:

- Select **Tools**, **Language** and **Thesaurus** (Ctrl + F7 will do the same).
- A task panel will appear on the right of the screen and a list of similar words will be displayed for you to choose from (Figure 22.13).

Undo

If you make a mistake you can undo your last action or actions. There are three ways to do this:

- Go to the **Edit** menu and choose **Undo**. There is actually a little phrase here to tell you what it is you are undoing. In this case **Typing**, but it could be any previous action, e.g. **Undo Insert** (Figure 22.14).

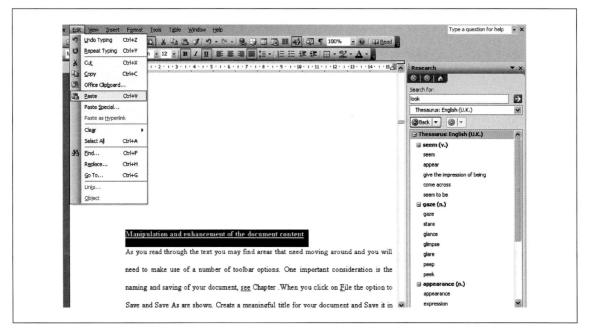

Figure 22.14

- Use the **Ctrl button + Z**
- Use the icon on the toolbar shown as a blue backward arrow

TIP

On the standard toolbar and under Edit you will find the undo option. If you want

to undo ↩ use this option and go back as many times as you need to until you are happy with the results.

Changing text

As you read through the text, you may find areas that need moving around or changing and to do this you will need to make use of a number of toolbar options.

Every time you click on a toolbar title (e.g. **Format**) take a note of the icon to the left of the option and also the **Ctrl** key options, as these can be used as alternative ways of accessing this function (Figure 22.14). Also be aware that when you click the right-hand button of the mouse similar options are offered (Figure 22.15).

For instance to 'Cut and Paste' or 'Copy and Paste' highlight the text. When you reach the end of the text press the right-hand button of the mouse and the options to **Cut** or **Copy** appear in a menu. Choose whichever is appropriate by clicking on the word with the left-hand button. Reposition the cursor by clicking at the point where you require the text to be, click the button on the right-hand side of the mouse again

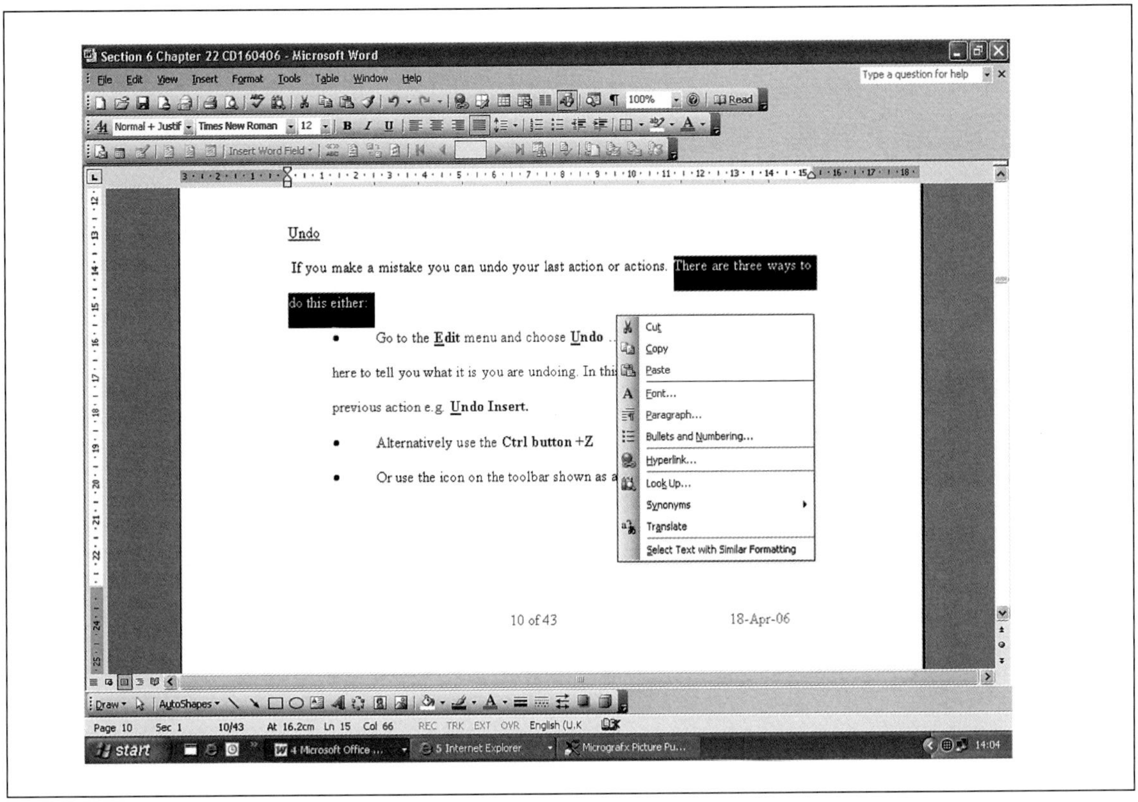

Figure 22.15

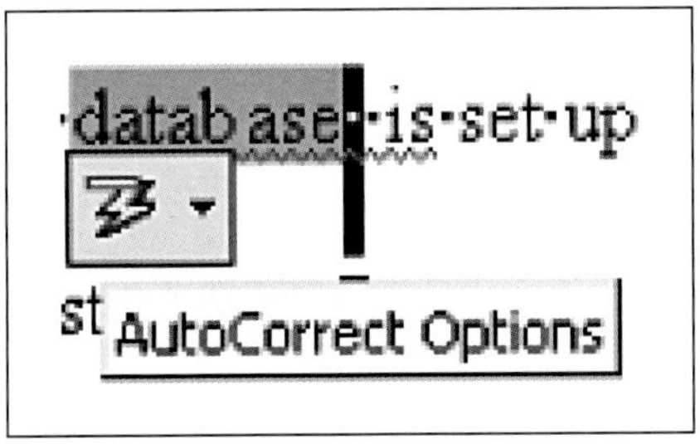

Figure 22.16

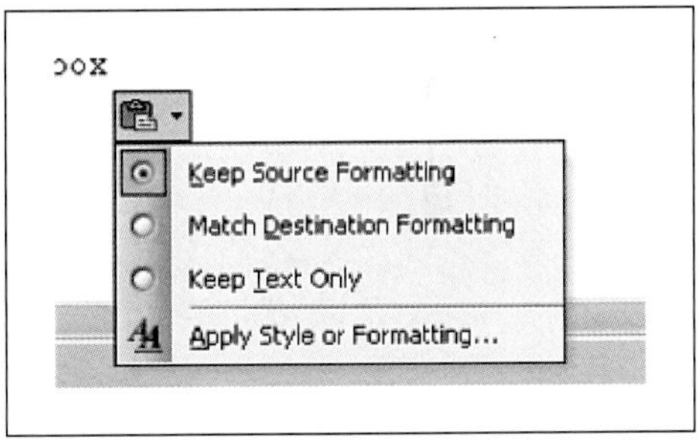

Figure 22.17

and select **Paste** (Figure 22.15). As you can see from the menu, there are alternative ways to do this, for example by clicking the relevant icons on the standard toolbar.

You may also see other icons appear on the screen. Sometimes a short blue line on its own or with a yellow arrow (Figure 22.16) will appear. If you click on these icons alternatives will be offered, for example **AutoCorrect**.

Similarly the icon shown in Figure 22.17 may appear when you move text around. For instance if you cut and paste a piece of text, the icon will suggest that you '**Match Destination Formatting**', that is keep the text the same as the section you have pasted into. If you do not want to select an option press the **Esc** button on the keyboard and it will disappear.

Ctrl button on the keyboard

The powerful **Ctrl** button is a gem of a button and you will find it handy within other Microsoft® programs. Using the **Ctrl** button in this example you can select sections of text from all over the document.

You may, for instance, want to go through the document and change the text so that all of the sentences containing the word Microsoft are shown in Bold. To do this, go to the first sentence and highlight it, scroll down the document to the next occurrence, hold the **Ctrl** button down *first* and then highlight the next section, scroll down again and when you reach the next section hold the **Ctrl** button down again and highlight (Figure 22.18).

Once you have found all of the relevant sections you can press the **B** icon or use the shortcut key (**Ctrl B**) and this will activate the change to all of the highlighted areas. The **Ctrl** key works in other places too, for instance if you have photographs on your computer and you want to pick out a selection only you can use the same technique.

Find and Replace

If you just need to replace one word with another, then use the Find and Replace option. For instance you may want a certain word to be changed so that it is displayed in the text as red and underlined. To do this:

- Go to **Edit** and **Replace**

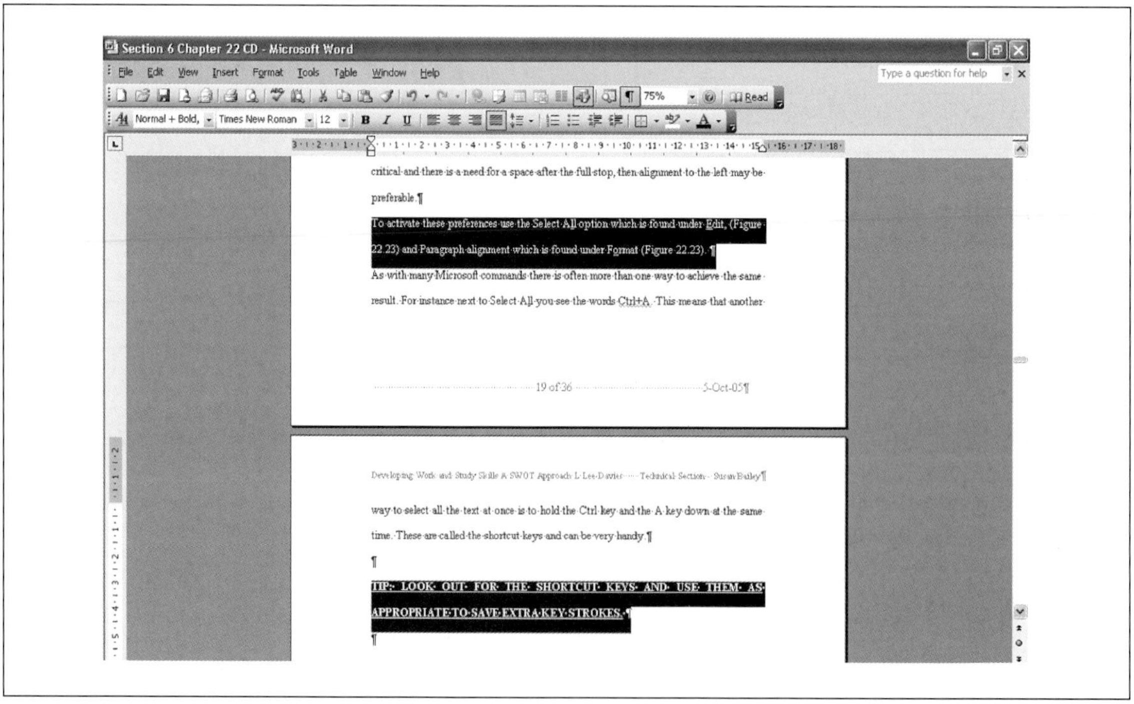

Figure 22.18

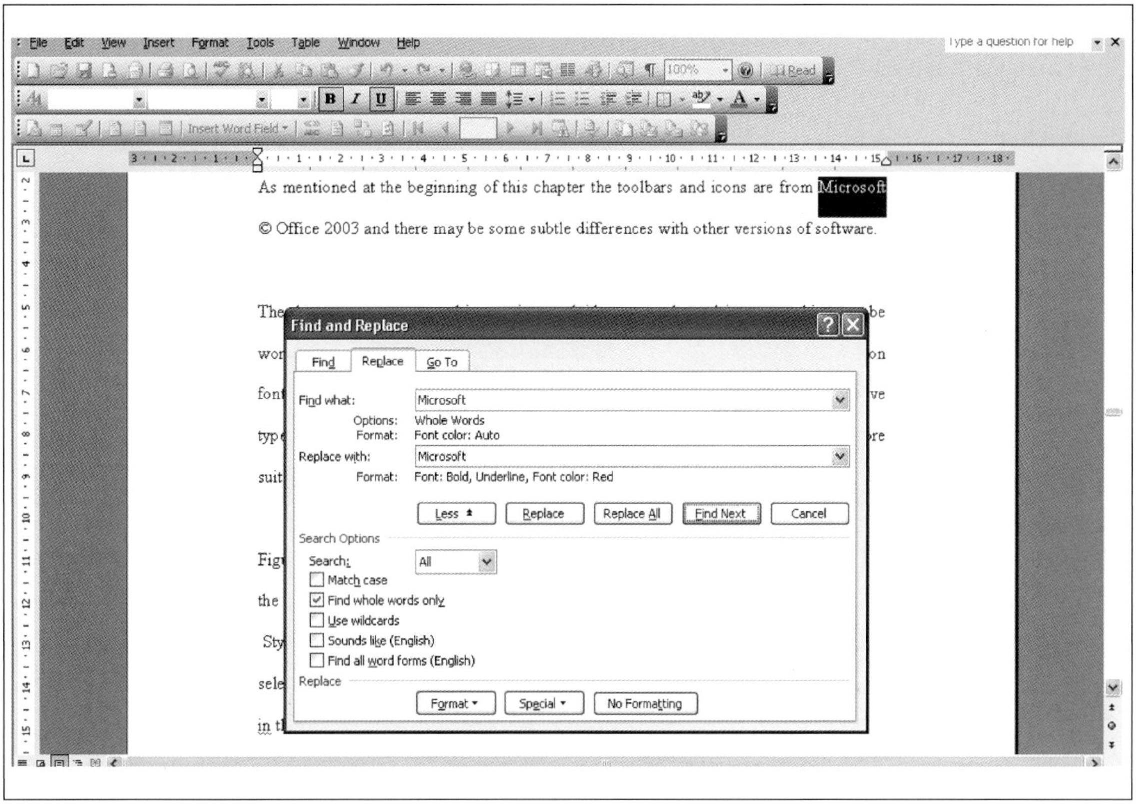

Figure 22.19

- Select the **More** option
- Put in the word you want to **Find** and click the option **Find whole words only**, in this case the word *Microsoft*
- Put in the replacement word, in this case the word, *Microsoft*, in red, bold and underlined. These options are found under **Format** (Figure 22.19)
- Use **Find Next** to move through the document and then **Replace**
- Alternatively you can choose **Replace All**

Alignment, paragraph setting and other enhancements

Alignment and paragraph setting, as with all other features, can be set up at the beginning. However, if a document has already been created, then alignment can be done by selecting the whole document. Although a report can be designed to reflect personal taste, the smartest design is probably justified text (i.e. text that is arranged to give a straight edge on both the right- and left-hand sides) with either 1.5 or double spacing. To activate these preferences:

- Go to **Edit** and **Select All** (Figure 22.20)

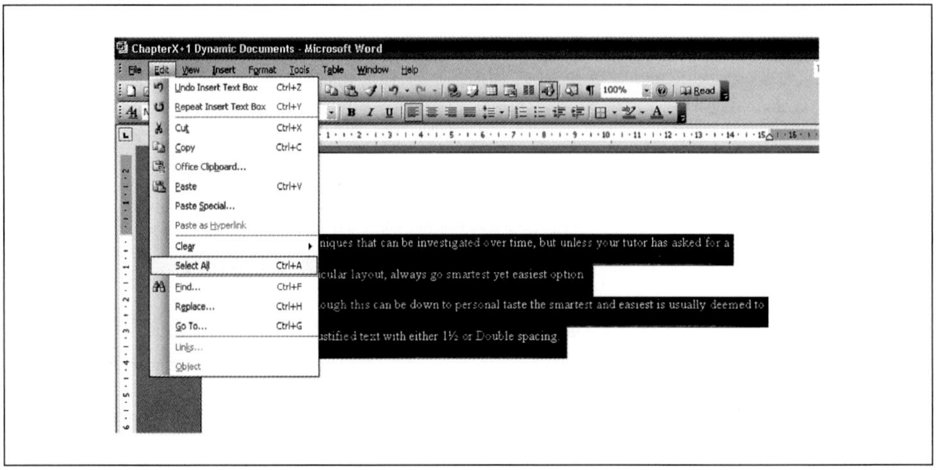

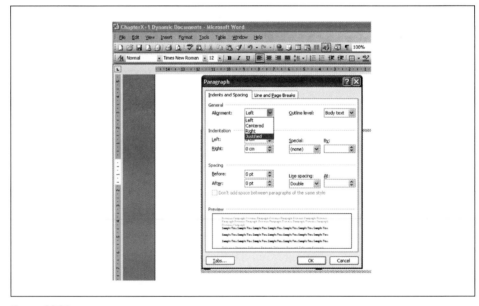

Figure 22.20

Figure 22.21

- **Format** and select **Paragraph** (Figure 22.21)
- Select **Alignment**: **Justified** and **Line Spacing: 1.5**

As with many Microsoft® commands there is often more than one way to achieve the same result. For instance next to **Select All**, you will see the words Ctrl+A and using this shortcut has the same effect.

TIP

Look out for the shortcut keys and use them as appropriate to save extra key strokes.

A further way of carrying out file management tasks is to select the text and click on the toolbar icon to change it. In Figure 22.22 the orange box on the formatting toolbar indicates that the text is at this time set to fully justified. However, when all the text is selected you can click on to any of the four alternatives (left, centre, right or justified). Next to the orange square on the right is the paragraph spacing icon which drops down to show spacing of 1.0, 1.5, 2.00 etc.

As mentioned at the beginning of this chapter the toolbars and icons are from Microsoft® Office 2003 and there may be some subtle differences with other versions of software.

The document you are working on can now be laid out smartly and at this stage it may be worth considering if the selected type of font and the font size look suitable. A common font is Times New Roman with a font size of 12. Once the text is selected then alternative types (Figure 22.23) and sizes can be experimented with to see if an alternative is more suitable.

Figure 22.23 also shows the styles and formatting selected, in this case normal + underlined.

Page breaks

To keep sections separate it is necessary to insert page breaks. You may also notice as you look through your document that you have created a condition known as 'widows and orphans'. If the last line of a paragraph is at the top of a new page, it is known as a widow; the first line of a paragraph at the bottom of a page is known as an orphan. Traditionally, this is to be avoided, as is the title of a section being on one page while the text is on the next (Figure 22.24).

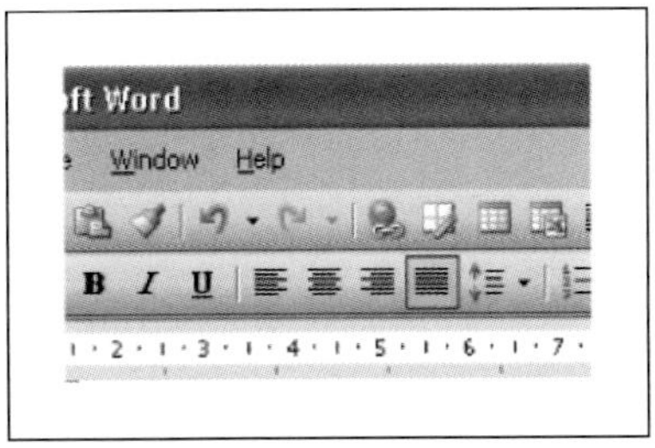

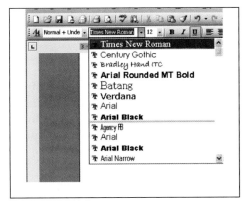

Figure 22.22

Figure 22.23

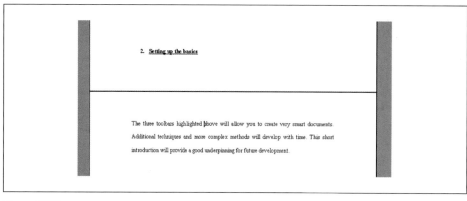

Figure 22.24

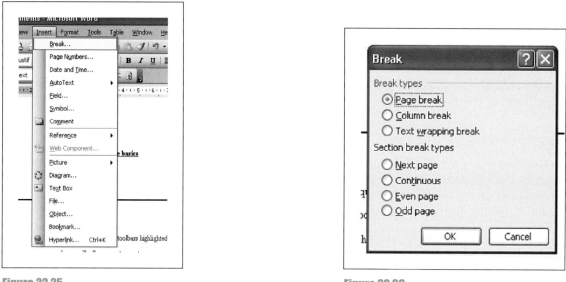

Figure 22.25   **Figure 22.26**

To insert a break, go to the beginning of the paragraph, select **Insert** (Figure 22.25) and then **Break**. Opt for **Page break** (Figure 22.26) and this will be inserted dividing off sections and bringing the 'widow' and 'orphan' together. The shortcut for this is to press the **Ctrl** button and **Return**. Alternatively pop in extra lines above the heading or use the more sophisticated control offered under **Paragraph** which keeps paragraphs together.

If you want to just change a section within the text, then you can use the option of a section break (Figure 22.26). When using section breaks you can chose an alternative set up for each section, for instance a landscape page instead of a portrait page.

ADVANCED TECHNIQUES

There are a number of techniques that can be used to smarten up documents and give them a crisp and professional feel, but these techniques require time and patience to get right. They are best practised after some initial skills have been gained with producing a simple document. These techniques include:

- Styles and formatting
- Alignment, paragraph setting and enhancements
- Headings
- Bullets and numbering

Styles and formatting

If you click on the styles and formatting icon  a display will appear on the right-hand side showing the styles and formatting you have used in your document (Figure 22.27).

If you scroll down you will also see Heading 1, Heading 2, etc. and if you place the cursor over the heading, the set-up for that style will be displayed (Figure 22.28).

To set up the headings at the beginning, create a new document and click on the styles and formatting icon. A list appears on the right that includes **Clear Formatting**, **Heading 1, 2** and **3** and **Normal** (Figure 22.29). If you want to change the format or add in numbering do so as detailed in the sections below. Once you are satisfied with the settings add headings and subheadings to your document, 'label' them as type 'Heading 1', 'Heading 2', etc. as you go. The setting up of the headings can be challenging, especially if they have been 'customised' in the past.

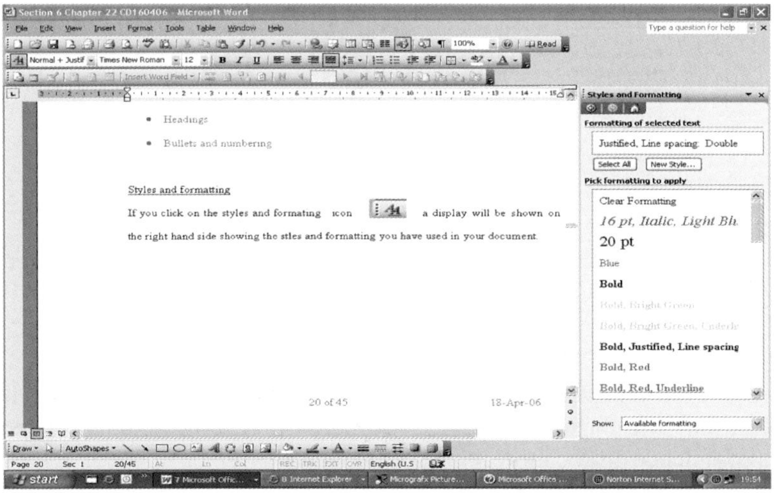

Figure 22.27

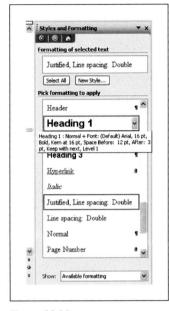

Figure 22.28

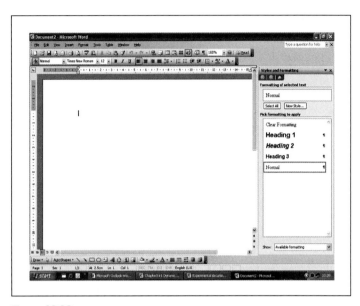

Figure 22.29

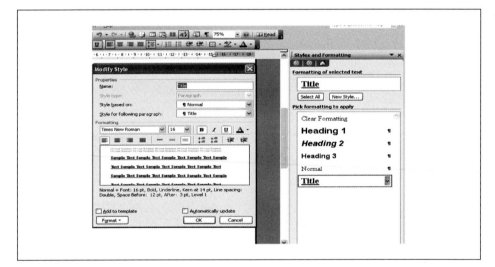

Figure 22.30

To prevent too much hassle in the early days of document production, it is suggested that only two or three heading styles and the default numbering system are used. As confidence grows, more sophisticated layouts can be applied.

If need extra heading types, these can be added by selecting **All styles**. Scrolling through the list you can find a new heading e.g. **Title**. This can be added by clicking on it. It will then appear on **Available formatting** (Figure 22.30).

Customising

At this stage it is recommended that minimum customising is used. However, the headings and titles should complement the rest of the text and use the same type of font.

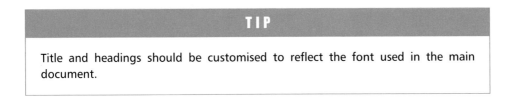

TIP

Title and headings should be customised to reflect the font used in the main document.

To modify the style (Figure 22.31):

- Position the cursor over a heading, e.g. Title
- From the drop down menu select **modify**
- The Modify Style panel will appear
- Select the font size, underline, colour options and indents of your choice and paragraph spacing if required

Figure 22.31 shows the selection of Times New Roman Font, Size 14, bold and underlined. Other formats can be chosen by clicking on the **Format** button.

Creating numbering

If you intend to create a table of contents (TOC) the numbering is the most important part. To create numbered headings and side headings (Figure 22.32):

- Position cursor over **Heading 1**
- Select **Modify** from the drop down menu

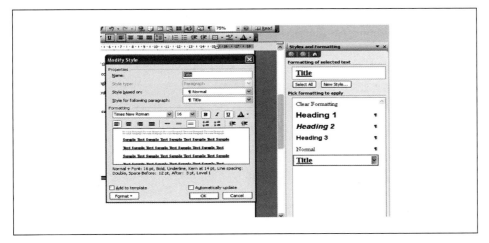

Figure 22.31

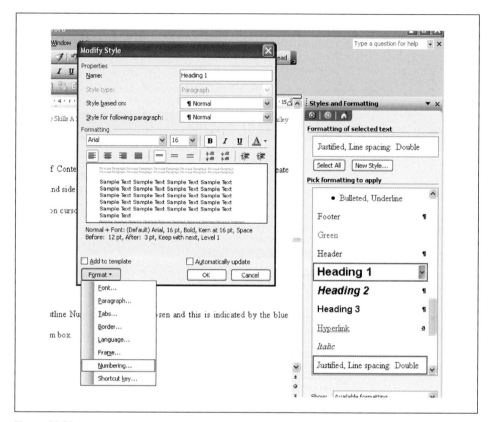

Figure 22.32

- Select **Format**
- Select **Numbering**
- Select tab **Outline Numbered** (Figure 22.32).

The easiest way to set up a numbering system is to choose an original set up. This is indicated when you click on one of the **Outline Numbered** boxes. If it is an original set up the **Reset** remains grey (Figure 22.33).

If you want another style, click on the style you require and if you are the user of the PC you can reset it. This will set it back to the original set up (Figure 22.34).

TIP
If an icon or option shows as grey it is not available to the user at this time.

The next stage is to add the detail of the numbers themselves. If you choose **Customize . . .** the screen in Figure 22.35 will appear. There are a few key areas to adjust:

- The number style should be set to 1, 2, 3.
- At level 1 the number format should be 1.

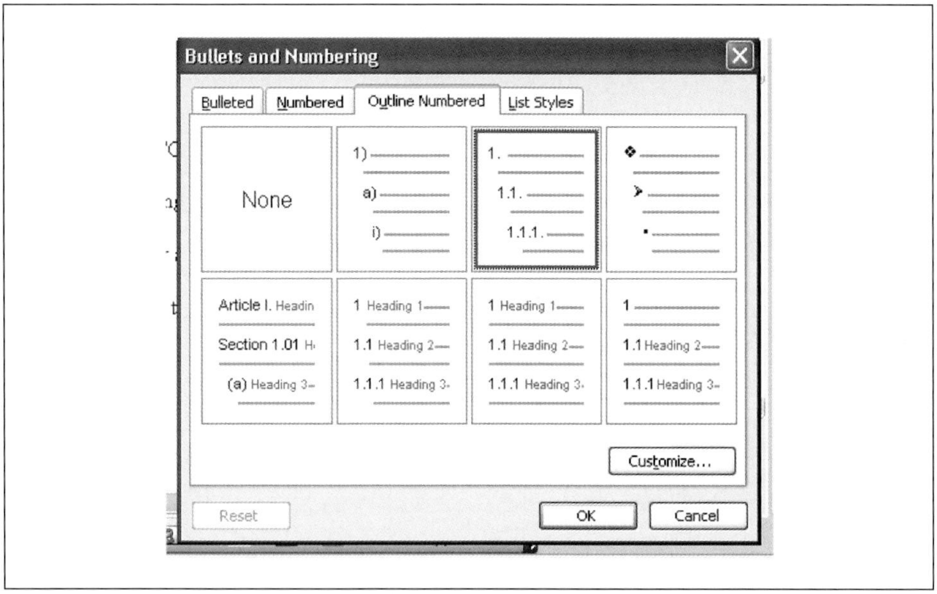

Figure 22.33

Figure 22.34

- At level 2 the number format should be 1.1.
- At level 3 the number format should be 1.1.1.
- Leave the number highlighted in grey, just add 1 or 1.1. as necessary to it.
- There is a **More** button which will give the options shown at the bottom of the Customize Outline Numbered List page (Figure 22.35).

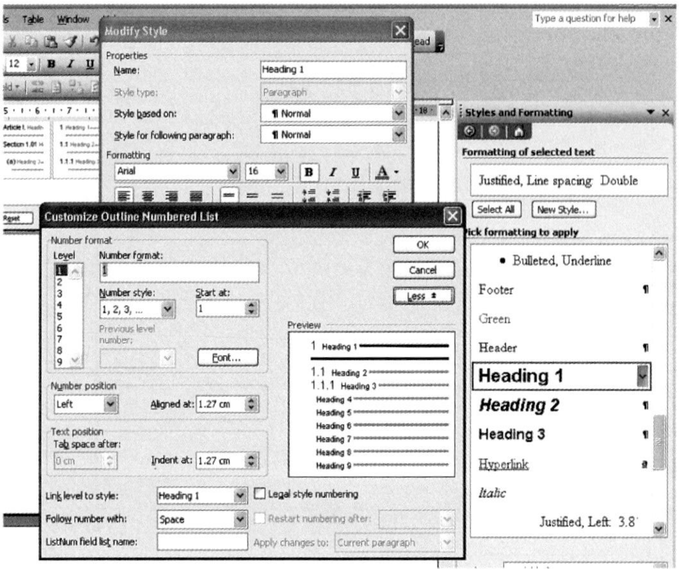

Figure 22.35

- Follow each number format with a space.
- Using the **Font** option, select font size, type and underlining as appropriate to the title format.
- For each option make sure that the **Restart Numbering** is *NOT* ticked.
- The styling and formatting panel will reflect the changes after customising.

TIP

Stick to a small number of heading types and styles to prevent too complex a set up.

Although headings and side headings can be done throughout the writing of the document, you may find it easier when *first* attempting layouts to wait until the end. That way the numbers and headings will follow a set sequence. If you add them in as you go along it is possible to get into a real mess. It is often not the text that troubles the new student, it's the technology!

To add the headings to a finished document, highlight the title heading and select **Title** (e.g. Dynamic Documents) (Figure 22.36).

Next select the main headings in each section (e.g. Introduction and Report Set Up) and select **Heading 1**. Then go into each section and select the next level of side

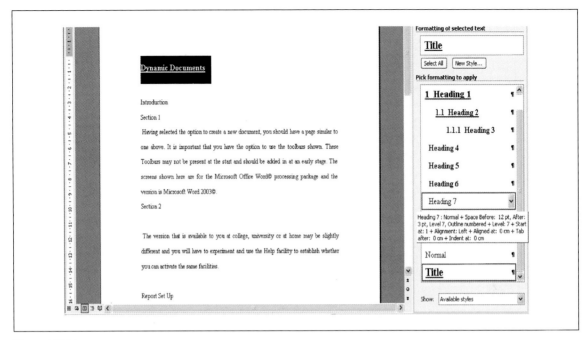

Figure 22.36

headings and select **Heading 2** (e.g. Section 1 and Section 2). This is probably the lowest level you need to go to.

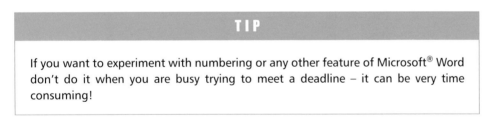

TIP

If you want to experiment with numbering or any other feature of Microsoft® Word don't do it when you are busy trying to meet a deadline – it can be very time consuming!

Table of contents

Now that the title and headings are in place a standard TOC can be added. Before starting this, go to the top of the document and **Insert** a new section, by using **Section break** instead of **Page break**. Click onto this new page and when the TOC is generated it will appear on this page. If you are not in the right position and the TOC appears inside the document, click on **Undo Typing** and start again. To create a TOC click on **Insert**, **Reference**, **Index** and **Tables** (Figure 22.37).

Once the index and tables window is displayed, there are various options which can be chosen. However, to achieve the standard layout as shown, click OK and the table will appear on the blank page. As with all techniques there is the facility to change the layout and this can be explored over time.

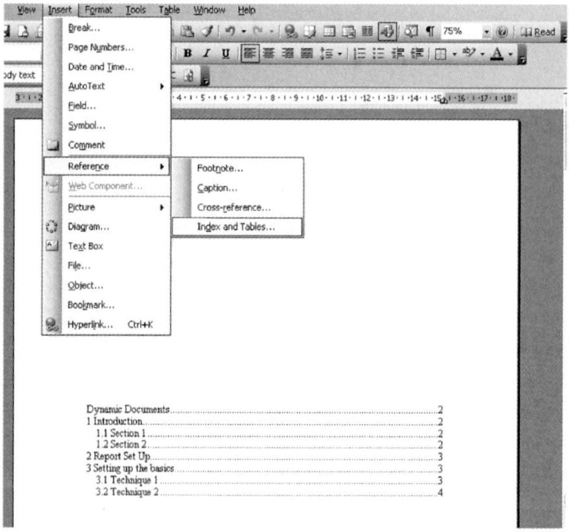

Figure 22.37

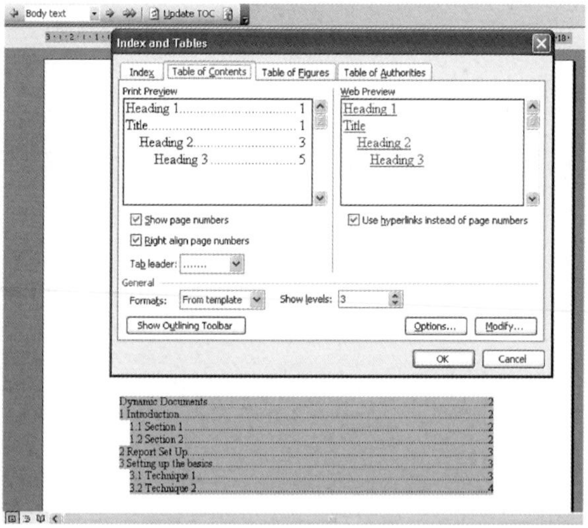

Figure 22.38

Once the TOC is in use, it is pertinent to go to **View** and **Toolbars** and tick the **Outlining Toolbar**. The **Outlining Toolbar** (Figure 22.38) has a number of facilities to support TOC including an update, which can be actioned if the document is changed. To update the table, right click on it and select **Update**.

FURTHER IMPROVEMENTS TO THE APPEARANCE OF YOUR DOCUMENT

Header and Footer

To add your own stamp and ownership to a document it is beneficial to add a header and footer. The contents of the header and footer should be simple and clear. To create a header and footer for your document go to **View** and select **Header and Footer**. The dotted **Header and Footer** areas will appear, as well as a toolbar that works with **Header and Footer** to give various facilities (Figure 22.39). To facilitate a clear document add your name and student number to the header and perhaps the document title. To the footer (selected by clicking on icon highlighted in Figure 22.40) add in the page no. and the number of pages together with a date. As you position the cursor over header and footer toolbar icons, a short phrase will appear indicating the function of the icon. You can also use the functions on the formatting toolbar to underline or centralise the text in the header and footer boxes.

TIP

It is advisable to put a blank line under the heading in the header so that it does not touch the main text (Figure 22.40).

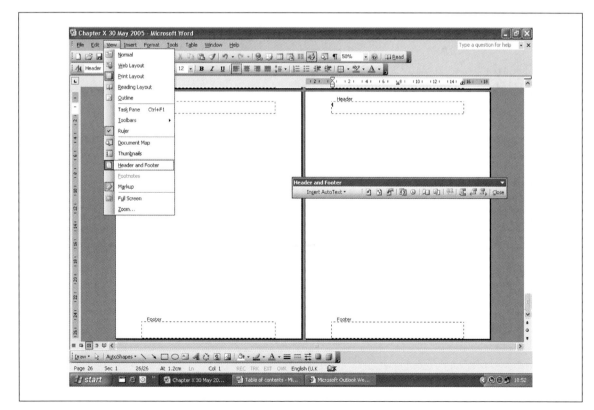

Figure 22.39

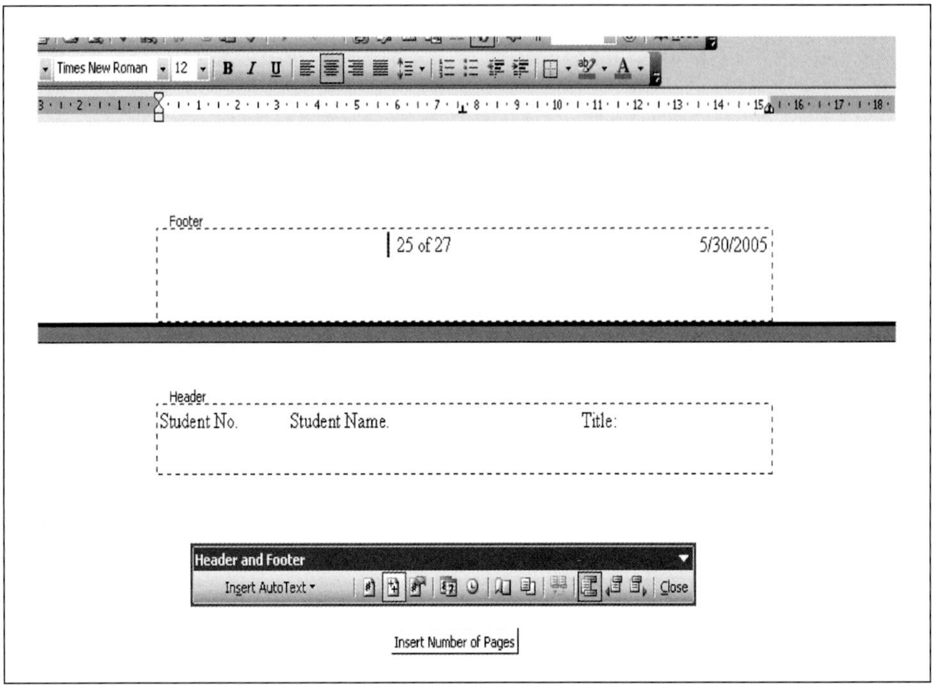

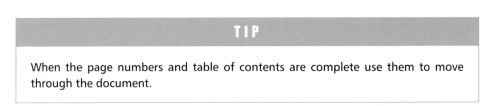

Figure 22.40

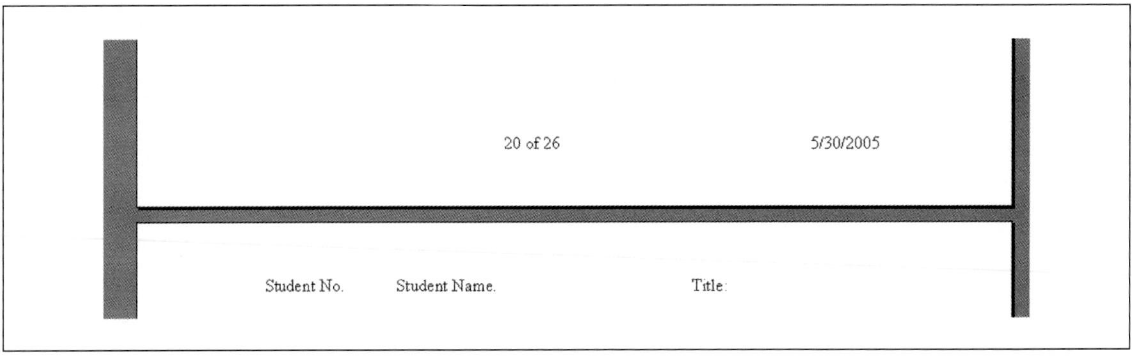

Figure 22.41

When the toolbar for the header and footer is closed, the contents will appear in grey on every page (Figure 22.41).

TIP

When the page numbers and table of contents are complete use them to move through the document.

Impressive front page

Compose the front page of your document on a separate sheet, unless you are familiar with working in sections. (Some techniques you will learn to make the best use of when you are more experienced. Choose the easy options initially to make sure you complete your work on time.) If you understand how sections work then your front page can become Section 1. A good front page reflects a professional delivery. In addition, check whether you are required to hand in a separate front sheet related to your course. This sheet may also indicate the format and presentation that the tutor requires and will probably show your course details.

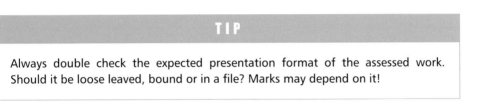

TIP

Always double check the expected presentation format of the assessed work. Should it be loose leaved, bound or in a file? Marks may depend on it!

It is also worth noting that it is very difficult for tutors to mark work in plastic sleeves!

A number of techniques can be used to improve a front page, but some of these techniques can also be employed in other areas of your work (Figure 22.42).

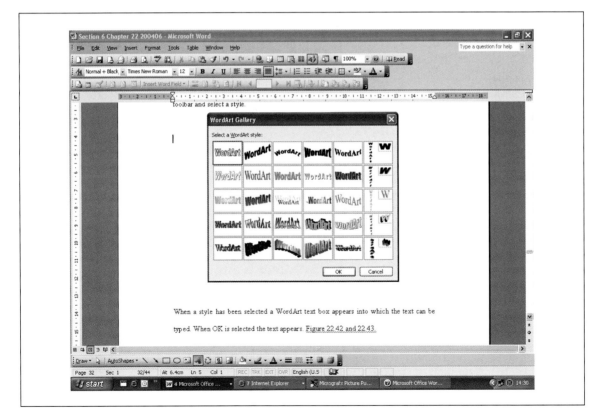

Figure 22.42

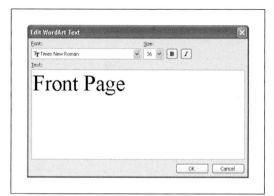

Figure 22.43

Figure 22.44

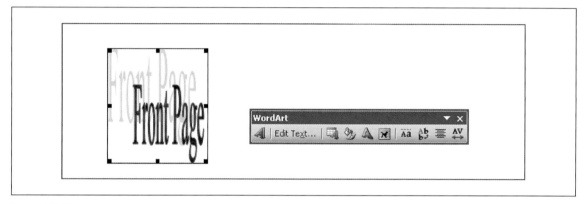

Figure 22.45

WordArt can be used to produce a more stylised title on the front page or, if

appropriate, in other parts of the document. To use WordArt select the blue  from the drawing toolbar and select a style (Figure 22.42).

When a style has been selected, a WordArt text box appears into which the text can be typed. When OK is selected the text appears (Figures 22.43 and 22.44).

WordArt also has a toolbar that allows manipulation of the text (Figure 22.45).

Pictures, diagrams and screen shots

On the front page and also in the text it may be necessary to add in a picture, a diagram or a screen shot. To find a suitable picture or a diagram go to **Insert** on the toolbar and select as appropriate (Figure 22.46).

A selection of pictures can be obtained by clicking on **ClipArt**. In addition photographs and pictures held in your files can be used as well as **New Drawings**, **AutoShapes**, **Organisational charts** and other types of charts.

These options can be selected through the **Insert** option; they also appear on the drawing toolbar (Figure 22.47). Sweeping the cursor along the toolbar will reveal

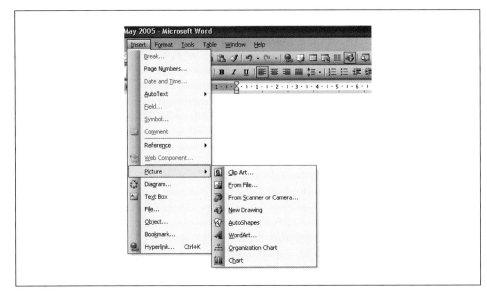

Figure 22.46

Figure 22.47

what each icon represents. It is also possible to see the icons when looking at the **Insert** menu, as the icon is shown to the left of the text where it exists.

When you add a text box, another box known as the Drawing Canvas (Figure 22.47) appears inviting you to 'Create your drawing here'. When you click inside the box a text box appears inside it. You can also paste your image into the box and then using the mouse, click on the corners of the image to stretch it out (Figure 22.48). Remember you will have an image within the drawing canvas, so it is important to make sure both boxes are manipulated to give a correct picture and full image.

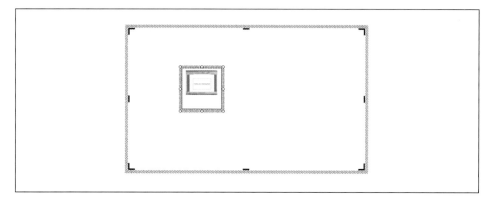

Figure 22.48

> # TIP
>
> Drag the text box and image out of the drawing canvas and delete the drawing canvas otherwise it will interfere with your document.

A picture, diagram or screen shot can be enclosed in a text box or it can stand alone as a picture. If it stands alone as a picture, it will help to reduce the size of the document. This set up enables you to move the picture, but it could place itself over the text. When you have downloaded the picture, click on the picture itself with the right-hand mouse button. Select **Format Picture**, go to **Layout** and choose the option **In front of the text** (Figure 22.49).

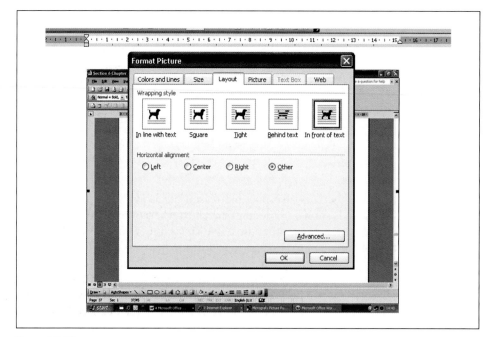

Figure 22.49

> **TIP**
>
> Make sure that there is no hidden text under your pictures!

If you need to include an image from the PC, sometimes referred to as a screen shot, organise the screen as you need it to look. Press the **Print Scrn** button at the top right of the keyboard and then open a document, usually a Word document or PowerPoint® slide, and click **Paste**. The screen image will appear on the page.

Figure 22.50 shows a screen dumped image in a text box. The text box is selected at this point, indicated by the dotted edge around the square. When the text box is selected the size can be changed, the sides moved in and out and the text box can be dragged to another position in the document.

> **TIP**
>
> Look for the changes in the cursor when it is positioned over the corner or side of a text box, a shape or a picture. A subtle change in the cursor shape indicates a different function.

When a two-ended arrow ↔ appears vertically or horizontally the image can be stretched, when it appears diagonally in the corner of an image the whole image can be enlarged proportionally. Other types of objects show the cursor in various guises. With an AutoShape there is a green circle • which allows the object to be rotated.

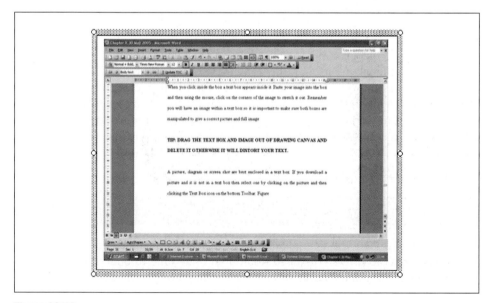

Figure 22.50

Figure 22.51

Access to a range of pictures for insertion into the text is available. Clicking on **Insert** **Picture** and **ClipArt** will display a clipboard of images (Figure 22.51). When a picture is chosen from the ClipArt selection, a blue arrow to the right of the picture drops down the options, click on **Insert**.

TIP

Once a screen dump appears in the document, click on the picture and then on the text box. This will enclose the picture in a text box and make it easier to manoeuvre or set it up as a picture as shown in Figure 22.49.

When you see the small black squares around the edge (Figure 22.52) you know that you are on the picture itself, rather than the text box. It is then possible to use the picture toolbar as shown below the picture. One option the picture toolbar offers is a crop tool (shown highlighted in Figure 22.51) which allows you to trim a picture.

When inserting text boxes and shapes into a document, move the text down to leave a space to accommodate them, otherwise the images position themselves over the text. Alternatively go back to **Format Picture** and then **Layout** to change how the text and the picture are blended together (Figure 22.49).

TIP

Never underestimate the time it will take to perfect the manipulation of pictures and text boxes to give the required results. Set aside time to understand how to change the shapes of the boxes and the picture formatting techniques.

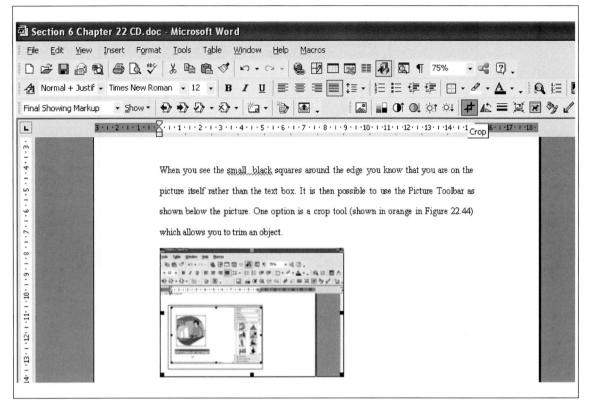

Figure 22.52

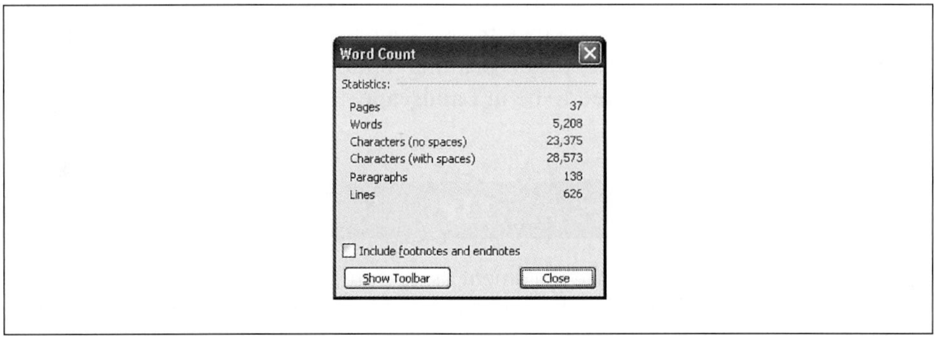

Figure 22.53

To finish off the document, you may have been requested to include the word count. The word count facility will either count the words in the whole document or the part of the document that has been highlighted. To see the word count select **Tools** and **Word Count**. Once calculated this can be added into the document (Figure 22.53).

Finally, **Save** the document and **Print**. Before printing go to **Print Preview** to check that each page looks correct, as the screen document can vary from the printed

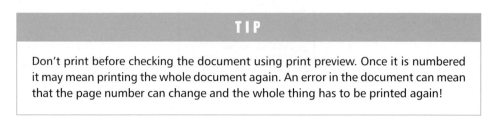

Figure 22.54

document. If you are including a spreadsheet, you may need to select **Landscape** for that particular page only. If so go to **File** and **Page Setup** and select **Landscape** and **Selected text** only. Check the other printing options before pressing **OK** (Figure 22.54). If several pages need to be in **Landscape**, then use section breaks.

TIP

Don't print before checking the document using print preview. Once it is numbered it may mean printing the whole document again. An error in the document can mean that the page number can change and the whole thing has to be printed again!

TIP

Many printers give an option to produce a draft copy of the document. This is often adequate for most assignments and saves a great deal of ink (Figure 22.55).

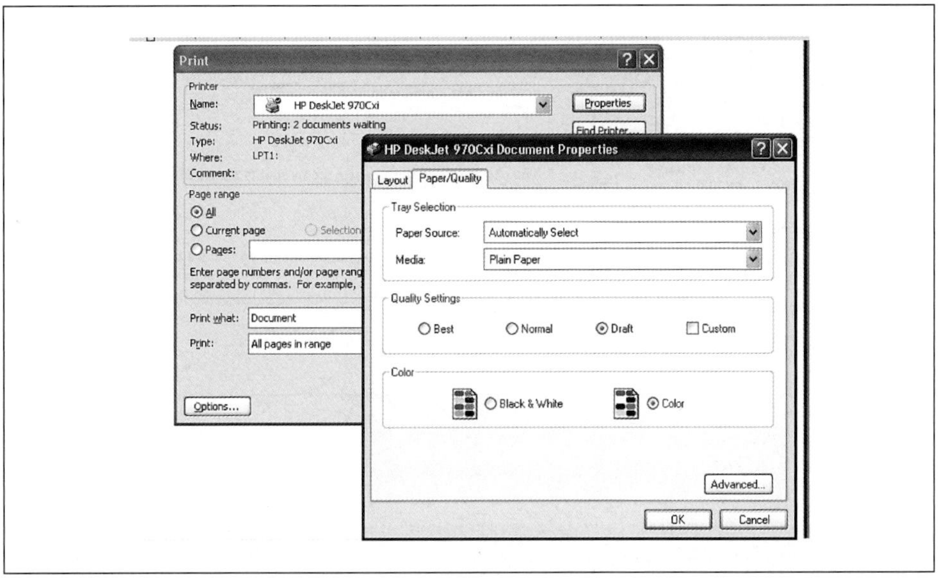

Figure 22.55

Finally put the finished document into a suitable document holder and submit your work.

By practising these techniques and accessing the following website you will be able to extend or consolidate your present skills set.

http://office.microsoft.com/en-gb/assistance/default.aspx.

TIP

Practise the creation of documents prior to working on set work for the course – it is often only when you need to do something that you learn how.

DOCUMENT RECOVERY

If you have set AutoRecovery on your PC and chosen a time between saves, you should find that if disaster strikes, like a power cut or someone switching off your PC by mistake, when you turn on the machine, the document will reappear more or less as you left it. Go back into Microsoft® Word and the recovered documents should appear on the left-hand side under **Document Recovery** (Figure 22.56).

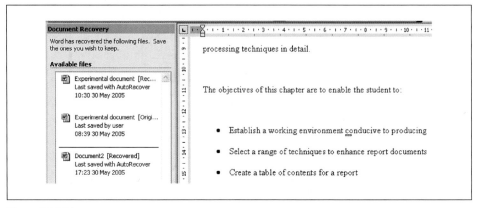

Figure 22.56

Summary

Producing reports and other documents are important in both business and university life. Presentation can make a big difference. It is important to make sure that documents contain the correct spellings and that the text is clear and easy to read.

A well laid out report which shows attention to detail, is pleasing to the eye and is welcomed by both managers and tutors alike. The use of page numbers, headers, footers and content pages enhances a document and makes it easy to reference. Additionally pictures, text variety, symbols and images can add clarity and interest to a document.

Good presentation takes practice!

TASK 1

Create a blank document and save it as 'Summary' document in a folder called *First Steps*.

TASK 2

Use the document created in Task 1, write, save and print in draft form a three-page summary of your experience which includes all of the following:

a. Enhanced text: e.g. bold, italics, coloured font

b. A font of Arial 12 and a paragraph spacing of 2.0

c. Justified text

d. A page break half way down the second page

e. A copyright symbol ©

f. A ClipArt image showing a student

g. A header showing your name and title

h. A footer showing a page number and the date

i. A screen shot of your university or college website

TASK 3

Revisit your document 'Summary' and modify it to include:

a. A front page

b. Headings

c. Table of contents

CHAPTER 23

Excelling to your advantage – data and mail merge

- To recognise the importance of accurate data
- To create a mail merged document using a spreadsheet as database

Spreadsheets can be used to produce excellent outputs for a range of key tasks. Traditionally the spreadsheet is associated with mathematical functions and these functions will be addressed in another section. However, the spreadsheet also lends itself to being used as a database and to producing charts and graphs of all descriptions. The emphasis of this section is to investigate useful ways of employing spreadsheets to give effective and meaningful output. Microsoft® Excel 2003 will be used to illustrate how data can be manipulated and presented; however, a number of software tools at university and in the workplace can be used to produce even more powerful and significant outputs.

The clever use of spreadsheets can be particularly useful in small businesses where the information technology (IT) department is small or even non-existent.

OVERVIEW OF SPREADSHEET

Format

Before launching into the creation of Microsoft® Excel documents, it is useful to study a basic spreadsheet (Figure 23.2). The toolbars contain many of the familiar icons and drop down lists which are present on Microsoft® Word documents and these can therefore be used to centre text, alter the format, cut and paste, etc. There are, however, a number of other icons that have significant mathematical and statistical significance.

It should be remembered that each cell in a spreadsheet document can be designated to hold data of a particular type. There is a full range of formats including numerical, text, currency and percentages. Selecting **Format** within a spreadsheet is very different to selecting **Format** in a Microsoft® Word document. If you select **Format**, (Figure 23.1) and then **Cells** on the spreadsheet toolbar the full range of categories is displayed (Figure 23.2). As in previous chapters, it should be noted that using the toolbar at the top of the page is not always the quickest way to activate a task. Always note the alternative ways of carrying out the same task. In the case of formatting a cell the two alternative ways of doing this are by selecting the icon shown in Figure 23.1 or pressing **Ctrl** and **1** at the same time.

Each cell has the equivalent of a grid reference, alphabetic along the top and numeric down the side; this means each cell has a unique location. If you write headings and labels onto a spreadsheet you can merge two or more cells together (click on icon shown in orange on the toolbar marked with a small a in the middle). It is also possible to use the borders option (Figure 23.3) to outline the text and give greater clarity.

These actions can be reversed using the toolbar as necessary, that is by clicking on the merge icon the text can be unmerged and by choosing no border (top left of borders) the border can be removed.

MAIL MERGE

The mail merge is a neat and clever technique which produces excellent results and saves endless hours of individual typing.

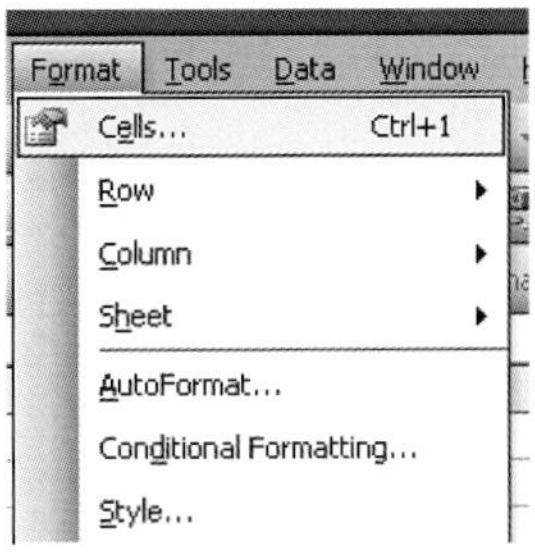

Figure 23.1

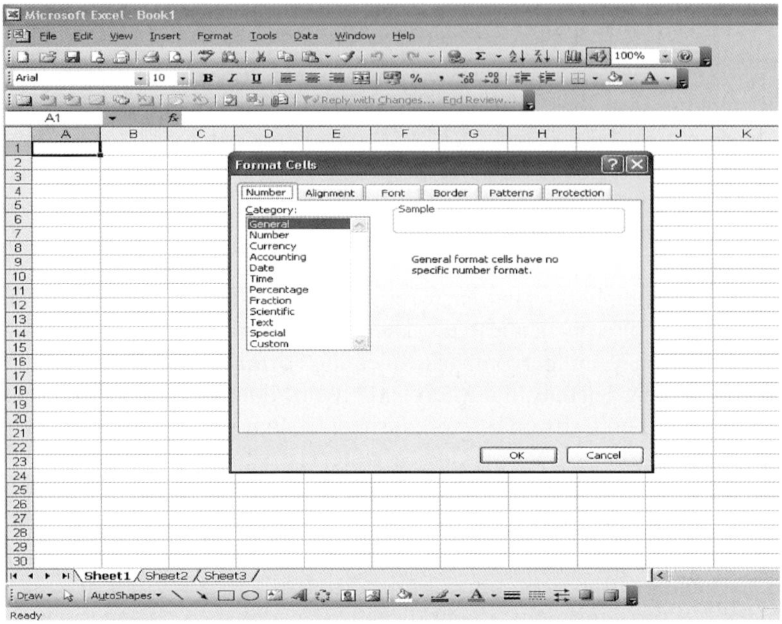

Figure 23.2

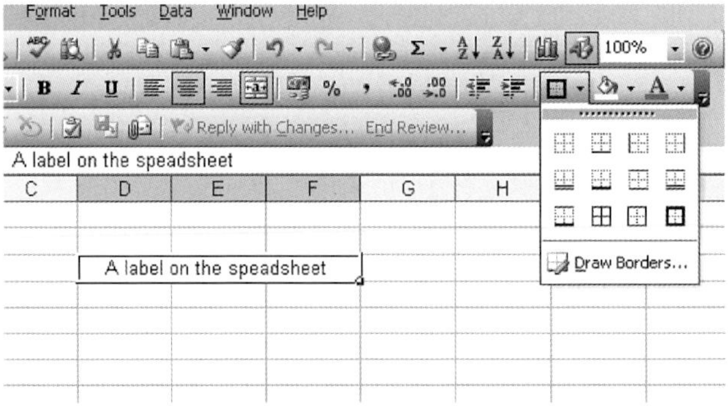

Figure 23.3

Being an efficient manager, team member, entrepreneur and partner can take its toll and the work–life balance tends to get eroded away. Therefore, when trying to add studying to the list of responsibilities and perhaps being a little new to student life, it is a relief to know that some aspects of spreadsheet work can be used at home and at work!

Take 'thank you letters' for example. Within a Microsoft® Excel spreadsheet you can set up a simple table of data which can be used over and over again. The key to

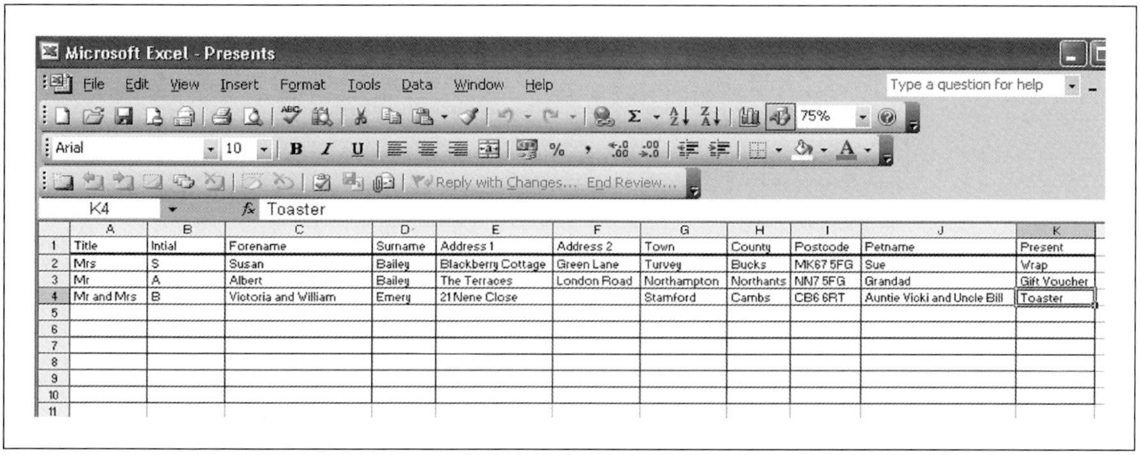

	A	B	C	D	E	F	G	H	I	J	K
1	Title	Intial	Forename	Surname	Address 1	Address 2	Town	County	Postcode	Petname	Present
2	Mrs	S	Susan	Bailey	Blackberry Cottage	Green Lane	Turvey	Bucks	MK67 5FG	Sue	Wrap
3	Mr	A	Albert	Bailey	The Terraces	London Road	Northampton	Northants	NN7 5FG	Grandad	Gift Voucher
4	Mr and Mrs	B	Victoria and William	Emery	21 Nene Close		Stamford	Cambs	CB6 6RT	Auntie Vicki and Uncle Bill	Toaster

Figure 23.4

preparing a table of data is ensuring that there are enough elements available to put together a meaningful letter and that the input of data is accurate. Figure 23.4 shows 11 fields of data, ranging from *Title* to *Present* along the top row.

TIP

When setting up a data table in Microsoft® Excel, look at letters you have written previously and highlight all of the variable data so that nothing is forgotten when you create a data table.

Often when creating a letter it is not until you try to insert data into the body of the text that it becomes apparent that one or two elements are missing. The field *Initial* is a common omission, but it is essential when you want to create an address or an address label, that is Mr **A** Bailey, but within the body of the letter you would refer to him as Mr Bailey. In the example shown Mr Bailey also has the Pet name of Granddad which could be used in the body of the text.

TIP

Always give each datasheet a unique name. Position the cursor on the word **Sheet No.**, click the right-hand mouse button, select **Rename** and replace the word Sheet No. with a more meaningful title, in this case *Presents* (Figure 23.5).

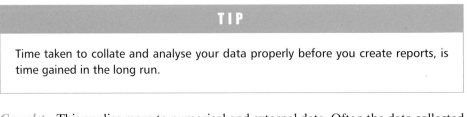

Figure 23.5

Accuracy of data

Good information comes from good quality data. Using the acronym ACCURATE (Management Information Systems 2000) we can unravel data and try to make sure that it is right on the first pass.

Accurate Data that are accurate means that the figures should add up. This sounds obvious but if you 'eyeball' your data, you can get a feel for errors. It is no good processing data unless you have scrutinised it well because once it reappears in a report you have the effort of having to revisit your original data to correct it, which wastes time and energy.

The other key element of creating data is to make sure that the capital letters are correctly input, for example Blackberry Cottage, MK67 5FG.

TIP

Time taken to collate and analyse your data properly before you create reports, is time gained in the long run.

Complete This applies more to numerical and external data. Often the data collected are incomplete and therefore give a false picture. For instance, some data only give figures for one year, however, if you are looking at house prices or stock market trends, it may be more useful to have two or three years' data for a more complete picture.

Cost beneficial Amazingly, many people collect data and provide statistics without thinking through whether the time taken to collect the data is going to be cost beneficial in the end and the results useful! Data should be collected efficiently and effectively and the presentation should be done in such a way that the target audience are in no doubt as to what the figures mean.

User-targeted When presenting data, it may be that you are talking to fellow colleagues in your division or you may be asked to give a presentation to the board. Either way, the delivery needs to be sensitive to their needs. Managers are usually only interested in bottom line figures, whereas your colleagues will want to know more details about their progress and future plans.

Relevant Do not be dragged down the path of providing interesting and pretty information from your data which is not at all relevant. Reports should be fit-for-purpose.

Authoritative Always be sure that you trust the source of your data. You may have used the internet to gather data, which is fine as long as you record where the data are from and when they were accessed. The danger is that you need to be happy with that source. Some data, such as that provided by Government statistics, large corporations or from your own workplace can usually be thought to have come from a trusted source. For other data undertake further investigation, make contact by e-mail if necessary and satisfy yourself that the data provided are from an authoritative source.

TIP

To prevent red faces in the boardroom, always be sure that you are providing information from trusted data sources.

Timely A friend of mine says there is more stress created by being late with a report than with getting it ready on time. With this in mind, work backwards from your delivery date and give yourself realistic targets to deliver the information. Then give yourself a day's leeway to cope with the unforeseen.

Easy-to-use Information should be presented clearly and in the right medium and using the right communication channel for the intended audience. Increasingly, your colleagues may be viewing your data on a PDA or Blackberry so clear, short headings and labels will aid their interpretation (Management Information Systems 2000).

Back to the mail merge

Before beginning the mail merge, take a moment to reconsider the data presented in the table with a more critical eye. Having 'eyeballed' the data, you are ready to merge

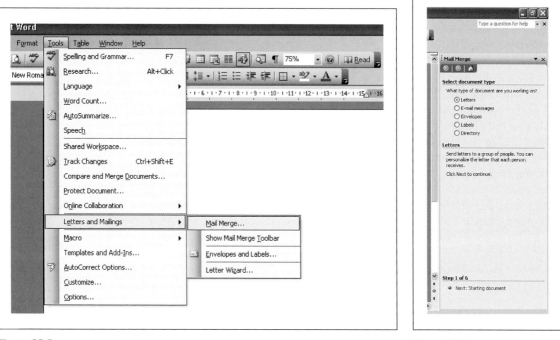

Figure 23.6   Figure 23.7

it in with a letter. This data can be used many times over in, for example, other letters, address labels or e-mail messages. Having already created the spreadsheet of data the next step is to merge it into a letter (Figures 23.6 and 23.7).

To do this:

- Open a **New** Microsoft® Word document
- Select **Tools** then **Letters and Mailings**
- Cascade down to the **Mail Merge** option

TIP

When you see the term *cascading* in a PC environment, it means opening up menu after menu, clicking on each one with the mouse (cascading), until you reach the option you need.

Although this option is to merge letters there are other options related to merging data. The **E-mail messages**, **Envelopes**, **Labels** and **Directory** options are well worth investigating as your confidence grows. Also, it may be handy to click on **Show Mail Merge Toolbar** in readiness for the other options (Figure 23.6).

> **TIP**
>
> Confidence to try new options expands as you move from known to unknown areas. When you have mastered one technique, try a comparable technique and look for similarities in the process.

This exercise will only concern itself with letters, but the labels option is also very useful. The labels option asks you to select a type of label and gives many options for label types. The labels are then collated and the label contents displayed as they will appear on the label.

> **TIP**
>
> To save wasting labels, print a test layout on a plain sheet of paper and then line up with the sheet of labels to make sure they align before printing for real.

Mail merge has step by step instructions which appear to the right of the screen. As you move through the instructions, you will be offered various alternatives. In addition the step reached is shown at the bottom of the panel, so if at anytime you make an incorrect decision then you can go back to the previous step and modify your response.

As advised before, it is easier to try a simple option and get it right, then experiment with alternatives at a later stage. In this example, selecting the options to **Use the current document** and **Use an existing list** (Figures 23.8 and 23.9) from the panel will give a straightforward example. From here:

- **Select recipients**
- **Browse** (browse means finding where you have saved your list of recipients on your computer (see Figure 23.4)
- Use the **Open** command to select the list

You will notice that when you go to **Select Table** (Figures 23.10, 23.11 and 23.12), the titles are displayed as shown at the bottom of the datasheet, this is why naming the data sheet *Presents* helps you to locate it. Note that each sheet name is followed by a $ sign.

> **TIP**
>
> Always label datasheets with a meaningful name (Figures 23.10–23.12).

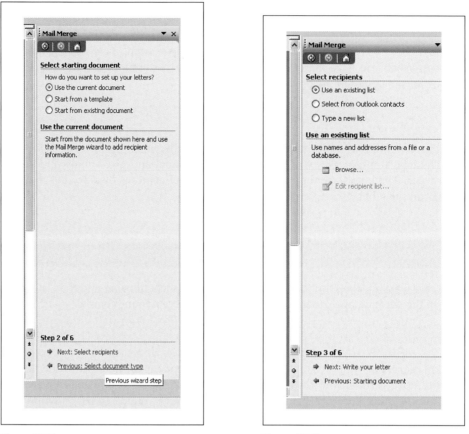

Figure 23.8

Figure 23.9

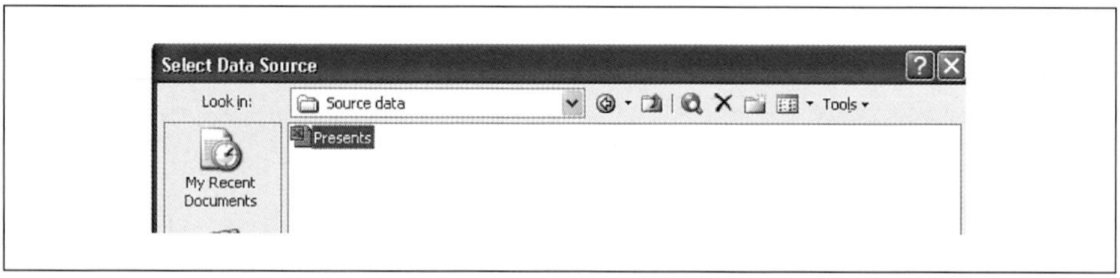

Figure 23.10

The mail merge recipients will now be displayed and using the tick box to the left of the names it is possible to select the appropriate recipients for the mail merge. In this case all are selected, but any editing of the lists should be done at this stage. When you are happy with the list, click **OK** (Figure 23.13).

Now that the recipients have been selected, the letter can be written. The whole point of a mail merge is to be able to create a whole batch of letters with different names and addresses on each letter. The stage is to create a letter with meaningful gaps (Figure 23.14).

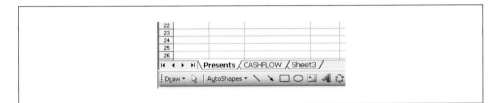

Figure 23.11

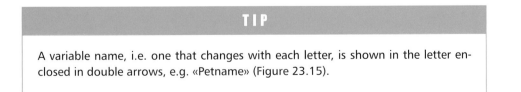

Figure 23.12

Start with the body of the letter and then add in spaces for the address, date and headed notepaper at the top. When you are happy with the letter select:

- **More items . . .** from the panel on the right (Figure 23.14)
- Select **Insert Merge Field** table

Now the fun begins. In each gap, an appropriate field needs to be added. So the word 'Dear' can either be followed by the petname or forename by highlighting one of them and clicking **Insert**, as appropriate. Carry on through the document until all of the necessary variables are inserted. Do not forget to leave appropriate spaces between variables and text. Sometimes it is easier to insert all of the variable names at once and then move them into the text.

TIP

A variable name, i.e. one that changes with each letter, is shown in the letter enclosed in double arrows, e.g. «Petname» (Figure 23.15).

Figure 23.13

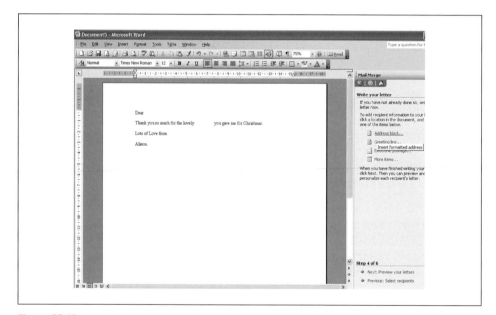

Figure 23.14

Step 4 is where you can preview your letter. It is at this stage that you can see how well the real data fits into the letter (see Figure 23.19).

You may be pleasantly surprised and find you have done it all right or disappointed as it may look a real jumble. This is not a worry because you can take one step back and make the appropriate change to the letter (Figure 23.16).

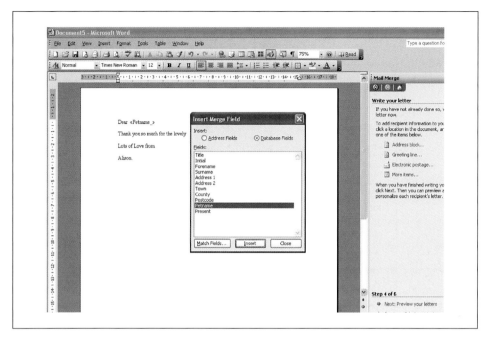

Figure 23.15

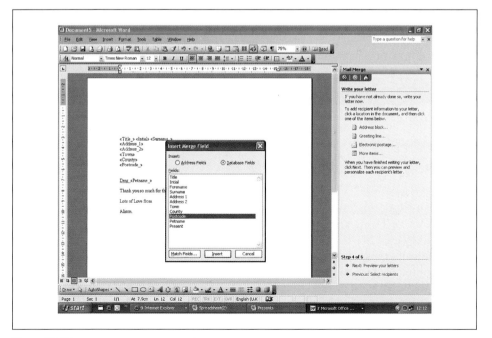

Figure 23.16

Figure 23.17   Figure 23.18

This is also a good time to add in a date at an appropriate location. By selecting **Insert** and clicking on the **Date and Time** option, you can ensure that every time the letters are generated in the future the correct date will appear (Figures 23.17 and 23.18).

The ground work is now completed and once you are happy with the previewed letters you can carry out Step 5 and **Complete the merge**.

> ### TIP
>
> If it all goes horribly wrong, just click on previous: rewrite your letter as appropriate and have another go!

You can check the letters to all the people in the file by using the double left and right arrows, or by clicking on Find a recipient in the panel on the right hand side (Figure 23.19).

When the merge is complete and any further personalisation is included, the letters can be printed (Figure 23.20).

Once the letters are printed, the whole file of merged documents can be saved or just the master letter showing the insertions. The Microsoft® Excel file of data can be added to and modified as needed.

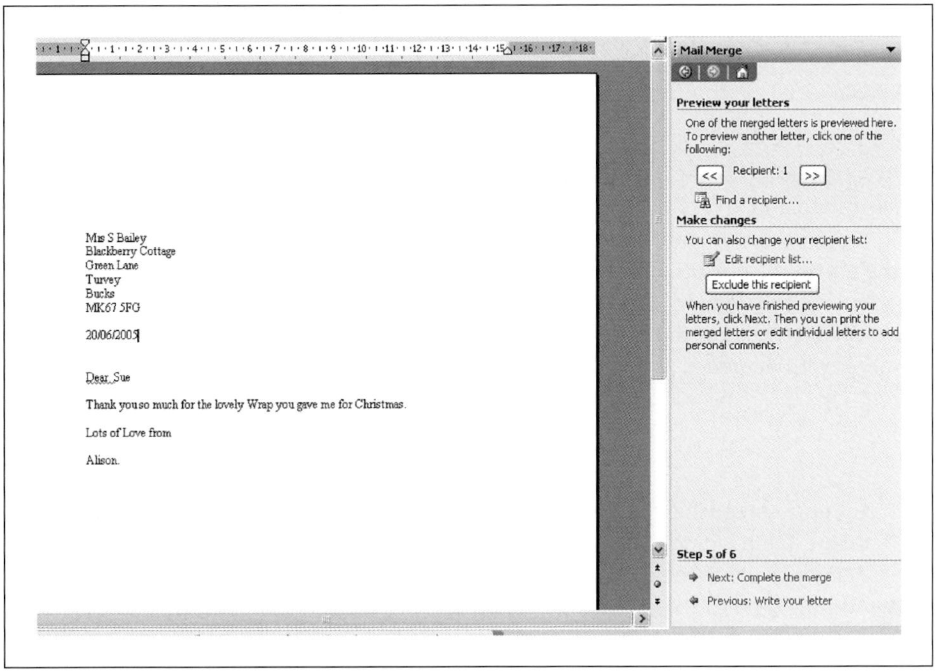

Figure 23.19

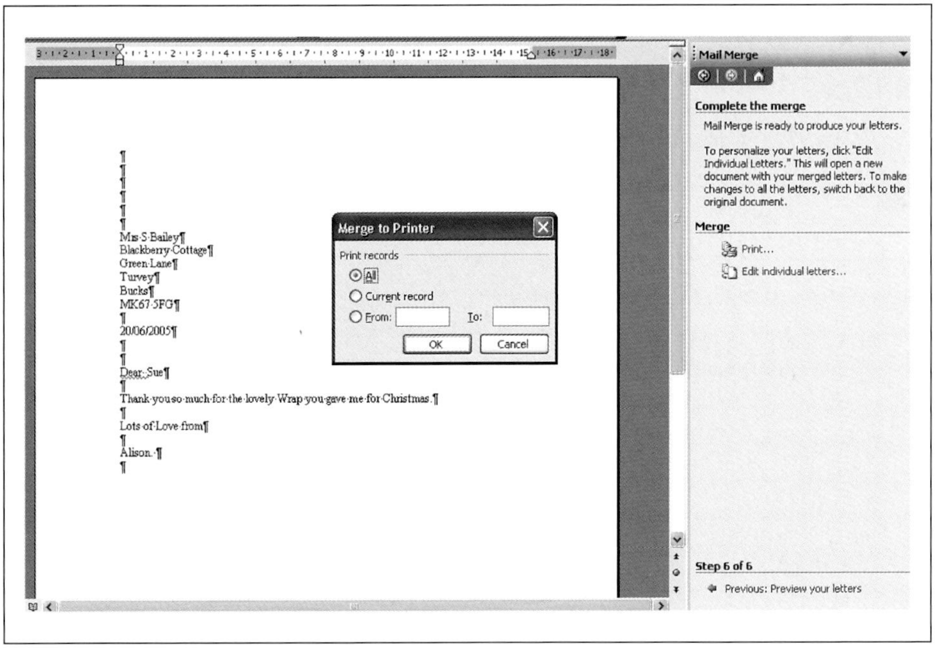

Figure 23.20

Summary

Accurate information stems from the input of accurate data. Student and manager alike should take responsibility for making sure data fit the ACCURATE acronym.

Merging documents and files of data together can produce excellent results at the touch of a button. However, careful examination of the original data and care in preparing the related documents creates smart letters and other documentation that reflect well on the originator. The key to success is to 'eyeball' your data and target your audience.

TASK 1

1 Set up a spreadsheet with data for eight customers.
2 Create the headings Title, Surname, Address Line 1, etc. plus a heading entitled Warehouse and one entitled % discount.
3 Add the data to the spreadsheet and check that it is ACCURATE.
4 Create a letter that offers each customer a % discount and gives them the location of their local warehouse, where the discount will apply.
5 Mail merge the two documents and print out two examples; adjust the addresses so that they fit a normal window envelope.

Reference

HNC/HND BTEC Core Unit 7 Management Information Systems: Business Course Book (2000) London: BPP Publishing Limited.

CHAPTER 24
Excelling to your advantage – graphs and charts

- To identify the key attributes of meaningful input and output
- To produce clearly labelled and impressive graphs and charts

A picture is worth a thousand words and likewise, so is a well-constructed graph or chart. To ensure a graph or chart paints a true picture, data ranges should be checked for accuracy and content and the display should be meaningful.

At the top levels of management the directors often do not have time to trawl through pages and pages of figures. Frequently the most vivid signal to them that changes are occurring is a peaking or falling graph. Similarly, production line output figures can be more easily tracked in a graphical format. It is then up to accountants or production supervisors to drill down and investigate why change has occurred and whether action is needed.

In both your work and studies you will be asked to work creatively with figures, perhaps researching or collating demographic data, sometimes analysing and displaying data. The skills gained in this chapter will give you the confidence to do this.

BASIC ELEMENTS

Cells and formatting

The fundamental element of a spreadsheet is the cell which is denoted by a grid reference (see Chapter 23 for more details). For instance, in Figure 24.1 February is in cell B1. Each cell can be set to a range of formats including number, currency, text and date. When creating data for graphs and charts you will need to specify the type of data you are using by formatting the cell. If you click into the cell and press **Ctrl + 1**, a choice of formats will be offered and an appropriate type can be chosen to match the data you are inputting.

TIP

Be aware of data types and select a format that is appropriate to your data.

Usually with a graph or chart you are comparing two, or even three, types of data. Common types of data could be months of the year, sales per unit or perhaps absenteeism per week.

Auto fill

To save time populating the titles on a spreadsheet, the auto fill option can be used. For instance if you were to put in a known series, for example January, February, March, etc. you can use the automatic fill option to fill in the rest of the series. To do this:

- Highlight the first two elements of the series.
- Hold the left mouse button down.
- From the handle in the bottom right corner (Figure 24.1) drag the mouse across the cells (ensure the cursor looks like a black cross).
- The series is automatically completed for you.

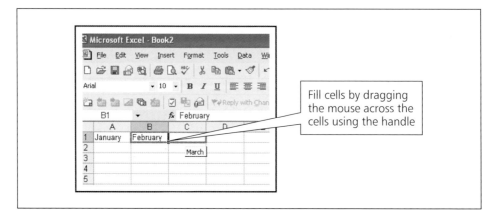

Fill cells by dragging the mouse across the cells using the handle

Figure 24.1

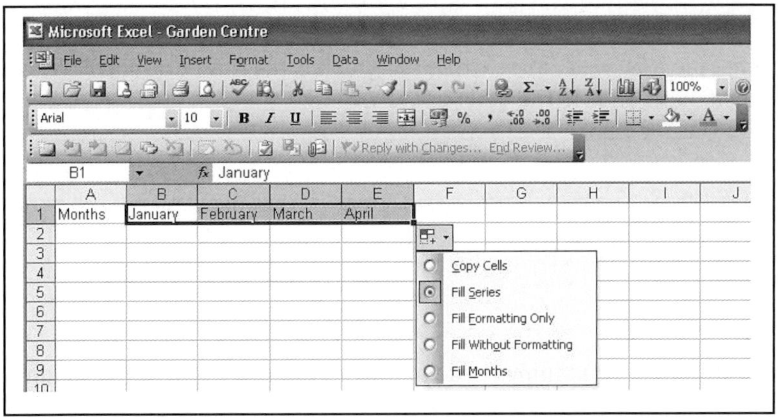

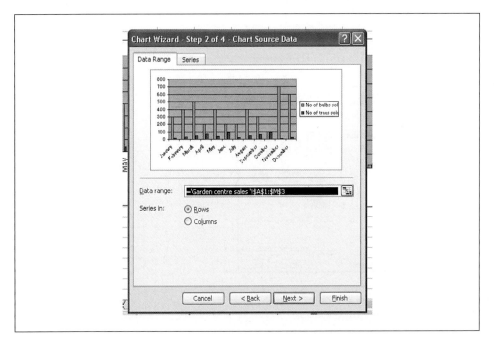

Figure 24.2

Alternatively, a small box will appear which will offer alternatives to filling the adjacent cells, in this case **Fill Months**. Then as you drag the mouse across the cells, the months will appear (Figure 24.2).

The data themselves can be input in rows (1, 2, 3, . . .) or in columns (A, B, C, . . .). Below is an example of sales in a garden centre. These data have been set up in rows which are denoted A1 to M3. The $ sign means the data is fixed in those locations (Figure 24.3).

Figure 24.3

TIP

Remember the axis which goes across the graph is the X axis, distinctive because a cross could mean an X!!! The other axis is Y.

HOW TO CREATE A GRAPH OR CHART FROM SCRATCH USING THE WIZARD

Checking the data

One of the most important things to do before you start is to check the validity and the robustness of your data. What was the source, who checked it, who tabulated it? Look at it and make sure that you feel confident it is right. Always revisit the source of your data if anything looks odd.

TIP

Always 'eyeball' your data before you input it.

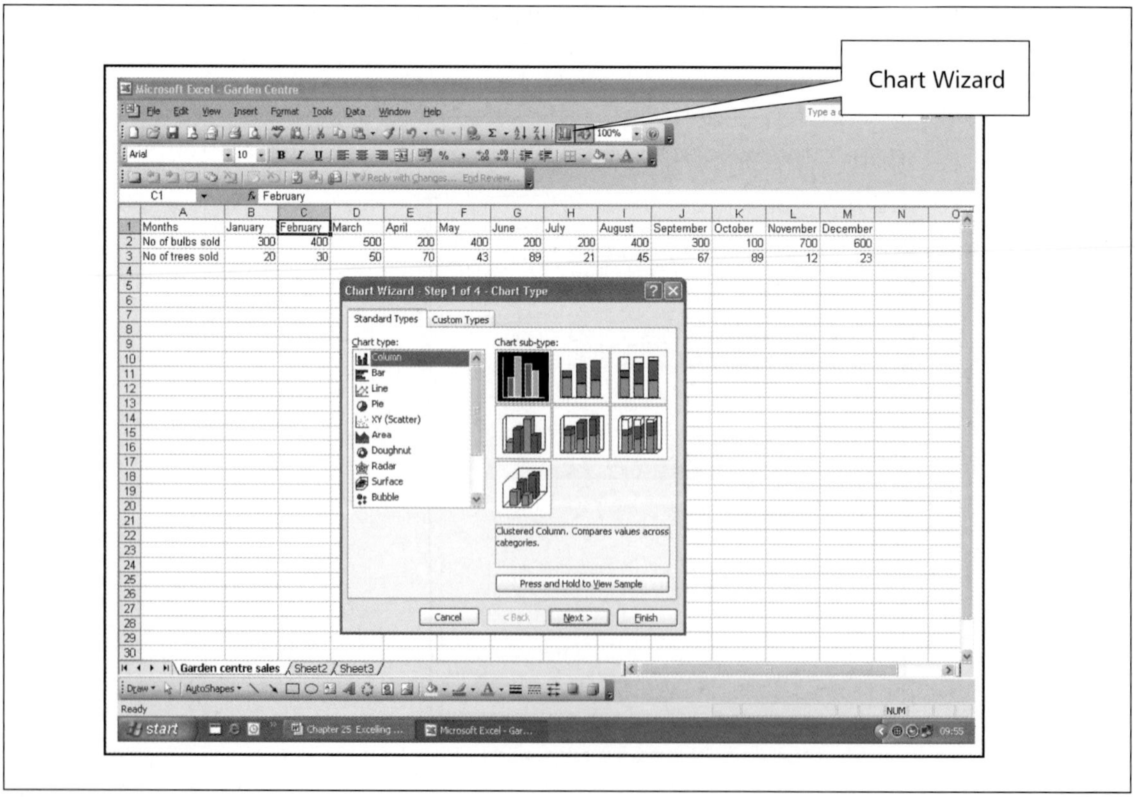

Figure 24.4

Microsoft® Excel 2003 offers a handy wizard for graph and chart production and by clicking on the chart icon the wizard is enabled.

Using the wizard:

- Select **Chart Type**, click on **Next** >.

- Highlight the data needed for the graph or chart by dragging the cursor over the data and the headings at the beginning or when prompted by the wizard (Figure 24.5).

- If the data are not in adjacent rows or columns use the **Ctrl** button on the keyboard to pick out each set of data, i.e. highlight first set of data, move to the next, press the **Ctrl** button, highlight the next set of data. The locations chosen will be displayed as the **Data range**.

- The wizard is capable of judging which way round the data should be and will display it accordingly; but make sure you check, as it is not foolproof.

- If necessary change **Series in:** to **Columns** or **Rows** as appropriate (Figure 24.5). Click on **Next** >.

- Add a chart title or other refinements (Figure 24.6). Note the tab top contains options that can be used to change titles, axes, gridlines, legend, data labels and data table. By experimenting, you can change the way your output is presented.

- Examples: The legend (or caption) can be given the meaningful title of *no. of bulbs sold* and *no. of trees sold*, instead of the standard default of *Series 1* and *Series 2*. This can be done by highlighting and including it in the **Data range** or

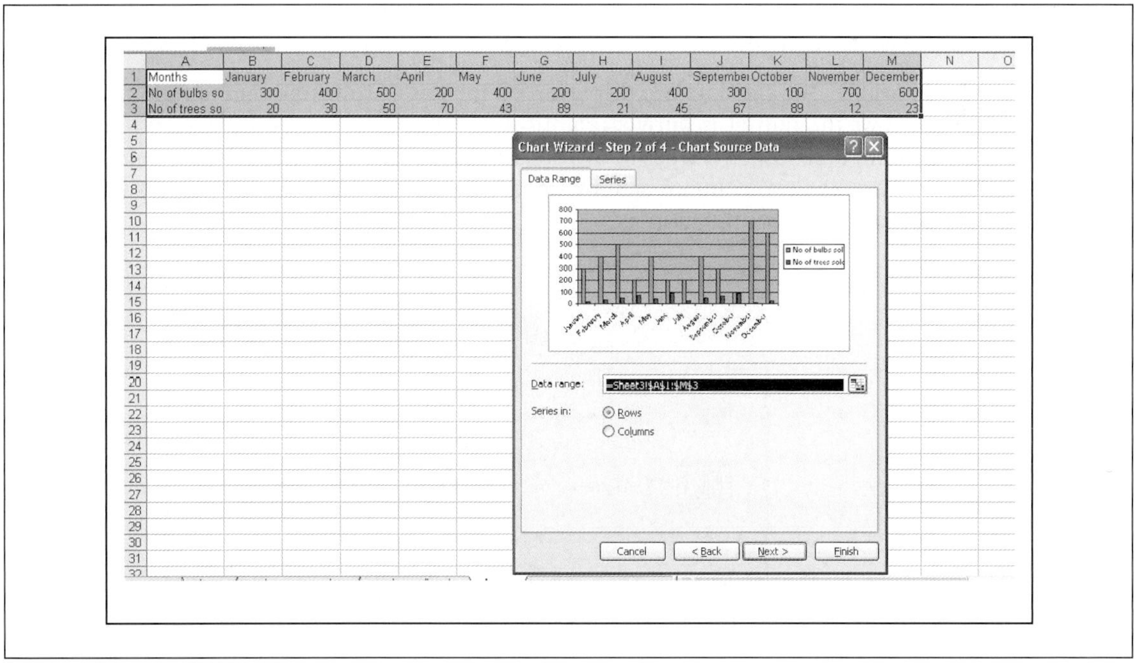

Figure 24.5

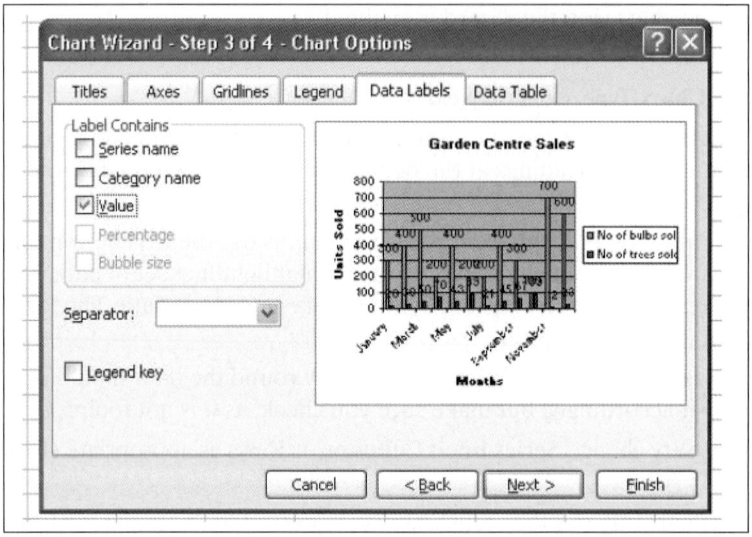

Figure 24.6

changing the title. Another example is shown in Figure 24.6, which shows that by selecting **Value**, the value appears above each column.

- Click on **Next** >.
- Choose a location for the new chart (Figure 24.7). **Finish**.
- If **As a new sheet** is chosen, label the new sheet appropriately.

Rows or columns

In Figure 24.8 the data are displayed on the left as rows and on the right as columns. In rows the output is fairly straightforward, but as columns the wizard presents the sales of bulbs and the trees in two separate graphs. This is not as easily comparable as showing the two columns side by side. Also it gives the X axis no value and relies on colour coding for the months.

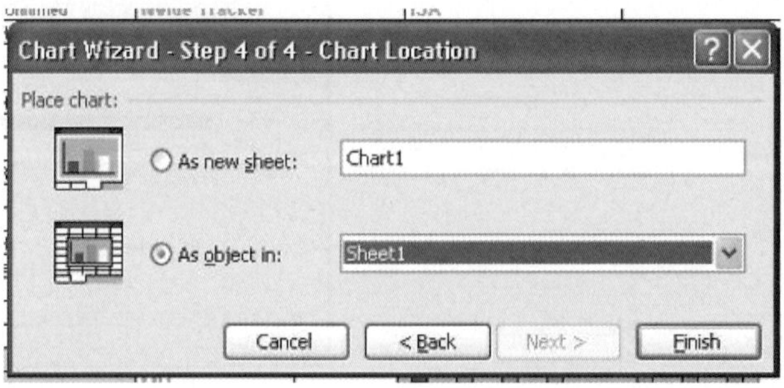

Figure 24.7

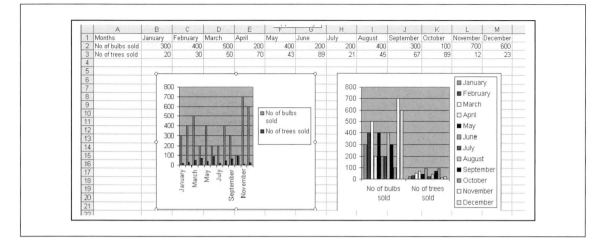

Figure 24.8

The excellent thing about using the wizard is that you can try all of the different options and the display will show you exactly what effect the particular action will have on the finished output.

TIP

Do not be afraid to experiment with graphs and charts. If you do not like the finished result, delete it and have another go!

Another change that can add clarity to your graph or chart is to show the original data and the legend keys at the bottom. As you can see, the original output from the wizard was cramped and difficult to read (Figure 24.9). However, when you click on **Finish** and the chart is displayed on the spreadsheet you can easily expand the display area so that the months display correctly and are not 'wrapped round'.

The smartly presented graph in Figure 24.10 displays the original data. To expand the chart, click on it and stretch it from the right-hand corner using the double-headed arrow.

TIP

When expanding a chart area, always do it from a corner point because expanding it from the bottom or the side will distort the graph.

Cosmetic changes to graphs

Once the graph appears on the datasheet various elements can be cosmetically changed to give a smarter appearance. Take the opportunity to experiment with the legend axis and main titles on the graph using the **Format** options.

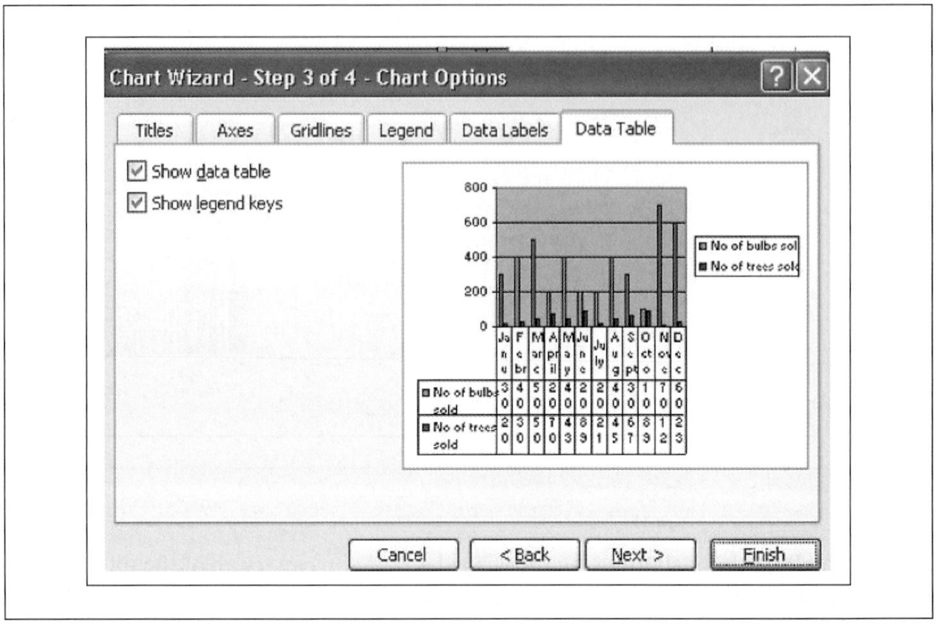

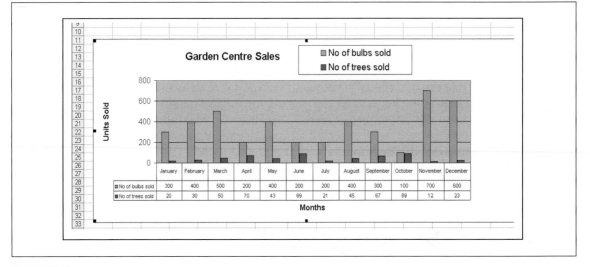

Figure 24.9

Figure 24.10

To make a change, first position the cursor over the area you want to change. Then click with the right-hand mouse button over one of the titles. The display will either show **Format Axis Title** or **Clear** as in Figure 24.11 or **Format Chart Title** or **Clear** if the cursor is over a title.

In Figure 24.11 the months January and March are displayed, but what happened to February? The reason February does not appear is because the font size is too big

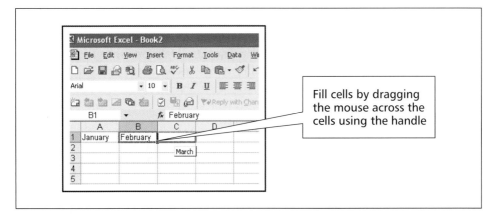

Figure 24.11

and the chart wizard has opted to display every other month. This gives an overview but not detail. Formatting the text allows the font size to be reduced so that all twelve months are displayed (Figure 24.12). Figure 24.12 shows the options given to **Format Chart Title**.

TIP

It can be useful to get rid of the chart legends, titles and just use text boxes. This gives more space for the chart.

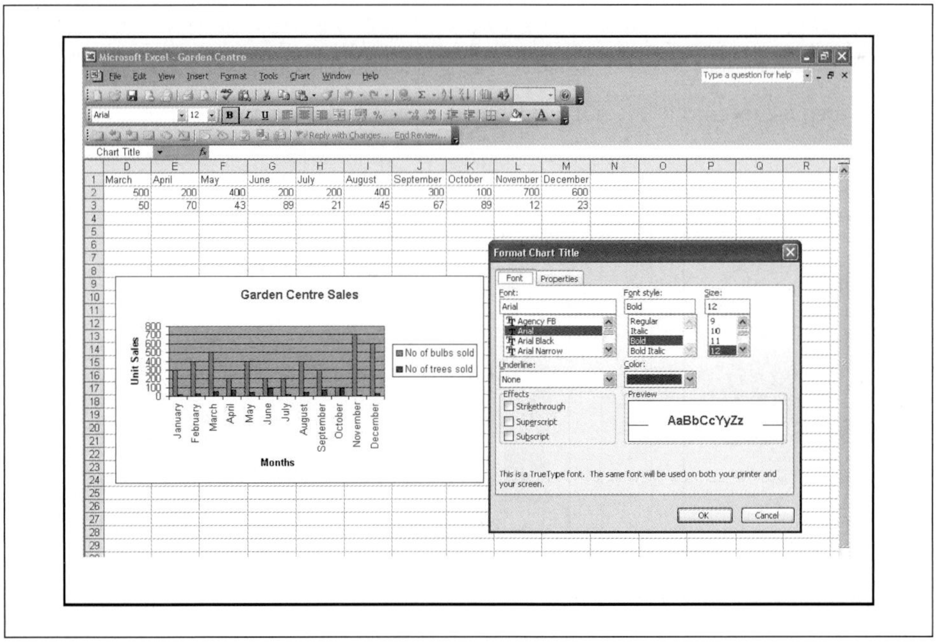

Figure 24.12

Altering the body of graphs or charts

To change features on your graph or chart, click on the finished chart with the right-hand mouse button. If you want to alter the chart itself, click on the graph and a display will show the options available. Headings were discussed in the previous section; in this section we will look at other aspects.

Data series

Placing the cursor over the columns or lines displays the value (Figure 24.13).

Clicking on the column itself with the right-hand mouse button produces a square in the centre of the column and a choice of options is displayed (Figure 24.14).

> **TIP**
>
> Click across the chart with the right-hand mouse button and note the available options. Experiment with each option in turn.

Format the Data Series will not only allow changes to font sizes and colours, but will also allow changes to the axis, Y error bars (which you will probably not need at this stage), data labels, series order and options.

There are hundreds of combinations to choose from with this one function, so use them as needed to give clarity to the final output (Figure 24.15).

Options can be used to change the gaps between the columns (Figure 24.16) but also notice that some options are 'greyed out' which means they are not available at this time.

> **TIP**
>
> If an area is greyed out it is not available as an option at this time.

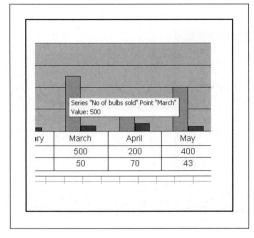

Figure 24.13

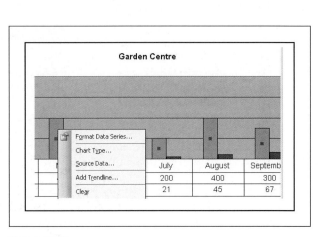

Figure 24.14

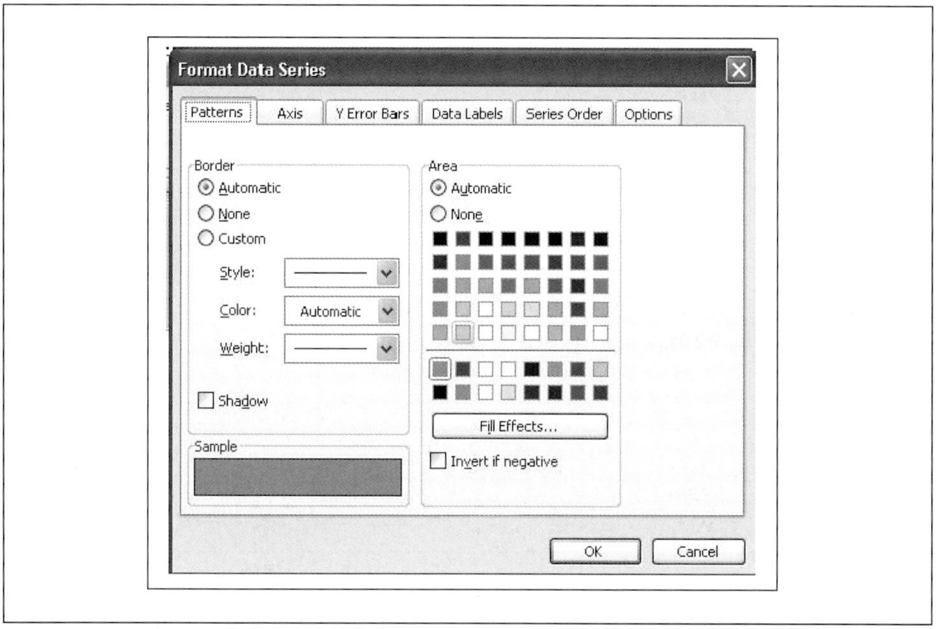

Figure 24.15

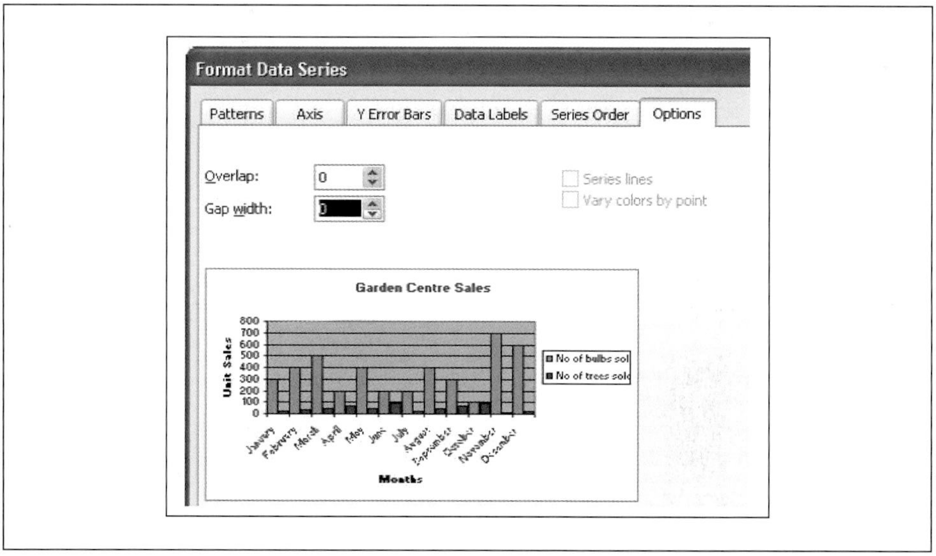

Figure 24.16

Choosing different types of graph, for example straight line, gives other types of options as well as features. The tabs are the same but some of the options are different. Experiment with these by changing to an alternative chart type (Figure 24.17).

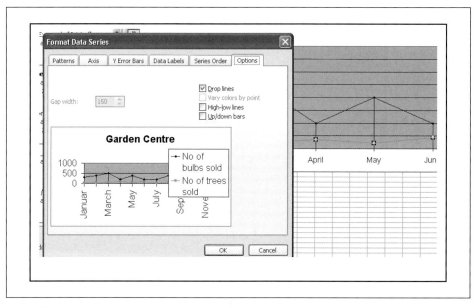

Figure 24.17

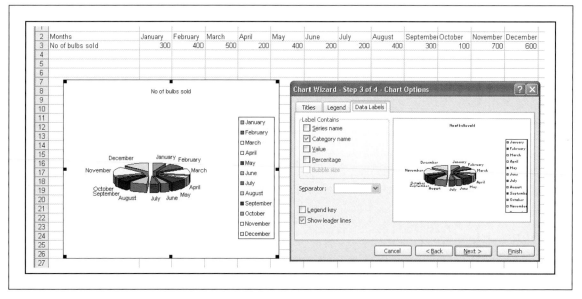

Figure 24.18

Pie charts can only be used for one dimensional/one source data and can create a striking output. In Figure 24.18 the source data shown are for bulbs only and the option to add the category name shows the months around the edge of the chart rather than just relying on the colour coding.

COMMON PITFALLS

Giving clarity to graphs and charts

As the producer of the graphs, it is easy to convince yourself that your presentation of the data is clear to all. However, one has only to look at the outputs from annual reports, financial institutions and newspapers to know that data are often presented creatively rather than accurately. There are some inventive ways of presenting data and there are some ways that it is best to avoid.

The fun chart

In may seem 'fun' to display the sales of bulbs and trees or whatever needs displaying using images. Figures 24.19 and 24.20 show images that could be used to represent 100 units sold of bulbs and trees. These images can then be shrunk or expanded appropriately to represent different units sold.

This may mean that the output looks pretty, but it is a nightmare to work out and not a professional way of displaying the data. That does not mean to say that your boss may not want you to be creative!

Disproportionate graphs

What is very noticeable from the graph shown in Figure 24.21 is how disproportionate the chart looks, namely because the bulb sales and the tree sales are both shown by unit.

This is one of the problems that graphical output can produce, when the data units are not properly considered. It is important to choose your scales wisely and you may have to go back to the original data source and consider a different way of representing it. Perhaps in this case the total sales or the total profit expressed in currency may give a better representation.

Figure 24.19

Figure 24.20

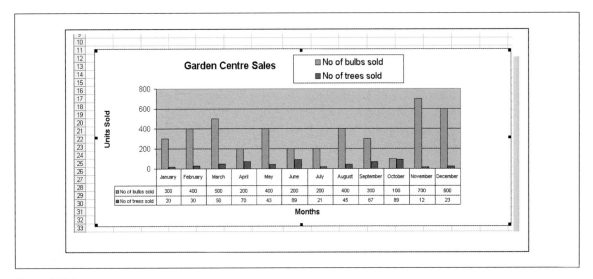

Figure 24.21

> ## TIP
>
> Always consider whether the representation of the data will give clarity in the final output, or at least, give the result you want!

The relativity dilemma

Figure 24.22 shows all bulbs sold by unit relative to one another. If you are comparing like for like sales, then units sold is an excellent comparison. If you are comparing re-tail outlets such as a small supermarket selling bulbs as a 'seasonal extra' and a garden centre selling thousands of units, then check that comparing two outlets on the same chart gives a meaningful output.

Another relativity dilemma is the axes. The chart on the left in Figure 24.22 has a zero point on the Y axis, whereas the chart on the right does not. It is easy to see that the sale of crocus bulbs outstrips the others, but starting the vertical axis at 300 makes hyacinth sales look non-existent, the zero axis gives credibility to the sales of all types of bulb. The tactic of starting an axis at a non-zero point is commonplace but it can distort the figures.

Well-defined axes

Another difference in the charts is that the Y axis on the left-hand chart is marked in 500 unit increments, whereas the right-hand chart has been altered using **Format Axis** to give 100 unit increments (Figure 24.23) and can therefore be read more accurately.

In Figure 24.23 the sales of bulbs is displayed as a percentage of the total and, although it shows that crocuses still outstrip the sales of the other bulbs, the results look more proportioned. This is a good opportunity to use a pie chart.

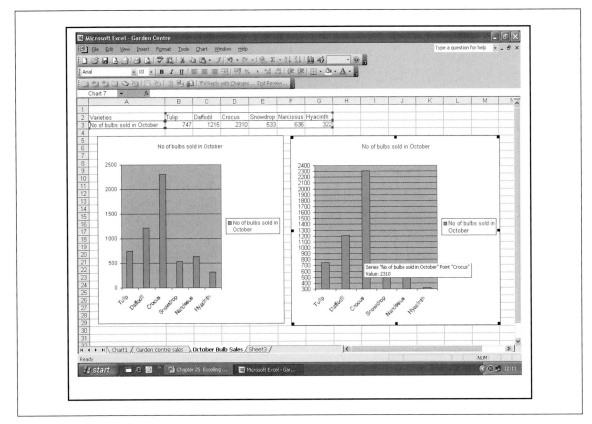

Figure 24.22

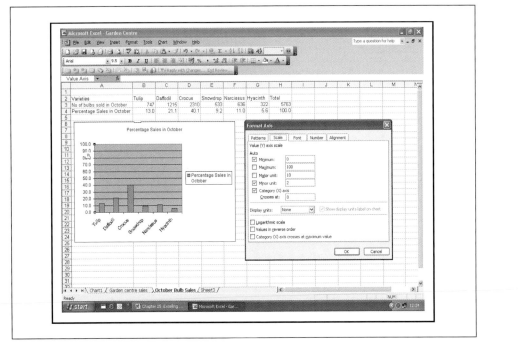

Figure 24.23

Using the chart wizard and a small space can often give a cramped and distorted view of the presented data. The ability to change the labelling detail and unit size on the X and Y axes can give greater clarity.

Trendline

Having prepared all of your data and displayed them in a well proportioned and meaningful way, it is possible to add in a trendline. A trendline can tell you whether things are looking up or are declining! You cannot put a trendline onto a pie chart or a three dimensional chart. To add a trendline click with the right-hand mouse button over a column or place on the graph and select **Add Trendline** (Figure 24.24).

However, not all charts are enhanced by this addition and sometimes trendlines are used inappropriately. For instance if you were to add a trendline to the chart on the left in Figure 24.25 it would show a decline, but if you add it to the chart on the right it shows an incline! The data are the same, the sales are the same, but the creator of the graph has put the bulb types in a different order. Therefore the trendline is meaningless and a complete waste of time.

TIP

Make sure a trendline makes sense.

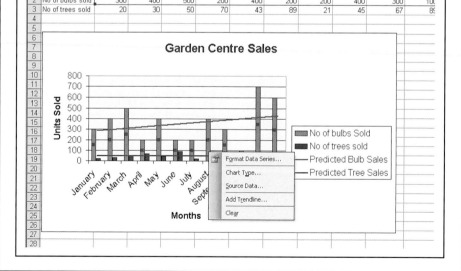

Figure 24.24

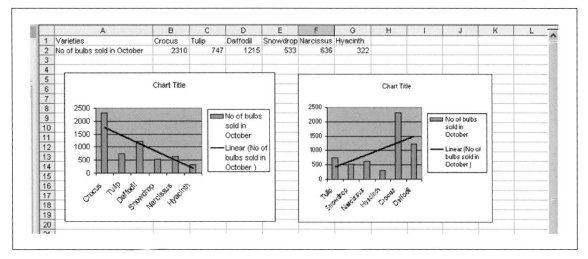

Figure 24.25

However, if you have year on year sales or monthly sales, a trendline can be an appropriate technique to use. In this case, there is still a flaw because most bulb sales will occur in the late autumn, so the trend will always go up at the end of the year. However, if you look at sales over five years, the trendline will be more meaningful.

If you click on the trendline you can change the patterns, type and options. In this case a name, Predicted Tree Sales, has been added to the trendline and the colour changed to match the columns (Figure 24.26).

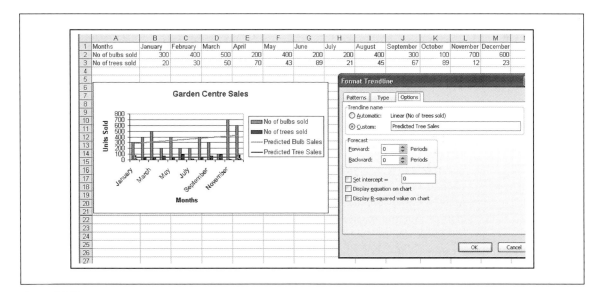

Figure 24.26

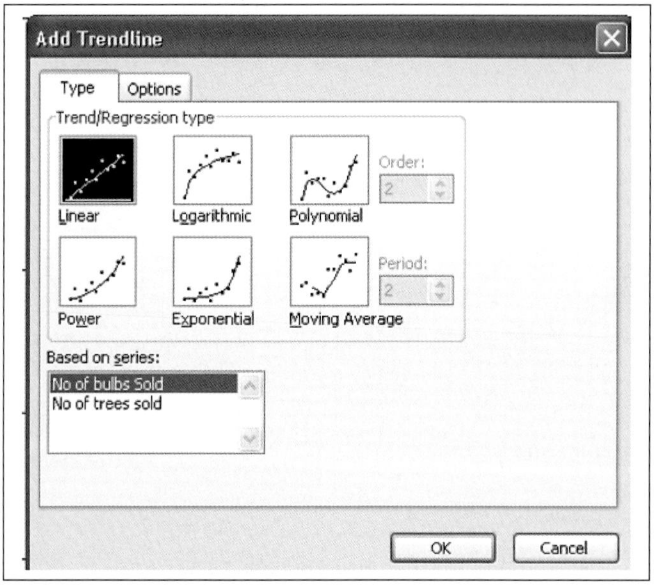

Figure 24.27

A trendline can be applied as a different type according to how the series needs to be displayed (Figure 24.27).

Summary

A well-constructed graph or chart can convey instant meaning and clarity. Managers can quickly recognise changes as they occur if well-checked and verified data are presented in a clear way. Data types can be represented in a variety of ways to represent currency, numbers, dates and text.

Chart wizards can produce a working graph or chart, but refinement of the parameters can give a much clearer picture. Experiment with all aspects of graph and chart production to give meaningful output, clearly displayed.

Avoid common mistakes with graph and chart production by ensuring that there is clarity. Avoid fun charts, disproportionate figures and the relativity dilemma. Make sure axes are well defined and appropriately scaled. Add trendlines if and only when appropriate.

The data below are the raw data issued by the Met Office for 2003 and 2004 (Met Office 2006) from the Oxford Station.

yyyy	mm	tmax degC	tmin degC	rain mm	sun hours
2003	1	7.6	1.8	81.4	87.7
2003	2	8.4	0.6	17.3	94.4
2003	3	13.3	2.7	25.2	154.8
2003	4	15.3	4.6	36.8	169.8
2003	5	17.5	8.1	48.1	191.2
2003	6	22.4	11.8	55.5	213.6
2003	7	23.7	13.4	53.8	192.0
2003	8	25.5	13.5	3.0	228.4
2003	9	21.3	8.1	17.4	175.3
2003	10	14.0	3.9	31.7	134.8
2003	11	12.0	5.7	89.6	78.9
2003	12	8.7	1.8	70.7	53.6
2004	1	8.8	2.7	66.1	62.7
2004	2	8.7	2.9	25.5	79.1
2004	3	10.9	3.4	51.8	100.5
2004	4	14.7	6.2	68.8	150.3
2004	5	18.0	8.6	41.1	195.5
2004	6	21.8	12.0	23.8	223.5
2004	7	22.0	12.2	83.1	169.6
2004	8	23.4	14.2	135.0	194.1
2004	9	20.1	11.7	28.9	174.3
2004	10	14.7	8.6	131.4	102.3
2004	11	10.9	5.8	34.2	52.5
2004	12	8.6	2.8	37.7	58.3

Figure 24.28

a. Put the data into a spreadsheet month by month
b. Set the format to accommodate the range of decimal figures
c. Create a pie chart of the sun, labelled by month for each year
d. Using a line graph, compare each month's rainfall between 2003 and 2004
e. For *each* year, use a chart to compare rain with sun per month

References

Levine, D. M. (2005) *Statistics for Managers Using Microsoft Excel* (International Edition), Upper Saddle River, NJ: Pearson.
Met Office (2006) [online]. [Accessed 18 April 2006]. Available from World Wide Web http://www.met-office.gov.uk/climate/uk/stationdata/oxforddata.txt

CHAPTER 25

Excelling to your advantage – figures, facts and statistics

- To employ formatting techniques
- To apply simple formula to a range of diverse data
- To utilise statistical functions and comprehend their relevance

Introduction

When the scientific calculator first appeared, it was a huge breakthrough. Mathematic and logarithmic tables were abandoned. When the calculator no longer offered rapid solutions to numerical problems, the next breakthrough was the spreadsheet.

Although initially the functions were limited, developments over the years have created a wealth of formulations that in theory solve most aspects of calculation in the mathematical world. Microsoft® Excel 2003 offers Financial, Date and Time, Math and Trig and Statistical formulae, as well as those related to databases and logic.

Once again the endless possibilities and the nature of your work will mean that you will have to develop mathematical skills steadily. As your skills develop you can pick, choose and practise the use of specific functions as they become useful or necessary.

It may be that in your work environment more specialised software is in use. However, an understanding of the principles of spreadsheet capabilities will provide a good underpinning and understanding. Given confidence with basic principles, the transition from 'known' to 'unknown' will become fairly painless!

SETTING UP A CELL

Toolbars

Most functions are available on the toolbars, but if the toolbars are not shown click on **View** and click the ones needed. Initially select **Formula Bar**, **Status bar**, **Standard**, **Formatting** and **Drawing** (Figure 25.1).

TIP

Familiarise yourself with the functions on each toolbar. Positioning the cursor over the icons on the toolbar reveals the function, e.g. merge and centre (Figure 25.2).

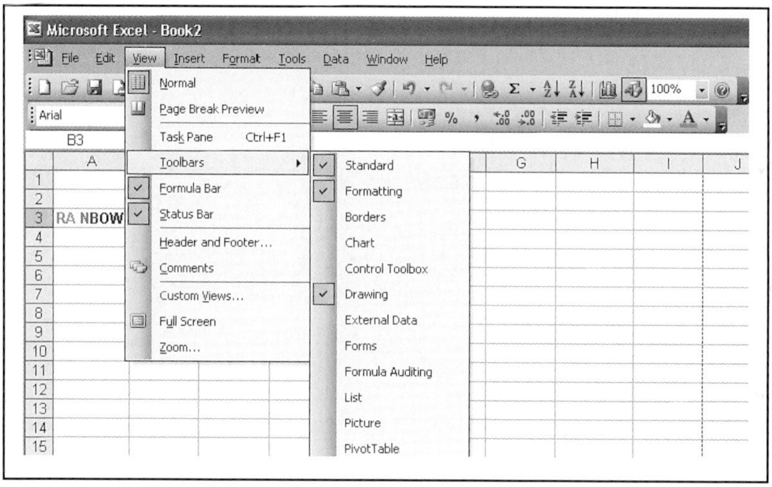

Figure 25.1

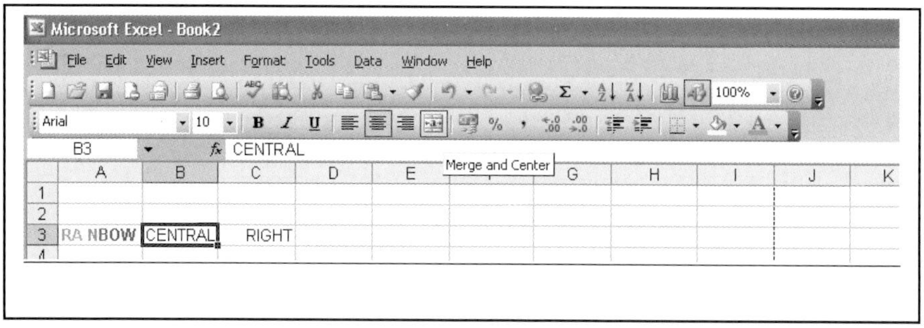

Figure 25.2

Text in cells

Changes to some aspects of the cell like bold text (**B**) and underline (<u>U</u>) are similar to Microsoft® Word documents. The main difference is that the contents of the cell appear in the formula bar and that is where the individual letters of a word or parts of a formula can be accessed.

In Figure 25.3 the letters of the word RAINBOW have been accessed individually and each letter has been highlighted in the formula bar and a colour chosen to represent it. The word **RAINBOW** is also in bold.

By clicking inside a box, it is possible to scan the tool bar and see immediately some aspects of the contents of the cell. Its grid position, A3, is shown in the name box above it and the **B** for bold is also highlighted on the toolbar.

The toolbars are divided into subsets with a pale grey divider between them, each dedicated to a different aspect of setting up the cells (Figure 25.4).

Some, as in Microsoft® Word, are dedicated to centring the contents of the cell (Figure 25.5), some are concerned with the grid, highlighting and font colour (Figure 25.6).

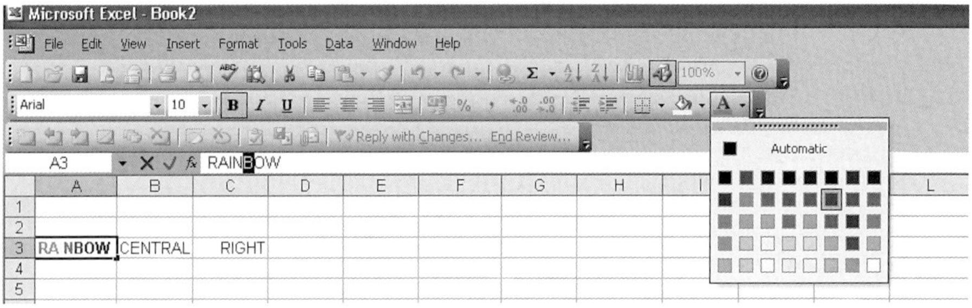

Figure 25.3

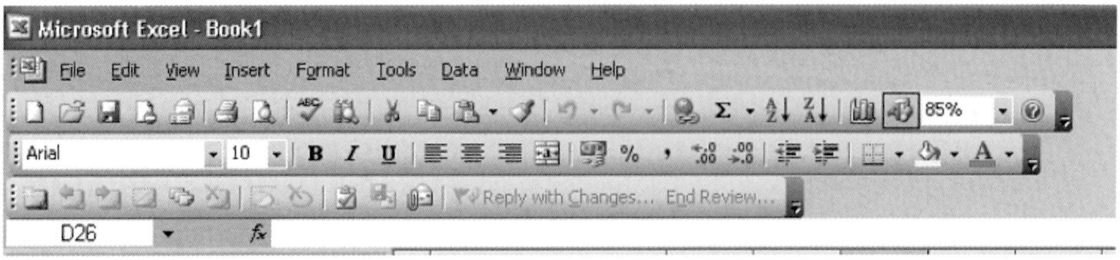

Figure 25.4

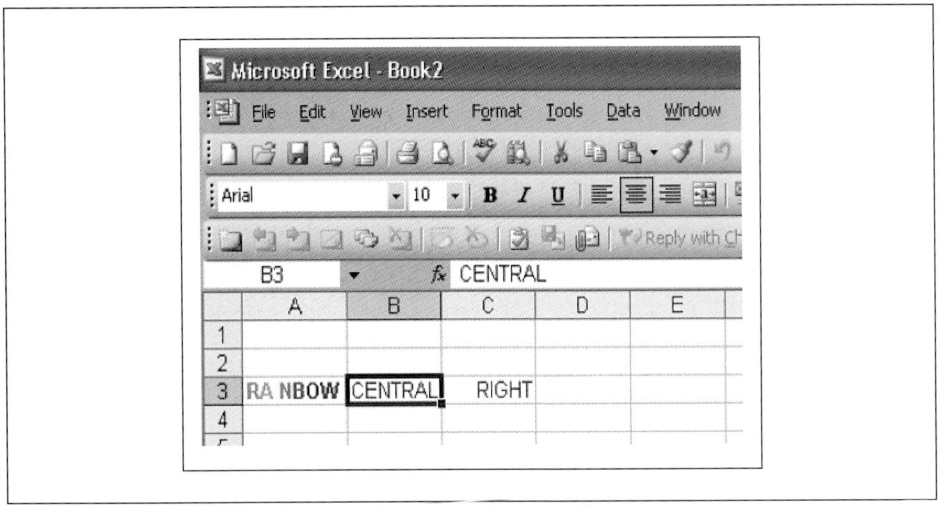

Figure 25.5

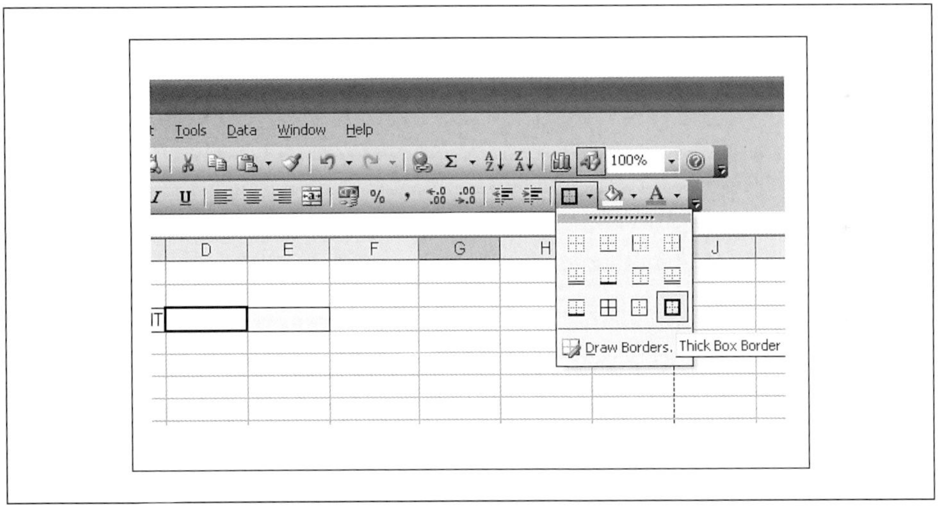

Figure 25.6

Figure 25.7

Numeric formats

The **Formatting** toolbar (Figure 25.7) shows the subsets that manipulate and enhance the numerical functions within the cell. They can also be accessed by

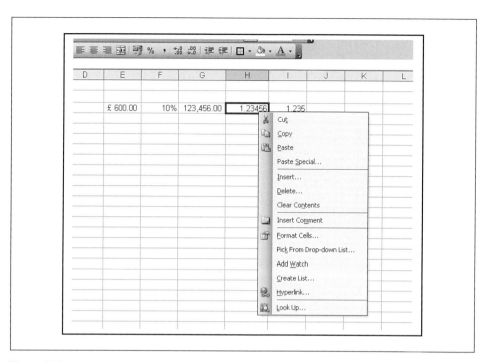

Figure 25.8

clicking with the right-hand mouse button when inside a cell and selecting **Format Cells** (Figure 25.8).

The toolbar can be used to set a cell to represent currency, percentage, a number with a comma in it, an increased number of places after the decimal or a decreased number of places after the decimal. An example of each of these is shown in Figure 25.8.

TIP

Format each cell to reflect the function it performs.

Currency

It may be that having chosen currency, the default is not the currency you need. This is when there is a need to use **Format Cells**. Figure 25.9 shows not only the number of different options a cell can be set to, but also the number of choices within each option. Something for everyone!

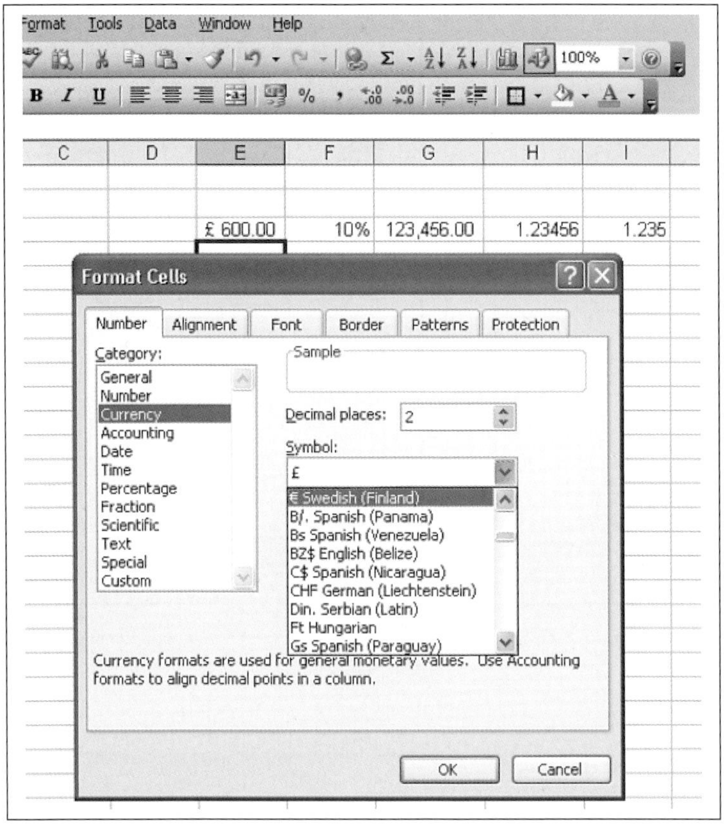

Figure 25.9

Negative numbers

If you set the figures to **Number** or **Currency** format, then there is an option of setting a negative number differently, for example to appear in red (Figure 25.10). The advantage of this is that when a number is negative it is visually and instantly apparent.

> **TIP**
>
> Use the formatting feature on the number and currency categories to highlight exceptions, e.g. negative numbers.

Date format

There is a huge range of different date formats (Figure 25.11), for example 14 March 2001. However, if the figures do not correspond to a date then the output will appear very odd indeed. Always be sure to use a format that is relevant to the country – beware of the difference between UK and US date formats.

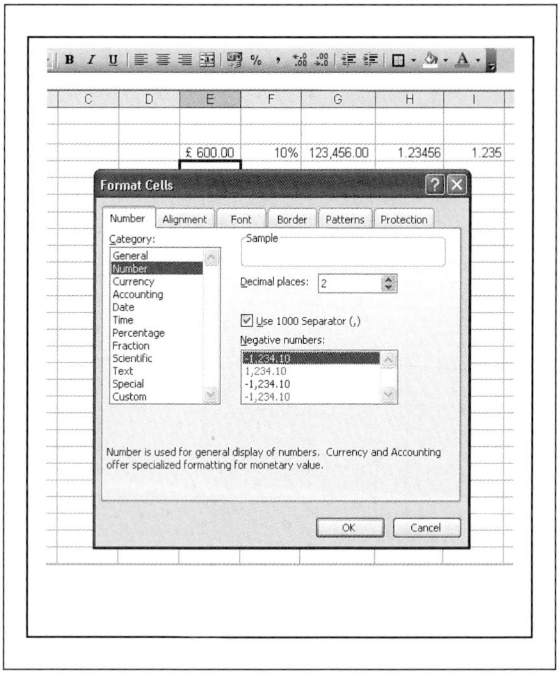

Figure 25.10

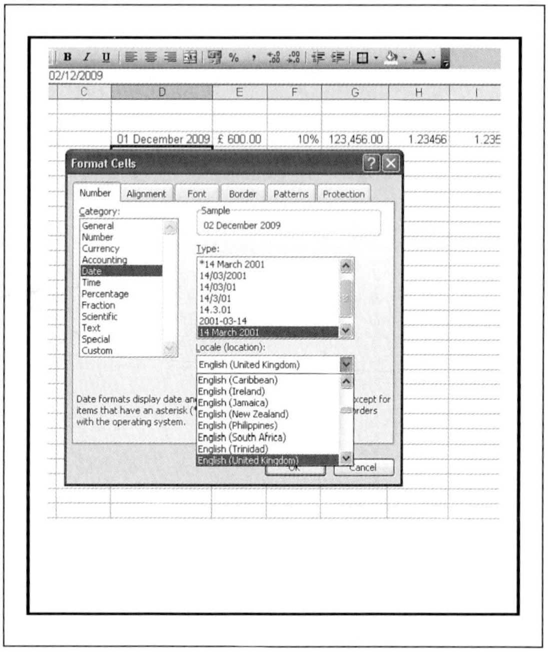

Figure 25.11

TIP

When creating spreadsheets always 'eyeball' the contents of the cells for oddities.

TECHNIQUES TO MANIPULATE AND HIGHLIGHT DATA

Conditional formatting

Having considered general number formatting, it is possible to use a more defined type of formatting, namely **Conditional Formatting**. It too can be used to highlight exceptions as they occur. An exception flags up a change from the norm.

If the spreadsheet cells are set up using conditional formatting, it is possible to define a rule that when it is true causes a different format to be output, thus highlighting the problem.

To do this:

- Select the cell to be formatted
- Select **Format**
- Select **Conditional formatting** (Figure 25.12)
- From the drop down list choose a condition, e.g. **less than** (Figure 25.13)
- Choose a **value**, e.g. 3500.

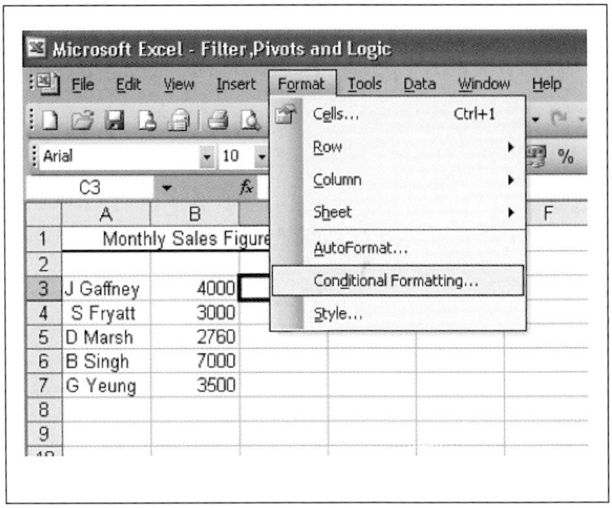

Figure 25.12

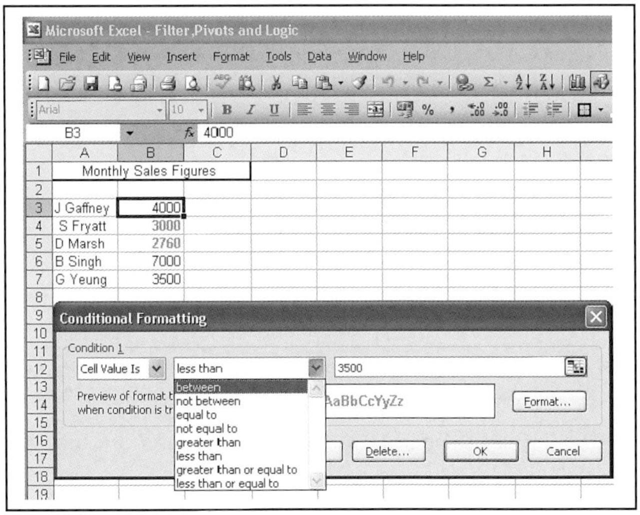

Figure 25.13

- Choose a format by clicking on the **Format** button (Figure 25.14)
- Set a second or third condition if needed
- Click **OK**

Selecting **Conditional formatting** in this example highlights those sales people achieving less than the target of 3500. It may also be used to highlight exceptionally good

Figure 25.14

sales people. In this case, by setting a second condition highlighting those achieving a figure of more than 6999. Note that conditional formatting sets the contents of the cell in a range of coloured text or block colour, or adds a border.

TIP

Experiment with conditional operations to make sure you are fully aware of how they work.

Using formulae to set conditions

In a similar way a formula can be set up to yield a warning text if certain conditions are true or false. In Figure 25.15 an IF statement is used and, according to whether a value is true or false, certain text appears. In this case if the sales are greater than or equal to 4000 then the text 'On or above target' appears, if false the text 'PROBLEM!!!' appears. If a formula like this is set up and you have 1000 items of data to examine, by devising a formula and then dragging the formula down certain traits can quickly be revealed.

Figure 25.15

Once you have set a formula you can repeat it by dragging it down the column of figures. To do this click with the left-hand mouse button on the cell, position the cursor on the bottom right-hand corner of the box and a cross will appear. Hold the left-hand mouse button down and drag the mouse down the cells until you reach the bottom of the column. As you do so the text will appear in the cell as in Figure 25.15. To make your results even clearer it is possible to just highlight the problem figures and leave blank text if the figures are acceptable.

TIP

Create formulae or conditions that highlight exceptions or problems.

Filters

A filter is also a useful tool for highlighting or selecting certain data. To set up select **AutoFilter** click on **Data**, **Filter** and then **AutoFilter** (Figure 25.16).

As a result, a small box containing an arrow appears at the top of each column (Figure 25.17) and when this is clicked on it reveals the range of data in that column plus other options that can be used to filter the data. These options include sorting and customising a filter.

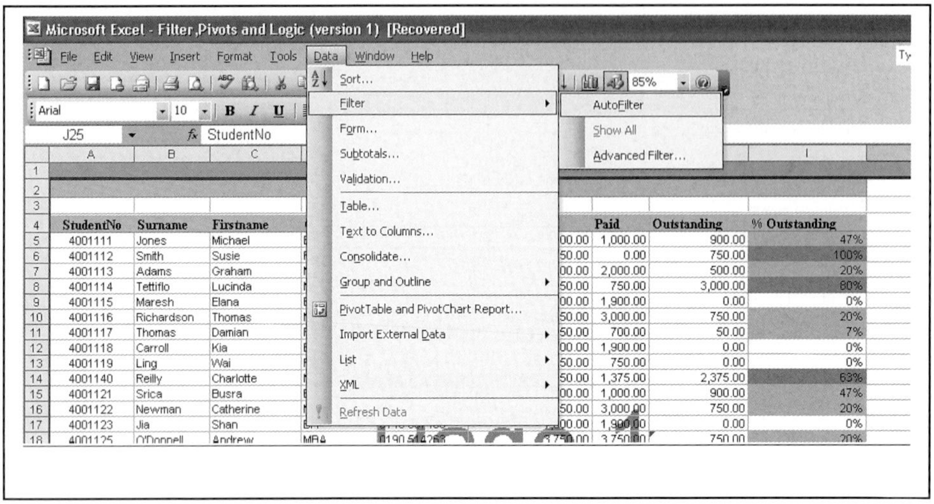

Figure 25.16

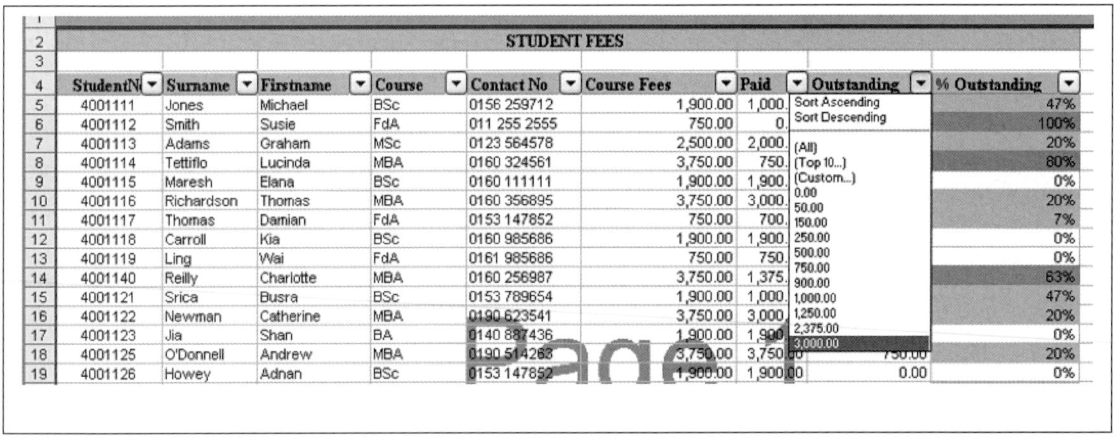

Figure 25.17

Figure 25.17 also shows **Conditional formatting** in place. It is used to reveal the percentage of debt outstanding. Debts of over 50 per cent show in red and all other debts show in pink. Looking at the filter drop down box relating to the amount of Outstanding Debt Figure the range can be seen. It shows that some students owe the sum of 3000 whilst others owe 0. The **(Custom . . .)** AutoFilter (Figure 25.17) can be set up as in Figure 25.18. Here it is used to find debts greater than 1000.

STUDENT FEES

StudentN	Surname	Firstname	Course	Contact No	Course Fees	Paid	Outstanding
4001111	Jones						900.00
4001112	Smith						750.00
4001113	Adams						500.00
4001114	Tettiflo						3,000.00
4001115	Maresh						0.00
4001116	Richard						750.00
4001117	Thomas						50.00
4001118	Carroll						0.00
4001119	Ling						0.00
4001140	Reilly						2,375.00
4001121	Srica						900.00
4001122	Newma						750.00
4001123	Jia						0.00
4001125	O'Donn						750.00
4001126	Howey						0.00
4001127	Condoll						900.00
4001128	Chandi						0.00
4001129	Byflad						0.00
4001130	Achmer	Richard	MSc	0123 654789	2,500.00	1,250.00	1,250.00
4001132	Willcocks	Sally	FdA	0153 789654	750.00	750.00	0.00

Custom AutoFilter dialog box:

Custom AutoFilter ✕

Show rows where:
Outstanding

is greater than ▾   1000 ▾

○ And ○ Or

▾   ▾

Use ? to represent any single character
Use * to represent any series of characters

OK   Cancel

Figure 25.18

TIP

Remember that in order restore the spreadsheet to show all entries, *go back to the column that has just been filtered* and select all (Figure 25.17). The last used column will be shown in blue.

Adding filters to your spreadsheet allows you to 'drill down' on the important aspects. If you add another column after the main spreadsheet is completed, highlight all of the data, remove the AutoFilter and then set it again.

SORTING DATA

Using AutoFilter options

The **Auto<u>F</u>ilter**, in the drop down box, gives the option to **Sort Ascending** or **Sort Descending** (Figure 25.17). It will sort the whole sheet keeping all the related records together.

Normal sort

If the filter is not on, a sort can be carried out by selecting **<u>D</u>ata** and **<u>S</u>ort** (Figure 25.19), or by using these icons.

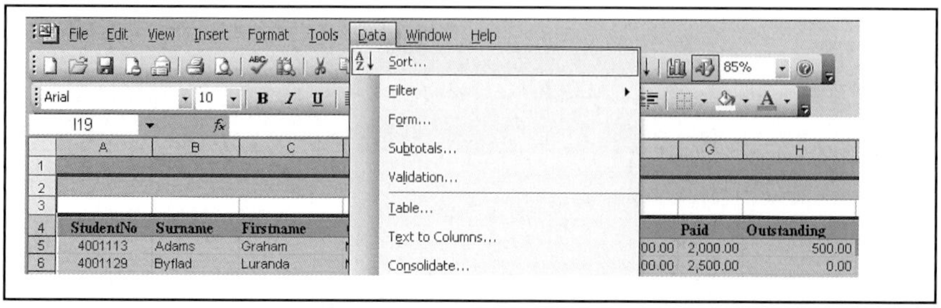

Figure 25.19

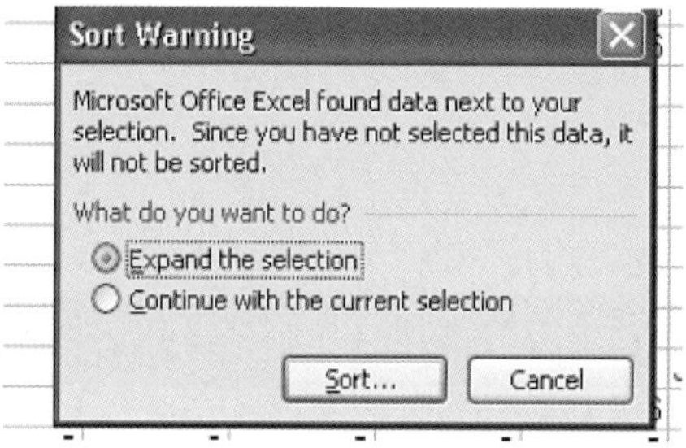

Figure 25.20

It is important to highlight all the items of data to be sorted to ensure that each record stays together. If you do not select the whole range of the spreadsheet, a warning will appear to ask if you want to expand your selection (Figure 25.20).

Imagine just sorting the Paid column, ascending or descending either way, without the rest of the data. Suddenly those who were fully paid up become debtors and those who were in debt have their debts cleared!

TIP

Beware when using a sort to highlight all of the related records before activating the sort.

Sort parameters

If you have headings on your spreadsheet, you will be able to choose which column to sort and whether to do it in ascending or descending order (Figure 25.21).

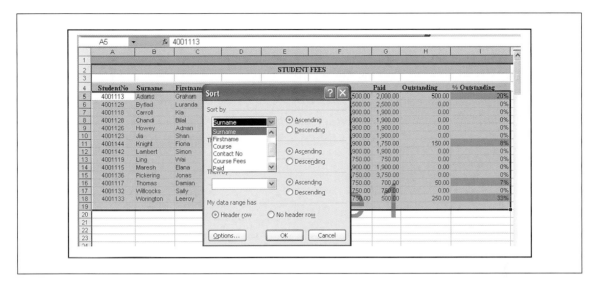

Figure 25.21

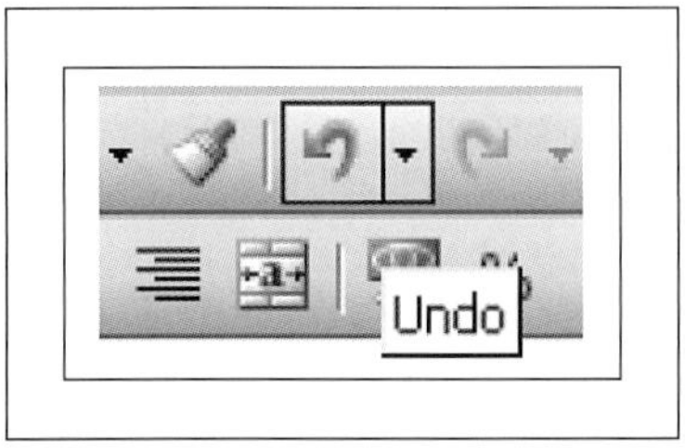

Figure 25.22

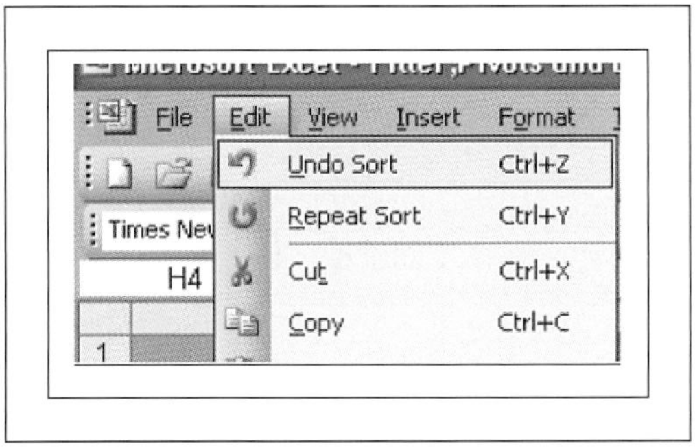

Figure 25.23

TIP

If you get in a mess with a sort, use the undo option Figure 25.22 or Figure 25.23. Rethink and start again. If you get into an even bigger mess close the spreadsheet without saving it!!!

Complex formulae

It is possible to set up quite complex spreadsheets to record day to day operations. Sometimes data such as attendance and absenteeism needs to be recorded. The spreadsheet in Figure 25.24 shows attendance for an IT class.

The students of the IT class are required to attend lectures denoted by L and either a practical (P) or a seminar(S) each week. If they attend both it is denoted by a B. Sometimes there are two practicals in a week or two seminars instead of a lecture. These are denoted by a 2. As the lecturer fills in the register the cells change

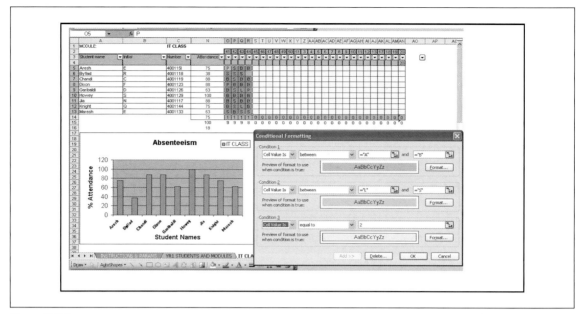

Figure 25.24

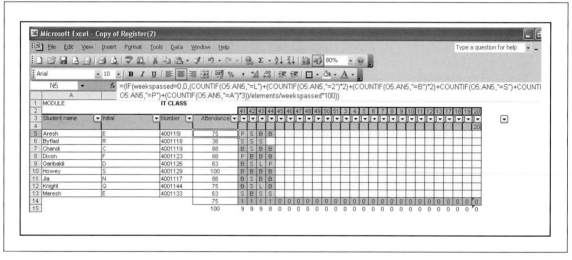

Figure 25.25

colour accordingly (Figure 25.25). Absenteeism is worked out with a long formula, which adds up the number of actual attendances as compared to the total number of sessions offered. The cells have been named as 'weekspassed' and 'elements' (Figures 25.26 and 25.27). Once cells or ranges are defined they can be used in a formula. In fact once formulae become this complex they are bordering on being very similar to programming and thus move into a different league. A chart to show percentage attendance can be created using the chart wizard as detailed earlier in this chapter. (Reproduced with permission of M. Van Bellen.)

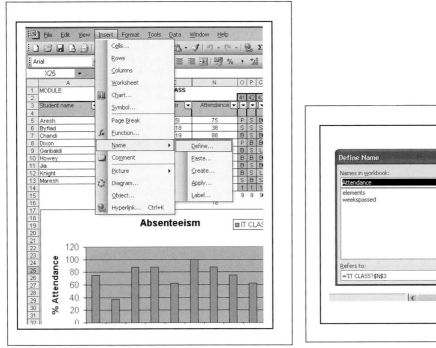

Figure 25.26

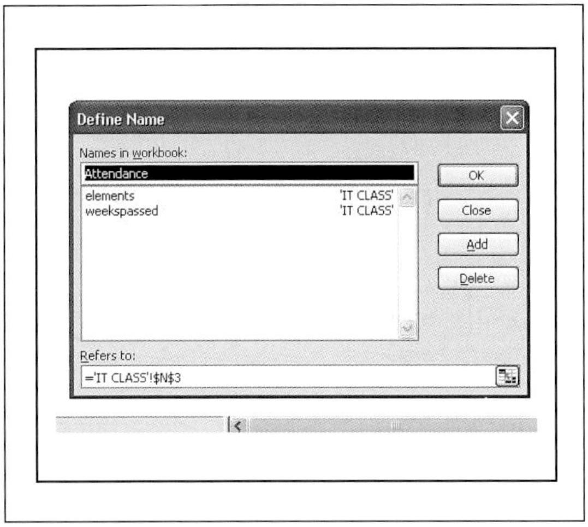

Figure 25.27

MANIPULATING NUMBERS

BODMAS

One of the principles behind mathematical formulae is BODMAS, which is a very early acronym meaning brackets, of, division, multiplication, addition and subtraction. This means that the order in which the elements of a formula are calculated will follow this principle. Therefore anything in brackets is calculated first, Of next, then division, etc. The above formulae are very straightforward, but as more advanced formulae are applied to your spreadsheets it is wise to check that the calculations occur in the right order and give the expected results. If the calculations are not in the right order, put brackets around key elements, so that they will be calculated first. For example $100 - 9 \times 10 = 10$ but $(100 - 9) \times 10 = 910$.

Formulae conventions in Microsoft® Excel

When creating a mathematical formula using Microsoft® Excel precede it with the $=$ sign. Use $+$ for plus, $-$ for minus, $*$ for multiplication and $/$ for division. Percentages should be represented by a decimal, for example 25 per cent would be represented as 0.25 or use the percentage option. The formula will appear in this box at the top of the spreadsheet.

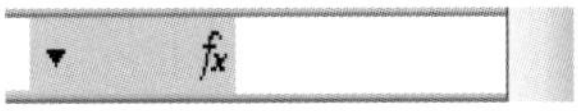

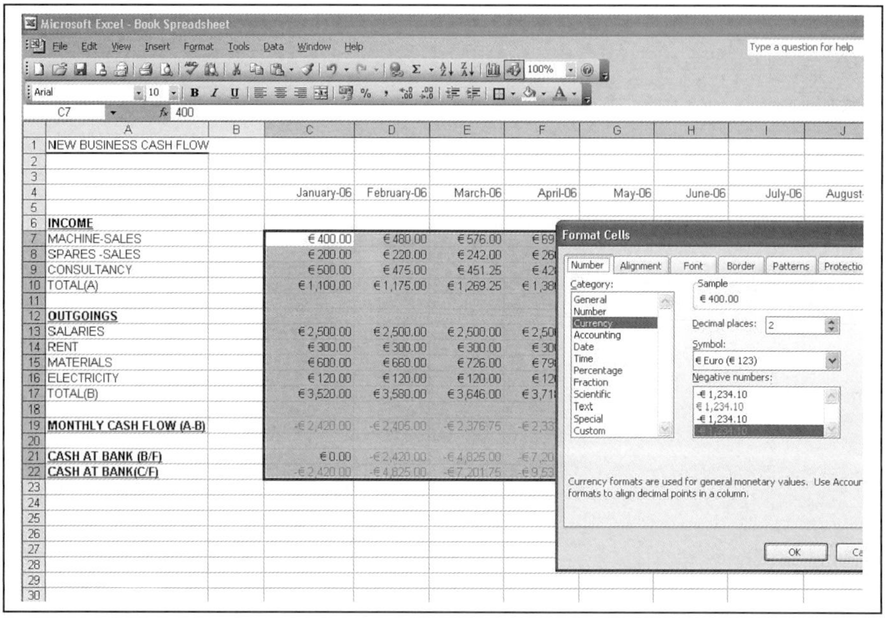

Figure 25.28

Setting up

Figure 25.28 shows a simple spreadsheet featuring the cash flow of a business. The cells containing the data are set to the currency format of the euro (€) and the option has been chosen to show negative numbers in red.

The months of the year have been set using English (US option) so that the month is shown in text (Figure 25.29). To save typing, the first three months were typed in and then the series was dragged to the end of the spreadsheet and the option **Fill Months** chosen (Figure 25.30).

In this example the monthly cash flow is dependent on the sales of machines, spares and consultancy income. The outgoings are for the salaries, rent, materials and electricity. The difference is the monthly cash flow figure, which initially is a negative number!

Spreadsheets can be used to manipulate numbers in a wide variety of ways and once a formula has been tested on a set of numbers and works, it can be dragged down rows or columns of figures to produce results.

What if . . .

Often, when looking at business figures, it is essential to make realistic assumptions about the future of the business. Once you have a spreadsheet set up you can manipulate the figures to test out the effect of changes in certain areas. The examples shown in Figures 23.31 to 23.34 show the machine sales increasing by 20 per cent a month (=C7+0.2*C7), spares by 10 per cent a month (=C8+0.1*C8), consultancy dropping by 5 per cent a month (=C9−0.05*C9) and materials rising 10 per cent a month (=C15+0.1*C15). These calculations will demonstrate a clear picture of how the overall state of the business will look in the next few years and help with the decision-making process.

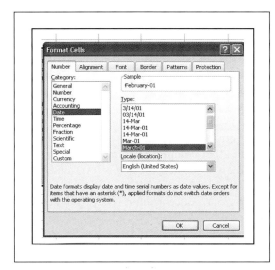

Figure 25.29

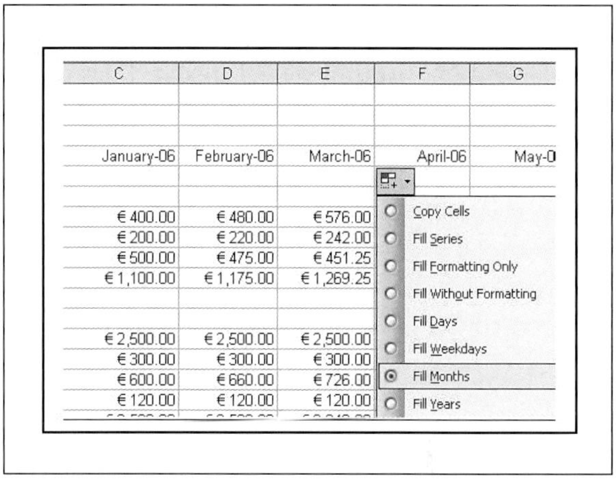

Figure 25.30

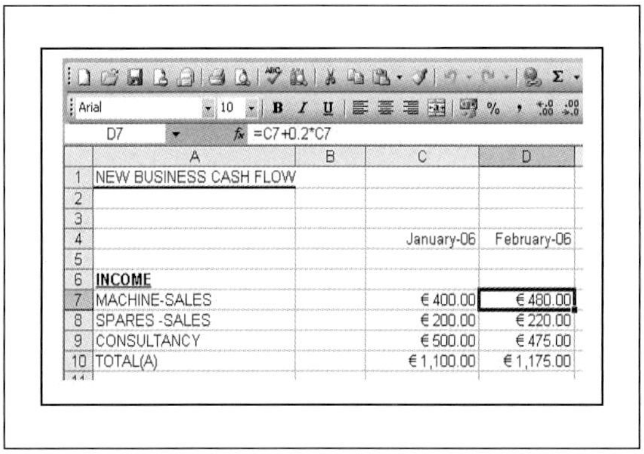

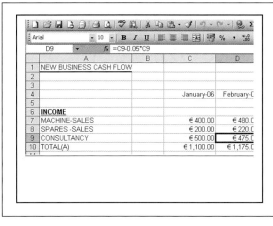

Figure 25.31

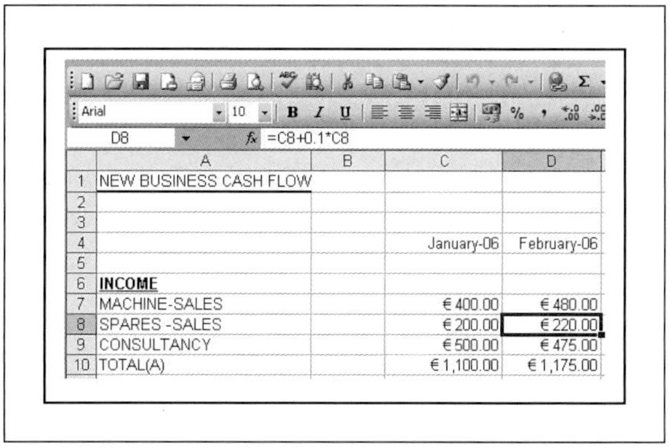

Figure 25.32

Figure 25.33

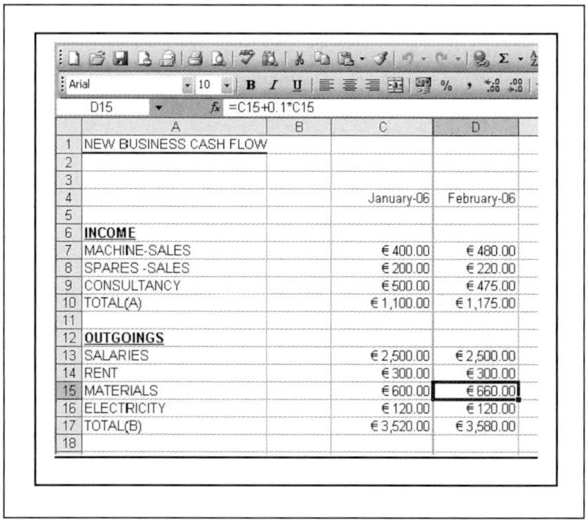

Figure 25.34

Autosum

The ability to add up a column of figures is one of the most common and useful facilities offered by Microsoft® Excel. To add up the column, click the cell where you need the answer to appear. Click on the AutoSum icon Σ (sigma sign) and a suggested column of figures appears. If this column is incorrect, position the cursor over the corner of the present column and reposition it over the correct area. Alternatively put in the two grid references for the column of figures which need to be added up (in this case E13 to E16 are to be auto summed). Press return and the answer appears in the cell. This formula can then be dragged across the other columns (Figure 25.35).

If hashes appear in the box (Figure 25.36), it is because the box is too small. Go to the top of the column and stretch it out, or double click on it.

Similarly if a number appears as in Figure 25.37, once again it is because the box is too small.

Figure 25.35

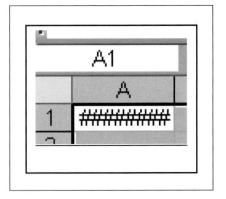

Figure 25.36

Figure 25.37

This usually occurs when you copy and paste figures from one spreadsheet to another. If anything else odd appears in the box, it is usually because the format has been set to something else – often decimal spaces – and needs to be changed.

TIP

When copying and pasting or adding new figures to a website, elongate the cell length as necessary and look out for incorrect data formats.

MORE USEFUL FACILITIES

Multiple worksheets

As your confidence with spreadsheets grows, you will start to create multiple worksheets per project. To use figures on one sheet (called OVERHEADS) with figures from another (called CASHFLOW):

- Go to the cell on the spreadsheet (OVERHEADS) where the figure needs to be and press =
- Go to the sheet where the figure is (CASHFLOW), click on it and press return
- The data will appear in the box on the OVERHEADS sheet

Figure 25.38 shows that the figure in box C24 is taken from a sheet named CASHFLOW. It shows that the position that the data came from is G22, but notice the $ in front of the G and the 22. The $ indicates that the address of the data that are being used in this calculation is absolute and will remain permanently set to the cell and sheet indicated.

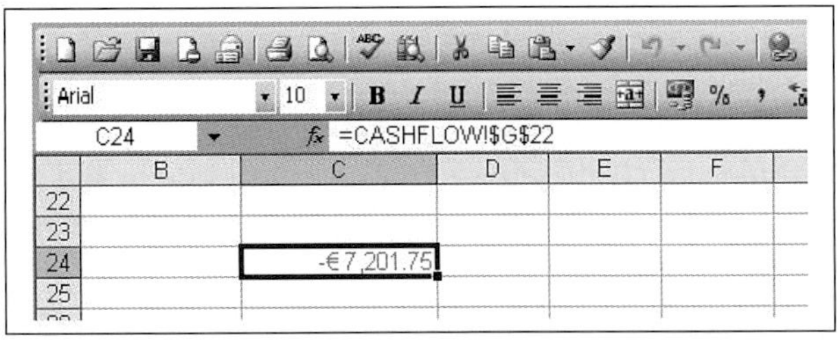

Figure 25.38

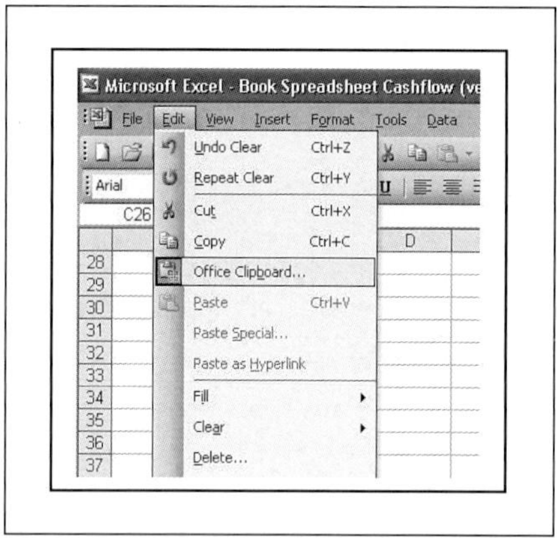

Figure 25.39

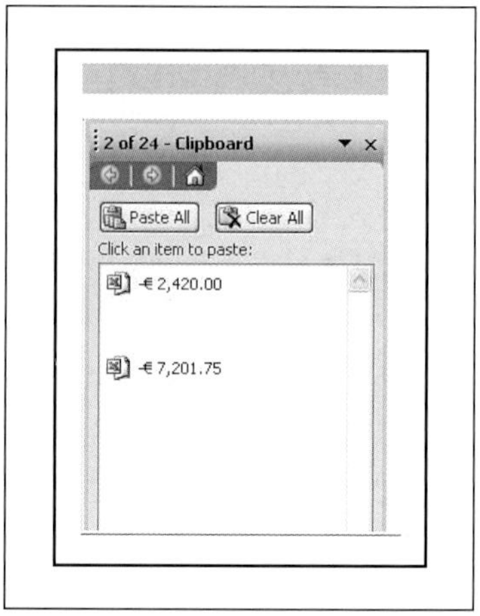

Figure 25.40

Clipboard

It may be that you require a number of items to be pasted into the spreadsheet. In such a case, it is useful to select the **Office Clipboard** (Figure 25.39) which is available under the **Edit** option. This will create a clipboard to the left of the spreadsheet (Figure 25.40) showing all of the items available to be copied over. The **Office Clipboard** is also available in Microsoft® Word.

TIP

When multiple items need to be pasted, open up an office clipboard.

Splitting the window

Figure 25.41 shows a feature which allows the screen to be split. This is handy when you have headings at the top or lists at the side of the spreadsheet, because a split keeps them in view at all times. Before selecting **Split** click on a cell between the titles. The split can be removed at any time selecting **Remove Split** (Figure 25.42).

Statistical options

When considering the statistical elements of spreadsheets, Microsoft® Excel offers a wide range of formulae and techniques to support both simple and complex statistical calculations. The drop down menu from the Σ sign shows a range of choices. For the attendance chart, an average attendance and a maximum attendance have been derived using the functions available (Figure 25.43).

However, if as a statistician you wish to consider other statistical formula such as standard deviation (i.e the statistical measure of the amount by which a set of values differs from the arithmetical mean or average), then you will have to go to the

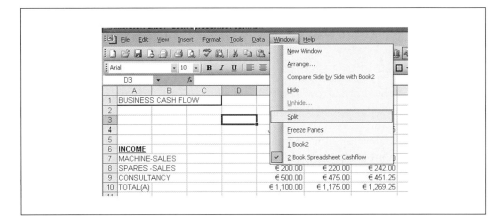

Figure 25.41

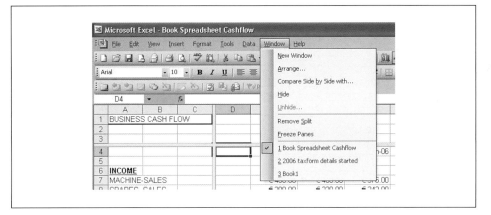

Figure 25.42

Figure 25.43

More **F**unctions options and choose **STDEVP**. The formula will then return a figure for the standard deviation (Figure 25.44).

Some other useful functions

When you select the down arrow next to the Σ sign, and select More **F**unctions, there is a very useful function called TODAY (Figure 25.45). If you select it and put onto your spreadsheet, the current date will always show on your spreadsheet.

As you begin to develop short formulae to support you work, you will probably find one or two functions really useful. There is a formula for net present value (NPV), pi (π) to 15 places of decimal (for the mathematicians), conversion from Binary to

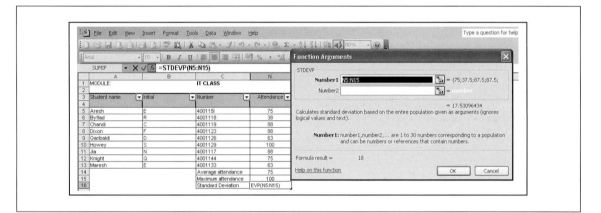

Figure 25.44

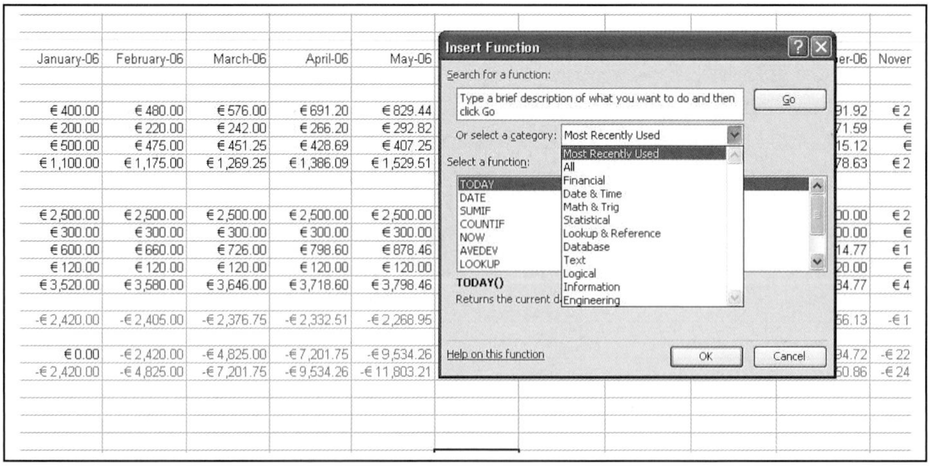

Figure 25.45

Hex (BIN2HEX) (for the computer buffs), COUNT, or COUNTIF. The trick is to find the ones that will save you time and energy, test them out and then use them.

One other function that may prove useful, especially if you are in the teaching profession, is the LOOKUP (Figures 25.46 and 25.47) function. Using a LOOKUP table, you can look up a percentage on a table of values and return a grade or visa versa (Figure 25.48). Again it is the table that takes the time, not the formula.

If you look at the example in Figure 25.48, you will see that the LOOKUP formula is shown in the paste function window. It is expressed as =LOOKUP (E2, J$2:J$16,K$2:K$16).

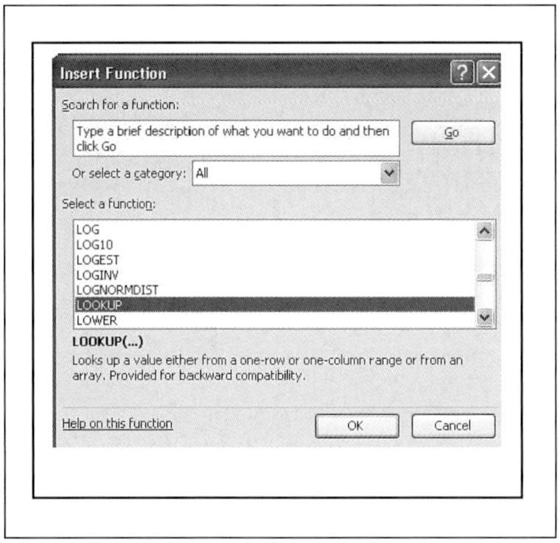

Figure 25.46

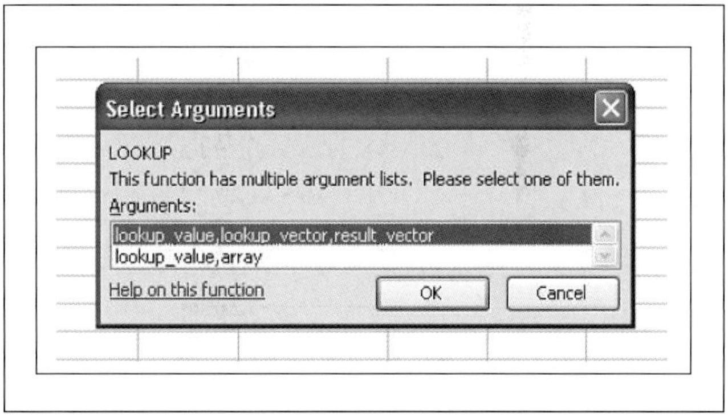

Figure 25.47

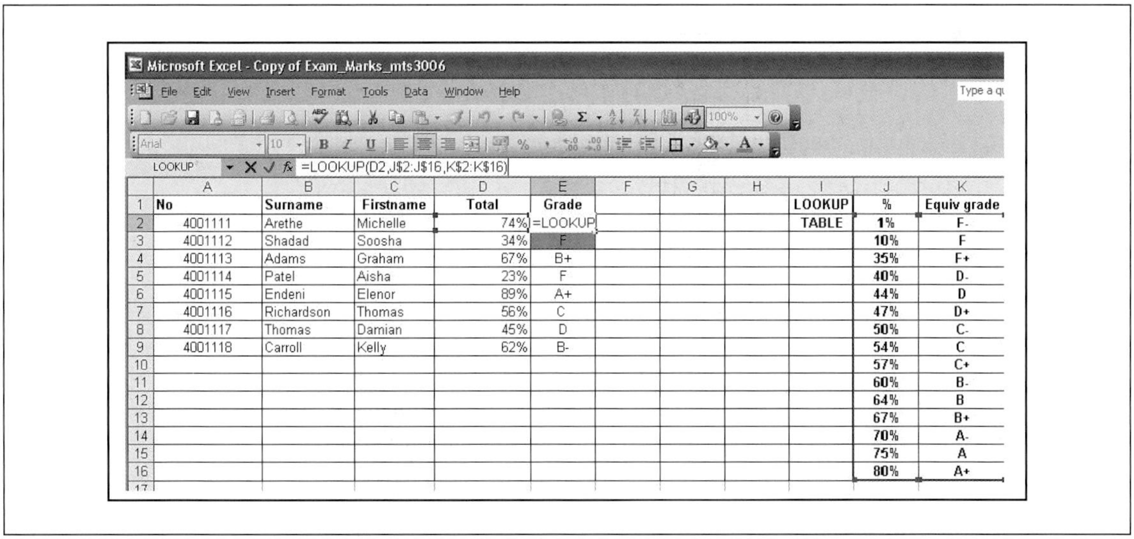

Figure 25.48

TIP

To see where the data for a formula is located on the spreadsheet, click at the end of formula on the fx line and the data will be displayed with a coloured box round it.

This function compares the total percentage in the cell E2 with the range in the LOOKUP table J$2 to J$16 until it finds a match. When it finds the value it returns the equivalent grade. So any percentage above 80% gets an A+, anything between 54% and 57% a C.

Points to be aware of when using formulae:

- The equal sign is the key to the formula, it will not work unless the = sign is present.
- A spread of values, i.e. the grades, are selected by their cell value at one end to their cell value at the other. In this case K2 to K16. the : in the middle shows it is a range (K2:K16).
- Do not leave commas or brackets out, they are important.
- LOOKUP tables need to be created in reverse order.
- The $ is very important as it denotes that the reference for the table remains fixed.

These are some of 329 functions available. The chances are you will probably use more than ten of these on a regular basis. However, some are quite intriguing like the IM-CONJUGATE which returns the complex conjugate of a complex number! However, if you do spot a gem of a calculation that supports your field of work, then you will probably be delighted to know that the formula exists as a function.

TIP

Study the functions available to ascertain if any can support your work.

Other statistical capabilities

Besides the vast array of functions already discussed, there are other capabilities available that support statistical work. Statistics and quantitative analysis are in a field of their own and often quite specialised software packages can be purchased to enable the calculation of some very sophisticated data. Microsoft® Excel is a versatile spreadsheet, but it does not have the sophistication of some other more specialised packages. However there are add-ons to Microsoft® Excel such as *XLStat Pro (Excel statistics) – statistics and data analysis software for Excel®* which can widen its functionality.

If this is your specialised field, you will be well briefed in the complex formulae that support statistical work. This final section serves to show you the type of capabilities that Microsoft® Excel can offer to support you. The techniques may be useful in quality control work, manpower planning and market research and forecasting.

In previous sections we have discussed the Mean and Standard Deviation functions. It is also useful for statistical purposes to be able to work out the mode (the most frequent value) and the median (middle value). These functions are both available in the statistical section in **More Functions**.

Trend analysis and moving averages

These can show how data changes over time and the chart wizard can support this by adding in trendlines, with the option of a trendline that is expressed as a **Moving Average** (Figure 25.49).

Graphs can also be used to ascertain if figures have a normal distribution or not (Figure 25.50).

These results show a fairly normal bell curve, but a skew either way may give reason to check the results, especially if previous years have shown a fairly regular pattern.

Regression and correlation coefficient

Regression is used to equate two variables and can be used for comparison and estimations. The correlation coefficient shows the relationship between ranges where

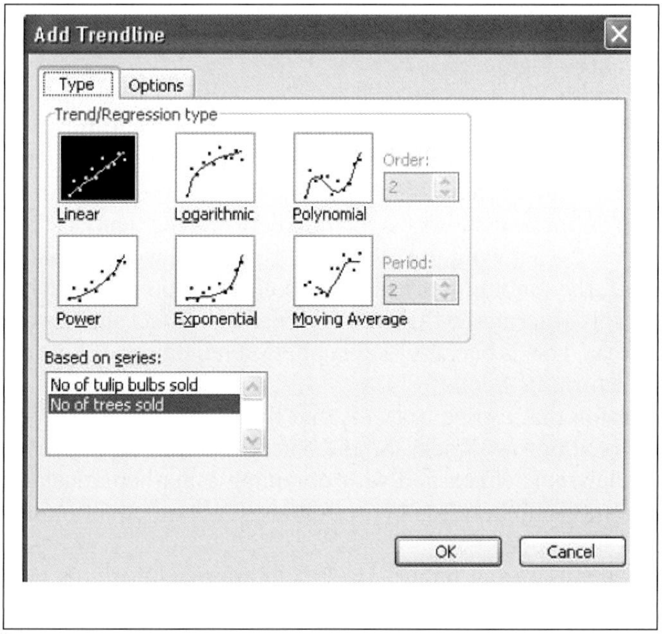

Figure 25.49

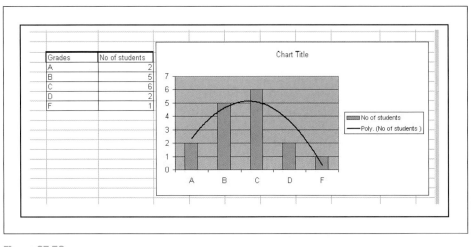

Figure 25.50

there is an upward or downward trend. How accurate that is, is determined by the spread of data.

There is a facility to produce the complicated banks of data relating to regression and correlation by selecting **Data Analysis** from the **Tools** menu. If **Data Analysis** is not available go to **Tools**, **Add-Ins** and select **Analysis ToolPak**. The **Data Analysis Menu** offers a range of operations including correlation and regression. The formulae relating to these operations are complex and need to be studied separately. However, once the principles are understood, the creation of the tables and graphs can easily be undertaken (Figure 25.51).

Figure 25.51 shows all of wealth of figures created by Microsoft® Excel from the two columns of data relating to the delivery and collection of milk bottles. The key factors are the correlation coefficient which is denoted by r squared, which in this case is 0.160945614. The value can be negative (e.g. falling) or positive but the nearer to 1 this figure is, the better as it shows correlation between the figures. The range can be between −1 and +1. So it would seem that all is not well with the milk bottle collection, for example, the amount delivered and collected do not correlate. However, if you study the graph, you can see that if the graphs were offset slightly then they would almost be identical. This is because of a lag between delivery of bottles, emptying of the bottles and returning them.

So the conclusion that can be drawn is that there is a delay lag in the returning of the milk bottles of about two weeks. So the bottles are coming back eventually!

Regression analysis is concerned with obtaining a mathematical equation which describes the relationship between two variables. Once an equation is derived it can be used for estimation purposes.

For instance, if you were a publican you could devise a formula to work out how much beer you will sell according to the temperature. Data have to collected over time to use as a basis for the calculation and, once the figures are fed into the

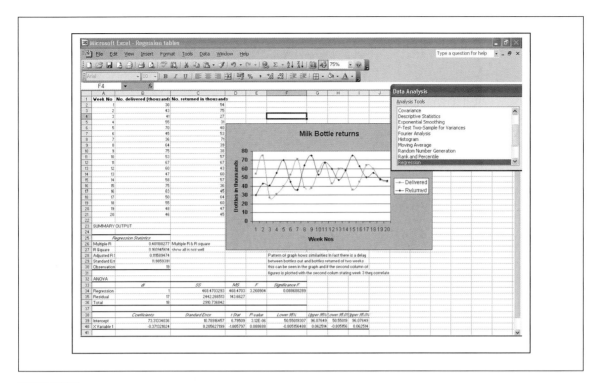

Figure 25.51

spreadsheet, the correlation coefficient has to be around 1. Perfect relationships are shown by 1 and −1. Otherwise, it means that the data collected are no good to start with and any equation will be a waste of time! However once Microsoft® Excel has been used to check this and create an equation, then the publican can pop in the estimated temperature for the day and work out how many pints he is likely to sell.

There are hundreds of formulae available as functions in Microsoft® Excel. However, just as with your multifunctional microwave at home, unless you are a specialist mathematician or statistician you will probably only use a couple of the functions on a regular basis!

Probability, planning and decision making

Using arithmetic, algebraic and financial expressions, it is possible to use programs such as Microsoft® Excel to create simulations, 'what ifs' and scenarios to support planning at strategic, tactical or operational levels. Businesses use a variety of techniques to assist their decision making and the introduction of sophisticated software such as (Decision Support Software) DSS, Expert systems and Executive Information Systems (EIS) using artificial intelligence (AI) creates even more opportunities.

Probability involves using specific formulae to derive how many single outcomes are possible. In the case of dice, cards or the lottery, the number of possible single outcomes are in each case 1 in 6, 1 in 52, 1 in 49 respectively:

Sometimes an event (e) is independent, that is the occurrence of that event does not influence the probability of another, like the toss of a coin. Sometimes an event (e) is dependent, that is one event affects another. For example, when the lottery is drawn, the probability of a certain number coming out depends on the number of balls already drawn.

Calculating probability If you look at your chances of winning the lottery, you have 6 numbers on your ticket and there are 49 different numbers. Probability = P(e1 then e2 etc) = P(e1) X P(e2), where e represents the chance each time. So the first number has 6 chances in 49 of being chosen, the second has 5 chances in 48, etc. There chances are 6/49*5/48*4/47*3/46*2/45*1/44)*100 which equals = 0.0000071511%, that is 1 in 13,983,816.

Diagrammatic techniques

Although not strictly a spreadsheet capability, it should be noted that tree diagrams, flowcharts, cause and effect (fishbone) diagrams can all be used to support decision making and brain storming sessions. The drawing tools available in a Microsoft® environment can be used to create these diagrams. These techniques help to break down complex problems and give better understanding so iteration or corrective action can be taken as necessary, and progress can be made.

Hiding, adding and deleting elements of the spreadsheet

Each **Cell**, **Row** and **Column** can be manipulated. On the **Edit** menu they can be deleted and on the **Insert** menu they can be added in. However, when spreadsheets become bulky, it may be wise to hide some of the columns or rows to give clarity. Choosing **Format** and then selecting **cell**, **Row** or **Column** allows you to **Hide** them or to standardise their size (Figure 25.52).

Security

Finally, having created your masterpiece, you may consider making it secure by adding a password. This means it cannot be opened unless the person has been given the password. A password can be added to a Microsoft® Word document too. To do this, Select **Tools** and then **Options**. Then click on the **Security** tab and add your password (Figure 25.53). There is also an option to 'protect' sheets or cells individually.

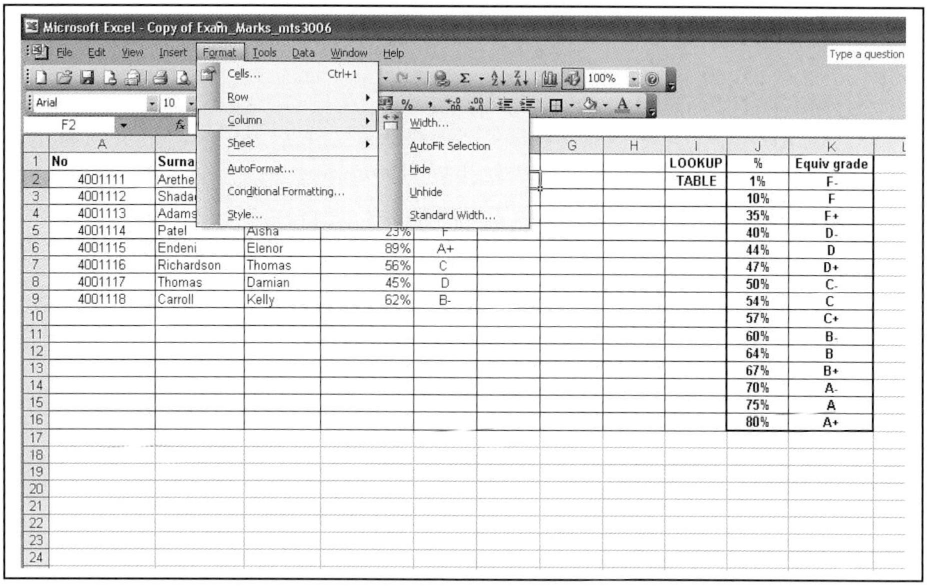

Figure 25.52

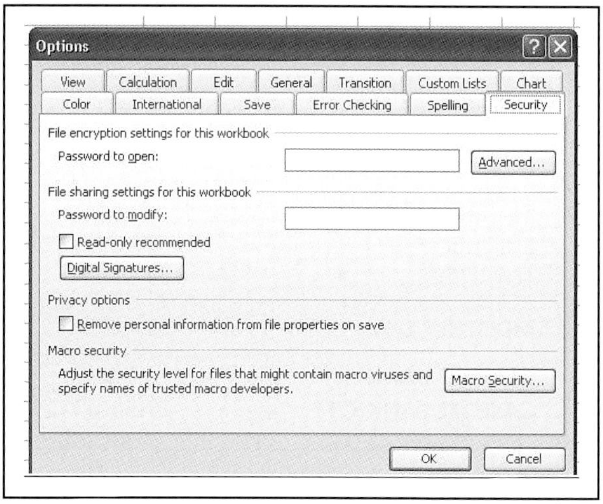

Figure 25.53

Summary

Microsoft® Excel 2003 offers a wealth of support for mathematical and statistical work. Having learnt to use the basic formatting techniques, a selection of work related functions should be investigated and practised.

Develop mathematical skills steadily; go from 'known' to 'unknown'. If formulae get too complex, try breaking them down into a number of easier ones. You could also take advice from colleagues and look at different ways of approaching the problem. Consider buying specialised software to do the task more cost effectively; remember your time is precious.

Use Microsoft® Excel to format your work so that changes and exceptions can be spotted easily. Utilise statistical and mathematical functions to support and enhance your work, but do not get bogged down. Ask your help desk or IT staff for support and advice.

TASK 1

Put the following data into a spreadsheet

	January-07
INCOME	
MACHINE-SALES	£400.00
SPARES-SALES	£200.00
CONSULTANCY	£500.00
TOTAL(A)	£1,100.00
OUTGOINGS	
SALARIES	£2,500.00
RENT	£300.00
MATERIAL	£600.00
ELECTRICITY	£120.00
TOTAL(B)	£3,520.00
MONTHLY CASH FLOW (A-B)	£2,420.00
CASH AT BANK (B/F)	£10,000.00
CASH AT BANK(C/F)	£7,580.00

Figure 25.54

Calculate when the monthly cash flow will become a positive: if sales go up 18 per cent per month, spares 9 per cent per month, consultancy comes down 6 per cent per month, electricity goes up 3 per cent per month and the wages go up by 10 per cent in a year's time.

The data below are the raw data issued by the Met Office for 2003 and 2004 (Met Office 2006) from the Oxford Station.

yyyy	mm	tmax degC	tmin degC	rain mm	sun hours
2003	1	7.6	1.8	81.4	87.7
2003	2	8.4	0.6	17.3	94.4
2003	3	13.3	2.7	25.2	154.8
2003	4	15.3	4.6	36.8	169.8
2003	5	17.5	8.1	48.1	191.2
2003	6	22.4	11.8	55.5	213.6
2003	7	23.7	13.4	53.8	192.0
2003	8	25.5	13.5	3.0	228.4
2003	9	21.3	8.1	17.4	175.3
2003	10	14.0	3.9	31.7	134.8
2003	11	12.0	5.7	89.6	78.9
2003	12	8.7	1.8	70.7	53.6
2004	1	8.8	2.7	66.1	62.7
2004	2	8.7	2.9	25.5	79.1
2004	3	10.9	3.4	51.8	100.5
2004	4	14.7	6.2	68.8	150.3
2004	5	18.0	8.6	41.1	195.5
2004	6	21.8	12.0	23.8	223.5
2004	7	22.0	12.2	83.1	169.6
2004	8	23.4	14.2	135.0	194.1
2004	9	20.1	11.7	28.9	174.3
2004	10	14.7	8.6	131.4	102.3
2004	11	10.9	5.8	34.2	52.5
2004	12	8.6	2.8	37.7	58.3

Figure 25.55

a. Put the data in a spreadsheet

b. Set up **Conditional Formatting** to make all rainfall over 35mm show up in red and under 10mm show up in blue

c. Add a new column called Average Temperature

d. Work out the average temperature (between max and min) for every month

e. Using that temperature, calculate the average, median, mode and standard deviation for 2003 and 2004

f. Using **Data Analysis** (regression), work out if there is any correlation between max temp and sun hours

g. Apply **AutoFilter** and **Sort** number of sun hours in ascending order

References

Levine, D. M. (2001) *Statistics for Managers Using Microsoft Excel* (International Edition), Pearson US

Met Office (2006) [online]. [Accessed 18 April 2006]. Available from World Wide Web http://www.met-office.gov.uk/climate/uk/stationdata/oxforddata.txt

CHAPTER 26
Database challenges

Learning objectives

- To recognise the principles behind data gathering
- To understand how databases function
- To recognise the key terms associated with databases
- To evaluate validation techniques
- To explain how and why tables of data are linked together in a relational database
- To understand how a database form is created and used
- To appreciate the principles of and need for data queries
- To comprehend how reports are constructed and output
- To be aware of current legislation relating to the handling and storage of data

Introduction

At this moment in time you are probably a live feature on tens if not hundreds of databases. Every time you shop, go to the doctor, subscribe to a magazine or start a new job, your details are logged and you become a number or item.

The proliferation of databases and the valuable nature of the data mean that not only are your details logged, but your details could be bought by some other agency. The first you will know about this is when you receive a stream of mail through your door that you did not expect. This chapter will highlight the key principles of data collection and give the reader a simplified overview of the nature of data storage and interrogation.

As a manager it is important to know the outline mechanics of certain software without having to know exactly how everything works. This chapter overviews the main elements of databases and offers insight into how databases work.

WHAT IS A DATABASE?

A database is the name used for a computer based storage area containing 'all of the information for one business application' (Bocij *et al.* 2003, p. 437). To create a database, various techniques are used to organise and manipulate the data. The most commonly used set up for a database is to put the data in **tables** and then link these tables together. This type of database is called a *relational database*.

Each table can stand alone and contains a unique collection of records (e.g. customer details). Within each table, the contents are said to represent, in technical terms, a 'collection of records for a similar entity' (Bocij *et al.* 2003, p. 437). Student records hold students as entity. The reason the tables can be linked together is that each record (i.e. details on one customer only) has a unique number associated with it. This unique number is known as the *primary key* and is used to form the link. Within each record there are a number of *fields*, again there is a technical term for a field: it is an attribute. Field is the physical term, attribute is the logical term.

The other main type of database is the *object-oriented database*. The way that an object-orientated database works is that the data and the procedures that process the data work together. This way the data become reusable objects which can be used over and over again. This data structure allows the object itself to be used for sophisticated and complex applications (Bocij *et al.* 2003) over and over again and the need for data tables is eliminated. Often object and relational databases can be mixed, for example by the Oracle SQL Server.

Whichever type of database is used in an organisation, the key principles of data collection, data accuracy, data input and the creation of meaningful output still exist. To illustrate some of the principles of data manipulation and the construction of a relational database, the Microsoft® Access 2003 database software will be used.

Once data exist in a database, they can be used in many ways. For instance, collecting existing data together in even larger database systems creates a data warehouse. A data warehouse is 'a database or collection of databases from different areas of a commercial organisation used as a tool for analysing overall business strategy as opposed to routine operations' (Encarta 2005). Once these large systems exist then data mining can be carried out. Data mining is defined as 'the locating of previously unknown patterns and relationships within data using a database application, for example the locating of customers with *common interests* in a retail establishment's database' (Encarta 2005). Buying trends and patterns, in data of all kinds, gives a competitive advantage to the owner and user of the data. The fact that these repositories and techniques exist means that during a person's lifetime their details will be held in a number of data warehouses. Equally important the day to day working life of most people will, somewhere along the line, involve creating data to be used in a database and subsequently in a data warehouse.

The advantages of a using a database

Data take up a lot of space and the key advantage should be that the database consists of data that is not duplicated anywhere else. It also needs to be consistent. However, for those who receive junk mail (is there someone out there who doesn't?) you will know that some companies have not achieved this yet. You may receive three pieces of junk mail, which is essentially all for you, but because there are slight 'typos' or missing elements in each address the recipient will get three sets, for example one for Mrs S Bailey, one for Mrs S B Ailey, and one for Mrs Bailey! Interestingly, you may find that looking carefully at the address may give you a clue as to who is selling your details on to other companies!

A good reason for the emergence of sophisticated database systems is that businesses demand more flexible data retrieval and reporting facilities. A fully functional, well-organised database system can fully support the needs of managerial decision makers at all levels.

Another advantage is that data are an important resource in an organisation and that they can be shared by many applications. Because of this, those in charge of the creation of a database, must plan carefully and make sure the data are well managed and controlled. After spending many years creating a database, it is essential that the staff are well trained to use it and that standards have been set. Techniques exist for preventing users from deleting and changing records, if they are not qualified to do so, and the system should be tested well enough to prevent the system 'hanging' if the wrong set of steps are taken. Similarly when data are input, restrictions can be put in place to prevent, or at least reduce, the input of erroneous or duplicate data. Data are a precious and expensive commodity. They must also be handled ethically. Government legislation has restricted the way that data can be used, but in-house the security of data is the key to organisational success.

Microsoft® Access 2003 is probably the most commonly available database and it is the one used throughout this chapter. It is not necessarily the one that you will use in an industrial or commercial environment; however, it does show some common principles.

DATA GATHERING

How are data gathered in the first place? It is possible to buy data, but a great deal of data will have come from old file based systems. Much new data is collected through market research, advertising campaigns and face to face services. At some point someone has to capture their data, either in a paper form or on the screen.

A great deal of data are collected through questionnaires and surveys. Collecting data usually starts with the collection of demographic data, for example age, sex, occupation, then moves on to the more specific details. Saunders *et al* (2003) conclude 'a valid question will enable accurate data to be collected'.

TIP

If you are involved with data collection, collect paper forms and questionnaires wherever you go. Print out copies of on-line forms. Fill them in and critically analyse them. This will help you to recognise and eliminate bad practice.

As surveys and questionnaires have been conducted by many people and organisations in the past, it may be useful to look at the question bank at this web address http://qb.soc.surrey.ac.uk. It contains a wealth of interesting information and examples.

Lessons learnt

You would imagine that after years of bureaucratic form filling and the extensive use of forms for internet access, that someone somewhere would get it right. Well, disappointingly, this is not true. Database set ups show a similar lack of vision. In the IT department, much head scratching can occur when the department is asked to sort the data in a legacy systems, that is a system that was set up to hold and process data in the past. Advances in the structure of a database and the need to add new fields of data can mean endless trawling through old data records in order to clean them up ready to use with a new system. In the next section a number of techniques are detailed that show how some erroneous data entry can be avoided.

Techniques for collecting accurate data – drop down menus and limited input

A great deal of data are collected via on-line forms and questionnaires. Much use is made of drop down menus. Drop down menus are used quite extensively for internet forms. For instance you may wish to book a flight on-line (Figure 26.1). When you are choosing a start destination, a drop down menu will appear. This limits the user's choice to the airports that the airline company flies to. Even cleverer is the fact that having chosen a start destination, the final destinations that drop down will only be the ones that are relevant. In this case, if flying from Prague with this airline, there is a choice of only seven destination airports.

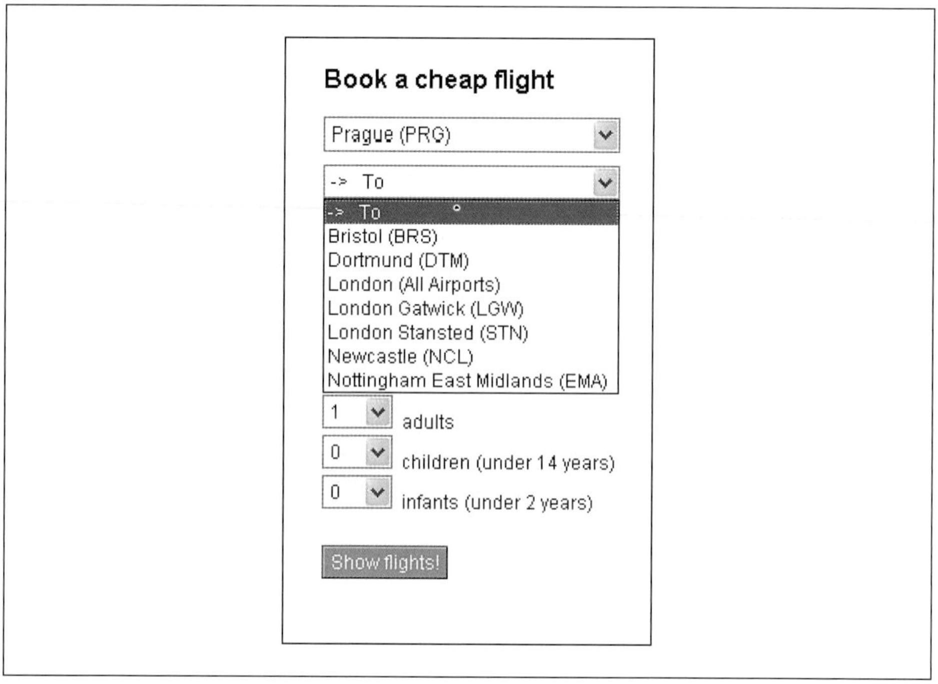

Figure 26.1

The drop down menu would have been set up during the design of the form and at the database design stage. On-line forms can limit the degree of freedom the user has in other ways. Sometimes there is a tick box, or the number of characters are limited in length or in format or in type. One of the most annoying features of the on-line form is the fact that you believe that you have completed it and then you submit it only to find there is something wrong with it.

Fortunately the design of on-line forms is improving; in the early days the form would come back blank and leave you scratching your head about why it had been rejected. Nowadays most forms have an asterisk to show the compulsory fields, and even more sophisticated versions tell you why the input you gave is unacceptable.

TIP

Eliminate collecting erroneous data wherever possible by limiting the user's choice to meaningful replies.

WARNING

Beware of the scrolling mouse. One turn of the wheel may change your choice – instead of Prague you could end up choosing Riga. Click anywhere outside the box before scrolling.

In order to have a better understanding of these techniques, the next section will show how a simple relational database is set up using Microsoft® Access. It will also show how various techniques are employed at the construction stage to help eliminate errors in data collection and storage.

DATABASE STRUCTURE – SETTING UP THE TABLES

Getting started

Open up Microsoft® Access. Go to **File** and select **New** and then select the **Blank Database** option (Figure 26.2).

Choose a folder for it to reside in and then give the database a meaningful name and select **Create**. It is worth knowing at this point that a Microsoft® Access database is like a Russian doll. The tables, forms, queries and reports all exist within the main database, in this case the trainer's database. As each element is created, the closing of the table, form, query or report causes it to be saved inside the database.

Once the database has been created, various database objects can be produced within it. On the left-hand side of the screen shown in Figure 26.3, the objects that are available are shown on the left-hand side.

To simplify the construction of this example, the only objects that will be used are **Tables** to build up tables to store meaningful data; **Queries** which are used to

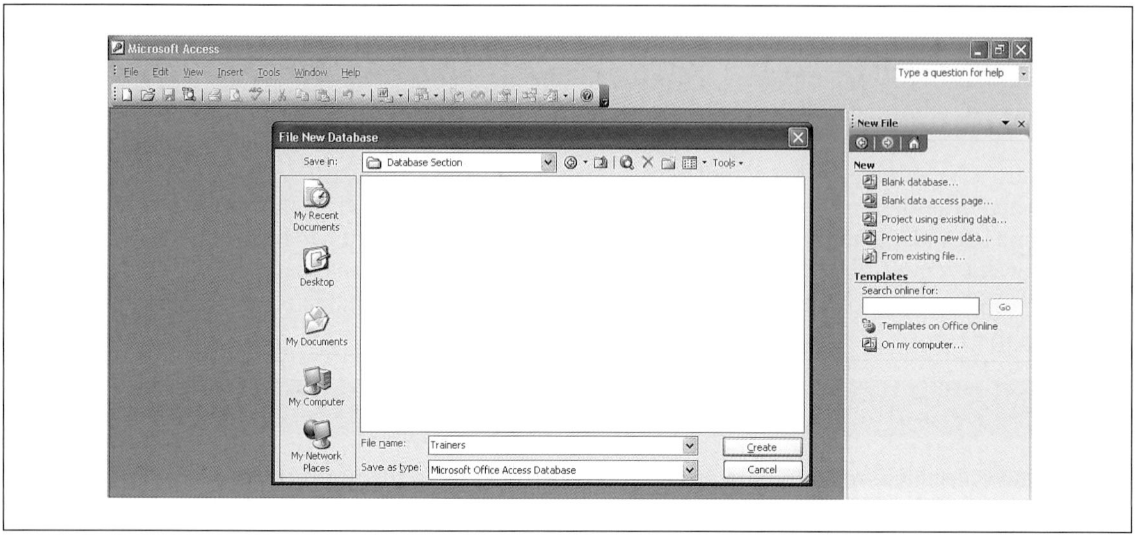

Figure 26.2

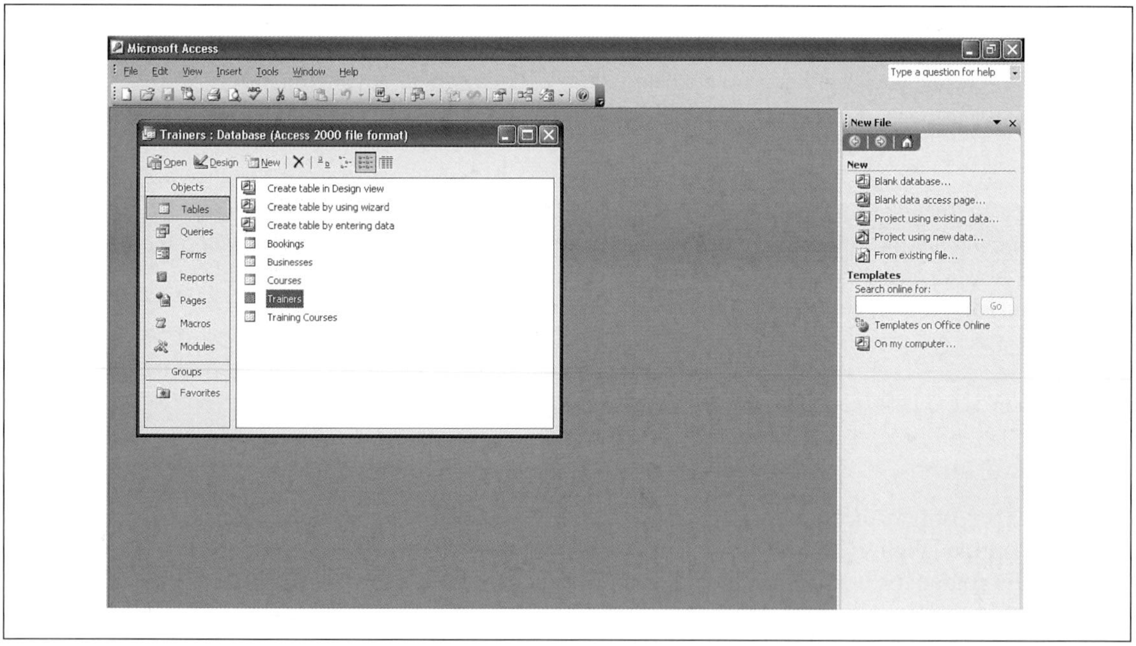

Figure 26.3

interrogate the available data and produce results from it; **Forms** which are be used to create forms; and finally **Reports** to show examples of the final outputs.

When the object is highlighted in orange (Figure 26.3) it shows the available options in each section (e.g. create a table in Design View) and the elements that have

Figure 26.4

been created already (e.g. Trainers) (Figure 26.4). Note the different icons that are used to show the difference between a create option and a created option.

As with all of the chapters in this technical part, the wealth of options and the complex nature of the task, means that it is only possible to cover the basics. Sometimes the creation of a table or report can be achieved more easily using a wizard and sometimes the wizard creates elements that are just too complex. Only time and experience will allow you to choose the best options.

Creating a table

Let us consider a very simple scenario. Presentations 'R' Us is a company running presentations and training for external companies. Presentations 'R' Us has a number of staff and so needs to know various things about each of the members of staff. Microsoft® Access can be used to set up a tables to hold this information.

To help to understand the design of a data table, the **Create Table in Design View** option will be used. (It is worth experimenting with the other two because they may prove more useful another time.) By selecting this option, the screen shown in Figure 26.5 appears, this is a blank screen where all the fields can be added. This screen

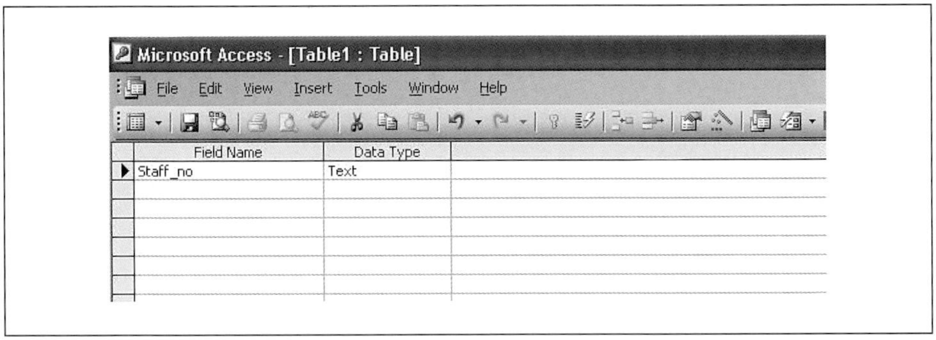

Figure 26.5

shows the first field has been created and named Staff_No, and is type Text. If text is chosen, the field can contain a combination of letters and numbers; however, if the staff number consists purely of numbers then the type can be set to Number. This is only the tip of the iceberg as far as fields and types are concerned.

A table that has Staff_no as its first field name indicates that the field names that follow should all be linked to the attributes that a staff member might have.

TIP

Do not duplicate fields except to link one table to another.

The underscore between 'Staff' and 'no' means that 'Staff_no' is seen as all one word or string. This convention is often used in database set ups as it makes the field name more recognisable when it is used for other operations. The Staff_no would form, in this particular case, the primary key. The primary key is used to identify the field in the table that will contain the unique identifier. Each record will thus be given a unique identifier, that is every staff member has to be allocated a unique number which will appear on their record and their record only. Figure 26.6 shows a small key in the toolbar above the table. To allocate the key to one of the fields, click in the box to the left of the field name, in this case Staff_no, and click on the key on the toolbar. Now other field names can be added (Figure 26.7).

The second field name is Title. For this field a LOOKUP table has been created, this means that when the details are added in later, a drop down menu will appear so that the person putting the data in can only choose from a list.

To create a LOOKUP table in Microsoft® Access, click into the **Data Type** column next to the **Field name** and select **Lookup Wizard** (Figure 26.8).

The window shown in Figure 26.9 will appear, offering a choice of using an existing table or typing in the values. As this is the first time this has been used, the elements will have to be typed in.

Having made that choice click on **Next** (Figure 26.10). This allows you to type in the values. Type in the first value, for example Mr, and then use the ↓ arrow on the keyboard to go to the next row and type in the next one, for example Mrs, until all of the values are in. Then click **Next**.

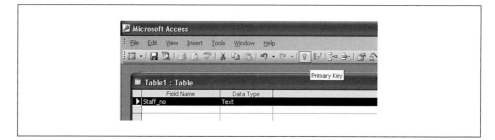

Figure 26.6

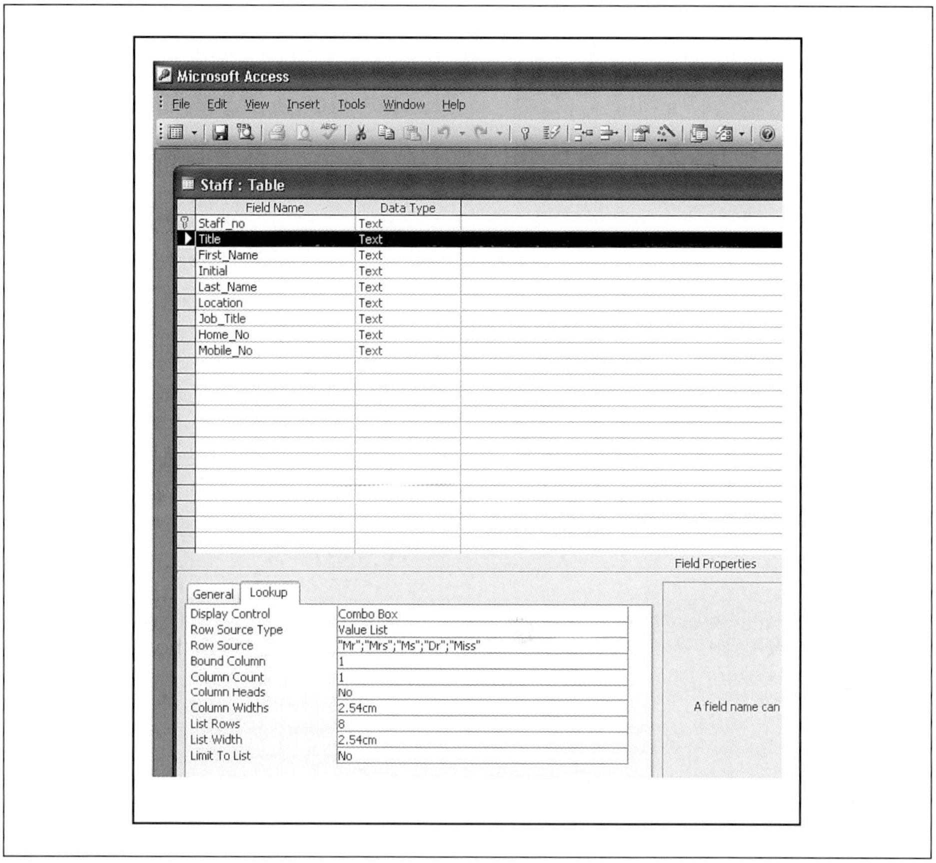

Figure 26.7

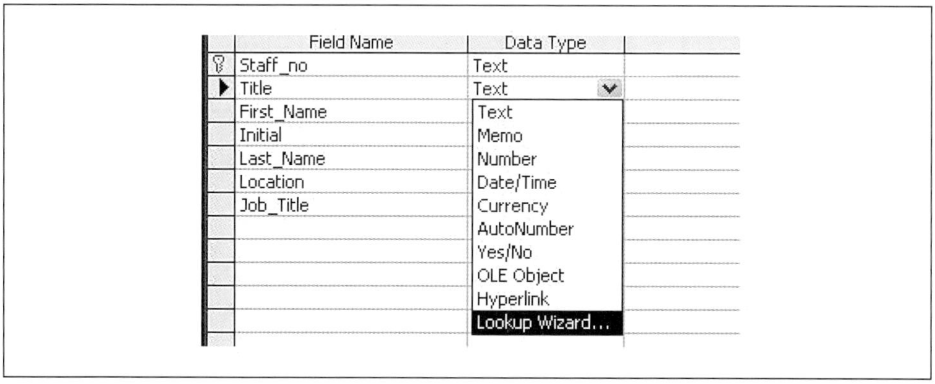

Figure 26.8

The next screen (Figure 26.11) allows for a name to be given to the set of values, in this case Titles, and when **Finish** is selected, the LOOKUP wizard closes.

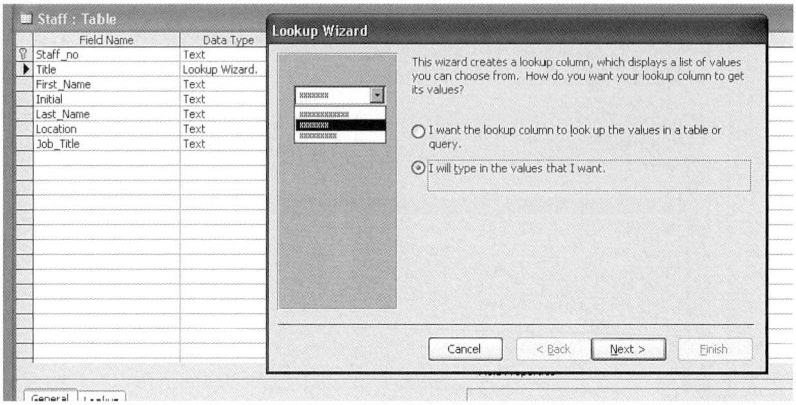

Figure 26.9

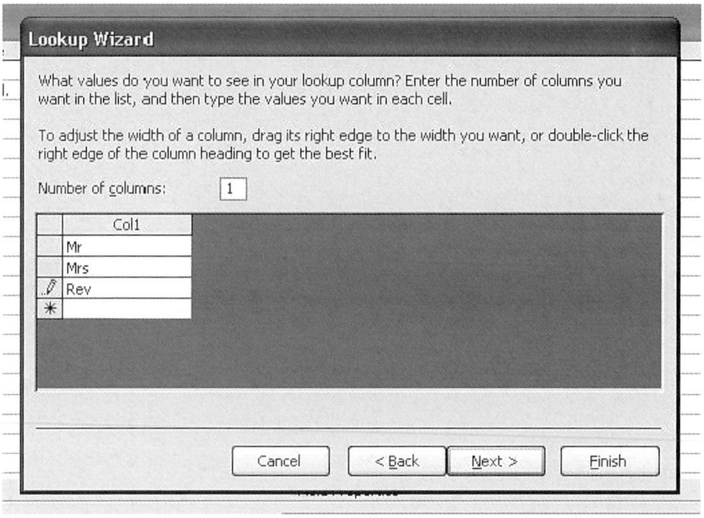

Figure 26.10

When returning to the table the word Text appears next to the field name, but at the bottom the values can be seen if the Lookup table for that field name is selected (Figure 26.12).

ACCURACY OF DATA AND TECHNIQUES THAT HELP

The building up of field names within a record needs careful thought. It should be noted that the database designer will always look to eliminate duplicate fields. For instance if you work in the human resources department, you will probably be

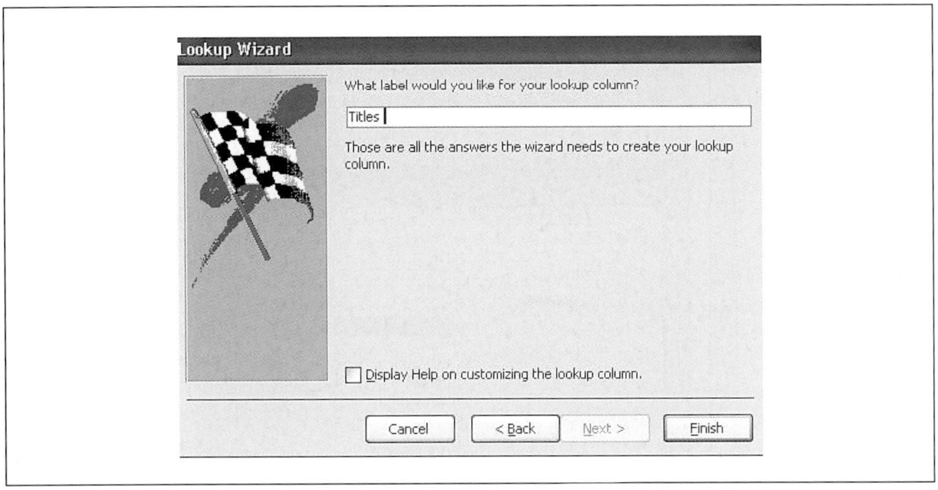

Lookup Wizard

What label would you like for your lookup column?

Titles

Those are all the answers the wizard needs to create your lookup column.

☐ Display Help on customizing the lookup column.

[Cancel] [< Back] [Next >] [Finish]

Figure 26.11

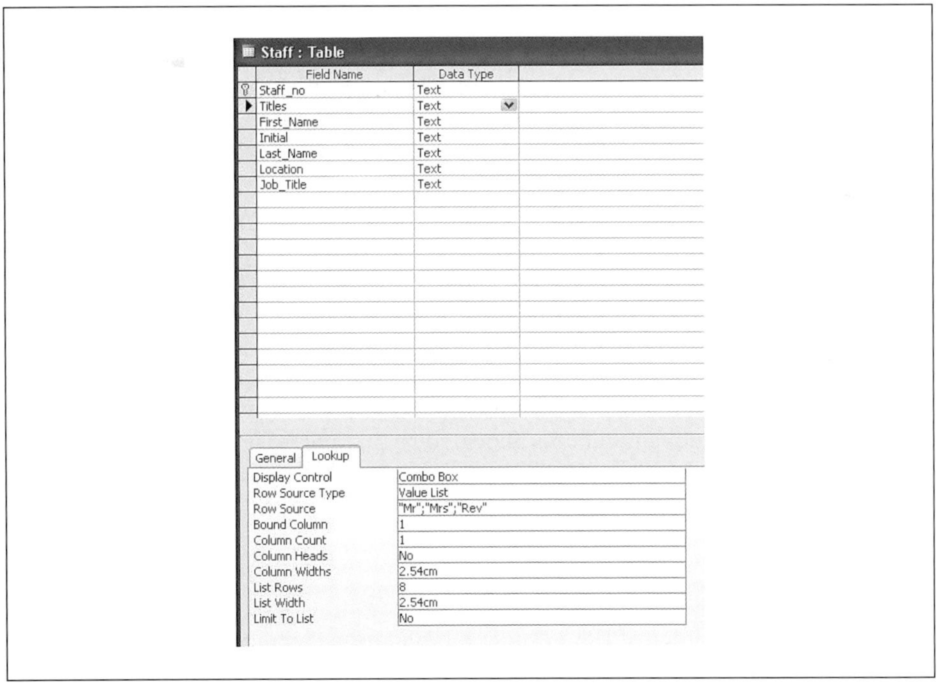

Staff : Table

Field Name	Data Type	
🔑 Staff_no	Text	
▶ Titles	Text	∨
First_Name	Text	
Initial	Text	
Last_Name	Text	
Location	Text	
Job_Title	Text	

General | Lookup

Display Control	Combo Box
Row Source Type	Value List
Row Source	"Mr";"Mrs";"Rev"
Bound Column	1
Column Count	1
Column Heads	No
Column Widths	2.54cm
List Rows	8
List Width	2.54cm
Limit To List	No

Figure 26.12

responsible for monitoring the training of staff and organising their appraisal schedules. When a database contains comprehensive staff records, the creation of a training plan or a timetable for appraisals for each staff member can be produced using the *present* staff records. To link these together the unique number which has been created for each member of staff can be used.

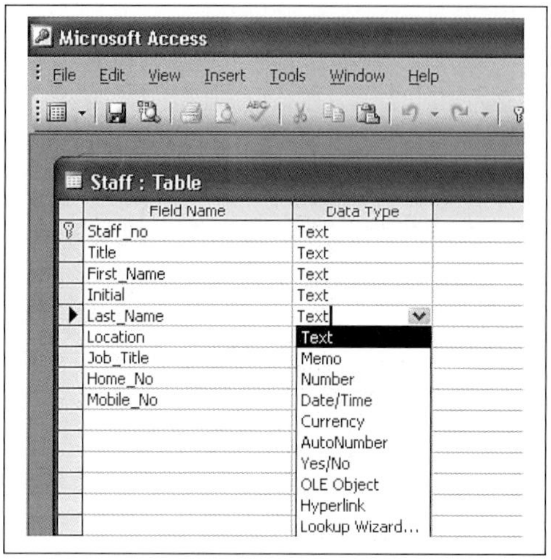

Figure 26.13

Once the number has been established, it can be used in other operations and the relevant fields can be extracted as necessary, for example First_Name if sending an invitation, Mobile_No if a contact point needed (Figure 26.13).

Figure 26.13 also shows that when setting up each **Field Name** a choice of **Data Types** is available. The selection of a specific type can help to eliminate the keying in of erroneous data. For instance if you create a field for a person's date of birth, you can use a **Date/Time** format. (However, when selecting a date/time format from the General area be careful not to pick an American version.) If you create a field for a rate per hour, you can use the **Currency** format so that the monetary elements show £, $ or any other appropriate currency symbol.

Creating unique numbers is sometimes more easily achieved by setting the **Data Type** for that field as **Autonumber**. This means that every time a new record is created the next sequential unique number is allocated to that record.

Sometimes when creating a questionnaire, the answers can be just 'yes' or 'no' – for instance do you own a personal computer? Again there is a Data Type that allows the person feeding the data in to use a tick box option.

Other validation techniques

Figure 26.14 shows a range of **Data Types** and validation techniques. Each of the techniques is another step towards preventing erroneous data being entered. The table shown has a collection of odd fields in it, so that as many combinations as possible can be illustrated here.

In Figure 26.14 the arrow is pointing to Date_of_birth. Therefore the **General** box and LOOKUP refer to that field only and the area where they are found is referred to as *field properties*.

Note that in this General area, the first line shows the format set to **Long Date**. However, there is a small blue arrow at the end of that box. This indicates that there is more than one option when selecting a date format. By clicking on the arrow, other formats will be displayed and can be selected as alternatives (Figure 26.15).

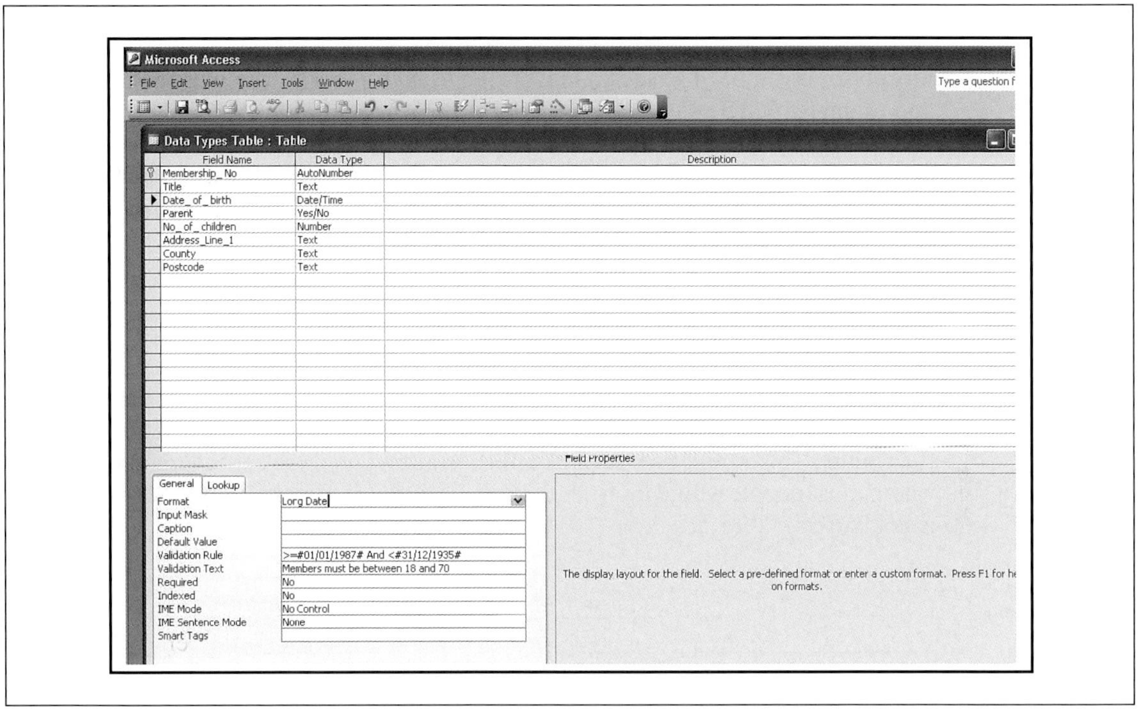

Figure 26.14

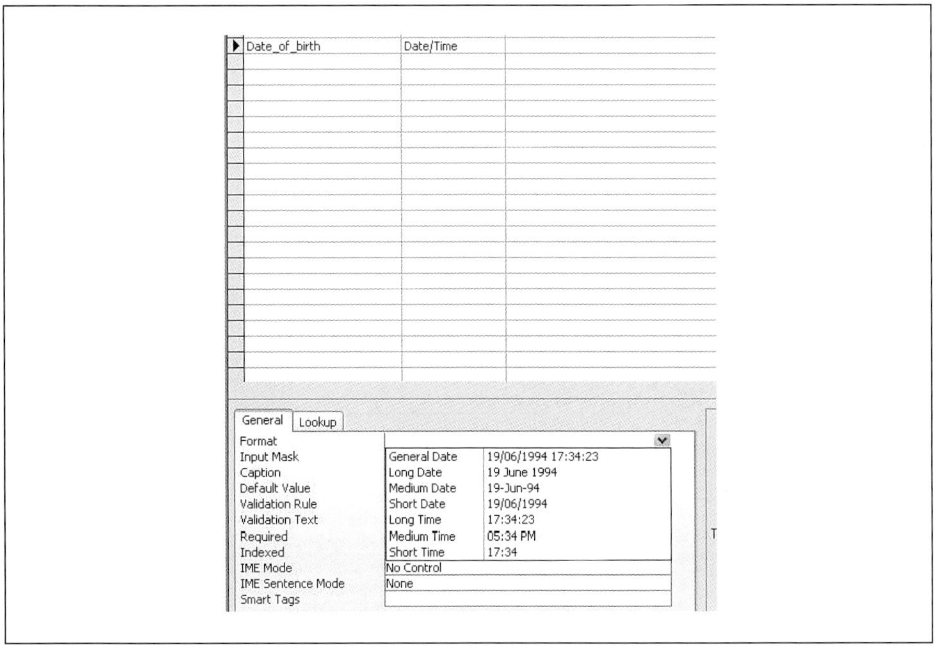

Figure 26.15

The illustration in Figure 26.14 also shows a **Validation Rule** and **Text**. When you click into some of these boxes, there will often be an explanation of the technique. Moreover, if you need to see an illustration of how it works, you can press the F1 key and examples will be shown to the right of the screen. In the example illustrated the **Validation Rule** has been set so that only dates of birth that indicate a new member is between 18 and 70 can be input. If the data fed in break this rule, the **Validation Text** will kick in to give an error message. Now where have you seen those annoying messages before!

DEFAULT VALUE AND INPUT MASKS

Two other field properties that can be set up in **General** are the **Default Value** and the **Input Mask**. The example in Figure 26.16 shows a default value of Northants as the county. This would be relevant if, for instance, you were setting up a local group where most people would be from the same county. It can always be over-written if it is not correct.

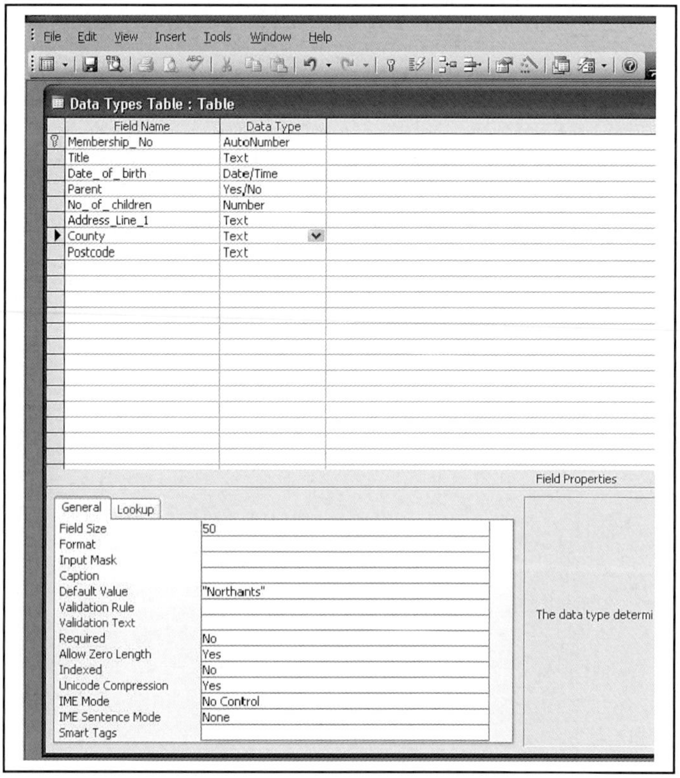

Figure 26.16

Finally in this section we will look at a technique which could be used to limit the type of characters that could be input; this is an **Input Mask**. As with a children's mask, where you can only see their eyes and tongue, the Input Mask limits what gets through. This is particularly useful when you request a postcode, telephone number, mobile number, web address or e-mail address. Each of these has something unique about them, a particular format. For instance postcodes follow a specific alpha and numeric pattern in the UK, telephone numbers begin with a 0, the district code and the actual number, mobile numbers are 11 digits and web addresses and e-mail addresses contain certain characteristics, for example www or @. By creating a mask, the special characters can be a permanent feature and the type of characters that are allowed can be set.

Figure 26.17 shows the table that appears when you are clicked on to the **Input Mask** line. The figure shows three things: a small box at the end of the **Input Mask** line which indicates the presence of a wizard, examples of a pattern for common masks and a simple mask. If you press F1 at this stage, the Microsoft® Access Help will appear to the right of the screen. This shows some examples, but more importantly it shows which mask characters restrict which entry. The following table lists these.

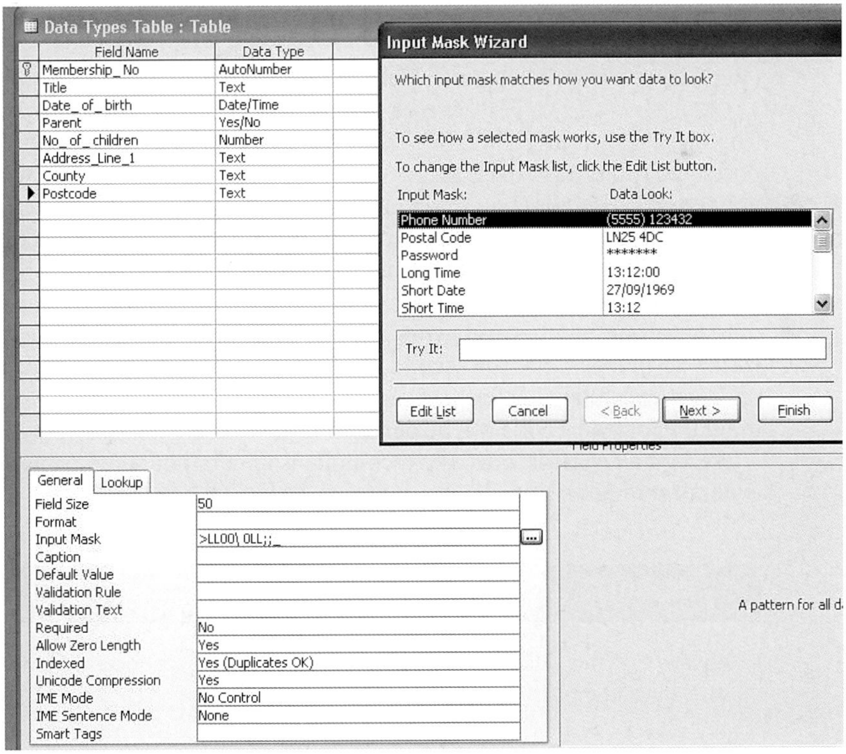

Figure 26.17

Character Description

0   Digit (0 to 9, entry required, plus [+] and minus [−] signs not allowed).

9   Digit or space (entry not required, plus and minus signs not allowed).

\#   Digit or space (entry not required; spaces are displayed as blanks while in Edit mode, but blanks are removed when data is saved; plus and minus signs allowed).

L   Letter (A to Z, entry required).

?   Letter (A to Z, entry optional).

A   Letter or digit (entry required).

a   Letter or digit (entry optional).

&   Any character or a space (entry required).

C   Any character or a space (entry optional).

. , : ; - /   Decimal placeholder and thousand, date, and time *separators* (the actual character used depends on the settings in the **Regional Settings Properties** dialog box in Windows Control Panel).

<   Causes all characters to be converted to lower case.

>   Causes all characters to be converted to upper case.

!   Causes the input mask to display from right to left, rather than from left to right. Characters typed into the mask always fill it from left to right. You can include the exclamation point anywhere in the input mask.

\   Causes the character that follows to be displayed as the literal character (for example, \A is displayed as just A).

(Reproduced from Microsoft® Help Menu)

The mask shown in Figure 26.17 of **>LL00\ 0LL;;** _was created by the wizard for a postcode. It has this effect: the > sign, causes all of the characters to be converted to upper case – this eliminates a jumble of upper and lower case characters. The LL indicate A–Z is required twice (i.e. compulsory). If an A to Z character is not typed in then the adding of more data is not possible until the user gets the right combination. The 00 indicates two numbers required. Now it could be argued that some postcodes only have one number following the two alpha characters. Replacing the second 0 with a 9 will mean that the second character is optional the \ and space indicates that the character following the \ will appear in the final data string. So when the data are input the following code will be permissible **NN75 9RT** but this code **N75 9RT** will not.

As with all wizards, once the technique is understood, then a mask specifically relevant to source data can be devised.

TIP

Always test the validation techniques you use with a good range of data to make sure all valid inputs will be accepted.

All of these techniques need to be discussed at the planning stages. The old adage Garbage In, Garbage Out (GIGO) applies as much today as it did 20 years ago! It may not be your job to create records for a database, but if you realise that techniques exist, then you can influence the way the data should be handled to make sure the data stored on your databases are as accurate as possible.

The word ACCURATE can be used as an acronym (Marketing Information Systems 2000) to indicate exactly what organisations should be working towards. If the data gathered are of good quality in all respects then the outputs will provide 'Good' and reliable information.

To reinforce the need to ensure all data are ACCURATE, this is probably a good point to re-emphasis what constitutes accurate data:

Accurate – 'Eyeball' to see if everything looks right

Complete – Have you thought of everything? Do you need external or comparative data?

Cost beneficial – Are you gaining anything from collecting this data? Will it cost more to collect and analyse than it is worth?

User-targeted – Remember your target audience: shop floor supervisor or director of the board. Lots of detail or just an overview?

Relevant – Just because data are interesting, it does not mean that they are relevant. Don't crowd the output with irrelevant data

Authoritative – Were the data obtained from a reliable source? Are you happy with it?

Timely – Ready on time; captured at the same time each day, week, month; available when needed

Easy to use – Information that is clearly presented and delivered via the right medium e.g. e-mail, Microsoft® PowerPoint slides, hard copy.

TIP

Using this acronym, ask yourself are these data accurate?

In general terms, use a character field, or **Text**, for a name or a numeric field for mathematical calculations such as salary. Anything like a house number or a phone number which you will *never* want to add up, set as a **Text** field.

You can also change the default number of characters Microsoft® Access assigns to a field by overtyping the number at the bottom of the screen. For instance surnames will rarely be more that 15 characters, say 20 at the most, so cut the number down from 50 to 20.

When the table is complete, click on the red cross ✖ at the corner of the window. As the window closes there will be an opportunity to a give the table a meaningful name (Figure 26.18).

Other tables can be created to fit into the overall design for the database. The table in Figure 26.19 will be used for Customer details and similarly others can be created for Course_Bookings (Figure 26.20) to contain all that needs to be known about course bookings!

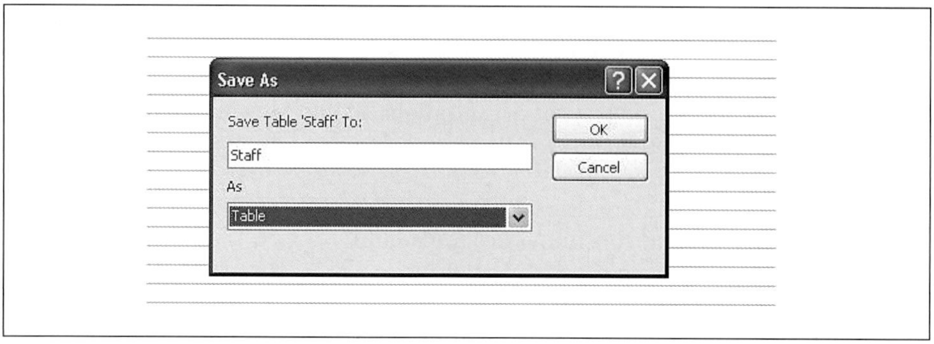

Figure 26.18

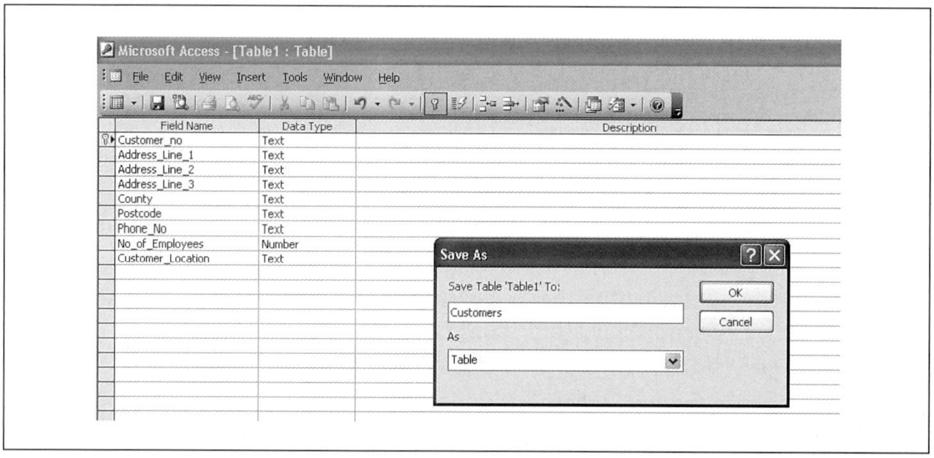

Figure 26.19

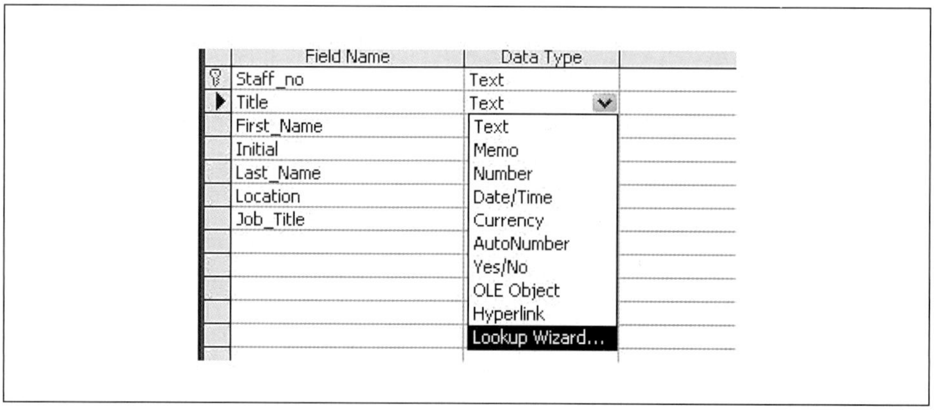

Figure 26.20

MAKING THE CONNECTION BETWEEN THE TABLES

The joining together of two or more tables means that a relationship between them has to be defined. This is a very important part of the process. For instance, a user of the system may want to link together the trainers who are available to run a course, with the businesses that need the course and the booking details. The icon on the toolbar shown in Figure 26.21 is the relationship icon.

When clicked, the relationship button will either show the tables that are already linked to one another *or* the show table icon can be clicked and a list of available tables will be shown (Figure 26.22).

As mentioned before data, should not be duplicated in multiple tables. If certain data only occur in one table, for instance a Staff Table, then when the details are changed they need only be changed in one area. Other tables that use the details from the Staff Table can be automatically refreshed with the new details.

However, the primary key will appear in other tables because that is the means by which the relationship is defined. When a primary key from one table appears in another table then it is called a *foreign key*.

TIP
You can always check whether a primary key has been set and where it appears by looking at the relationship table, it appears in bold, e.g. Booking_Ref.

In Figure 26.22 the Staff_No in the Staff Table is linked to the Course_Bookings Table. In the Course_Bookings table it is referred to as Trainer_No, this is because

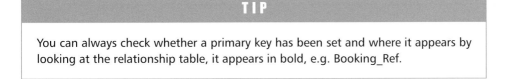

Figure 26.21

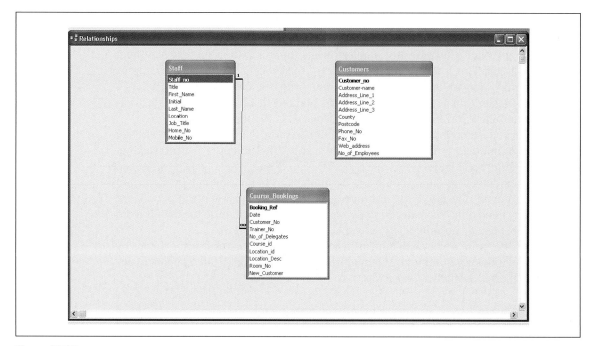

Figure 26.22

that title is more appropriate for that table. However, it is identical in **Data Type** and field size to Staff_No so the two can be linked together without a problem. The good thing is that if more details are need on the trainer then they can be gathered from the staff table.

TIP
If you are involved with systems design, consider all of the options that might be needed, both short and long term.

To connect two tables, click on the field that connects the two tables together, for example Staff_No, then, holding the mouse button down, drag across to the table that contains Trainer_No, in this case Course_Bookings. As you drop over Trainer_No a box will appear (Figure 26.23). The box shows the two related items. Two key things that can be considered at this time are the **Relationship Type** and **Enforce Referential Integrity**.

Relationship type

The types that you will encounter will be *One to One*, *One to Many* or *Many to Many*. So what do these relationships mean? Well if two entities have a One to One relationship it means that there is a single link between them. So in the case of Courses then perhaps one trainer can only teach on one course because they are not

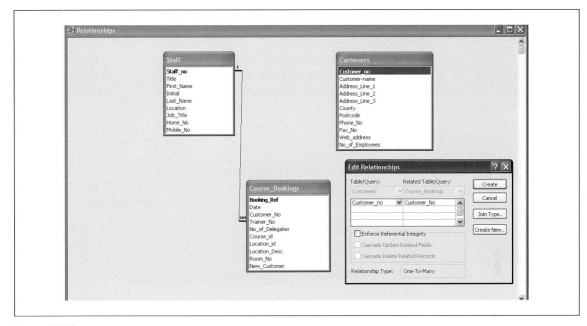

Figure 26.23

specialised in any other. But for One to Many, a business can make lots of bookings, and a trainer can be involved on lots of bookings too. The diagram denotes this with 1(One) at one end of the link and a ∞ (Many) at the other end. So talking this through, you would say that a business can make one or many bookings, but each booking will be with one and only one business. Similarly when you go to the doctor, there are lots of doctors and lots of patients (Many to Many) but when it come to an appointment, a patient can make many appointments, but each appointment will be with one and only one doctor.

When designing a database, it is also useful to remember that some relationships are *mandatory* and some *optional*, for example if you work in the UK it is mandatory to have a National Insurance No., but it is optional to be a member of a trade union.

Figure 26.23 shows that the relationship in this case is One to Many, that is to say that a business can make as many bookings as it needs, but for each booking there will only be one business on the individual booking form.

Enforce Referential Integrity

When the **Enforce Referential Integrity** box is ticked then a check will be made to ensure that the two items being linked are of the same type. This is a set of rules used to ensure that relationships between tables are valid and it is always advisable to set this. It also ensures that the related items cannot be deleted or changed. If it is not set, the two symbols representing one (1) and many (∞) will not show on the relationship diagram. If this is acceptable, the link will be made as shown in the diagram, but if not an error message will show and the field types will have to be checked.

TIP

If you have a problem with referential integrity (Figure 24.24) click with the right-hand mouse button over the table. This will give a link (Figure 24.25) directly to the table design to allow you to see where the problem is.

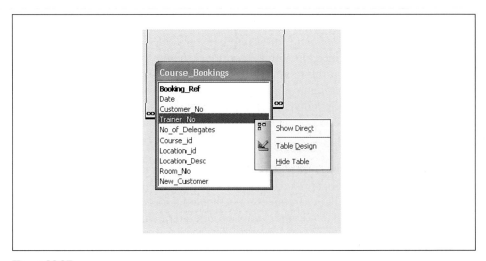

Figure 26.24

Figure 26.25

Other facilities exist at this point that enable records to be updated. However, as with all programs, it is easy to try and drill down too deep at an early stage and lose the reader. So suffice to say that when you are ready, there are many more sophisticated features to explore.

INPUTTING DATA

Having designed the correct number of fields and deliberated on the type and limitations of data they will hold, it is time to actually put some data into the database. On the toolbar you will notice these two icons, this one is the design icon  and this one is  the Datasheet View. It is extremely important to get the design right before putting real data in; changes later on can be costly and time consuming.

The design for the Course_bookings database is shown in Figure 26.26.

The Datasheet View is shown in Figure 26.27.

By toggling between the two icons, Design and Datasheet, it is possible to see how the design is looking. Note that where the **Data Type** is a number, a 0 appears automatically, also the new customer has a box because the answer has been set to Yes or No only. You will note it is set blank for No, but if you click inside the box a tick will appear for Yes.

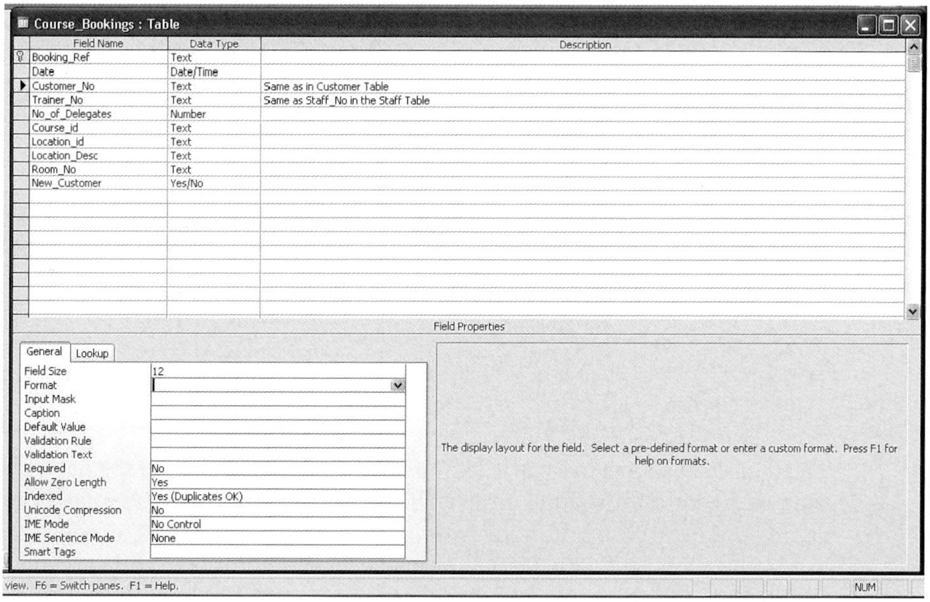

Figure 26.26

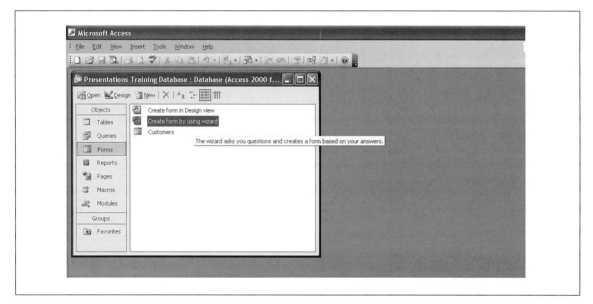

Figure 26.27

Figure 26.28

TIP

Work through the design with mock data before releasing for general use.

Adding data with a datasheet or form

The datasheet shown in Figure 26.27 can be used to add in all of the data, but it is possible to create a form quite easily. The form can then provide an additional way of adding the data. More advanced still is Form within a Form. You will often see this used in business and commerce. For instance, in a library the top part will show your details and at the bottom will be a list of your current books.

To create a form easily, click on **Form** in the **Objects** list and then double click on **Create form by using wizard** (Figure 26.28).

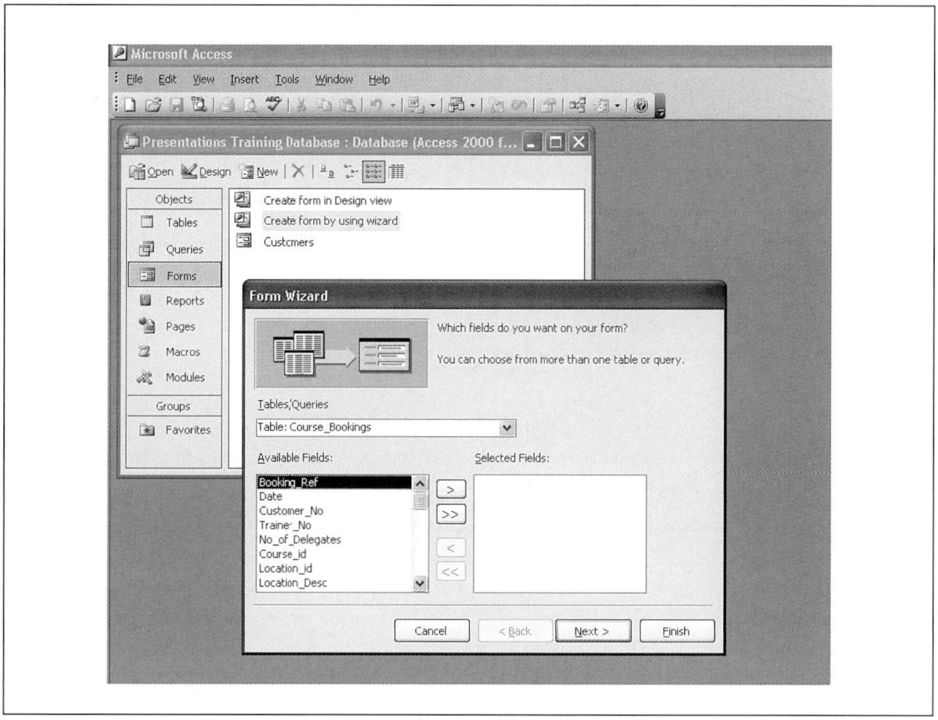

Figure 26.29

There are two main things to note about the **Form Wizard** screen. One is that you can choose to make a form from any of the Tables or Queries that currently exist. To select the one you want, there is a drop down arrow. Note that the table Course_Bookings is the one selected in Figure 26.29. Underneath this the **Available Fields** are shown. The **Selected Fields** are the ones that will appear on the form.

To select *all* available fields the double arrow `>>` should be used. To select just one or two, each one should be highlighted and then the single arrow `>` used to carry them across. This convention is often used in other programs and enables fields to be moved back and forth until the right ones are chosen.

The benefit of using the wizard is that you can try all sorts of combinations of design, and if you do not like the result you can delete and try again.

TIP

If you change the data table you will have to go back and recreate the matching form.

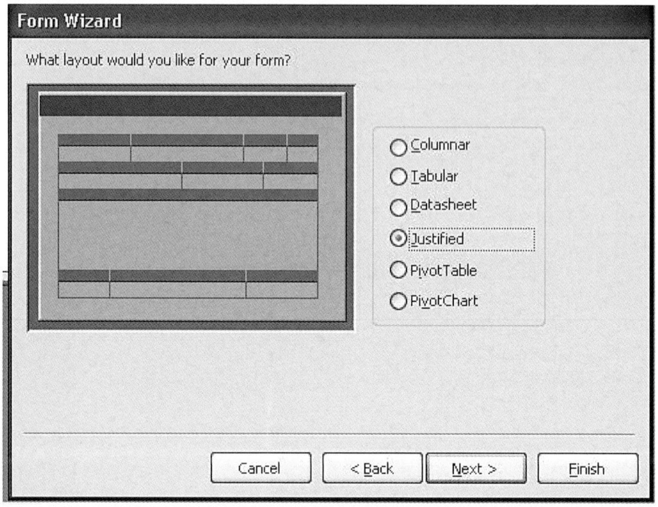

Figure 26.30

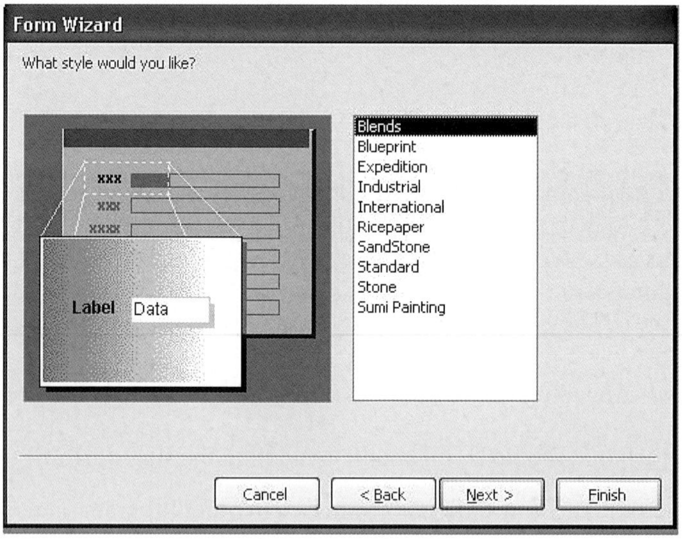

Figure 26.31

The wizard offers a wealth of combinations for form creation (Figures 26.30 and 26.31), the choice is yours. In addition, the form can be further modified by clicking on the form itself and selecting the design mode  . Forms, as with all of the elements of the database construction (tables, reports, etc.), should be given a meaningful name (Figure 26.32).

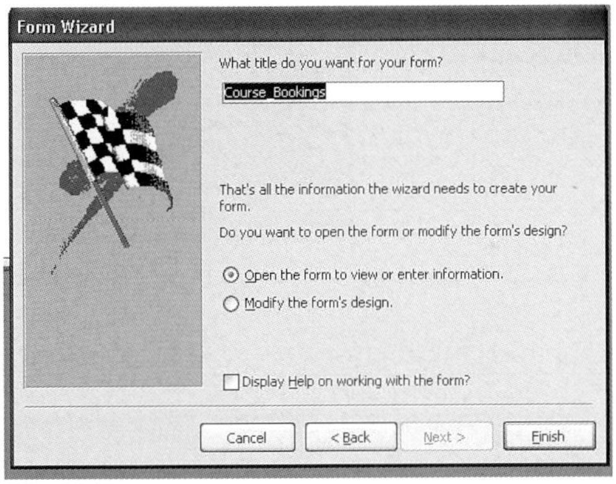

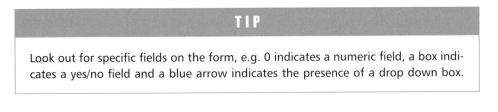

Figure 26.32

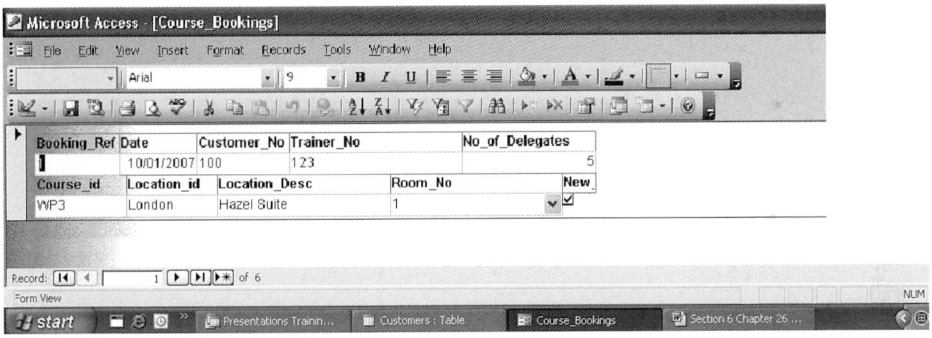

Figure 26.33

Once the steps are complete the form appears on the screen and can be populated (Figure 26.33). The bottom of the screen (Figure 26.34) shows the number of records and which record you are viewing. The asterisk should be clicked to create a new record.

TIP
Look out for specific fields on the form, e.g. 0 indicates a numeric field, a box indicates a yes/no field and a blue arrow indicates the presence of a drop down box.

What is a Query?

Queries are used to interrogate databases. The wizard can be used to simplify this process (Figure 26.34), but basically the facility allows you to set certain criteria or rules and search the contents of all or part of the tables in the database to see if the criteria or rules are matched. Over time, it is possible to use very skilful techniques to

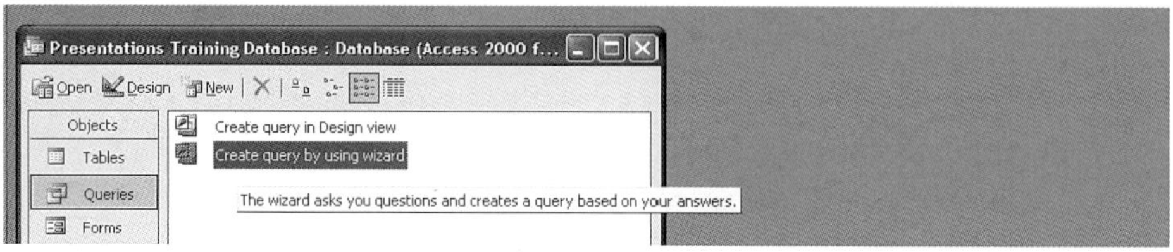

Figure 26.34

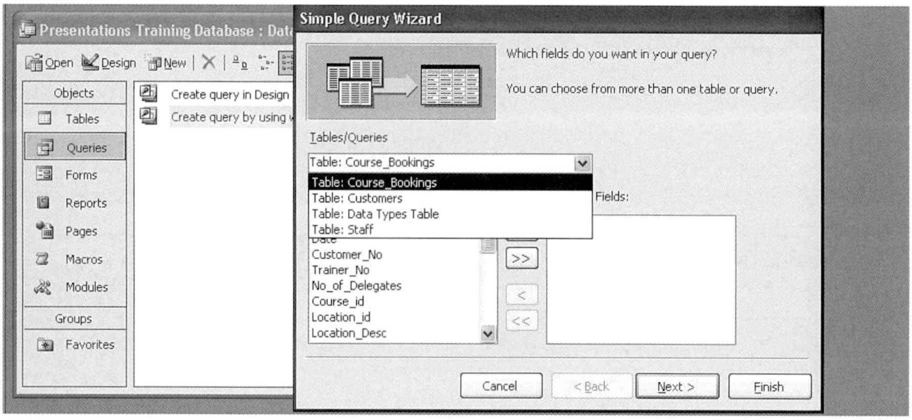

Figure 26.35

interrogate and extract interesting facts and figures from databases and move away from using the wizard to creating queries from scratch.

The wizard can use any **Table or Query** available and will produce a table based on the selected items. Note the use of arrows again to move and select data (Figure 26.35).

In the Query that has been created below, it should be noted that two tables are being used with fields from both displayed below. This is where the **Relational database** comes into its own, by linking tables together and using relevant data from each without duplication.

Once the design is complete (Figure 26.36), criteria can be specified in order to work even further down into the database, in order to pick up certain information. In this case the criterion is to find all instances that match the staff member called

Mandy. When the Run button is pressed [ ] the results of that query will appear (Figure 26.37).

Along with the records relating to Mandy are all of the other fields shown in the design (Figure 26.36). If they are not needed, the small green tick can be removed and they will not appear.

Similarly dates can be used to extract data relevant to timetables and schedules (Figures 26.38 and 26.39). Again, this is only the tip of the iceberg and serves to show the essence of how complex database interrogation can be.

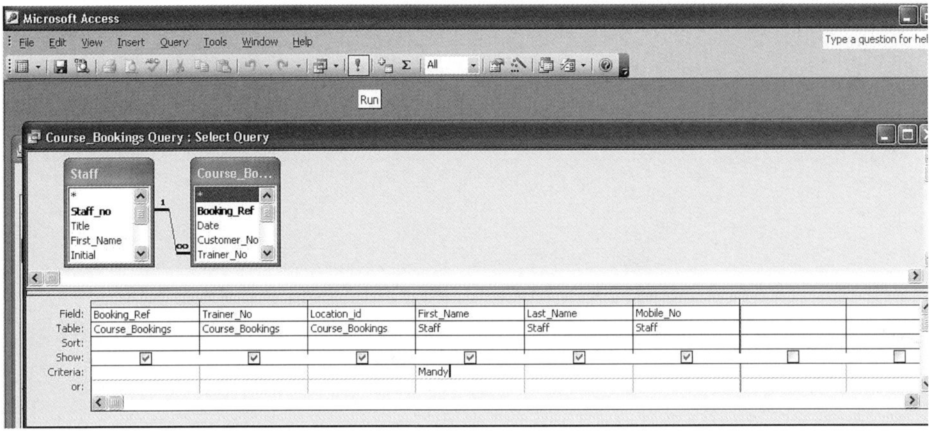

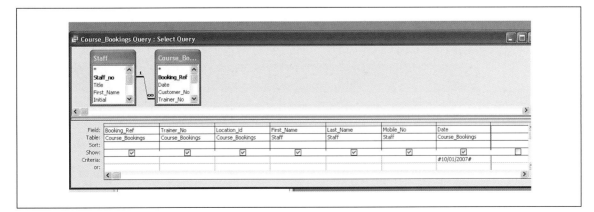

Figure 26.36

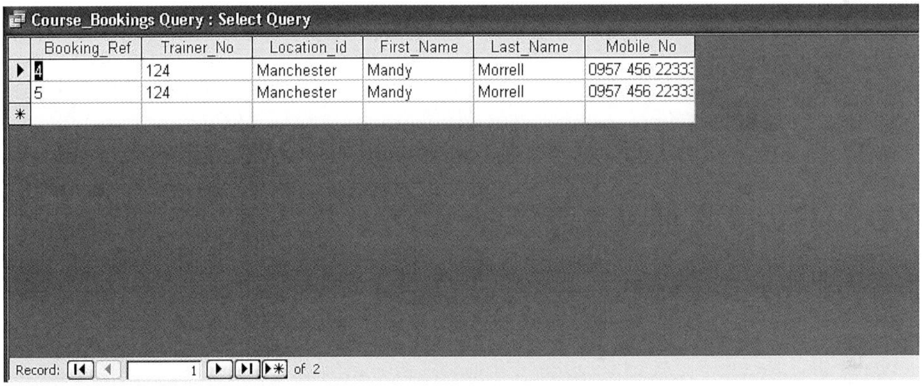

Figure 26.37

Figure 26.38

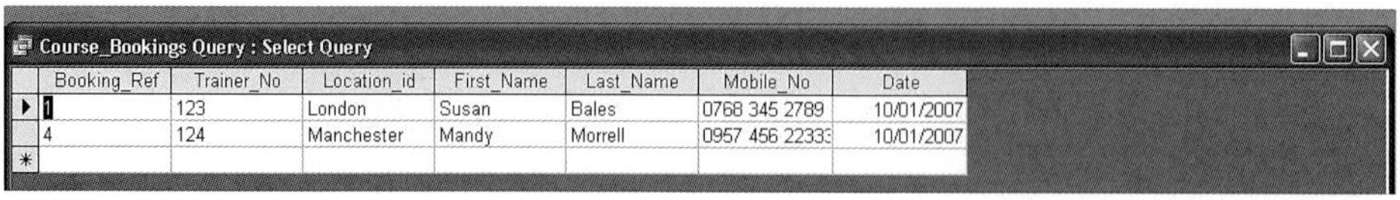

Figure 26.39

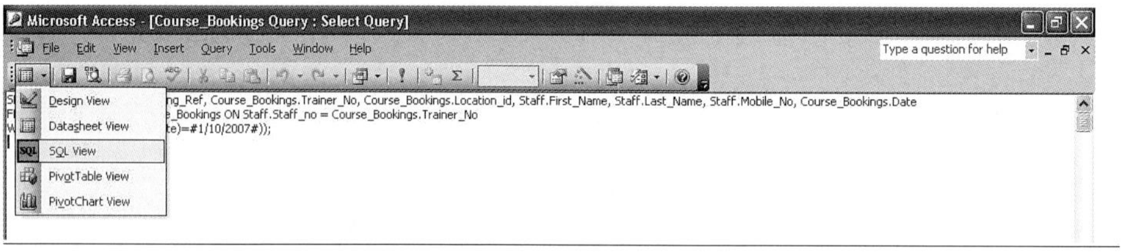

Figure 26.40

To complete this section on queries, Figure 26.40 shows the SQL view. Many people in the software industry can write and understand SQL code. It strings together information from data tables and commands that serve to produce results from a given set of data. Figure 26.40 shows the string of commands and information that produced the results in Figure 26.39.

REPORTS

The output from all of this activity is usually a report, although on-line interrogation can be used as well.

The report can again be taken from any table or Query that has been created. It is also possible to mix and match data from a variety of sources (e.g. different fields from different tables or Queries). This can give a much more comprehensive output (Figure 26.41).

TIP
Look for similar modes of operation within the database functions.

The report wizard allows different headings to be moved to the top of the report, ascending of descending lists and a variety of pre-determined styles (Figures 26.42, 26.43 and 26.44).

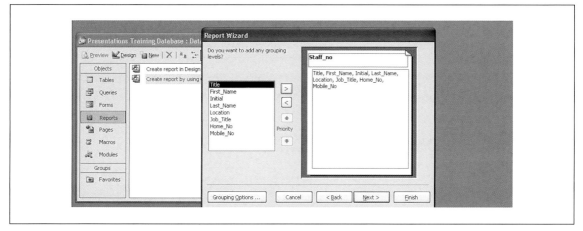

Figure 26.41

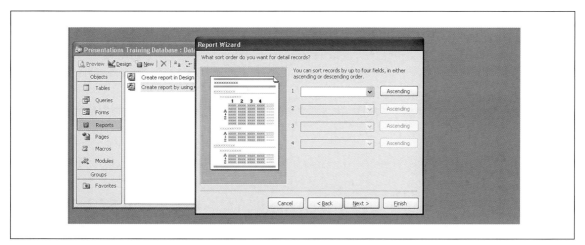

Figure 26.42

Figure 26.43

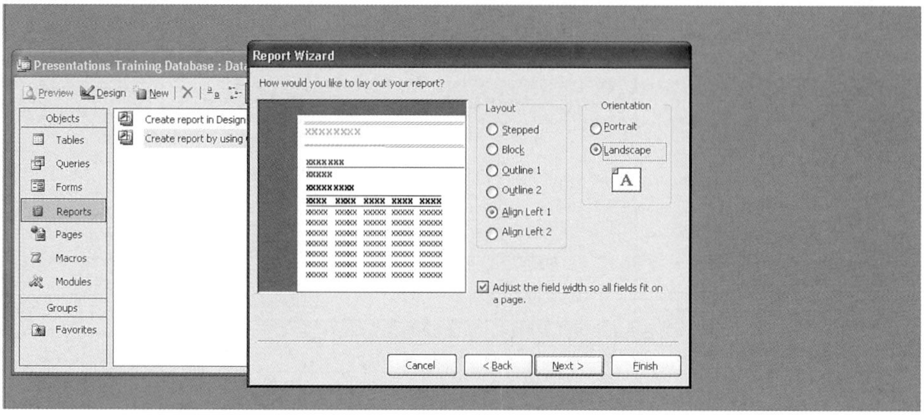

Figure 26.44

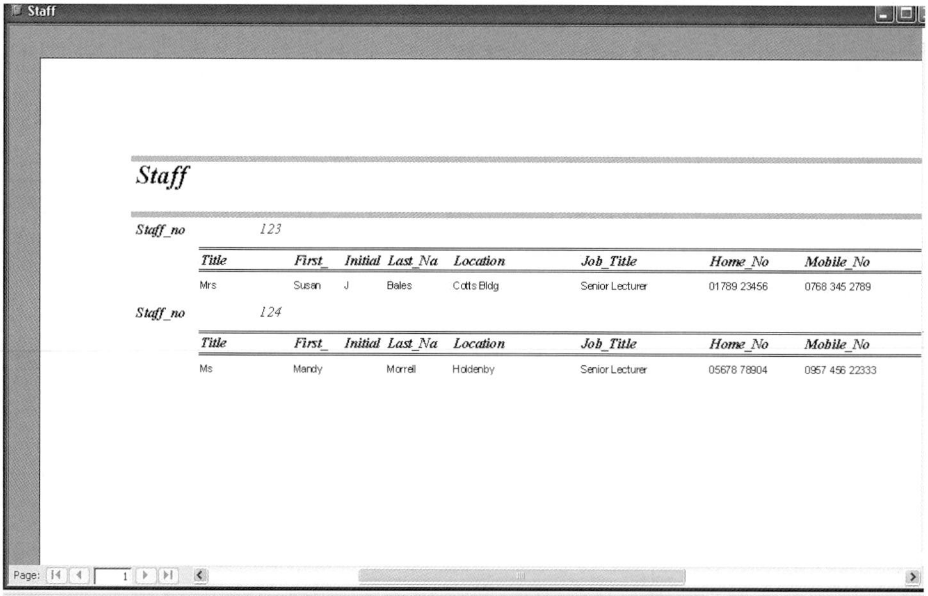

Figure 26.45

The finished output from the report can leave much to be desired (Figure 26.45). In this case the headings need to be adjusted and stretched out, the underlining needs to be altered and the design looks cramped. Again, the final report can be tweaked by

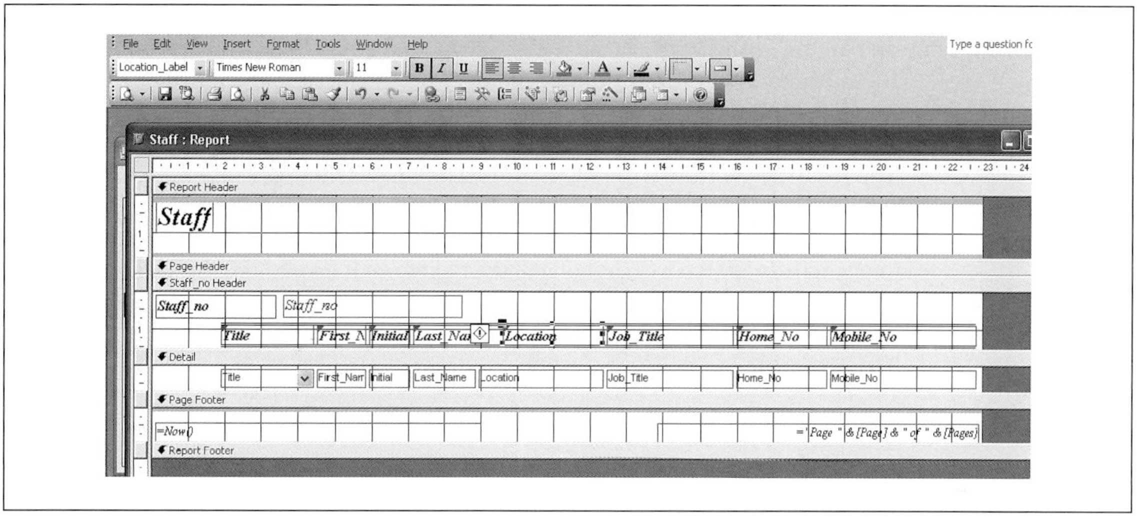

Figure 26.46

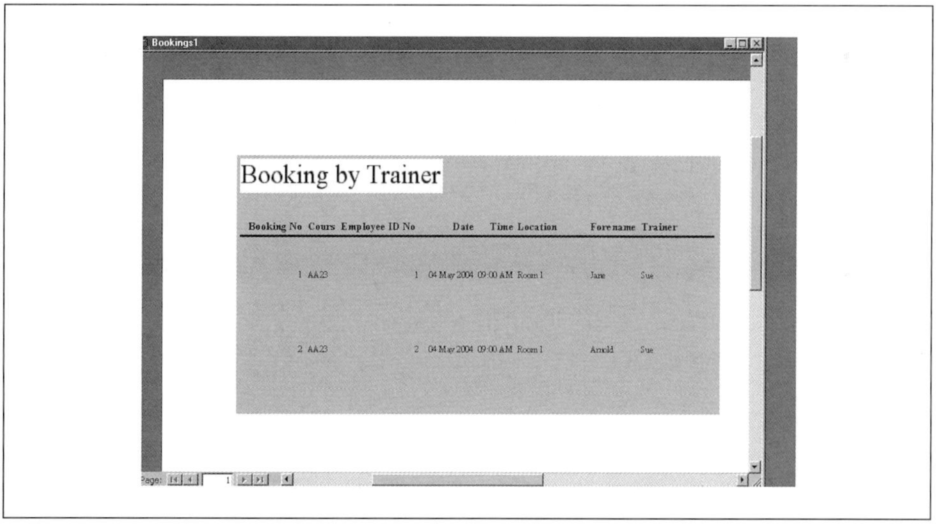

Figure 26.47

clicking on the report and selecting the **Design View** and making relevant changes (Figure 26.46) to give a smarter and more polished result (Figure 26.47).

Switchboard

To finish off the design, it is possible to create a switchboard. This is a variation on a form and it allows the user to click directly into a certain form or report as soon as the database opens. It is one of a huge number of facilities available under the **Tools** menu (Figure 26.48).

By selecting **Edit** on the **Default** menu (Figure 26.49) and then **New** on the **Edit** menu (Figure 26.50), a new command can be added (Figure 26.51). It is possible to see the switchboard items in the **Tables** and **Forms** sections.

The result of creating a switchboard is that a new front piece is created. When the switchboard design is complete, go back to **Tools** and select **Startup** (Figure 26.52) and select **Switchboard** from the drop down list under **Display Form/Page**. Once that is done and the database closed down, the next time it is opened, the switchboard will be displayed (Figure 26.53). This is also a handy technique for only allowing access to certain parts of the database.

The result can look something like the design in Figure 26.53.

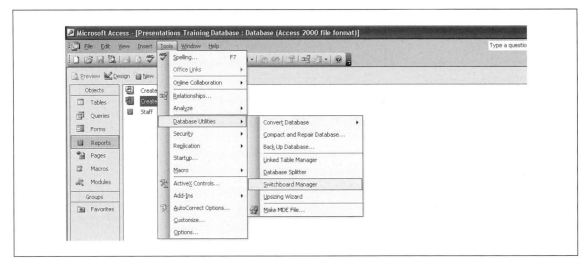

Figure 26.48

Figure 26.49

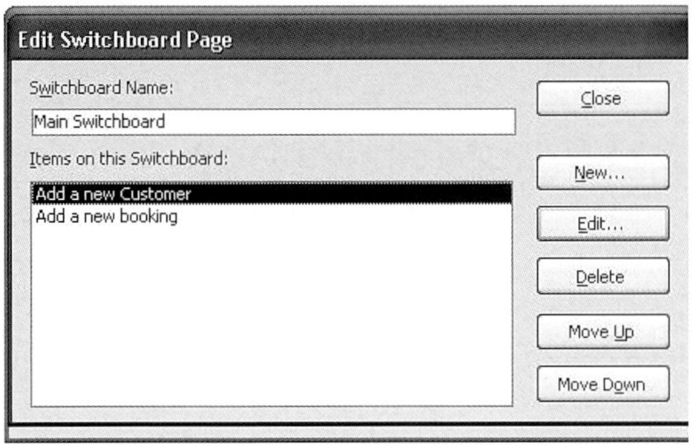

Figure 26.50

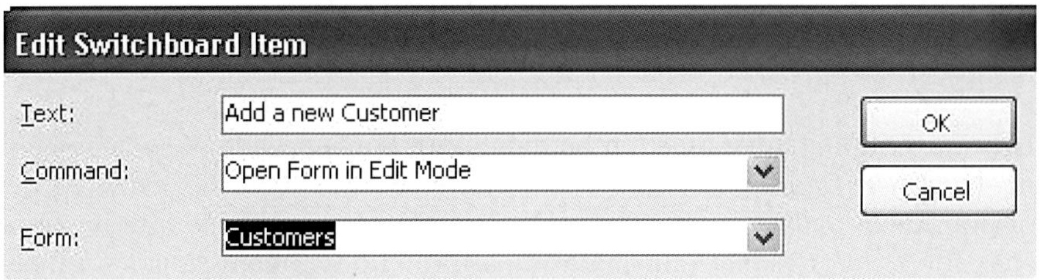

Figure 26.51

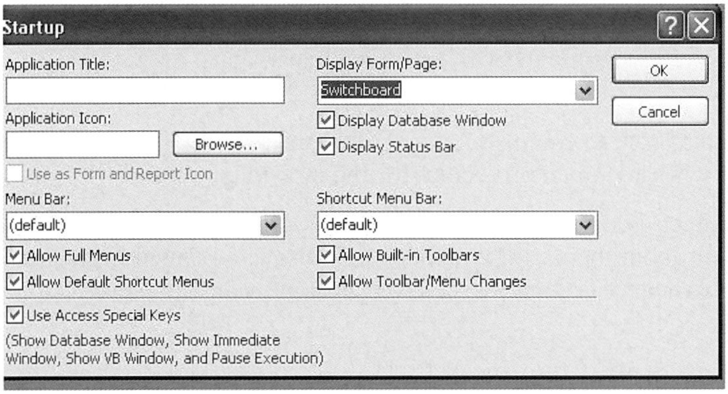

Figure 26.52

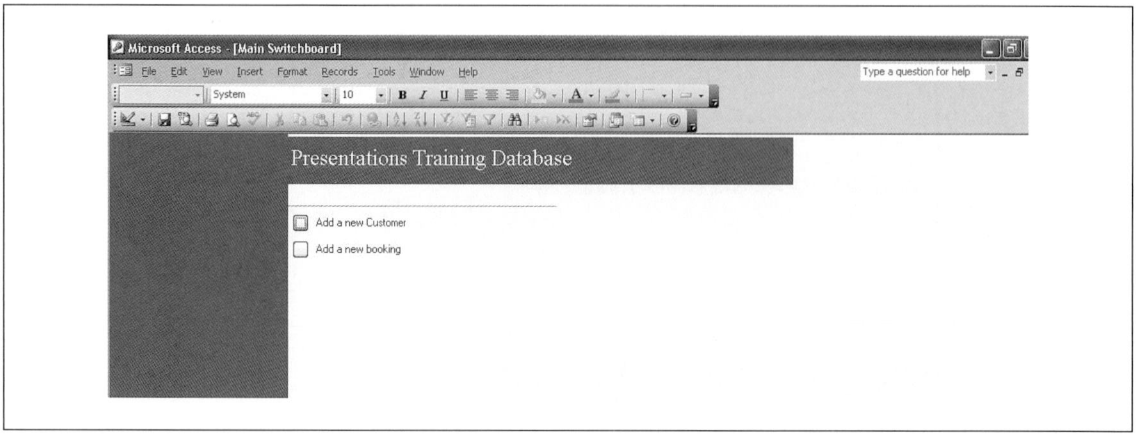

Figure 26.53

THE LEGAL SIDE OF DATA COLLECTION AND STORAGE

It is worth noting in this section on databases, the legal side of collecting and storing data. '*The Data Protection Act 1998* seeks to strike a balance between the rights of individuals and the sometimes competing interests of those with legitimate reasons for using personal information' (Information Commissioner's Office 2005). There are eight principles of good practice that must be adhered to, namely that data are:

1 fairly and lawfully processed
2 processed for limited purposes
3 adequate, relevant and not excessive
4 accurate and up to date
5 not kept longer than necessary
6 processed in accordance with the individual's rights
7 secure
8 not transferred to countries outside the European Economic area unless the country has adequate protection for the individual

This Act protects people from being bombarded with mail as they can now be asked if information about them can be passed on. It also allows an individual to know what information is held on a computer and within some manual records.

The Freedom of Information Act

This Act came into force on 1 January 2005. It enables people to gain access to information held by public authorities. Some data are published by public authorities. If it is not published 'any person has the right to make a request for information held by a public authority. The authority must usually respond to this request within 20 working days' (Information Commissioner's Office 2005).

Summary

This chapter has enabled the reader to understand some of the jargon and key terms used in the creation of databases. In a commercial environment the role of the manager is often advisory and he or she will not be expected to get involved in the actual design. However, as he or she is often the end-user, a clear and comprehensive understanding of data gathering, database design and storage techniques is essential. It is also useful to know how validation techniques can be used to prevent erroneous data being input.

The elements of database design as introduced in this chapter help to give an idea of what is possible. How a form is created, a query set up and a report output helps to create a feel for the mechanics of a database without going into the detail. The chapter also serves to refresh the reader on their legal obligations and to be aware of current legislation relating to the handling and storage of data.

Databases are notoriously complex, but no business can survive without collecting processing and outputting data, so a good understanding paves the way for future challenges.

TASK 1

Set up a three tables for a DVD club and link them together.
  a. Design a simple form that all members can complete
  b. Remember to put on the form a tick box that permits you to keep the information on a database
  c. Input the fields into a data table for the members using Member_ No as the primary key then First_Name, Surname, Title, Address, Town, Postcode, Mobile_Telephone_No
  d. Create a data table for DVDs using DVD_No, Name, Type
  e. Create a table for booking of DVDs using Booking _No, Date_borrowed, Date_to_be_returned, DVD_No, Member_No
  f. Include some validation techniques
  g. Link them together
  h. Create a form for each

TASK 2

Add data to the database
a. Using the form, put five records into Member, ten into DVD and ten Bookings. Remember you can only make a booking for members and DVDs that exist in your tables.
   1 Members
   2 DVDs
   3 Booking – put in a full range of dates in March and April for Date_to_be_returned
b. Print out each one as a report.

TASK 3

Interrogate the database
a. Set up a query using Member_no, Mobile_Telephone_No, DVD_No, DVD_Name, Date_Borrowed
b. Set up a query to see which DVDs are overdue by choosing a date in mid- April
c. Print it as a report that says at the top *Overdue DVDs for April*

References

Bocij, P., Chaffey, D., Greasley, A. and Hickie, S. (2003) *Business Information Systems, Technology, Development and Management for e-business* 2nd edn, London: FT Prentice Hall.

Management Information Systems (2000) London: BPP Publishing.

Information Commissioners Office [online] Accessed on 2 October 2005 http://www.informationcommissioner.gov.uk

Saunders, M., Lewis, P. and Thornhill, A. (2003) *Research Methods for Business Students*. 3rd edn, Harlow: FT Prentice Hall.

The Question Bank Social Surveys Online [online] 2 October 2005 http://qb.soc.surrey.ac.uk

CHAPTER 27
Powerful presentations

Learning objectives

- To create a simple, but effective, presentation
- To experiment with additional timesaving features
- To manipulate slides to create a slick delivery

Introduction

Throughout your life as a student or as a manager you will, on numerous occasions, be asked to do a presentation. Too often people present overcrowded slides using complex wizardry and read extensively from their notes. Consequently the potential powerfulness of their presentation is lost.

The purpose of this chapter is to allow you to quickly produce a worthwhile and credible presentation that will give you the confidence to deliver it professionally.

WHAT IS POWERPOINT®?

PowerPoint® is part of the Microsoft® Office suite which allows you to produce presentations:

- electronically, e.g. on screen, disk, etc.
- on paper, in the form of handouts
- on transparencies for users with an overhead projector (OHP)

Additionally it allows you to annotate your slides with notes which help you make an effective presentation.

The wealth of creative options

It is always advisable to plan out what you are going to put onto your slides. The actual construction of the slides needs to be fairly simplistic, but your notes and the flow of the delivery need to be thought through. A picture or a good graph is priceless and you can look confidently at your audience while explaining the detail of your brilliant slide.

To start the proceedings you will need to open a blank Microsoft® PowerPoint presentation. When you open a Microsoft® PowerPoint presentation, the **General** area will offer a straightforward version of a presentation file. You will also note that there is an entire section labelled **Presentations**. This contains a variety of versions that have been pre-formatted. It may be worth browsing through this selection prior to starting your own slides to see if there is something more suitable for your particular requirement.

CREATING YOUR SLIDES

When you open the **Presentation** from the **General** area, the first screen will be displayed. On this screen you will see many familiar toolbars and you will have the ability to manipulate the text, centre it, embolden it just as you would be able to in a Microsoft® Word document. At this early stage, make sure that you have the drawing toolbar available to you (Figure 27.1), as this will be useful to you in constructing your slide show.

Microsoft® PowerPoint 2003 allows you to choose a number of different PowerPoint® slide layouts. Figure 27.2 shows a title slide.

> **TIP**
>
> Don't clutter you slides with too much detail, dazzle the audience with your patter instead.

To create a powerful presentation it is not necessary to use the whole variety of layouts available, just selecting one or two key ones will give you the output that you need.

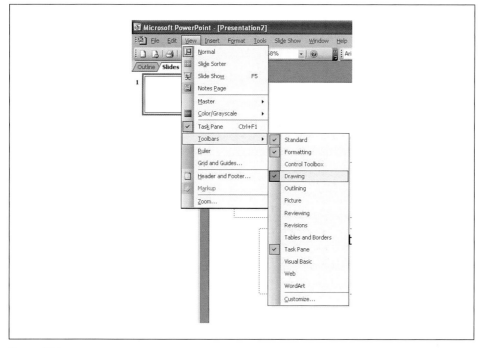

Figure 27.1

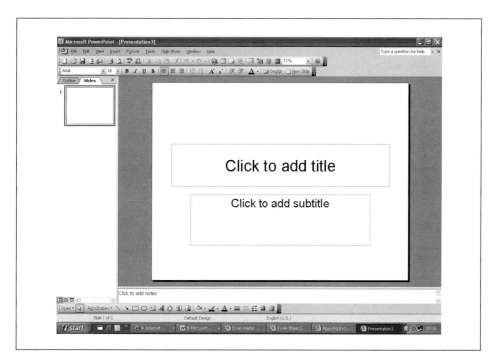

Figure 27.2

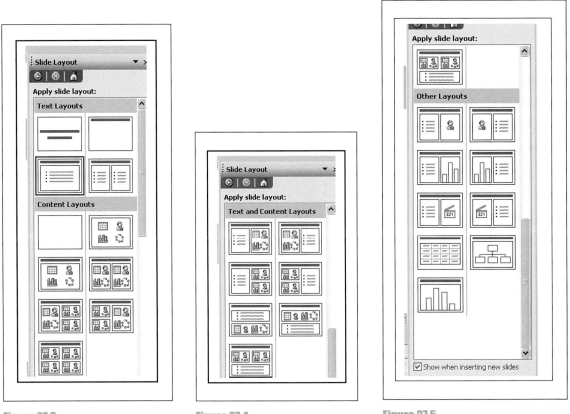

Figure 27.3   **Figure 27.4**   **Figure 27.5**

Figures 27.3, 27.4 and 27.5 show that there are layouts containing diagrams, graphs, video clips, organisational charts, as well as a variety of layouts for text. All of these will be useful to you in time and again there is an opportunity to experiment with them when the pressure is off – that is when you have finished you last assignment! Bullet points are a familiar feature of PowerPoint® presentations and should be used to clarify your thoughts and act as a trigger in your presentation.

TIP

Use bullet points to trigger your patter.

Getting started

This may be the first presentation you have embarked on and you could spend four or five hours perfecting it. So this section will give you an outline of a simplistic approach leaving you plenty of time in your leisure to put the 'whiz bang' into it if you need to.

Isolating one of the slide options in the **Content Layouts**, it is possible to identify the six main symbols Microsoft® PowerPoint uses to represent things that might be pertinent to your presentation layout (Figure 27.6). The wealth of layouts, some with text or title, some without, can be chosen according to the needs of the presentation.

As you get more proficient with Microsoft® PowerPoint, you may like to set up a **Master slide** which is a kind of template for your own presentations. This can contain things such as your company logo and colours representing the company image, or your personal contact details.

However, this is not a task to embark on at this stage, but merely a note to let you know that you can create your own style when you have the time (Figures 27.7 and 27.8).

Getting back to the basic design, when you open your presentation template for the first time, it is worth noting that under **Format** there are some existing **Slide Designs** (Figure 27.9). This Microsoft® PowerPoint option allows you to choose from

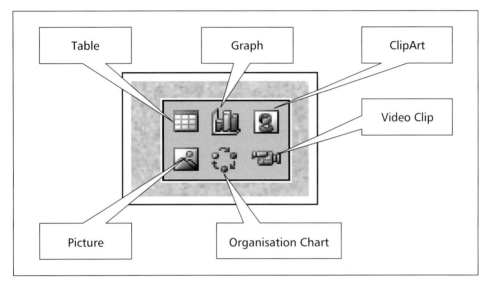

Figure 27.6

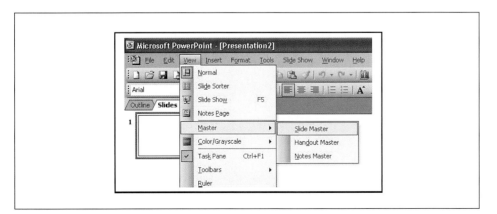

Figure 27.7

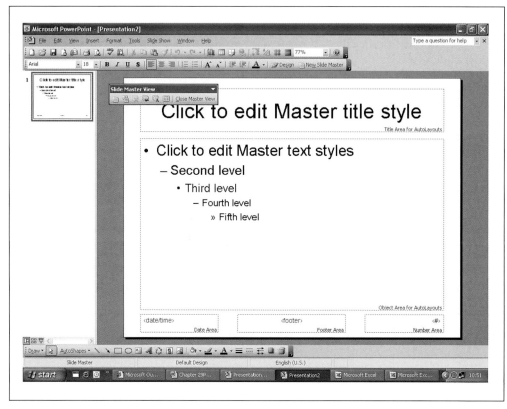

Figure 27.8

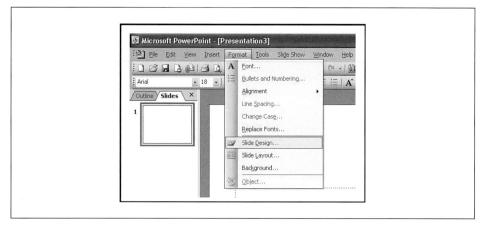

Figure 27.9

a selection of designs. You may like to use these rather than setting up your own. Or you may just use the **Background** option which is also available under **Format**.

When you select slide design a selection of pre-prepared layouts (Figure 27.10) is displayed on the right-hand side of the screen. This will include any you have set up yourself.

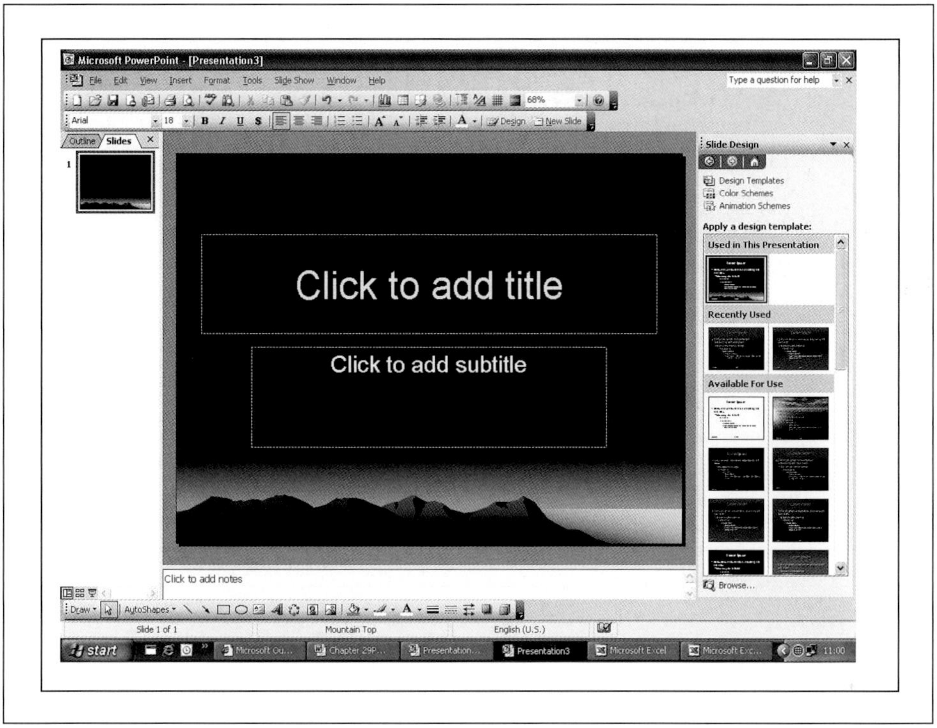

Figure 27.10

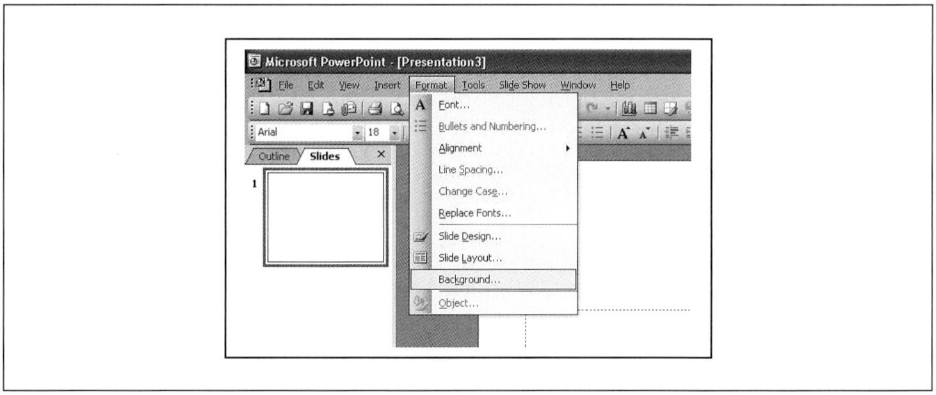

Figure 27.11

BASIC LAYOUTS

To set up a simple presentation, restrict yourself to using some of the more common templates. For this exercise, just use a simple **Background** to give your slides a little texture and interest (Figure 27.11).

Select **Format** and then **Background** and a screen will appear. Note there is a blue down arrow, clicking on this arrow will reveal the choice of **Automatic**; a range of

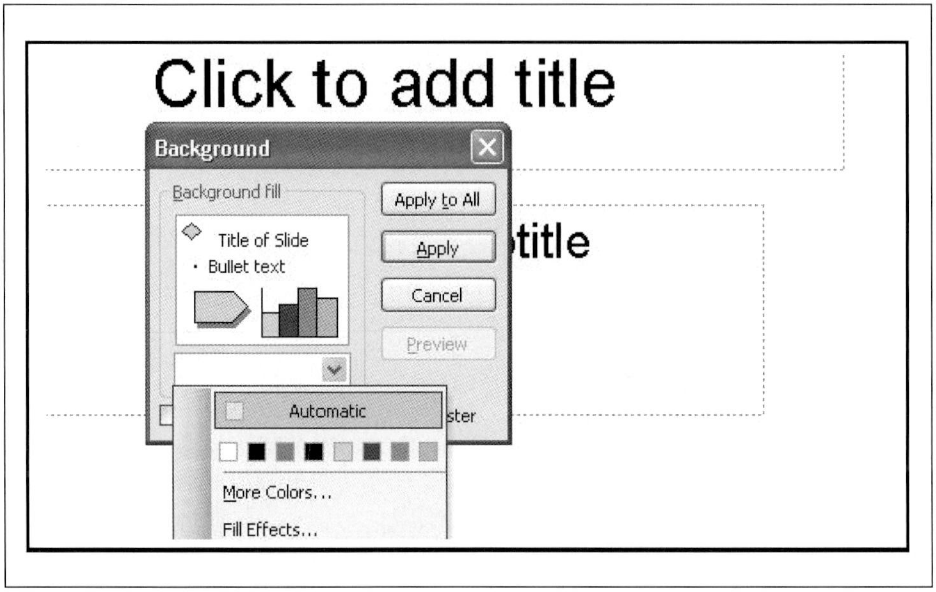

Figure 27.12

colours that you have used in the past and then the option for **More Colours** or **Fill Effects** (Figure 27.12).

This is another area where a variety of combinations are available and you will probably find a personal favourite from the wealth of colours and textures offered. To create a textured background, select **Fill Effects** and from the next screen (Figure 27.13) select **Textures** and then click on one of the options. Pick something that will be readable, but not distracting. The option that you have is to apply this to one or all of your slides (Figure 27.14).

Slide layout

It should be noted that, when selecting **Slide Layout**, you are once again presented with a variety of templates. To demonstrate this, a number of pertinent layouts will be used.

To access the layouts, select **Format**, **Slide Layout** and a panel of templates will be displayed on the right of your slide for you to pick from (Figure 27.15).

The first slide should introduce your and your subject. By clicking into each box you can add your own text. For example, **Click to add Title**, **Click to add subtitle**, as shown in Figure 27.16.

TIP

You can change the font style and size using the normal formatting toolbar. Text boxes can be stretched if the text runs over a little.

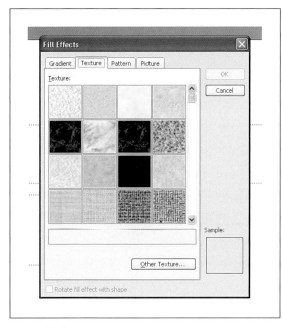

Figure 27.13

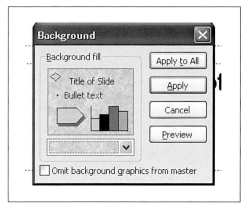

Figure 27.14

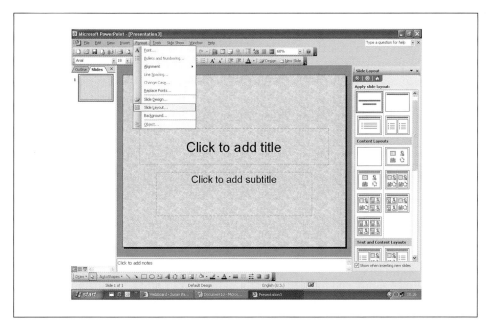

Figure 27.15

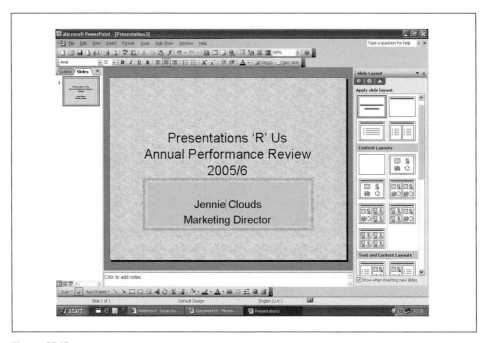

Figure 27.16

Having told the audience who you are, you will use a slightly different template (Figure 27.17) to continue with your presentation.

From the top of the toolbar select **Insert** and then **Insert New Slide**. The options for a new slide appear on the right. It is also possible to click on **Slide Layout** and apply the layout to an existing slide or add in a new one (Figure 27.18). When you have used presentations for a while, Microsoft® PowerPoint will display the ones you have used regularly, at the top of the selection.

Figure 27.19 shows a good layout for an overview slide, whilst Figure 27.20 shows a layout that can explain the points a little more clearly, without overloading the viewer.

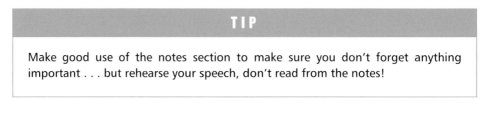

TIP

Make good use of the notes section to make sure you don't forget anything important . . . but rehearse your speech, don't read from the notes!

For your own sanity and to keep clear thoughts in your mind, use the notes option. To do this you will note a box underneath the slide which says **Click to add notes** (Figure 27.21). This example shows a full and detailed set of notes, very useful in times of panic!!!

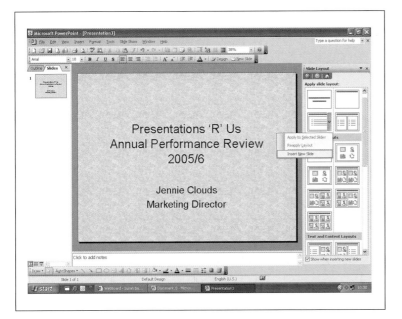

Figure 27.17

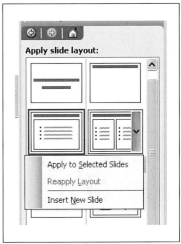

Figure 27.18

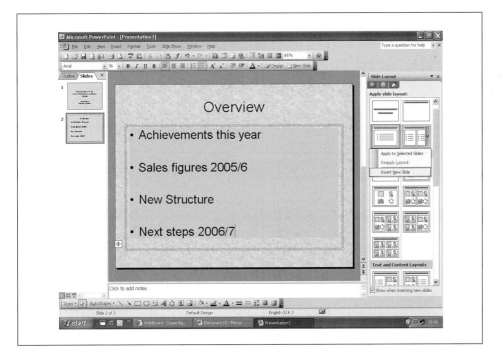

Figure 27.19

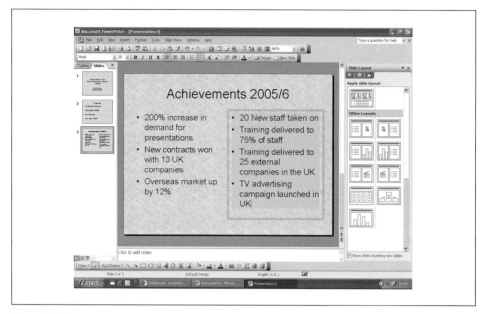

Figure 27.20

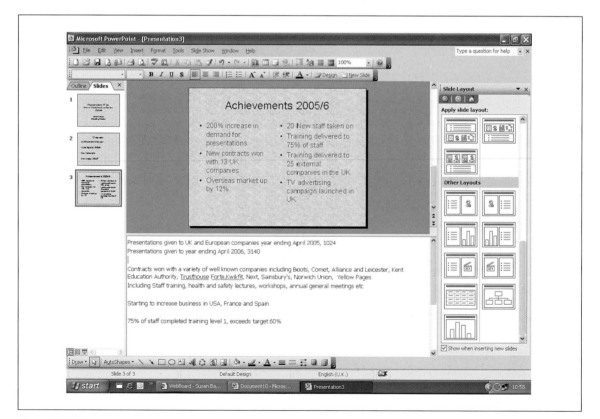

Figure 27.21

Other options

Some of the **Slide Layouts** allow the user to add a graph. The option chosen may be for a title and a chart (Figure 27.22), but at other times a chart with text may be more appropriate. This gives you all the same options as you would have in Microsoft® Excel. Your choice is to construct the graph in Microsoft® Excel and then add it in or construct it at the point of presentation. Microsoft® PowerPoint will give you a graph format and you can overtype the default data and add your own titles if you wish (Figures 27.23 and 27.24).

You also have the option to change the chart type (Figures 27.25 and 27.26).

A useful slide in a business environment is an organisational chart. When selecting the organisational chart option, there is a variety of options (Figure 27.27) besides the standard hierarchical set up. If the hierarchical chart becomes too detailed, it is difficult to read it, so be brief. Also think about your audience, perhaps another version would be better.

By clicking onto the boxes, names can be added (Figure 27.28).

At each stage of the structure it is possible to put a branch in a new direction, add a variety of workers and choose layouts to match the organisation's requirements. To add co-workers and subordinates and make other additions, click on the line coming into the box you want to assign, click with the right-hand mouse button and choose from the selection (Figure 27.29).

Other **Slide Layouts** give the opportunity to add in pictures, logos, ClipArt or video (Figure 27.30).

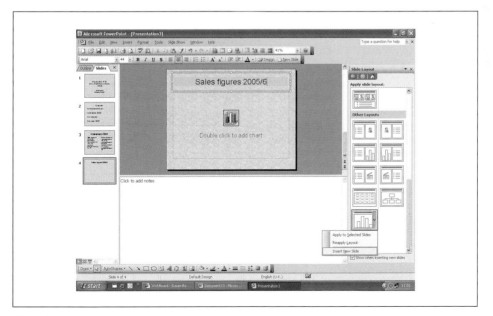

Figure 27.22

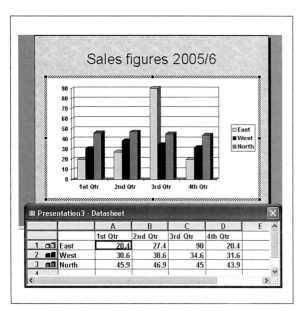

Figure 27.23

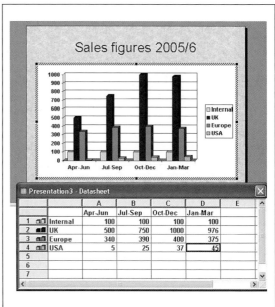

Figure 27.24

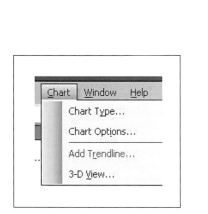

Figure 27.25

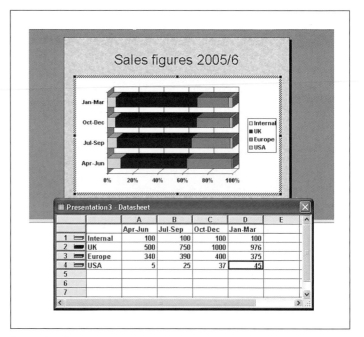

Figure 27.26

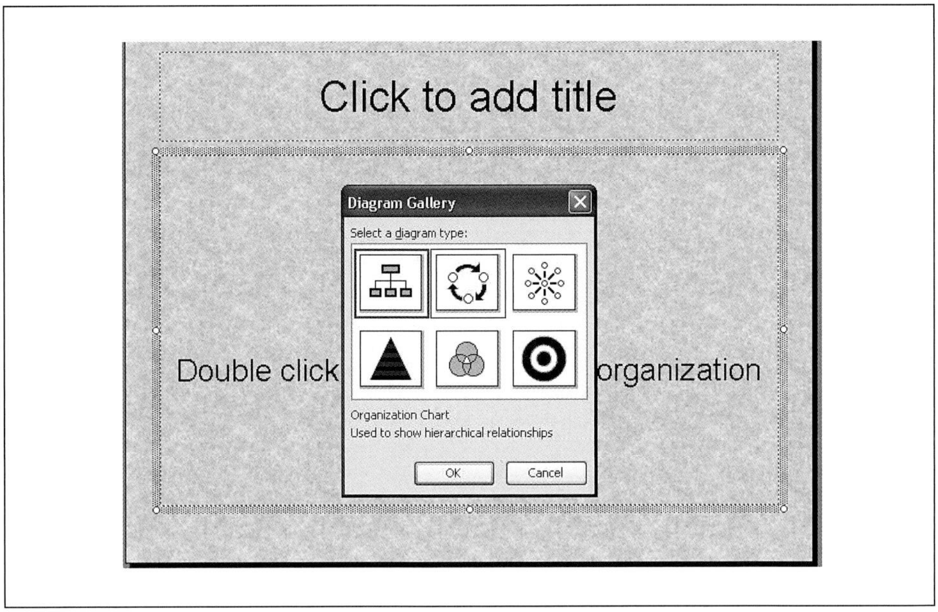

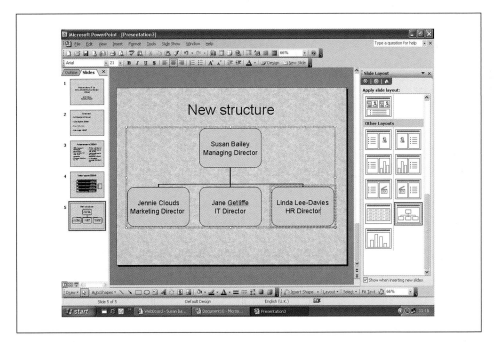

Figure 27.27

Figure 27.28

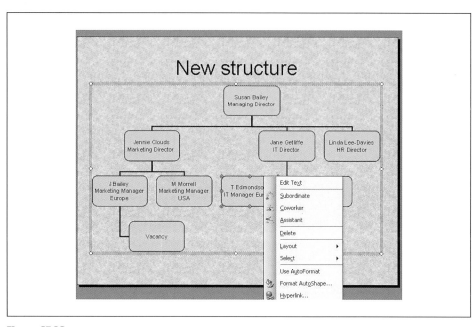

Figure 27.29

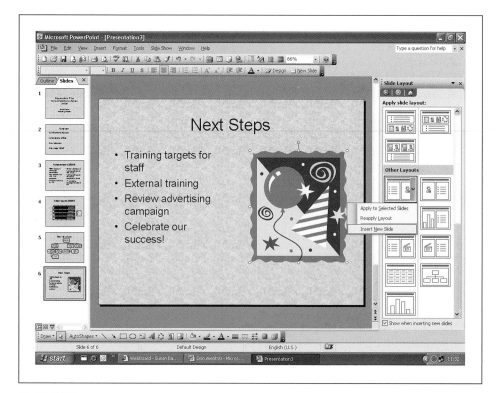

Figure 27.30

This set of slides has deliberately avoided the use of 'whizzy' slides. Often the audience has fallen asleep waiting for the text to finally 'tumble' into place or has felt dizzy having seen slides checker board in and out.

However, for those of you who cannot resist the odd 'whizzy' moment, here is brief overview of the possibilities.

CUSTOMISING TECHNIQUES

Under the **Slide Show** option there is a range of possibilities. By just selecting **View Show** the slide show will begin to run. Alternatively the function key F5 will have the same effect. At each click of the left mouse button the next slide will appear. If you need to go back or stop, a click on the right mouse button will reveal a menu and the **Previous** slide can be selected or the slide show stopped. Pressing the **Esc** button on the keyboard will also stop the show and the Page Up or Down keys on the keyboard can be used to scroll up and down the slides.

In this section there are other options that allow the user to set up a slide show with timings, and even **Record Narration**. This is particularly handy if the show is to run continuously without human intervention (Figure 27.31).

In addition to these, **Action Buttons** can be set up on a slide. When they are pressed the slide show can then be set to go to a different location in the slide sequence (Figure 27.32).

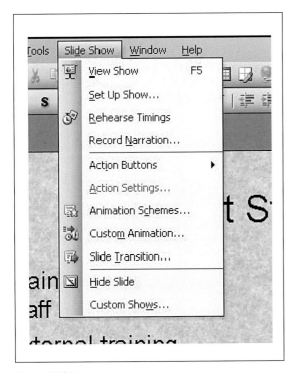

Figure 27.31

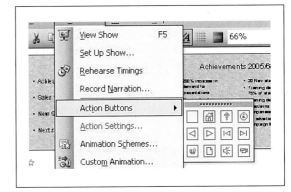

Figure 27.32

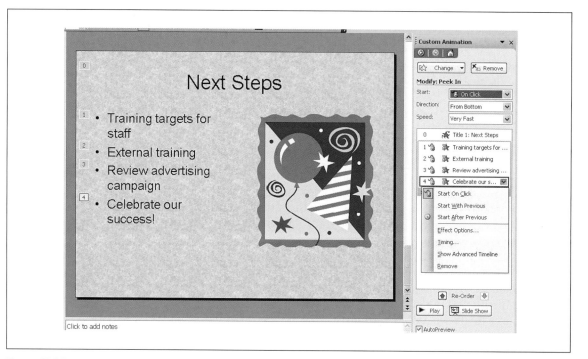

Figure 27.33

Other useful, if somewhat over used, options include **Animation Schemes** and **Custom Animation**. Figure 27.33 shows the essence of how **Custom Animation** works. When this option is chosen, a set of numbers appear on the slide. Once each item can be identified, an animation technique can be applied. The mouse icon indicates the action that happens on the mouse click, and there is a wealth of effects and timings that can be added at your leisure.

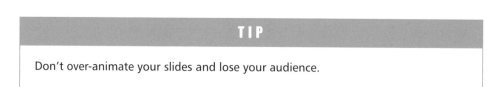

TIP

Don't over-animate your slides and lose your audience.

The other key animation technique which can be applied is transition. This is the technique which creates an effect as you move from one slide to the next. When **Slide Transition** is selected, a range of actions are offered, for example box in, dissolve, etc. When one is chosen a small grey star is seen at the bottom of the slide (Figure 27.34).

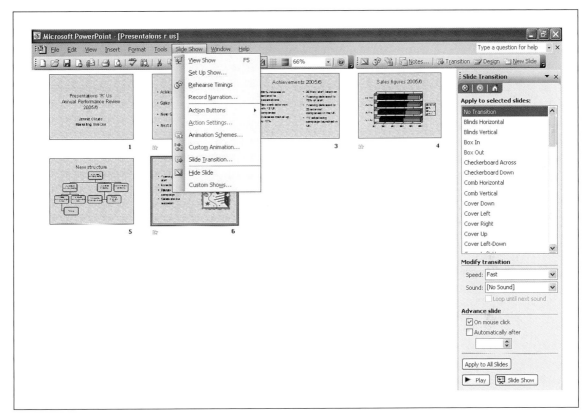

Figure 27.34

Manipulating and changing the slides

Clicking on the **Slide Sorter** option ▢▢ as indicated in Figure 27.35, gives a view of all of the slides. Once they are in this format, the mouse can be used to drag and drop them to different positions. Slides can also be deleted by clicking on them and pressing the delete button or new slides from another presentation can be added in.

PRINTING YOUR PRESENTATION

You can print your presentation in various ways, for example:

- each slide as seen in the presentation
- handouts
- handouts with room for lecture notes to be added
- screen dumps plus your crib notes

Clicking on **File**, then **Print Preview** (Figure 27.36) shows you what the finished product will look like (Figure 27.37).

It is possible to print out each slide individually or as a set (Figure 27.38).

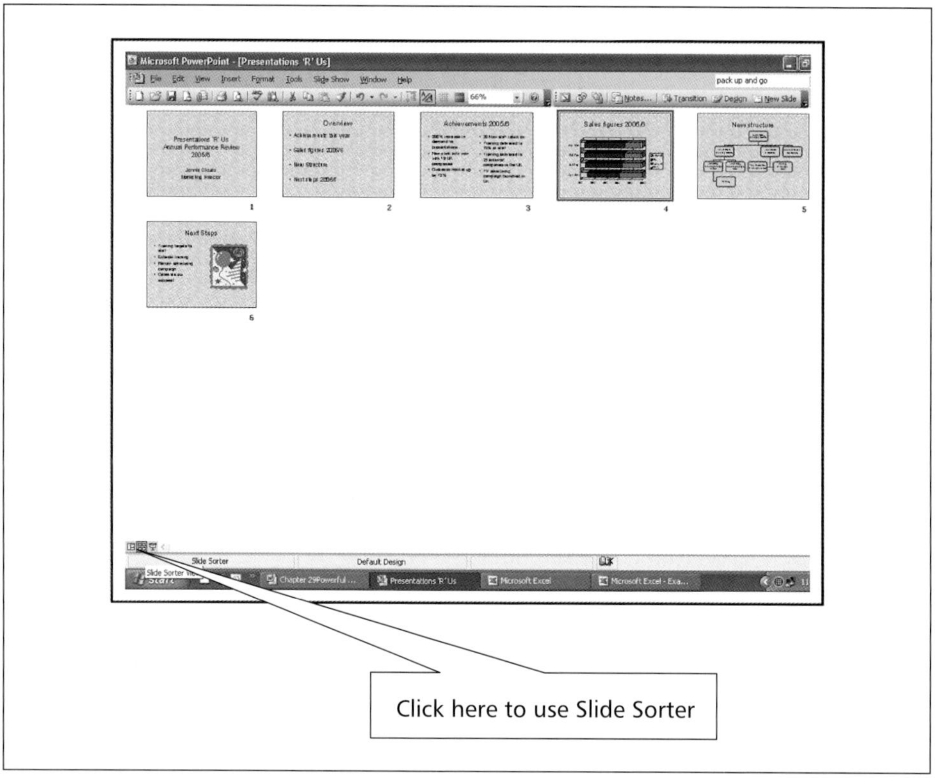

Figure 27.35

> Click here to use Slide Sorter

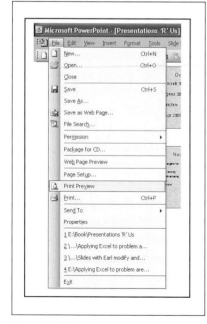

Figure 27.36

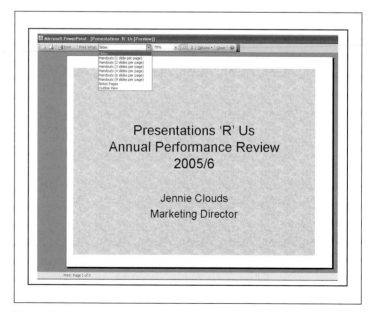

Figure 27.37

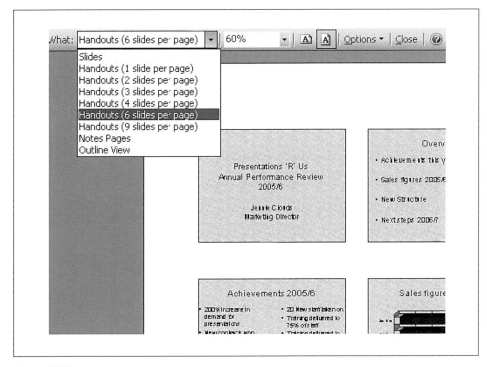

Figure 27.38

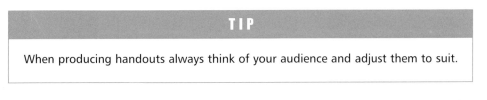

TIP

When producing handouts always think of your audience and adjust them to suit.

Slides Slides give screen dumps of the presentation. These are useful if you are going to use an OHP for your presentation. Print these out either directly onto acetates or print onto paper and photocopy onto acetates.

Handouts When printing handouts, you can choose how many slides you have per sheet. Three slides allows room for your audience to make notes by each slide (Figure 27.39).

If you choose more slides per sheet you also have an option to allow you to choose which order they are printed in, that is whether they read across the page or read down in columns as in a newspaper (Figure 27.40).

Printing out the Notes Page shows the slide and the notes. This can be used as guidance for the final presentation (Figure 27.41).

Finally, an Outline View will remind you of the headings and main points as shown on each of the slides. These can also be very useful for your own notes too (Figure 27.42).

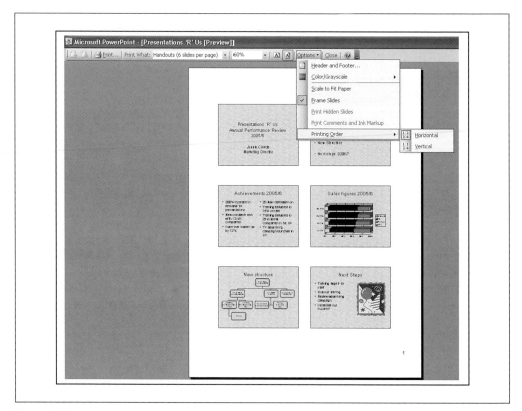

Figure 27.39

Figure 27.40

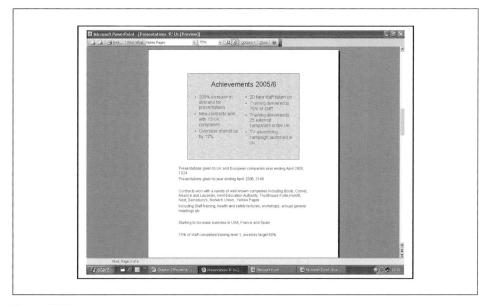

Figure 27.41

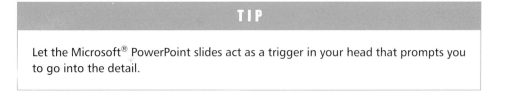

Figure 27.42

TIP

Let the Microsoft® PowerPoint slides act as a trigger in your head that prompts you to go into the detail.

Summary

Organisations today seem to expect presentations on a set of Microsoft® PowerPoint slides. Often in the pursuit of the 'whizzy' delivery, the clarity of the actual presentation can be lost. This chapter shows how to put together a clear and consist set of slides, without overpowering the audience.

The chapter highlights the wealth of *useful* features that exist in Microsoft® PowerPoint, such as the organisational chart and the ability to add diagrams and pictures. The presenter can prepare for a presentation by adding notes to the slide and can create for the audience some useful handouts to support the delivery. Presentations should rely on quality, not quantity and wizardry to get the point over. Work smartly to produce a slick delivery with a meaningful presentation.

TASK 1

1 Set up a slide show of six slides about your favourite hobby or pastime

2 Use a slide design from the templates offered – not too dark or busy

3 Incorporate

  a. A variety of slide designs
  b. One transition
  c. One animation

4 Add notes to the notes page

5 Prepare a handout with all six slides on it

6 Deliver the presentation to a few friends – limiting yourself to five minutes!

Index